The Complete Guide
to High-end Audio

The Complete Guide to High-end Audio

Robert Harley

A
Acapella Publishing
P. O. Box 80805
Albuquerque, New Mexico 87198-0805 USA

International Standard Book Number:
Hardcover: 0-9640849-1-0
Paper: 0-9640849-0-2

Cover Concept and Design: *Daniel Bish*
Cover Illustration: *Gregory Truett Smith*
Illustrations: *Evalee Harley*, except where otherwise credited
Technical Reviewers: *A. J. Conti, Gary Gomes, Bill Low, Peter W. Mitchell, Arthur Noxon*

This book was produced by Evalee Harley using Microsoft Word, MacDraw Pro, and QuarkXPress on a Macintosh IIx, then output using a high-resolution imagesetter. Copies were printed via offset lithography.

7 8 9 10

Printed in the United States of America

To Evalee

Contents

9   Turntables, Tonearms, and Cartridges: The LP Playback System   265

13   Audio for Home Theater   345

Appendix A: Sound and Hearing   363

Foreword

By Keith Jarrett

Music is the sonic motion of intention. With words, sound can be divorced from meaning by taking away the physical quality of speech. But music's meaning is *in* its physical quality: its sound. When a musician plays something a certain way and we can't hear the intent (the reason) behind it, we are hearing wasted motion, and register it as such because we haven't been given enough clues about the intent. We can then grow to think that everything is only gesture, and miss the real thing.

The media through which we hear music (our systems, rooms, etc.) cannot be separated from our ability to experience the music. It isn't the same *music* on a different system because we cannot separate music's rhetoric (its words) from its physical reality (its delivery). This makes the "delivery systems" (our stereos) more important than we might think they are. Can they *tell* us what the musicians on the recording are telling us?

As a musician, I often—too often—had the following experience: I would play a concert, hear the tape afterward, and wonder what was missing. I would remember incredible things in the concert that just weren't on the tape. The notes were there, but notes are not music. Where was the music, the *intention*?

We could think of it this way: On the tape, the rhetoric had no meaning. Had I trusted the tape and not my memory of the actual event, I would have never grown to understand that, even though the sound is on tape, it doesn't mean you've recorded the *music*. If you've heard a certain CD on a certain system, it doesn't necessarily mean that you've heard what's on the CD. We must learn to trust the responses of our own system—our ears—to music systems. Of course, this demands that we be in touch with ourselves—no easy thing.

People to whom music is important need to get close to the intention in a recording, and there's only one way to do this in the home: learn about the world of audio equipment. Use your (and others') ears to help remove whatever hinders you from the musical experience on the recording. Of course, it's not only the reproduction side that needs care—but that's the only side the listener has control over.

For instance, it's demonstrable that by merely flipping a two-pronged AC plug on a CD player, or even a turntable, a record you thought you didn't like can become a favorite—just because the polarity was wrong. Since music cannot be divorced from its emotional content, the *sound* of a record can determine whether you think you like the *music*. And vice versa, when you can't listen to music you really think you like because of how it was *recorded*.

Obviously, the musical experience is a delicate, complex thing, and we humans are more sensitive than we sometimes think. But we have the option to tune our music systems to better balance the equation. We can get closer to what we want if we *know* what we want.

There are stereo components that approximate the musical experience at many different price levels. We all know what our financial limitations are; but, given the desire to improve our systems, we *can* do it.

It by no means follows that musicians have to be audiophiles. Though I've been recording since 1965, I didn't seriously think about much of this until the last decade. But audiophiles and music lovers push the envelope, and we all benefit. Also, the more serious audiophiles are determined to keep their minds and ears open, keep learning, and try to remain patient during the process. Doing this thing right can take time.

There are a lot of people out there listening to all of these components for us. I recommend *using* this fact, and *carefully* reading others' evaluations, until you can tell whether a reviewer's preferences in sound match your own priorities. You *can* sort of get to know these guys over a period of time.

But, of course, it's *your* ears that count. I think you should pay attention to their needs. After all, we're talking nutrition in an age of diet soft drinks.

Preface

This book is for anyone who enjoys music. It is about enriching our lives through the joy of high-quality music reproduction in the home. My goal in writing it has been to make the technology we call high-end audio accessible to *all* music lovers—not just those with a big bank account or a technical bent. Owning a high-quality music play-back system is enormously rewarding. I want to share that experience with everyone who appreciates music.

Of all the ways in which humanity is united, perhaps the most powerful is our *need* for music. Music stirs our souls, moves our emotions, stimulates our intellects, enriches our lives. The higher the quality with which music is reproduced, the deeper and more intense our involvement with it becomes. High-end audio is nothing less than the quest for reproducing music with all the passion and emotion of the live event.

Ironically, only a tiny percentage of the population knows how wonderful reproduced music can sound through a good system. Hearing a high-end system for the first time can be a startling experience. The loudspeakers vanish, replaced by the performers in the room. The music's emotion and expression are suddenly *right there* in front of you. Music you've heard a hundred times has a depth and an intensity previously unrealized. You can almost see the expressions on the performers' faces as the music's meaning touches you at the deepest level. You melt into the chair, not wanting the music to stop.

Although the technology to produce this powerful experience is readily available, high-end audio reaches only a very small portion of the music-loving public. The high-end audio industry has—without realizing it—erected barriers between itself and many music lovers. Because high-end audio grew out of a do-it-yourself hobbyist spirit, the assumption tends to be that its customers are technophiles rather than music lovers. The result has been either complete ignorance among the general population that high-end audio components even exist, or the mistaken belief that you need a degree in electrical engineering to walk into a specialty audio retailer.

Owning a high-quality music playback system shouldn't be an intimidating prospect. This book takes the mystery and apprehension out of buying and using such a system by explaining high-end audio in clear, direct language. I also hope to involve those music lovers who have been turned off by the technical jargon, elitism, and/or sexism of high-end audio.

This last barrier between the high-end industry and its potential customers—sexism—is an important one to bring down. High-end audio has traditionally been a male-dominated pursuit. But women enjoy and appreciate music just as much as men do—why shouldn't they be as involved in high-quality music reproduction? By learning about high-end audio and how to make wise purchasing decisions through this book, women need no longer be excluded from this rewarding pursuit. And if the reader of this book is a man, include your partner in choosing components and enjoying the system. High-end audio can be a bonding experience between a couple rather than the source of friction it so often is.

Although this book contains enough technical detail for even the most advanced audiophile, it is basic enough to arm a non-technical person with the knowledge they need to buy and enjoy their first high-quality music-reproduction system. At the next level, this book is a bridge between the new audiophile and the specialist magazines, which tend to assume a high level of knowledge about the subject. It will bring you up to speed so that you may better understand and enjoy the high-end press—particularly the product reviews. Finally, a thorough reading should make you very knowledgeable about high-end audio.

To make *The Complete Guide to High-end Audio* easily accessible to every level of music enthusiast, I've broken down the chapters on specific audio component categories into clearly identified sections:

1) *What the component does*
2) *How to choose that component and make wise purchasing decisions*
3) *What to listen for in evaluating that component*
4) *How the component works*
5) *How to interpret the component's specifications and measurements*

The beginner can quickly find out what a preamplifier does, for example, while the technical enthusiast can just as easily learn how an R/2R ladder digital-to-analog converter works. Each chapter is structured with the most basic information first, progressing to the more advanced sections later in the chapter. When you reach your limit of technical understanding, simply skip ahead to the beginning of the next chapter. The book is designed so that a first reading might include only the basics of each component's role in a playback system, or how to make informed purchasing decisions. Subsequent readings can deepen your knowledge of specific topics.

And don't be intimidated by all the technical information in this book—you don't need to understand it to enjoy high-quality music in the home. I've included it for those audiophiles who want a deeper understanding of high-end audio technology, and to make this book truly *The Complete Guide to High-end Audio*.

At whatever level you choose to pursue high-end audio, what really matters is that you enjoy the music. I hope this book helps you do just that.

Robert Harley
Santa Fe
March, 1993

About the Author

Robert Harley is Consulting Technical Editor of *Stereophile*, America's oldest and largest subjective-review magazine. His more than 300 published equipment reviews and articles on high-quality music reproduction have helped thousands of music lovers improve their hi-fi systems.

Robert Harley holds a degree in recording engineering, and has taught a college degree program in that field. He has worked as a recording engineer and studio owner, compact disc mastering engineer, technical writer, and audio journalist. He is a member of the Audio Engineering Society, and has written or co-written several papers for presentation at AES conventions.

Acknowledgments

A book like this one can never be brought to life by a single person. Instead, it is the culmination of the direct and indirect efforts of many individuals to whom I am indebted.

First and foremost, I'd like to thank my wife, Evalee, for her tremendous contribution to my life and to this project. She single-handedly converted my word-processor files and rough sketches into the book you are now holding. She gave much of herself to make this book a reality.

I am grateful to the experts in specific fields of audio who provided technical review for this book: Gary Gomes, A.J. Conti, Art Noxon, Bill Low, and, especially, Peter W. Mitchell, who seems to be an expert in *every* area of audio.

My research for this book relied heavily on the writings of my audio journalist colleagues, particularly John Atkinson, Martin Colloms, Dick Olsher, and Peter W. Mitchell. Their technical expositions in product reviews and articles over the past decade were an invaluable source of information.

Special acknowledgment goes to *Stereophile* magazine founder J. Gordon Holt. He was the first audio writer to describe how an audio component *sounded* rather than how it *measured*. Gordon laid the foundation—nearly forty years ago—for the entire field of subjective evaluation of audio equipment, and developed the unique language of describing reproduced music that we all take for granted today.

I'd like to thank all the readers of *Stereophile* who have called me for advice over the years; your questions told me what I needed to include in this book.

The combination of my desire to write and my interest in music and audio technology springs from my family. My parents instilled in me a love of the printed word that has immeasurably enriched my life. My brother Steve's willingness to share his stereo and record collection with his little brother was undoubtedly the seed that germinated, nearly twenty-five years later, into this book.

Many others contributed selflessly to this project. I thank Keith Jarrett for his eloquent foreword; Richard Lehnert for his valued editorial guidance; Daniel Bish and Gregory Truett Smith for the unique cover; the many high-end equipment manufacturers who supplied graphics and photographs; *Stereophile* magazine for the Audio Precision and MLSSA graphs, and for allowing me to reprint short sections of text from my previous writings; Tom Gillett, Mrs. R.D. Pauley, and Scott Smith; and Larry Fine, author of *The Piano Book*, for sharing with me his insights into and experience in self-publishing.

I'd also like to acknowledge the writings of Robert Pirsig. His "reconciliation of two apparently disparate modes of thought" makes it perfectly natural to describe, in the same article, an audio component's soundstage bloom as well as its reproduction of a –90dBFS, 1kHz undithered sinewave.

1 What Is High-end Audio?

High-end audio is about passion—passion for music, and for how well it is reproduced. High-end audio is the quest to re-create in the listener's home the musical message of the composer or performer with the maximum realism, emotion, and intensity. Because music is important, re-creating it with the highest possible fidelity is important.

High-end audio products constitute a unique subset of music-reproduction components that bear little similarity to the "stereo systems" sold in department stores. A music-reproduction system isn't a home appliance such as a washing machine or toaster; it is a vehicle for expressing the vast emotional and intellectual potential of the music encoded on our records and CDs. The higher the quality of reproduction, the deeper our connection with the music.

The high-end ethos—that music and the quality of its reproduction matter—is manifested in high-end audio products. They are designed by dedicated enthusiasts who combine technical skill and musical sensitivity to craft components that take us one step closer to the original musical event. High-end products are designed by ear, built by hand, and exist for one reason—to enhance the experience of music listening.

A common misconception among the hi-fi consuming public is that high-end audio means high-*priced* audio. In the mass-market mind, high-end audio is nothing more than elaborate stereo equipment with fancy features and price tags aimed at millionaires. Sure, the performance may be a little better than the hi-fi you find at your local appliance store, but who can afford it? Moreover, high-end audio is seen as being only for trained, discriminating listeners, snobs, or gadget freaks—but not for the average person on the street.

High-end audio is none of these things.

First, the term "high-end" refers to the products' *performance*, not their price. Many true high-end systems cost no more—and often *less*—than the all-in-one rack systems sold in department stores. I've heard many inexpensive systems that capture the essence of what high-quality music reproduction is all about—systems easily within the budgets of average consumers. Although many high-end components *are* high-priced, this doesn't mean that you have to take out a second mortgage to

A high-end audio system can cost less than $1200. . .

NAD/PSB photo courtesy Lenbrook Industries, Ltd. Pickering, ON Canada

. . . or more than $120,000.

Courtesy Apogee Acoustics, Inc.

have high-quality music reproduction in your home. A great-sounding system can be less expensive than you might think.

Second, high-end audio is about communicating the musical experience, not adding elaborate, difficult-to-operate features. In fact, high-end systems are much *easier* to use than mass-market mid-fi systems. This is because the high-end ethic eliminates useless features, instead putting the money into sound quality. High-end audio is for music lovers, not electronics whizzes.

Third, *anyone* who likes music can immediately appreciate the value of high-quality sound reproduction. It doesn't take a "golden ear" to know what sounds good. The differences between good and mediocre music reproduction are instantly obvious. The reaction—usually pleasure and surprise—of someone hearing a true high-end audio system for the first time underscores that high-end audio can be appreciated by everyone. If you enjoy music, you'll enjoy it more through a high-end system. It's that simple.

Finally, the goal of high-end audio is to make the equipment "disappear"; when that happens, we know that we have reached the highest state of communication between musician and listener. High-end audio isn't about equipment; it's about music.

The high-end credo holds that the less the musical signal is processed, the better. Any electronic circuit, wire, tone control, or switch degrades the signal—and thus the musical experience. This is why you won't find graphic equalizers, "spatial enhancers," "sub-harmonic synthesizers," or other such gimmicks on high-end equipment. Such devices are not only departures from musical reality, they add unnecessary circuitry to the signal path. By minimizing the amount of electronics between you and the musicians, high-end audio products can maximize the directness of the musical experience. Less is more.

Imagine yourself standing at the edge of the Grand Canyon, feeling overwhelmed by its grandeur. You experience not only the vastness of this massive sculpture carved deep into the earth, but all its smaller features jump out at you as well, vivid and alive. You can discern fine gradations of hue in the rock layers. The distinctions between the many shades of red are readily apparent. Fine details of the huge formations are easily resolved simply by your looking at them, thus deepening your appreciation. The contrasts of light and shadow highlight the apparently infinite maze of cracks and crevasses. The longer and closer you look, the more you see. The wealth of sensory input keeps you standing silently at the edge, in awe of nature's unfathomable beauty.

Now imagine yourself looking at the Grand Canyon through a window made of many thicknesses of glass, each one less than perfectly transparent. One pane has a slight grayish opacity that dulls the vivid hues and obliterates the subtle distinctions between similar shades of color. The fine granular structure of the next pane diminishes your ability to resolve features in the rock. Another pane reduces the contrast between light and shadow, turning the Canyon's immense depth and breadth into a flat canvas. Finally, the windowframe itself constricts your view, destroying the Canyon's overall impact. Instead of the direct and immediate reality of standing at the edge of the Grand Canyon, what you see is gray, murky, lifeless, and synthetic. You may as well be watching it on television.

Hearing reproduced music through a mediocre playback system is like looking at the Grand Canyon through those panes of glass. Each component in the playback chain—CD player, turntable, preamplifier, power amplifier, loudspeakers, and the cables that connect them—in some way distorts the signal passing through it. One product may add a coarse, grainy character to instrumental textures. Another may reduce the dynamic contrasts between loud and soft, muting the composer's or performer's expression. Yet another may cast a thick, murky pall over the music, destroying its subtle tonal colors and overlaying all instruments with an undifferentiated timbre. Finally, the windowframe—that is, the electronic and mechanical playback system—diminishes the expanse that is the musicians' artistic intent.

High-end audio is about removing as many panes of glass as possible, and making those that remain as transparent as they can be. The fewer the panes, and the less effect each has on the information passing through it, the closer we get to the live experience and the deeper our connection with the musical message.

Why are high-end audio products more transparent windows on the musical event than mass-market "stereo systems"? High-end products are designed to *sound* good—that is, like the real thing. They're not necessarily designed to perform well on some arbitrary technical specification. The true high-end designer *listens* to the product during its development, changing parts and trying different techniques to produce the most realistic sound possible. He combines technical skill with musical sensitivity to create a product that best conveys the musical experience. This dedication often becomes a zealous pursuit, involving many hundreds of listening hours and painstaking attention to every factor that influences the sound. Often, a more expensive part will be included to improve the product's sound, while the retail price remains the same. The higher cost of this musically superior part comes off the company's bottom line. Why? Because the high-end designer cares deeply about music and its reproduction.

Conversely, mass-market audio components are often designed to look good "on paper"—on the specification sheet—sometimes at the expense of sound quality. A good example of this is the "THD wars" of the 1970s and '80s. THD stands for Total Harmonic Distortion, a specification widely used by uneducated consumers as a measure of amplifier quality. (If you've done this, don't worry; before I learned more about audio, I also looked at THD figures.) The lower the THD, the better the amplifier was perceived to be. This led the electronics giants to produce products with vanishingly low THD numbers. It became a contest to see which brand had the most zeros after the decimal point in its THD specification (0.001%, for example). Many buyers bought receivers or amplifiers solely on this specification.

Although low THD is a worthy design goal, the problem arose in *how* those extremely low distortion figures were obtained. A technique to reduce distortion in amplifiers is called "feedback"—taking part of the output signal and feeding it back to the input. Large amounts of feedback reduce THD, but cause all kinds of other problems that degrade the amplifier's musical qualities. Did the electronics giants care that their products' sound quality was worse? Not a chance. The only thing that mattered was making a commodity which would sell in greater quantity. They traded musical performance for an insignificant technical specification that was sold to the public as being important. Those buyers choosing components on the basis of a specification sheet rather than listening ended up with poor-sounding systems. Ironically, the amplifiers that had the lowest THDs probably had the lowest quality of sound as well.

This example illustrates the vast difference between mass-market manufacturers' and high-end companies' conceptions of what an audio component should do. High-end manufacturers care more about how the product sounds than how it performs on the test bench. They know that their audience of musically sensitive listeners will buy on the basis of sound quality, not of specifications.

High-end products are not only designed by ear, but are often hand-built by skilled craftspeople who take pride in their work. The assemblers are often audiophiles themselves, building the products with as much care as if the products were to be installed in their own homes. This meticulous attention to detail results in a better quality of construction, or "build quality." Better build quality can not only improve a product's sound, but also increases its long-term reliability. Moreover, beautifully handcrafted components can inspire a pride in ownership that the makers of mass-produced products can't hope to match.

High-end audio products are often backed by better customer service than mid-fi products. Because high-end manufacturers care more about their products and customers, they generally offer longer warranties, more liberal exchange policies, and better service. It is not uncommon for high-end manufacturers to repair products out of warranty at no charge. This isn't to say you should expect such treatment, only that it sometimes happens in high-end and is unthinkable with mass-market products. High-end companies care about their customers.

These attributes also apply to high-end specialty retailers. The high-end dealer shares a passion for quality music reproduction and commitment to customer service. If you're used to buying audio components at a mass-market dealer, you'll be pleasantly surprised by a visit to a high-end store. Rather than trying to get you to buy something that may not be right for you, the responsible high-end dealer will strive to assemble a system that will provide the greatest long-term musical pleasure. Such a dealer will put your musical satisfaction ahead of this month's bottom line.

Finally, most high-end products are designed and built in America by American companies. In fact, American-made audio components are highly regarded throughout the world. More than 40% of all American high-end audio production is exported to foreign countries, particularly the Far East. This is true even though high-end products cost about twice as much abroad as they do in the U.S., owing to shipping, import duties, and importer profit. The enthusiasm for American high-end products abroad is even more remarkable when one remembers the popular American misconception that the best audio equipment is made in Japan.

On a deeper level, I believe that high-end products are fundamentally different from mass-market products. From their conception, purpose, design, construction, and marketing, to how they are used, high-end components are very different from their mid-fi cousins.

What distinguishes a high-end from a mass-market product is the designer's caring attitude toward music. He isn't creating boxes to be sold like any other commodity; he's making musical instruments whose performance will affect how his customers experience music. The high-end component is a physical manifestation of a deeply felt concern about how well music is reproduced, and, by extension, how much it is enjoyed by the listener.

The high-end designer builds products he would want to listen to himself. Because he cares about music, it matters to him how a faceless listener, perhaps thousands of miles away, experiences the joy of music. The greater the listener's involvement in the music, the better the designer has done his job.

To the high-end designer, electronic or mechanical design isn't merely a technical undertaking—it's an act of love and devotion. Each aspect of a product's design, technical as well as musical, is examined in a way that would surprise those unaccustomed to such commitment. The ethos of music reproduction goes to the very core of his being; it's not a job he merely shows up for every day. The result is a much more powerful and intimate involvement in the music for the listener than is possible with products designed without this dedication.

What *is* high-end audio? What is high-end sound? It is when the playback system is forgotten, seemingly replaced by the performers in your listening room. It is when you feel the composer or performer speaking across time and space *to you*. It is feeling a physical rush during a musical climax. It is the ineffable roller-coaster ride of emotion the composer somehow managed to encode in a combination of sounds. It is when the physical world disappears, leaving only your consciousness and the music.

That is high-end.

2 Choosing a High-end Audio System

Introduction

Choosing a high-quality music reproduction system is one of the most important purchasing decisions you'll make in your life. Unlike buying home appliances, your selections in components will influence how deeply you appreciate and enjoy an art form—music. A great-sounding system can even change your lifestyle as music assumes a greater importance in your life. A hi-fi system is a vehicle for exploring the world of music; the better the system, the farther and wider that vehicle will take you.

Although selecting hi-fi components may seem a daunting task, a little knowledge and preparation go a long way toward realizing your dream system—and staying within your budget. The informed shopper knows that choosing the right components, matching those components to each other, and careful setup are more important than a big bank account. This chapter will teach you to become a wise shopper and show you the path to assembling the most musically and aesthetically satisfying system possible for your money.

A high-end audio system is made up of many components, each with a specific job. These components generally fall into three basic categories: source components, control components, and playback components.

A source component is any device that recovers the audio signal from an information storage medium. A compact disc player, which recovers an audio signal from a CD, is a source component. Other sources include turntables, tuners, and tape decks. Source components are also called the *front end* because they are at the very beginning of the playback chain.

The control component is the preamplifier; it receives signals from the source components and controls which one is sent to the power amplifier for listening. The preamplifier is the heart of a hi-fi system; all the source components run through the preamplifier, which also controls the volume and signal routing.

Playback components are the power amplifier and loudspeakers, which work together to convert the preamplifier's output into music.

If you're a newcomer to audio, you may first want to read the introductory sections of Chapters 5–12 before shopping for a system. Each of these chapters is devoted to a specific component, with an introductory section explaining the component's function, terminology, and features. Later sections in each chapter go into specific detail about selecting that component on musical and technical bases.

In this chapter, we'll look at how to choose a high-end system. The major topics include:

- *Setting your budget*

- *Complete vs. incremental purchases*

- *Choosing the system best suited to your needs*

- *Allocating your budget to specific components*

- *Upgrading a single component*

- *How to read magazine reviews of audio equipment*

- *System matching*

- *Do's and don'ts of selecting components*

- *Your relationship with the retailer*

- *Setting up your system for the best sound*

Setting Your Budget

How much should you spend on a music playback system?

That depends on two things—your priorities in life and your financial means. Let's take the priorities first. One person may consider a $2000 stereo system an extravagance, yet not bat an eye at blowing $7000 on a two-week European vacation. Conversely, another person of similar means would find a $7000 vacation a waste of money when there is so much great hi-fi on the wish list. The first person probably considers music as merely a dispensable diversion while driving to work. To the second person, however, enjoying and appreciating music is a vital aspect of human existence. How much of your disposable income you should spend on a hi-fi system is simply a matter of how important music is to you, and only you can decide that. Owning a good hi-fi system will probably elevate music listening to a much higher priority in your life.

The second factor—your financial means—can often suggest a hi-fi budget. According to a 1991 survey of *Stereophile* readers, the average hi-fi system as a percentage of annual income was just under 10% (an average hi-fi cost of $6300 out of an average income of $66,000). The mean income of *Stereophile* readers was $80,700, with a mean system cost of $9100. Survey respondents also planned to spend an average of $2154 on hi-fi in the coming year. These are loose generalizations; high-end systems range in cost from less than $1200 to more than $200,000. And don't let these figures intimidate you: *Stereophile* readers are dedicated enthusiasts and not necessarily representative of all music lovers. You can put together a musically-satisfying system for much less than the figures cited.

I strongly urge you, however, to establish a significant budget for your high-end system. The expenditure may seem high at the time, but you will be rewarded night after night and year after year with your favorite music wonderfully reproduced. A year or two from now, as you enjoy your system, the money spent will have been forgotten, but the pleasure will continue—a good music-playback system is a lasting and fulfilling investment. Moreover, if you buy a quality system now, you won't want to sell it or trade it in for something better later. It is sometimes false economy to "save" money on a less than adequate system. Do it right the first time.

There's another way of determining how much to spend for a hi-fi system: Find the level of quality you're happy with and let that set your budget. Visit your dealer and have him play systems of various levels of quality. You may find yourself satisfied with a moderately priced system—or you may discover how good reproduced music can sound with the best equipment, and just have to have it.

The Complete vs. the Incremental Purchase

After you've established a budget, you must decide which of the following three ways of buying a hi-fi is best for you. These are:

1) Buy an entire system made up of the finest components.
2) Buy an entire system made up of components within a limited budget.
3) Buy just a few components now and add to the system as finances permit.

The first option doesn't require much thought—just a large bank account. The purchaser of this system needn't worry about budgets, upgrading, and adding components later. Other elements of buying a high-end system (I'll talk about these later) do apply to the cost-no-object audiophile: allocating the budget to specific components, dealing with the retailer, and home auditioning. But this sort of listener isn't under the same financial constraints that force the tough choices inherent in the other two options. Just choose a topnotch system and start enjoying it.

Most of us, however, don't enjoy such a luxury. We must live within the set budgets of options 2 or 3. Option 2 is to spend the entire budget on a complete system now. In option 3, you'll spend your entire budget on just a few, higher-quality components and add the other pieces later as money becomes available. We'll call Option 2 the *complete purchase,* and Option 3 the *incremental purchase.* There are advantages and disadvantages to each approach.

Buying an entire system at once means that the overall budget must be spread among all the components comprising a system. Consequently, you'll have less to spend on each component. You may not get the quality of components you'd hoped for, but the system will be complete and you can start enjoying it right away. This type of purchase is more suited to the music lover who doesn't want to think about equipment. He wants a system he can set up, forget, and use to enjoy music. There are many listeners for whom this approach is ideal.

The listener more inclined to treat audio as a hobby, or one who has her sights set on a more ambitious system, will buy just a few components now and add to the system as finances permit. This listener may spend the same amount of money as our first listener, but on just a pair of loudspeakers instead of on a whole system. She will use her old receiver or integrated amplifier, turntable, or CD player until she can afford the electronics and sources she really wants. Her system will be limited by the receiver's performance; she won't immediately get the benefit of her high-end loudspeakers. But when she *does* buy her dream electronics, she'll have a truly first-rate system. This approach requires more patience, commitment, and, in the long term, more money. But it is one way to end up with a superlative system.

The audiophile buying a system piece by piece can benefit from rapidly changing technology. She can start with components that don't change much over the years—power amplifiers, for example—and wait to buy those products likely to get better and cheaper over time—such as digital processors, CD players, and CD transports.

Another benefit of adding components to your system one at a time is the ability to audition components in that system before buying. Rather than putting together a whole system in a store based on your own auditioning or a salesperson's recommendations, the incremental buyer can carefully audition components and choose the best musical match for the rest of the system. This is a big advantage when assembling a hi-fi best suited to your musical tastes. This piece-by-piece approach is more for the hobbyist, and demands a deeper level of commitment to audio. It also requires a great deal more patience.

In short, if you want to get a good system, forget about the hardware, and just enjoy music, buy the entire system now. Given the same initial expenditure, you won't end up with the same-quality system as if you'd bought pieces slowly, but you'll be spending less money in the long run and can have the benefit of high-end music playback immediately. Moreover, you can go about your life without thinking about what piece of audio hardware to buy next. The complete purchase is recommended for the music lover who isn't an audio hobbyist. Many music lovers taking this approach, however, find themselves upgrading their systems piece by piece after discovering the rewards of owning a high-end audio system.

Conversely, the music lover on a budget who has set her sights on a more ambitious system, and who takes a more active role in audio equipment, will probably build a system gradually. This listener will more likely read product reviews in magazines, visit the dealer often, and take equipment home for evaluation. By doing so, she'll become a better listener, a more critical audiophile, and develop a broader knowledge of audio equipment.

Whichever approach you take, the information in the rest of this chapter—selecting a system suited to your listening, allocating the budget to specific components, dealing with the retailer, and system setup— apply equally well.

Choosing the System Best Suited to Your Needs

Just as a pickup truck is better suited to the farmer and a compact car to the city dweller, a hi-fi system ideal for a small New York City apartment would be entirely inadequate in a large suburban home. The hi-fi system must not only match your musical taste, as described in the next chapter, but must also suit your room and listening needs. (The following section is only an overview of how to choose the best system. More detailed information on how to select specific components is contained in Chapters 5–12.)

Many of the guidelines are fairly obvious. First, match the loudspeaker size to your listening room. Large, full-range loudspeakers don't work well in small rooms, and vice versa. Not only are large loudspeakers physically dominating, they tend to overload the room with bass energy. A loudspeaker that sounds fine in a 17' by 25' room will likely be thick, boomy, and bottom-heavy in a 12' by 15' room. The bass performance you paid dearly for (it's expensive to get correct deep-bass reproduction) will work against you if the loudspeaker is put in a small room. For the same money, you could buy a superb minimonitor whose build cost was put into making the upper bass, midrange, and treble superlative. You win both ways with the minimonitor: your room won't be overloaded by bass, and the minimonitor will likely have much better soundstaging and tonal purity. There are other benefits: minimonitors, with their limited low-frequency extension, are less likely to annoy neighbors. You can thus listen to music louder without bothering anyone. Further, placement is much easier in small rooms.

Conversely, a minimonitor just won't fill a large room with sound. The sense of power, dynamic drive, deep bass extension, and feeling of physical impact so satisfying in some music just doesn't happen with minimonitors. If you've got the room and the budget, a full-range, floorstanding loudspeaker is the best choice.

Another important consideration is amplifier power. The amplifier should be matched to the loudspeakers and the room. A larger room requires more amplifier power, as does a loudspeaker of low sensitivity. These issues are described in detail in the power amplifier and loudspeaker chapters (6 and 7).

Value vs. Luxury Components

High-end audio components run the gamut from utilitarian-looking boxes to lavish, gold-plated, cost-no-object shrines. The packaging doesn't always reflect the quality of the electronics inside, but rather the manufacturer's product philosophy. Some companies try to offer the best sound for the least money by putting excellent electronics in inexpensive chassis. These are the so-called "value" products. Manufacturers of "luxury" components may put the same level of electronics in a lavish chassis with a 1"-thick front panel, lacquer-filled engraving, expensive metalwork, and custom machined input jacks or terminal posts.

A designer of *very* expensive electronics once told me that he could sell his products for *half* the price if he used a cheap chassis. He felt, however, that the level of design and execution in his electronics deserved no less than the ultimate in packaging.

Some buyers demand elegant appearance and a luxury feel; others merely want the best sound for the least money. To some music lovers, appearance and elegant packaging are secondary to sound quality; they don't care what it looks like so long as it sounds good. Conversely, some audiophiles are willing to pay for gorgeous cosmetics, battleship build quality, and all the trimmings that make some products exude elegance and luxury.

When choosing high-end components, match your needs with the manufacturer's product philosophy. That way, you won't waste money on thick faceplates you don't care about, or, conversely, spend money on a product that doesn't do justice to your home decor.

Another type of product puts mediocre or even poor electronics in a fancy, eye-catching package. Their market is the less musically sophisticated buyer who chooses on appearance and status (or the company's past reputation) rather than sound quality. These so-called "boutique" brands are not high-end, however, and should be avoided.

A related topic is convenience vs. cost. Some products include convenience features that add to the component's price without improving the sound quality. Remote control on a preamplifier is a good example. The remote-control function—if done right—can double a preamp's cost, but doesn't result in better sound quality. When choosing components, consider the tradeoffs between sound quality, convenience, and price.

Allocating Your Budget to Specific Components

There are no set rules for how much of your total budget you should spend on each component in your system. Mass-market mid-fi magazines have been telling their readers for years to spend most of a hi-fi budget on the loudspeakers because they ultimately produce the sound. This thinking also suggests that all amplifiers and CD players sound alike; why waste money on expensive amplifiers and digital sources?

The high-end listener makes different assumptions about music reproduction. A fundamental tenet of high-end audio holds that if the signal isn't good at the beginning of the reproduction chain, nothing downstream can ever improve it. In fact, the signal will only be degraded by any product it flows through. High-end audio equipment simply minimizes that degradation. If your CD player is bright, hard, and unmusical, the final sound will be bright, hard, and unmusical. Similarly, the total system's performance is limited by the resolution of the worst component in the signal path. You may have superb loudspeakers and an excellent turntable and cartridge, but they'll be wasted with a poor-quality preamp in the signal chain. Quality matching between components is essential to getting the most sound for your budget.

High-quality loudspeakers at the end of a chain containing a bad-sounding component can even make the system sound worse than lower-quality loudspeakers. The high-resolution loudspeakers reveal all the imperfections of the electronics upstream of them. This situation has been likened to having a large picture window in your home. If the view is of the Northern California coastline, you want that window to be as clean and transparent as possible. But if the window looks out over a garbage dump, you'd prefer a window that somewhat obscured the view.

I've listened to $400 loudspeakers driven by $30,000 worth of electronics, and $9000 loudspeakers driven by budget integrated amplifiers. I can state categorically that the electronics and source components are every bit as important as—or more important than—the loudspeakers. Although the loudspeakers significantly influence the overall sound, high-quality source components (turntable and CD player) and good electronics (preamplifier and power amplifier) are essential to realizing a musical high-end system.

For the following exercise, I assembled an imaginary system of the components I'd choose if my audio budget totaled $6000. Here are the costs per item:

Preamplifier:	$1000
Power amplifier:	1200
Digital source:	1300
Loudspeakers:	2000
Interconnects and cables:	500
Total:	$6000

As you can see, loudspeakers consumed exactly a third of the budget, the digital source took up another 22%, the preamp 17%, and 20% went to a power amplifier. The remaining 8% was spent on interconnects and cables. These numbers and percentages aren't cast in stone, but they're a good starting point in allocating your budget. If you wanted to include a turntable, tonearm, and cartridge, the budget for the other components would have to be reduced.

Another approach with this budget would be to buy an inexpensive CD player ($500) and put the $800 saved into better loudspeakers or electronics. Then, as finances permitted, you could add a digital processor and drive it with the CD player's digital output jack (see Chapter 8). You'll have music in the meantime, and end up with a better-sounding system in the long run.

The 33% figure for loudspeakers is very flexible. There seems to be an important threshold in loudspeaker performance at about $2000. Loudspeakers costing more than $2000 are often disproportionately better than those under $2000, so you may want to shift more of the total budget to loudspeakers to cross this threshold. As described in Chapter 7, many moderately priced loudspeakers outperform much more expensive models. Use Chapter 7's guidelines on choosing loudspeakers to get the most performance for your loudspeaker dollar.

Here's another sample budget, this one based on a maximum expenditure of $2000:

```
Amplification: ......................................$ 750
Digital source: .....................................400
Loudspeakers: ......................................750
Interconnects and cables: ......................100
Total: ................................................$2000
```

This system will use an integrated amplifier instead of a separate preamplifier and power amplifier, and a CD player instead of separate CD transport and digital processor. Again, I selected components that experience suggested would be a good match, and tallied the percentages after choosing the components. Interestingly, the breakdown was very similar to that in the first example: 37% (vs. 33%) on loudspeakers, 20% (vs. 25%) on a digital source, 37% (same) on amplification, and 5% (vs. 8%) on interconnects and cables.

I've heard systems at this price level that are absolutely stunning musically. When carefully chosen and set up, a $2000 high-end system can achieve the essence of what high-quality music reproduction is all about—communicating the musical message. I've even heard a whole system with a list price of $850 that was musical and enjoyable. The point isn't how much you spend on a hi-fi, but how carefully you can choose components to make a satisfying system within your budget.

You should also save some of your budget for an AC power conditioner and accessories. I advise against buying a power conditioner and accessories when you buy the system. Take the system home, get it set up and optimized, *then* add a power conditioner and start experimenting with accessories. Here's why: AC conditioners don't always make an improvement. In fact, they can degrade the sound. There are many variables with AC power conditioners, including the quality of AC from your wall, the method of AC conditioning, and the number and nature of the components plugged into the conditioner. It is therefore best to try the conditioner at home before buying.

There's another good reason for adding an AC line conditioner later: By getting to know how your system sounds without an AC conditioner, you'll be better able to judge if the conditioner is an improvement. Remember that a change in sound isn't always for the better. The same logic holds true for accessories such as cones, feet, and tube dampers: You'll be in a much better position to judge their effectiveness—or lack of it—by knowing your system intimately before installing accessories. Hold some of your budget—perhaps a few hundred dollars—for accessories. If they don't make a difference, you've now got a few hundred dollars to spend on records or CDs. (A full survey of accessories is included in Chapter 12.)

Upgrading a Single Component

Many audiophiles gradually improve their systems by replacing one component at a time. The trick to getting the most improvement for the money is to replace the least good component in your system. A poor-sounding preamp won't let you hear how good your digital processor is, for example. Conversely, a very clean and transparent preamp used with a grainy and hard digital source will only let you hear just how grainy and hard the digital source is. The system should be of similar quality throughout. If there's a quality mismatch, however, it should be in favor of high-quality source components.

Determining which component to upgrade can be difficult. This is where a good high-end audio retailer's advice is invaluable—he can often pinpoint which component you should upgrade. Another way is to borrow components from a friend and see how they sound in your system. Listen for which component makes the biggest improvement in the sound. Finally, you can get an idea of the relative quality of your components by carefully reading the high-end audio magazines, particularly their recommended components sections. If your system is composed of all Class B-rated products, and you've got a Class D-rated CD player, you know where to start.

In Chapter 1, I likened music listening through a playback system to looking at the Grand Canyon through a series of panes of glass. Each pane distorts the image in a different way. The fewer and more transparent the panes are, the clearer the view, and the closer the connection to the direct experience.

The analogy is useful for getting the most sonic improvement for the least money when upgrading a single component in your high-end system. Think of each component as a pane of glass in a window. Some of the panes are relatively clear, while others tend to have an ugly coating that distorts the image. The pane closest to you is the loudspeaker; the next closest pane is the power amplifier; next comes the preamp; and the last pane is the signal source (CD player or turntable). Your view on the music—the system's overall transparency—is the sum of the panes. You may have a few very transparent panes, but the view is still clouded by the most opaque panes.

The key to upgrading a hi-fi system is to get rid of the dirtiest, most colored pane of glass in the series. Find the component that degrades the music performance the most and replace it. This technique gives you the biggest improvement in sound quality for the money spent.

Conversely, putting a very transparent pane closest to you—the loudspeaker—only reveals in greater detail what's wrong with the other panes—the power amplifier, preamplifier, and source components. A high-resolution loudspeaker at the end of a mediocre electronics chain can actually sound worse than the same system with a lower-quality loudspeaker.

Following this logic, we can see that a hi-fi system can never be any better than its source components. If the first pane of glass—the source component—is ugly, colored, and distorts the image, the result will be an ugly, colored, and distorted view. The transparent panes after the first pane can never remove the distortion. In fact, the transparency of the other panes only serves to highlight just how bad the first pane is. To achieve a high-quality playback system, the place to start is often with the source components.

Improving your playback system is like replacing a colored pane of glass with a more transparent one. As you upgrade your system and remove veils, you can start to see that other panes you thought were transparent actually have some flaws you couldn't detect before. The next upgrade step is to identify and replace what is now the weakest component in the system. This can easily become an ongoing process.

Unfortunately, as the level of quality of your playback system rises, your standard of what constitutes good performance rises with it. You become ever more critical, upgrading component after component in the search for musical satisfaction. This pursuit can become an addiction and ultimately *diminish* the ability to enjoy music. The next chapter includes an editorial I wrote for *Stereophile* magazine examining this subject.

How to Read Magazine Reviews

I've deliberately avoided recommending specific products in this book. By the time you would have read the recommendations, the products would likely have been updated or discontinued. The best source for up-to-date advice on components is product reviews in high-end audio magazines. Because most of these magazines are published monthly, they can stay on top of new products and offer buying advice. Many magazine reviewers are highly skilled listeners, technically competent, and uncompromising in their willingness to report truthfully about audio products. There's a saying in journalism that epitomizes the ethic of many high-end product reviewers: "without fear or favor." The competent review provides unbiased and educated opinion about the sound, build quality, and value of individual products. Because high-end reviewers hear lots of products under good conditions, they are in an ideal position to assess the relative merits and drawbacks and report their informed opinions. The best reviewers have a combination good ears, honesty, and technical competence.

You'll notice a big difference between reviews in high-end magazines and reviews in the so-called "mainstream slicks." The mass-market, mainstream magazines are advertiser-driven; their constituents are their advertisers. Conversely, high-end magazines are usually reader-driven; the magazines' goal is to serve their readers, not their advertisers. Consequently, high-end magazines often publish negative reviews, while mass-market magazines generally do not. Moreover, high-end magazines are much more discriminating about what makes a good component that can be recommended to readers. Mass-market magazines cater to the average person in the street, who, they believe—in my view, mistakenly—doesn't care about aspects of music reproduction important to the audiophile. The high-end product review is thus not only more honest, but much more discriminating in determining what is a worthy product. If you're reading a hi-fi magazine that never criticizes products, beware. Not all audio components are worth buying; therefore not all magazine reviews should conclude with a recommendation.

As someone who makes his living reviewing high-end audio products, I'll let you in on a few secrets which can help you use magazine reviews to your advantage. First, associate the review you're reading with the reviewer. Before reading the review, look at the byline and keep in mind who's writing the review. This way, you'll quickly learn different reviewers' tastes in music and equipment. Seek the guidance of reviewers with musical sensibilities similar to your own.

Second, don't assign equal weight to all reviews or reviewers. Audio reviewing is like any other field of expertise—there are many different levels of competence. Some reviewers have practiced their craft for decades, while others are newcomers who lack the seasoned veteran's commitment to the profession. Consider the reviewer's reputation, experience, and track record when giving a review credence. Also consider the reviewer's standards for what makes a good product. Just as there's a big difference between a movie recommendation given by Joel Siegel (*Good Morning America*) and Andrew Sarris (*The Village Voice*), so too are there differences in product recommendations from high-end reviewers.

Finally, listen to the products yourself. If two components are compared in a review, compare those products to hear if your perceptions match the reviewer's. Even if you aren't in the market for the product under review, listening to the components will sharpen your skills and put the reviewer's value judgments in perspective.

A common mistake among audiophiles looking for guidance is to select components on the basis of a rave review without fully auditioning the product for themselves. It's much easier to buy a product because a particular reviewer liked it than it is to research the product's merits and shortcomings for yourself. Buying products solely on the basis of a review is fraught with danger. Never forget that a review is nothing more than one person's opinion, however informed and educated that opinion might be. Moreover, if the reviewer's tastes differ from yours, you may end up with a component you don't like. We all have different priorities in judging reproduced sound quality; what the reviewer values most—soundstaging, for example—may be lower in your sonic hierarchy. *Your* priorities are the most important consideration when choosing music-playback components. Trust your own ears.

Sharp-eyed readers can find out which products a reviewer really thinks are special. Most reviewers list the reference system in which they audition new products. When a particular product shows up in the reference system review after review, you can be sure that the reviewer thinks that product is especially good. Another sure sign of a superb product is if the reviewer buys the product himself.

A final word about product reviews: Don't stop enjoying music if a component you've already purchased gets a negative review. You enjoyed music through that product before the review appeared—Why should another person's opinion intrude on your musical satisfaction? Magazine reviews—positive and negative—carry too much weight in readers' minds, and in the marketplace. (Remember, you heard this from a professional reviewer.)

In sum, reviews can be very useful provided you:

- Get to know individual reviewers' sonic and musical priorities. Find a reviewer on your sonic and musical wavelength, then trust his or her opinion.

- Compare your impressions of products to the reviewer's impressions. This will not only give you a feel for the reviewer's tastes and skill, but the exercise will make you a better listener.

- Don't assign the same weight to all reviews. Consider the reviewer's reputation and experience in the field. How many similar products has the reviewer auditioned? If a reviewer has heard virtually every serious digital processor, for example, his or her opinion will be worth more than the reviewer who has only heard a few models.

- Don't buy—or summarily reject—products solely on the basis of a review. Use product recommendations as a starting point for your own auditioning. Listen to the product yourself to decide if that product is for you. Let *your* ears decide.

System Matching

It is a truism of high-end audio that an inexpensive system can often outperform a more costly and ambitious rig. I've heard modest systems costing, say, $1500 that are more musically involving than $15,000 behemoths. Why?

Part of the answer is that some well-designed budget components sound better than ill-conceived or poorly executed esoteric products. But the most important factor in a playback system's musicality is *system matching*. System matching is the art of putting together components that complement each other sonically so that the overall result is a musicality beyond what each of the components could achieve if combined with less compatible products. The concept of synergy—that the whole is greater than the sum of the parts—is very important in creating the best-sounding system for the least money.

System matching is the last step in choosing an audio system. You should have first defined the system in terms of your individual needs, set your budget, and established a relationship with a local specialty audio retailer. After you've narrowed down your choices, which products you select will greatly depend on system matching.

Knowing what components work best with other components is best learned by listening experience, skill, and access to a wide range of equipment. Many of you don't have the time—or access to many diverse components—to find out for yourselves what equipment works best with other equipment. Consequently, you must rely on experts for general guidance, and on your own ears for choosing specific equipment combinations.

The two best sources for this information are magazine reviews and your local dealer. Your dealer will have the greatest knowledge about products he carries, and can make system-matching recommendations based on his experience assembling systems for his customers. Your dealer will likely have auditioned the products he sells in a variety of configurations; you can benefit from his experience by following his system-matching recommendations.

The other source of system-matching tips is magazine reviews. Product reviews published in reputable magazines will often name the associated equipment used in evaluating the product under review. The reviewer will sometimes describe his or her experiences with other equipment not directly part of the review. For example, a loudspeaker review may include a report on how the loudspeaker sounded when driven by three or four different power amplifiers. The sonic characteristics of each combination will be described, giving the reader an insight into which amplifier was the best match for that loudspeaker. More important, however, the sonic descriptions and value judgments expressed can suggest the *type* of amplifier best suited to that loudspeaker. By *type* I mean both technical performance (tubed vs. transistor, power output, output impedance, etc.) and general sonic characteristics (hard treble, forward presentation, well-controlled bass, etc.).

Let's say the reviewer drove the loudspeakers with four amplifiers: a low-powered but sweet-sounding integrated amplifier, a high-output–impedance tubed design, a medium- to high-powered inexpensive solid-state unit, and a massive solid-state amplifier that requires two people to lug it into the listening room. The reviewer reports that the integrated amplifier just didn't have enough power to produce sufficient volume, and that the sound lacked dynamics. The high-output-impedance tubed amplifier was mushy in the bass and had a reduced sense of pace and rhythm. The inexpensive solid-state amplifier had terrific bass control, but its forward presentation and grainy treble made it less than ideal with the loudspeaker under review. (All of these terms—like "forward," "grainy," and "pace"—are defined in the next chapter.) Finally, the reviewer concludes that the solid-state behemoth is the only suitable amplifier for this particular loudspeaker.

This doesn't mean that the most expensive amplifier will always work the best with all loudspeakers. I can think of loudspeakers in which this scenario would be completely different. Another loudspeaker would sound just fine with the integrated amplifier, suggesting that using the huge solid-state unit would be overkill. However, if the loudspeaker was a little tizzy in the treble and lean in the midbass, the tubed amplifier would tend to ameliorate these tendencies. Finally, if the loudspeaker wasn't that sensitive to treble grain, but needed to be driven by an amplifier with control and authority in the bass, the inexpensive solid-state unit would be a good choice—and the most cost-effective.

These reports of system matching can extend beyond the specific products reported on in the review. A fairly good idea of which *type* of sonic and technical performance is best suited to a particular product can be gained from a careful reading of product reviews. For example, you may conclude that a particular loudspeaker needs to be driven by a large, high-current amplifier. This knowledge can then point you in the right direction for equipment to audition yourself; you can rule out low-powered designs.

By reading magazine reviews, following your dealer's advice, and listening to combinations of products for yourself, you can assemble a well-matched system that squeezes the highest musical performance from your hi-fi budget.

Do's and Don'ts of Selecting Components

Some audiophiles are tempted to buy certain products for the wrong reasons. For example, many high-end products are marketed on the basis of some technical aspect of their design. A power amplifier may, for example, be touted as having "over 200,000μF of filter capacitance," "32 high-current output devices," and a "discrete JFET input stage." While these may be laudable attributes, they don't guarantee that the amplifier will produce good sound. Don't be swayed by technical claims. Listen to the product for yourself.

Just as you shouldn't make a purchasing decision based on specifications, neither should you base your decision solely on brand name. Many high-end manufacturers with solid reputations sometimes produce mediocre-sounding products. A high-end marquee doesn't necessarily mean high-end sound. Again, let your ears be your guide. I'm often pleasantly surprised to find moderately priced products that sound as good—or very nearly as good—as products costing two or three times as much.

You should, however, consider the company's longevity, reputation for build quality, customer service record, and product reliability when choosing components. High-end manufacturers run the gamut from one-man garage operations to companies with hundreds of employees and advanced design and manufacturing facilities. The garage operation may produce good-sounding products, but may not be in business next year. This not only makes it hard to get service, but also greatly lowers the product's resale value.

High-end manufacturers also have very different policies regarding service. Some repair their products grudgingly, and/or charge high fees for fixing products out of warranty. Others bend over backward to keep their valued customers happy. In fact, some high-end audio companies go to extraordinary lengths to please their customers. One amplifier manufacturer who received an out-of-warranty product for repair not only fixed the amplifier free of charge, but replaced the customer's scratched faceplate at no cost! It pays in the long run to do business with manufacturers who have reputations for good customer service.

Another factor to consider before laying down your hard-earned cash is how long the product has been on the market. Without warning, manufacturers discontinue products and replace them with new ones, or update a product to "Mark II" status. When this happens, the value of the older product drops immediately. Don't get stuck with a product at the end of its production run. If you know an excellent product is about to be discontinued, you can often buy the floor sample at a discount. This is a good way of saving money, provided the discount is significant. You end up with a lower price and all the service and support inherent in buying from an authorized and reputable dealer rather than a private party.

The best source of advance information on new products and what's about to be discontinued are *Stereophile*'s reports from the semiannual Consumer Electronics Shows and *Stereophile*'s own annual High-End Hi-Fi Shows.

Your Relationship with the Retailer

Your local specialty audio retailer plays a vital role in the high-end audio industry. He's more than just an equipment dealer; he is usually a dedicated audio and music enthusiast himself. He knows his products and is often the best person to advise you on selecting equipment and system setup. The good specialty audio retailer doesn't sell you boxes of electronics; he provides you with the satisfaction of great-sounding music in your home.

If you've bought audio equipment only from mass-market retailers in the past, you should completely realign your expectations of your relationship with the high-end dealer. How you've bought mass-market audio equipment will be very different from how you'll buy a high-end system.

Consider the very different relationships between seller and buyer in the following scenarios. In the first situation, a used-car dealer in downtown Los Angeles is trying to sell a car to someone from out of town. The seller has only one shot at the buyer, and he intends to make the most of it. The seller doesn't care about return business, the customer's satisfaction with the purchase, or what the customer will tell his friends about the dealer. It will be an adversarial relationship from start to finish.

Then consider a new-car dealer in Great Falls, Montana, selling a car to another Great Falls resident. For this dealer, return business is vital to survival. So is customer satisfaction, quality service, providing expert advice on models and options, finding exactly the right car for the particular buyer, and giving the customer an occasional ride to work when he drops off his car for service. He knows his customers by name, and has developed mutually beneficial, long-term relationships with them.

If buying a mass-market hi-fi system is like negotiating with a used-car dealer in downtown L.A., selecting a high-end music system should be made within a relationship similar to the one enjoyed between the Montana dealer and his customers.

Take the time to establish a relationship with your local dealer. Make friends with him—it'll pay off in the long run. Get to know a particular salesperson, and, if possible, the store's owner. Tell them your musical tastes, needs, lifestyle, and budget—then let them offer equipment suggestions. They know their products best, and can offer specific component recommendations. The good stores will regard you as a valued, long-term customer, not someone at whom they have one shot at making a sale. Don't shop just for equipment—shop for the retailer with the greatest honesty and competence.

Keep in mind, however, that dealers will naturally favor the brands they carry. Be suspicious of dealers who badmouth competing brands that have earned good reputations in the high-end audio press. The best starting point in assembling your system is a healthy mix of your dealer's recommendations and unbiased, competent magazine reviews.

The high-end retailing business is very different from the mass-market merchandising of the low-quality "home entertainment" products sold in appliance emporiums. The specialty retailer's annual turnover is vastly lower than that of the mid-fi store down the street. Consequently, the specialty retailer's profit margin must be larger for him to stay in business. Don't expect him to offer huge discounts and price cuts on equipment to take a sale from a mid-fi store. Because the high-end dealer offers so much more than just pushing a box over the counter, his prices just can't be competitive. Instead, you should be prepared to pay full list price—or very close to it—on a system purchase.

Here's why. The specialty retailer often operates on a net profit margin of about 5%. After paying his employees, rent, lights, heat, insurance, advertising, and a host of other expenses, the dealer can expect to put in his pocket about five cents out of every dollar spent in his store. Now, if he discounts his price by 5%, he is essentially working for free, and only keeping his doors open a little longer. If the dealer offers a discount or marks down demonstration or discontinued units, you should take advantage of these opportunities. But don't expect the dealer to discount; he deserves the full margin provided by the product's suggested retail price.

In return for paying full price, however, you should receive a level of service and professionalism second to none. Expect the best from your dealer. Spend as much time as you feel is necessary auditioning components in the showroom before you buy. Listen to components at home in your own system before you buy. Ask the retailer to set up your system for you. Exploit the dealer's wide knowledge of what components are best for the money. Use his knowledge of system matching to get the best sound possible on a given budget. And if one of your components needs repair, don't be afraid to ask for a loaner until yours is fixed. The dealer should bend over backward to accommodate your needs.

If you give the high-end dealer your loyalty, you can expect this red-carpet treatment. This relationship can be undermined, however, if you buy a product the dealer sells from a competitor, or by mail, to save a few dollars. The higher price charged by the dealer may seem hard to justify at first, but in the long run you'll benefit from his expertise and commitment to you as a customer. If the product purchased elsewhere doesn't sound good in your system, don't expect your local dealer to help you out. Further, don't abuse the home audition privilege. Take home only those products you are seriously considering buying. If the dealer let everyone take equipment home for an audition, he'd have nothing in the store to demonstrate. The home audition should be used to confirm that you've selected the right component through store auditioning, magazine reviews, and the dealer's recommendations.

If you don't live close to any high-end dealers, there are several very good mail-order companies that offer excellent audio advice over the phone. They provide as much service as possible by phone, including money-back guarantees, product exchanges, and component matching suggestions. You can't audition components in a store, but you can often listen to them in your system and get a refund if the product isn't what you'd hoped.

In short, if you treat your dealer right, you can expect his full expertise and commitment to getting you the best sound possible. There's absolutely no substitute for the skilled dealer's services and commitment to your satisfaction.

Used Equipment

Used products often sell for half the component's original list price, making used gear a tempting alternative. The lower prices on used high-end components provide an opportunity to get a high-quality system for the same budget as a less ambitious new system. Moreover, buying used gear lets you audition many components at length. If you find a product you like, keep it. If you don't like the sound of your used purchase, you can often sell it for no less than what you paid.

There are two ways of buying used equipment: from a dealer, and from a private party. A retailer may charge a little more for used products, but often offers a short warranty (60 or 90 days), and sometimes exchange privileges. Buying used gear from a reputable retailer is a lot less risky than dealing with a private party (unless you're buying from a friend).

The audiophile inclined to buy used equipment can often get great deals. Some audiophiles simply *must* own the latest and greatest product, no matter the cost. They'll buy a state-of-the-art component one year, only to sell it the next to acquire the current top-of-the-line. These audiophiles generally take good care of the equipment and sell it at bargain-basement prices. If you can find such a person, have him put your name at the top of his calling list when he's ready to sell. You can end up with a superb system for a fraction of the original selling price.

A few pitfalls await the buyer of used equipment, however. The following disadvantages of used equipment apply mostly to buying from a private party rather than from a reputable dealer. First, there are no assurances that the component is working properly. The product could have a defect not apparent during a cursory examination. Second, the used product could be so outdated that its performance falls far short of new gear selling for the same price—or less—than the used component. This is especially true of CD players, CD transports, and digital processors. Third, a used product carries no warranty; you'll have to pay for any repair work. Finally, you must ask why the person is selling the used equipment. All too often, a music lover doesn't do his homework and buys a product that doesn't satisfy musically or work well within the rest of his system. If you see lots of people selling the same product, beware—it's a sign that the product has a fundamental musical flaw. Finally, buying used equipment from a private party eliminates all the factors that make your local specialty retailer such an asset when selecting equipment. You don't get the dealer's expert opinions, home audition, trade or upgrade policy, dealer setup, warranty, dealer service, loaner units, and all the other benefits you get from buying new at a dealer.

Approach used components with caution; they can be a windfall—or a nightmare.

About Product Upgrades

Many manufacturers improve their products and offer existing customers the option of upgrading their component to current performance. This is the "Mark II" (or III or IV) designation on some products. The dealer can usually handle sending your component back to the factory. Some manufacturers prefer to deal with the customer directly, saving the dealer markup and keeping the upgrade price lower.

Setting Up Your System for the Best Sound

How your system is set up and installed in your home can make a big difference in the system's musical performance. There are many setup techniques whose individual audible differences may be very small, but which can dramatically increase a system's performance when combined. System setup requires listening skill (covered in the next chapter), patience, and a desire to extract the last bit of performance from your system. There's nothing more rewarding than realizing a significant audible improvement without spending a dime.

All system setup should be based on a foundation of good loudspeaker placement. (This topic is so important that I've devoted a large section of Chapter 4 to it.) Once you've made this coarse adjustment, you can work on refinements. As your system's sound improves, you'll become more attuned to small performance variations. It's like the Grand Prix driver who notices the difference of a half pound of air pressure in his tires; at a certain level of performance, small differences become important.

Chapters 4–11 include specific setup procedures for each component in the playback chain; Chapter 12 covers the accessories that will help you get the most out of your system.

Here's a summary of the system setup techniques detailed in the later chapters.

- Position the loudspeakers and listening seat for the best sound. Without proper loudspeaker and listener placement, none of the other setup techniques will matter (see Chapter 4).

- Add acoustic treatments to the listening room. They can have profound effects on the system's performance, and make the difference between mediocre and superlative sound. Acoustic treatments are covered in detail in Chapter 4.

- Keep interconnects away from AC cords. If they must meet, position them at right angles to each other instead of parallel (see Chapter 11).

- Separate digital data interconnects (between a separate CD transport and digital processor) from analog interconnects. The very high frequencies carried in digital cables can radiate noise and pollute analog signals (see Chapter 8).

- Turn off your digital components when playing LPs.

- Keep interconnects and loudspeaker cables as short as possible, but always the same length between left and right (see Chapter 11).

- Position components for adequate ventilation. Overheating will shorten product life.

- Assure good contact between loudspeaker cables and binding posts. Get the spade lug fully on the binding post and tighten with a nut driver (see Chapter 11).

- Clean plugs and jacks periodically with contact cleaner (see Chapter 12).

- Maintain adequate distance between the preamplifier and power amplifier. The power amp's large transformer can radiate 60Hz hum. This is more critical in preamplifiers with phono stages or with separate phono preamps (see Chapter 6).

- Install the equipment on a sturdy stand. Vibration can degrade system performance, particularly that of turntables (covered in more detail in Chapters 9 and 12).

- Use a polarity meter or voltmeter to determine the best AC plug polarity (described in Chapter 12).

- Don't use light dimmers in the listening room or fluorescent lighting.

- Experiment with AC power conditioners. They make a huge improvement in some systems, none in others, and can sometimes degrade system performance. Listen before you buy (see Chapter 12).

- Try accessories such as isolation feet and high-end AC power cords. Buy them with the provision that you can return them for a full refund (see Chapter 12).

Component Selection Summary

When choosing a high-end system or component, follow these ten guidelines:

1) Establish your budget. Buy a component or system you'll be happy with in the long run, not one that will "do" for now. Do it right the first time.

2) Be an informed consumer. Learn all you can about high-end audio. Study magazine reviews, visit your local specialty retailer, and read the rest of this book. Do your homework.

3) Develop a relationship with your dealer. He can be the best source of information in choosing components and assembling a system.

4) Find components that work synergistically together. Again, your dealer knows his products and can offer suggestions.

5) Select products based on their musical qualities, not technical performance, specifications, price, or brand name.

6) Choose carefully; many lower-priced components can outperform higher-priced ones. Take your time and maintain high standards—there are some great bargains out there.

7) Buy products from companies with good reputations for value, customer service, and reliability. Also, match the company's product philosophy (cost-no-object vs. best value for the money) to your needs.

8) When possible, listen to prospective components in your system at home before buying.

9) Follow the setup guidelines in this and the subsequent chapters to get the most from your system. Enlist the aid of your dealer in system setup.

10) Add accessories *after* your system is set up.

If you read the rest of this book, subscribe to a reputable high-end magazine, and follow these guidelines, you're well on you way to making the best purchasing decisions—and having high-quality music reproduction in your home.

I have one last piece of advice. After you get your system set up, forget about the hardware. It's time to start enjoying music.

3 Becoming a Better Listener

Critical listening is the practice of evaluating the quality of audio equipment by careful analytical listening. Critical listening is very different from listening for pleasure; the goal isn't to enjoy the musical experience, but to determine if a system or component sounds good or bad, and what *specific characteristics* of the sound make it good or bad. We want to critically examine what we're hearing so that we can form value judgments about the reproduced sound. We can use this information to evaluate and choose components, and to set up a system.

Evaluating audio equipment by ear is essential—today's technical measurements simply aren't advanced enough to characterize the musical performance of audio products. The human hearing mechanism is vastly more sensitive and complex than the most sophisticated test equipment now available. Though technical performance is a valid consideration when choosing equipment, the ear should always be the final arbiter of good sound. Moreover, the musical significance of sonic differences between components can only be judged subjectively. This is best expressed by Michael Polanyi in his book, *Personal Knowledge* (Harper Torchbooks TB 1158):

> *"Whenever we find connoisseurship operating within science or technology we may assume it persists only because it has not been possible to replace it by a measurable grading."*

Because we use connoisseurship in the evaluation of audio products, the process is more an aesthetic endeavor than a purely technical one. Good technical performance can contribute to high-quality musical performance, but it doesn't tell us what we really want to know: how well the product communicates the musical message. To find that out, we must listen.

In my full-time job as Consulting Technical Editor for *Stereophile* magazine, I listen to audio products extensively under ideal conditions, then measure their technical performance in the test laboratory. My experience overwhelmingly indicates that we learn much more about the quality of an audio component in the listening room than in the test lab.

Knowing what sounds good and what doesn't is easy; most people can tell the difference between excellent and poor sound. But discovering *why* a product is musically satisfying or not, and the ability to recognize and describe differences in sound quality, are learned skills. Like all skills, that of critical listening improves with practice. The more you listen, the better a listener you'll become. As your ear improves, you'll be able to distinguish smaller and smaller differences in reproduced sound quality—and be able to describe *how* two presentations are different, and why one is better.

This chapter defines the language of critical listening, describes what to listen for, and outlines the procedures for setting up valid listening comparisons. It will either get you started in critical listening, or help you become a more highly skilled listener.

Audiophile Values

A general discussion of audiophile values is important in understanding the next sections of this chapter. We can make some broad statements about what we like and dislike in reproduced music, and what is important to us as audiophiles.

Good sound is only a means to an end—musical satisfaction—not the end itself. If a neighbor or colleague invites you over to hear his hi-fi system, you can tell immediately whether he's a music lover or a "hi-fi buff" more interested in sound than in music. If he plays the music very loud, then turns it down after 30 seconds to seek your opinion (approval), he's probably not a music lover. If, however, he sits you down, asks what kind of music *you* like, plays it at a reasonable volume, and says or does nothing for the next 20 minutes while you both listen, it's likely that this person holds audiophile values or simply cares a lot about music.

In the first example, the acquaintance tried to impress you with *sound*. In the second case, your friend also wanted to impress you with his system, but by its ability to express the *music*, not shake the walls. This is the fundamental difference between "hi-fi enthusiasts" and music lovers.

(You can use the same test to immediately tell what kind of hi-fi store you're in. And if anyone pulls out a CD of trains, sonic booms, Shuttle launches, or jet takeoffs, run for cover.)

I've noticed an unusual trend when playing my system for friends and acquaintances not involved in audio. I sit them down in the "sweet spot" (the seating position that provides the best sound) and put on some music I think they'll like. Rather than sitting there for the whole piece or song, they tend to jump up immediately and tell me how good it sounds. They've apparently been conditioned by the kind of razzle-dazzle demonstrations in some hi-fi stores or friends' houses. When *you* begin listening—at someone's house or a dealer's showroom—don't feel the need to express an opinion about the sound. Sit and listen attentively with eyes closed, letting the *music*—not the sound—tell you how good the system is.

When listening in a group, don't be swayed by others' opinions. If they're skilled listeners, try to understand what they're talking about. Listen to their descriptions and compare their impressions with your own. In fact, this is the best way to recognize the specific sonic characteristics we'll talk about later in this chapter. But don't go along with what everyone else says. If you don't hear a difference between two digital cables, for example, don't be afraid to say so. In addition, you should be completely truthful when asked for an opinion about a system. If the sound is bad, say so.

All audio components affect the signal passing through them. Some products add artifacts, such as a grainy treble or a lumpy bass. Others subtract parts of the signal—for example, a loudspeaker that doesn't go very low in the bass. (These terms are defined later in this chapter.) A fundamental audiophile value holds that sins of commission (adding something to the music) are far worse than sins of omission (removing something from the music). If parts of the music are missing, we can subconsciously fill in what isn't there and still enjoy the music. But if the playback system adds an artificial character to the sound, we are constantly reminded that we're hearing a reproduction and not just music.

Let's illustrate this sins-of-commission/omission dichotomy with two loudspeakers. The first loudspeaker—a three-way system with a 15" woofer in a very large cabinet—sells for a moderate price in a mass-market appliance store; it plays loudly and develops lots of bass. The second loudspeaker sells for about the same price, but is a small two-way system with a 6" woofer. It doesn't play nearly as loudly, and produces much less bass. If you needed a refrigerator dolly to move the first loudspeaker, you can almost hold the second loudspeaker in your out-stretched hand.

The behemoth loudspeaker has some problems. The bass is boomy, thick, and overwhelming. All the bass notes seem to have the same pitch. The very prominent treble is coarse and grainy, and the midrange has a big peak of excess energy that makes singers sound as if they have colds.

The small loudspeaker has no such problems. The treble is smooth and clear, and the mids are pure and open. It has, however, very little bass by comparison, won't play very loudly, and doesn't produce a physical sensation of sound hitting your body.

The first loudspeaker commits sins of commission, *adding* unnatural artifacts to the sound. The bass peaks that made it boomy, the grain overlaying the treble, and the midrange colorations are all additive distortions.

The second loudspeaker's faults, however, were of omission. It *removed* certain elements of the music—low bass and the ability to play loudly—but left the remainder of the music intact. It didn't add grain to the treble, thickness to the bass, or colorations to the midrange.

There is no doubt that the second loudspeaker will be more musically satisfying. The first loudspeaker's additive distortions are not only much more musically objectionable, they also constantly remind us that we are listening to artificially reproduced music. The second loudspeaker's flaws are of a nature that allows us to forget that we are listening to loudspeakers. Addition is far worse than subtraction.

Another audiophile value holds that even small differences in the quality of the musical presentation are important. Because music matters to us, we get excited by *any* improvement in sound quality. Moreover, there isn't a linear relationship between the magnitude of a sonic difference and its musical significance.

While reviewing a revelatory new state-of-the-art digital-to-analog converter, I listened to a piece of music I'd heard hundreds of times before. The piece, performed by a five-member group, had vocals and very long instrumental breaks. During the instrumental breaks, the vocalist played percussion instruments. Through lesser-quality digital processors, the percussion had always been just another sound fused into the music's tapestry; I'd never heard it as a separate instrument played by the vocalist. The group seemed to become a four-piece ensemble when the vocalist wasn't singing; I never heard the percussion as separate from the rest of the music.

The new digital processor was particularly good at resolving individual instruments and presenting them not as just more sounds homogenized into the overall musical fabric, but as distinct entities. Consequently, when the instrumental break came, I heard the percussion as a separate, more prominent instrument. In my mind's eye, and for the first time, the vocalist never left—she remained "on stage," playing the percussion instruments. Just by this "small" change in the presentation, the band went from being a quartet to a quintet during the instrumental breaks.

The "objective" difference in the electrical signal must have been minuscule; the subjective musical consequences were profound.

This is why small differences in the musical presentation are important—if we care deeply enough about music and about how well it is reproduced. "Small" improvements can have large subjective consequences. This example highlights the inability of measurements alone to characterize audio equipment performance.

Much of music's expression and meaning can be found in such minutiae of detail, subtlety, and nuance. When such subtlety is conveyed by the playback system, we feel a vastly deeper communication with the musicians. Their intent and expression are more vivid, allowing us to more deeply appreciate their artistry. For example, if we compare two performances of Max Reger's Sonata in D Major for solo violin—one competent, the other superlative—we could say that, on an objective basis, they were virtually identical. Both performers played the same notes at about the same tempo. The difference in expression is in the nuances, the inspired subtleties of rubato, tempo, emphasis, length of notes, and volume that bring the performance to life and convey the piece's musical meaning and intent. This example is analogous to the difference between mediocre and superb music playback systems, and why small differences in sound quality can matter so much. High-end audio is about reproducing these nuances so that we can come one step closer to the musical expression.

The sad but universal truth about audio equipment is that, any time you put a signal into an audio component, it never comes out better at the other end. We therefore want to keep the signal path as simple as possible, to remove any unnecessary electronics from between us and the music. This is why we get rid of equalizers and other such "enhancers" from our playback systems. The less done to the signal, the better.

Pitfalls of Becoming a Critical Listener

There are some dangers inherent in developing critical listening skills. The first is an inability to distinguish between critical listening and listening for pleasure. Once started on the path of critiquing sound quality, it's all too easy to forget that the reason we're involved in audio is because we love music. We start thinking that every time we hear music we must have an opinion about what's right and what's wrong with the sound. This is the surest path toward the disease humorously known as *Audiophilia nervosa*. Symptoms of *Audiophilia nervosa* include constantly changing equipment, playing only one track of a disc or LP at a time instead of the whole record, changing cables for certain music, and in general "listening to the hardware" instead of to the music.

But high-end audio is about making the hardware disappear. When listening for pleasure—which should be the vast majority of your listening time—forget about the system. Forget about critical listening. Shift into critical-listening mode only when you need to make a value judgment, or just for practice to become a better listener. Draw the line between critical listening and listening for pleasure—and don't cross it.

There is also the related danger that your standards of sound quality will rise to such a height that you can't enjoy music unless it's perfectly reproduced—in other words, to the point that you can't enjoy music, period. Lower your expectations of sound quality when you can't control it. Although it's not very high-quality reproduction, I get a great deal of pleasure from my car stereo. Don't let being an audiophile interfere with your enjoyment of music anytime, anywhere.

Sonic Descriptions and their Meanings

The biggest problem in critical listening is finding words to express our perceptions and experiences. We hear things in reproduced music that are difficult to identify and put into words. A listening vocabulary is essential not only to conveying to others what we hear, but also to recognizing and understanding our own perceptions. If we can attach a descriptive name to a perception, we can more easily recognize that perception when we experience it again.

A perfect example of the bond between words and perceptions is found in Michael Polanyi's *Personal Knowledge* (Harper Torchbooks TB 1158). His description of the radiology student's experience is identical to that of the audiophile becoming a skilled critical listener:

"Think of a medical student attending a course in the X-ray diagnosis of pulmonary diseases. He watches in a darkened room shadowy traces on a fluorescent screen placed against a patient's chest, and hears the radiologist commenting to his assistants in technical language, on the significant features of these shadows. At first the student is completely puzzled. For he can see in the X-ray picture of a chest only the shadows of the heart and the ribs, with a few spidery blotches between them. The experts seem to be romancing about figments of their imagination; he can see nothing that they are talking about. Then as he goes on listening for a few weeks, looking carefully at ever new pictures of different cases, a tentative understanding will dawn on him; he will gradually

forget about the ribs and begin to see the lungs. And eventually, if he perseveres intelligently, a rich panorama of significant details will be revealed to him; of physiological variations and pathological changes, of scars, of chronic infections and signs of acute disease. He has entered a new world. He still sees only a fraction of what the experts can see, but the pictures are definitely making sense now and so do most of the comments made on them. He is about to grasp what he is being taught; it has clicked. Thus, at the moment when he has learned the language of pulmonary radiology, the student will also have learned to understand pulmonary radiograms. The two can only happen together. Both halves of the problem set to us by an unintelligible text, referring to an unintelligible subject, jointly guide our efforts to solve them, and they are solved eventually together by discovering a conception which comprises a joint understanding of both the words and the things."

Just as the student learns to understand pulmonary radiograms at the moment he learns the language of pulmonary radiology, the audiophile learns to identify specific sonic characteristics when he learns the language of critical listening. The bond between words and ideas is inextricable.

By describing in detail the specific sonic characteristics of how electronic components change the sound of music passing through them, I hope to attune you to recognizing those same characteristics when you listen. After reading this next section, listen to two products for yourself and try to hear what I'm describing. It can be any two products—if you have a portable CD player, hook it up to your system and compare it to your home CD player. Even comparing a CD and a cassette made from that CD will get you started. The important thing is to start listening analytically. If you don't hear the sonic differences immediately, keep listening. The more you listen, the more sensitive you'll become to those differences.

Every listener hears a little differently. What I listen for during critical listening may be different from another listener's sonic checklist. Moreover, the different values placed on different aspects of the sonic presentation are matters of taste. I occasionally spend time listening critically in my listening room with visiting manufacturers and designers of high-end equipment—many of them highly skilled listeners. While we share many commonalities in determining what sounds good, there is a wide range of perception about what aspects of the presentation are important. For example, some listeners value correct reproduction of timbre above all else. A product may have outstanding bass, spectacular soundstaging, and clean treble, but if the timbre is synthetic or hard, those other good qualities don't matter to that listener. Conversely, another listener may find soundstaging of utmost importance. Finally, a layer of treble grain that is hardly noticed by one listener may be unacceptable to another. We all hear differently and value different things in music reproduction. Different listeners not only hear differently, but a single listener's musical perceptions and acuity vary with the time of day, mood, and state of relaxation.

The following description of what I listen for is a reflection of my own tastes, mixed with what I've learned from other skilled listeners. You may have your own sonic priorities, but the important thing is that we all hear and describe the same characteristics with the same language. The descriptive terms presented here can be found in my and other writers' product reviews for *Stereophile*. There is general agreement about what these terms mean, but shades of meaning vary among individual listeners.

When I listen critically to an audio component to characterize its sonic and musical performance and form value judgments about that product, I first follow the set-up procedures described later in this chapter. They are vital to forming accurate impressions of products, but secondary to the following discussion.

The sonic terms and characteristics defined here apply to audio components in general. Advice on what to listen for when choosing specific components is included in Chapters 5–13. Note that we often describe differences in terms of a frequency-response difference (i.e., "too much treble"). The component may have flat treble response, but the distortions it introduces give the impression of too much treble.

It's also useful to understand the broad terms that describe the audio frequency band. The range of human hearing, which spans ten octaves from about 16Hz (cycles per second) to 20,000Hz, or 20 kilohertz (20kHz), can be divided into the specific regions described below.

Frequency Range		
Lower Limit	Upper Limit	Description
20	40	Deep Bass
40	80	Midbass
80	160	Upper Bass
160	320	Lower Midrange
320	640	(Middle) Midrange
640	1280	Upper Midrange
1280	2560	Lower Treble
2560	5120	Middle Treble
5120	10240	Upper Treble
10240	20480	Top Octave

This rough guide will help you understand the following terms and definitions. A full characterization of how a product "sounds" will include aspects of each of these sonic qualities.

Tonal Balance

The first aspect of the musical presentation to listen for is the product's overall *tonal balance*. How well balanced are the bass, midrange, and treble? If it sounds as though there is too much treble, we call the presentation *bright*. The impression of too little treble produces a *dull* or *rolled off* sound. If the bass overwhelms the rest of the music, we say the presentation is *heavy* or *weighty*. If we hear too little bass, we call the presentation *thin, lightweight, uptilted,* or *lean*.

A product's tonal balance is a significant—and often overwhelming—aspect of its sonic signature.

Overall Perspective

The term *perspective* describes the apparent distance between the listener and the music. Perspective is largely a function of the recording (particularly the distance between the performers and the microphones), but is also affected by components in the playback system. Some products push the presentation *forward*, toward the listener; others sound more distant, or *laid-back*. The forward product presents the music in front of the loudspeakers; the laid-back product makes the music appear slightly behind the loudspeakers. Put another way, the forward product sounds as though the musicians have taken a few steps toward you; the laid-back products give the impression that the musicians have taken a few steps back. Yet another way of describing perspective is by row number in the concert hall. Some products put the listener in Row D, others give you the impression that you're sitting in Row S.

Several other terms describe perspective. *Dry* generally means lacking reverberation and space, but can also apply to a forward perspective. Other watchwords for a forward presentation are *immediate, incisive, vivid, aggressive,* and *present*. Terms associated with laid-back include *lush, easygoing,* and *gentle*. These terms also apply to musical timbres, described later.

Forward products produce a greater sense of the instrument's *presence* before you, but can quickly become fatiguing. Conversely, if the presentation is too laid-back, the music is uninvolving and lacking in immediacy. If the product under evaluation distorts the perspective captured during the recording, I prefer that it err in the direction of being laid-back. When a product is overly immediate, I feel as though the music is coming *at* me, assaulting my ears. The reaction is to close up, to try to keep the music at arm's length. Conversely, a laid-back presentation invites the listener in, pulling her gently forward *into* the music, allowing her the space to explore its subtleties. It's like the difference between having a conversation with someone who is aggressive, gets in your face, and talks too much, compared with someone who stands back, speaking quietly and sparsely.

In loudspeakers, perspective is often the result of a peak or dip in the midrange (a peak is too much energy, a dip is too little). In fact, the midrange between 1kHz and 3kHz is called the *presence region* because it provides a sense of presence and immediacy. The human voice harmonics span the presence region thus, the voice is greatly affected by a product's perspective.

Untrained listeners who can't specifically identify whether a reproduced musical presentation is forward or laid-back will feel a tension that usually translates into a desire to turn down the music if the presentation is too forward. Conversely, a laid-back presentation can make the music uninvolving rather than riveting.

Note that the terms associated with overall perspective can be used to describe specific aspects of the presentation (such as the treble) in addition to describing to the overall perspective. If we say the treble is forward, we mean that it is overly prominent, causing it to sound as though it is closer to the listener than the rest of the music.

The Treble

Good treble is essential to high-quality music reproduction. In fact, many otherwise excellent audio products fail to satisfy musically because of poor treble performance.

The treble characteristics we want to avoid are described by the terms *bright, tizzy, forward, aggressive, hard, brittle, edgy, dry, white, bleached, wiry, metallic, sterile, analytical, screechy,* and *grainy*. Treble problems are pervasive; look how many adjectives we use to describe them.

If a product has too much apparent treble, it overstates sounds that are already rich in high frequencies. Examples are overemphasized cymbals, excessive sibilance ("s" and "ch" sounds) in vocals, and violins that sound thin. A product with too much apparent treble is called *bright*. Brightness is a prominence in the treble region, primarily between 3kHz and 6kHz. Brightness can be caused by a rising frequency response in loudspeakers, or poor electronic design. Many CD players and solid-state amplifiers add prominence to the treble, although they measure as having a flat frequency response.

Tizzy describes too much upper treble (5kHz-20kHz), characterized as a *whitening* of the treble. Tizzy cymbals have an emphasis on the upper harmonics, the sizzle and air that rides over the main cymbal sound. Tizziness gives cymbals more of an "sssss" than a "sssshhhh" sound.

Forward, if applied to treble, is very similar to *bright*; both describe too much treble. A forward treble, however, also tends to be dry, lacking space and air around it.

Many of the terms listed above have virtually identical meanings. *Hard*, *brittle*, and *metallic* all describe an unpleasant treble characteristic that reminds one of metal being struck. In fact, the unique harmonic structure created from metal-on-metal impact is very similar to the distortion characteristics of a solid-state amplifier driven past its power limitations.

I find the sound of the saxophone to be a good gauge of hard, brittle, and metallic treble, particularly lower treble. If reproduced incorrectly, sax can take on a thin, reedy, very unpleasant tone. The antithesis of this sound is *rich*, *warm*, and *full*. When the sax's upper harmonics are reproduced with a metallic character, the whole instrument's sound collapses. Interestingly, the sound of the saxophone has the most complex harmonic structure of any instrument. It's no wonder that it is so revealing of treble problems.

White and *bleached* have meanings very similar to *bright*, but I associate them more with a thinness in the treble, often caused by a lack of energy (or what sounds like a lack of energy) in the upper midrange. With no supporting harmonic structure beneath it, the treble becomes threadbare and thin, much like an overexposed photograph. Cymbals should have a gong-like low-frequency component with a sheen over it. If cymbals sound like bursts of white noise (the sound you hear between radio stations), what you're probably hearing is a *white* or *bleached* sound.

A particularly annoying treble characteristic is *graininess*. Treble grain is a coarseness overlaying treble textures. It is most noticeable (to me, anyway) on solo violin, massed violins, flute, and female voice. On flute, treble grain is recognizable as a roughness or fuzzy sound that seems to ride on top of the flute's dynamic envelope. (That is, the grain follows the flute's volume.) Grain makes violins sound as though they are being played with hacksaw blades rather than bows. This is a gross exaggeration, but one that conveys the idea of the coarse texture added by grain.

Treble grain can be of any texture, from very fine to coarse and rough. Think of 400 grit sandpaper and 80 grit sandpaper. The more coarse the grain, the more objectionable it is. The preceding discussion of grain applies in even larger measure to midrange textures, which we'll discuss later.

Treble problems can foster the interesting perception that the treble isn't integrated into the music's harmonic tapestry, but is riding on top of it. The top end seems somehow separate from the music, not an integral part of the presentation. When this happens, we are aware of the treble as a distinct entity, not as just another aspect of the music. If the treble calls attention to itself, be suspicious.

The most common sources of these problems are, in a rough order of descending magnitude: tweeters in loudspeakers, overly reflective listening rooms, digital source components (usually the CD player or digital processor), preamplifiers, power amplifiers, cables, and dirty AC power sources.

So far, I've discussed only problems that emphasize treble. Some products tend to make the treble softer and less prominent than live music. This characteristic is often designed into the product, either to compensate for treble flaws in other components in the system, or make the product sound more palatable. Deliberately softening the treble is the designer's shortcut; if he can't get the treble right, he just makes it less offensive by softening it.

Here are the terms that describe good treble performance, listed in ascending order of magnitude: *smooth, sweet, soft, silky, gentle, liquid,* and *lush*. When the treble becomes overly smooth, we say it is *romantic, rolled-off,* or *syrupy*. Smooth, sweet, and silky treble are compliments; rolled-off and syrupy suggest that the component goes too far in treble smoothness, and is therefore *colored*.

A rolled-off and syrupy treble may be blessed relief after hearing bright, hard, and grainy treble, but it isn't musically satisfying in the long run. Such a presentation tends to become *bland, uninvolving, slow, thick, closed-in,* and *lacking detail*. All these terms describe the effects of a treble presentation that errs too far on the side of smoothness. The presentation will lack *life, air, openness, extension,* and a sense of *space* if the treble is too soft. The music sounds *closed-in* rather than being big and open.

The best treble presentation is one that sounds most like real music. It should have lots of energy—cymbals can, after all, sound quite aggressive in real life—yet not have a synthetic, grainy, or dry character. We don't hear these characteristics in live music; we shouldn't hear them in reproduced music. More important, the treble should sound like an integral part of the music, not a detached noise riding on top of it. If a component has a colored treble presentation, however, it is far less musically objectionable if it errs on the side of smoothness rather than brightness.

The Midrange

J. Gordon Holt, *Stereophile*'s founder and the father of subjective audio equipment evaluation, once wrote, "If the midrange isn't right, nothing else matters."

The midrange is important for several reasons. First, most of the musical energy is in the midrange, particularly the important lower harmonics of most instruments. Not only does this region contain most of the musical energy, but our ear is much more sensitive to midrange and lower treble than to bass and upper treble. Specifically, we are the most sensitive to sounds between about 800Hz and 3kHz, both to low volume and small frequency-response changes within this band. The ear's threshold of hearing—i.e., the softest sound we can hear—is dramatically lower in the midband than at the frequency extremes. We've developed this additional midband acuity probably because the energy of most of the sounds we hear every day—the human voice, rustling leaves, the sounds of other animals—is concentrated in the midrange.

Midrange colorations can be extremely annoying. Loudspeakers with peaks and dips in the mids sound very unnatural; the midrange is absolutely the worst place for loudspeaker imperfections. Confining our discussion to loudspeakers for the moment, midrange colorations overlay the music with a common characteristic that emphasizes certain sounds. The male speaking voice is particularly revealing of midrange anomalies. Some sounds seem to stick out from the others. These colorations are often described by comparisons with vowel sounds. A particular coloration may impart an "aaww" sound. A coloration lower in frequency may emphasize "ooohhh" sounds. A higher-pitched coloration may sound like the vowel sound "eeeee." Another coloration may be called *hooty*.

Some midrange colorations can be likened to the sound of someone speaking through cupped hands. Try reading this sentence while cupping your hands around your mouth. Open and close your hands and listen to how the sound of your voice changes. That's the kind of midrange coloration we sometimes hear from loudspeakers—particularly mass-market ones.

In short, if recordings of male speaking voice sound monotonous, tiring, and resonant, it is probably the result of peaks and dips in the loudspeaker's response. (These colorations are most apparent on male voice when listening to just one loudspeaker.)

Terms to describe poor midrange performance include *peaky, colored, chesty, boxy, nasal, congested, honky,* and *thick. Chesty* describes a lower-midrange coloration that makes vocalists sound as though they have colds. *Boxy* refers to the impression that the sound is coming out of a box instead of existing in open space. *Nasal* is usually associated with a narrow peak, producing a sound similar to talking with your nose pinched. Honky is similar to nasal, but higher in frequency and broader in bandwidth.

Loudspeaker design has progressed so much in the past ten years that horrible midrange colorations are largely a thing of the past (at least in loudspeakers with high-end aspirations). Still, colorations persist—particularly in inexpensive loudspeakers—but they tend to be more subtle.

One type of lower-midrange coloration that still afflicts even moderately priced high-end loudspeakers is caused by vibration of the loudspeaker's cabinet. The loudspeaker will resonate at certain frequencies, launching acoustic energy from the cabinet when those frequencies are excited. Cabinet resonances are heard as certain notes "sticking out" or "jumping forward." This problem is clearly audible on solo piano; ascending or descending left-hand lines reveal certain notes that change character. These problem notes jump out because they have more energy; some of the sound is being produced by the loudspeaker cabinet, not only the loudspeaker's drive units. The same thing happens with musical instruments; the musician's expression "wolf tone" describes the same phenomenon. This problem also afflicts the upper bass. In Chapter 7 I talk in much greater detail about loudspeaker cabinet vibration.

As described previously under "Perspective," too much midrange energy can make the presentation seem forward and "in your face." A broad dip in the midrange response can give an impression of greater distance between you and the presentation.

When choosing loudspeakers, be especially attuned to the midrange colorations described. What is a very minor—even barely noticeable—problem heard during a brief audition can turn into a major irritant over extended listening.

The preceding descriptions apply primarily to midrange problems introduced by loudspeakers. Expanding the discussion to include electronics (preamps and power amps) and source components (LP playback or a digital source) introduces different aspects of midrange performance that we should be aware of.

An important factor in midrange performance is how instrumental *textures* are reproduced. Texture is the physical impression of the instrument's sound—its fabric rather than its tone. The closest musical term for texture is *timbre*, defined by *Webster's Ninth New Collegiate Dictionary* as "The quality given to a sound by its overtones; the quality of tone distinctive of a particular singing voice or instrument." Sonic artifacts added by electronics often affect instrumental and vocal textures.

The term *grainy*, introduced in the description of treble problems, also applies to the midrange. In fact, midrange grain can be more objectionable than treble grain. Midrange grain is characterized by a coarseness of instrumental and vocal textures; the instrument's texture is granular rather than smooth.

Midrange textures can also sound hard and brittle. Hard textures are apparent on massed voices; a choir sounds *glassy*, *shiny*, and *synthetic*. This problem gets worse as the choir's volume increases. At low levels, we may not hear these problems. But as the choir swells, the sound becomes hard and irritating. Piano is also very revealing of hard midrange textures, the higher notes sounding annoyingly *brittle*. When the midrange lacks these unpleasant artifacts, we say the textures are *liquid*, *smooth*, *sweet*, *velvety*, and *lush*.

A related midrange problem is *stridency*. I think of stridency as a combination of thinness (lack of warmth), hardness, and forwardness, all in the midrange. Strident vocals emphasize mouth noises and overlay the texture with a whitish grain. A saxophone can thus sound thin and reedy, though in a different way from that described as treble grain. A strident sax is hard, more forward in the mids, and granular in texture. Stridency can be caused by an apparent thinness in the lower midrange that makes the upper midrange too prominent. A product described as "strident" has been severely criticized.

Many of these midrange and treble problems are grouped together under the term *harshness*.

Other midrange characteristics affect such areas as clarity, transparency, and detail. These are discussed later, under more specific categories.

Bass

Bass performance is the most misunderstood aspect of reproduced sound, among both the general public and hi-fi buffs. The popular belief is that the more bass, the better. This is reflected in ads for "subwoofers" that promise "earthshaking bass" and the ability to "rattle pant legs and stun small animals." The ultimate expression of this perversity is boom trucks that have absurd amounts of extraordinarily bad bass reproduction.

But we want to know how the product reproduces *music*, not earthquakes. What matters to the music lover isn't *quantity* of bass, but the *quality* of that bass. We don't just want the physical feeling that bass provides; we want to hear subtlety and nuance. We want to hear precise pitch, lack of coloration, and the sharp attack of plucked acoustic bass. We want to hear every note and nuance in fast, intricate bass playing, not a muddled roar. If Ray Brown, Stanley Clarke, John Patitucci, or Eddie Gomez is working out, we want to hear *exactly* what they're doing. In fact, if the bass is poorly reproduced, we'd rather not hear any bass at all.

Correct bass reproduction is essential to satisfying musical reproduction. Low frequencies constitute music's tonal foundation and rhythmic anchor. Unfortunately, bass is difficult to reproduce, whether by source components, power amplifiers, or—especially—loudspeakers and rooms.

Perhaps the most prevalent bass problem is lack of *pitch definition* or *articulation*. These two terms describe the ability to hear bass as individual notes, each having an attack, a decay, and a specific pitch (these terms are explained in Appendix A). We should hear the texture of the bass, whether the sonorous resonance of a bowed double bass or the unique character of a Fender Precision. Low frequencies contain a surprising amount of detail when reproduced correctly.

When the bass is reproduced without pitch definition and articulation, the low end degenerates into a dull roar going on beneath the music. We hear low-frequency content, but it isn't musically related to what's going on above it. We don't hear precise notes, but a blur of sound. The individual dynamic envelopes of instruments are completely lost. In music in which the bass plays an important rhythmic role—rock, electric blues, and some jazz—the bass guitar and kick drum seem to lag behind the rest of the music, putting a drag on the rhythm. Moreover, the kick drum's dynamic envelope is buried in the bass guitar's sound, obscuring its musical contribution. These conditions are made worse by the common mid-fi affliction of too much bass.

Terms descriptive of this kind of bass include *muddy, thick, boomy, bloated, tubby, soft, fat, congested, loose,* and *slow.*

Terms that describe excellent bass reproduction include *taut, quick, clean, articulate, agile, tight,* and *precise.* Good bass has been likened to a trampoline stretched taut; poor bass is a trampoline hanging slackly.

The amount of bass in the musical presentation is very important; if we hear too much, the music is overwhelmed. Excessive bass is a constant reminder that we're listening to reproduced music. This overabundance of bass is described as *heavy.*

If we hear too little bass, the presentation is *thin, lean, threadbare,* or *overdamped.* An overly lean presentation robs music of its rhythm and drive. The full, purring sound of bass guitar is missing, the depth and majesty of double bass or cello is gone, and the orchestra loses its sense of power. Thin bass makes a double bass sound like a cello, a cello like a viola. The rhythmically satisfying weight and impact of bass drum is reduced to a shadow of its former power. Instruments' harmonics are emphasized in relation to the fundamentals, giving the impression of well-worn cloth that's lost its supporting structure. A thin or lean presentation lacks *warmth* and *body.* As described earlier in this chapter in the discussion of sins of commission and omission, an overly lean bass is preferable to fat and boomy bass.

Two terms related to what I've just described about bass amount are *extension* or *depth*. Extension is how deep the bass goes—not the bass and upper bass described by *lean* or *weighty*, but the very bottom end of the audible spectrum. This is the realm of kick drum and pipe organ. All but the very best systems *roll off* these lowermost frequencies. Fortunately, deep extension isn't a prerequisite to high-quality music reproduction. If the system has good bass down to about 35Hz, we don't feel anything is missing. Pipe-organ enthusiasts, however, will want deeper extension and are willing to pay for it. Reproducing the bottom octave correctly can be very expensive.

Just as colorations caused by frequency-response peaks and dips can make the midrange unnatural, bass can be colored by peaks and dips. Bass colorations create a monotonous, droning characteristic that quickly becomes tiring. In the most extreme example, *one-note bass*, the bass seems to have only one pitch. This impression is created by a large peak in the system's frequency response at a specific frequency. This pitch is then reproduced more loudly than other pitches. One-note bass is also described as being *thumpy*. Ironically, this undesirable condition is *maximized* in boom trucks. The playback system is tuned to put out all its energy at one frequency for maximum physical impact. The drivers of those vehicles don't seem to care that they're losing the wealth of musical information conveyed by the bass.

Many of the terms used to describe midrange colorations apply to the bass (mostly the upper bass). *Chesty*, *thick*, and *congested* are all useful in describing colored bass reproduction. Bass lacking these colorations is called *smooth* or *clean*.

Much of music's dynamic power—the ability to convey wide differences between loud and soft—is contained in the bass. Though I'll discuss dynamics later in this section, bass dynamics bear special discussion—they are that important to satisfying music reproduction.

A system or component that has excellent bass dynamics will provide a sense of sudden impact and explosive power. Bass drum will jump out of the presentation with startling power. The dynamic envelope of acoustic or electric bass is accurately conveyed, allowing the music full rhythmic expression. We call these components *punchy*, and use the terms *impact* and *slam* to describe good bass dynamics.

A related aspect is *speed*, though, as applied to bass, "speed" is somewhat of a misnomer. Low frequencies inherently have slower attacks than higher frequencies, making the term technically incorrect. But the *musical* difference between a component having "slow" or "fast" bass is profound. A product with fast, tight, punchy bass produces a much greater rhythmic involvement with the music. This is examined in more detail later.

Although reproducing the sudden attack of a bass drum is vital, equally important is the system's ability to reproduce a fast decay (how a note ends). The bass note shouldn't continue after a drum whack has stopped. Many loudspeakers store energy in their mechanical structures and radiate that energy slightly after the note itself. When this happens, the bass has *overhang*, a condition that makes kick drum, for example, *bloated* and *slow*. Music in which the drummer used double bass drums is particularly revealing of bass overhang. If the two drums merge into a single sound, overhang is probably to blame. You should hear the attack and decay of each drum as distinct entities. Components that don't adequately convey the dynamic envelope of low-frequency instruments rob music of its power and rhythmic drive.

Soundstaging

Soundstaging is the apparent physical size of the musical presentation. When we close our eyes in front of a good playback system, we "see" the instrumentalists and singers before us, often existing within an acoustic space such as a concert hall. The soundstage has the physical properties of *width* and *depth*, producing a sense of great size and space in the listening room. Soundstaging overlaps with *imaging*, or the way instruments appear as objects hanging in three-dimensional space within the recorded acoustic.

Of all the ways music reproduction is astounding, soundstaging is without question the most miraculous. Think about it. The two loudspeakers are driven by two-dimensional electrical signals that are nothing more than voltages that vary over time. From those two voltages, a huge, three-dimensional panorama unfolds before us. We don't hear the music as a flat canvas with individual instruments fused together; we hear the first violinist to the left front of the presentation, the oboe farther back and toward the center, the brass behind the basses on the right, and the tambourine behind all the other instruments at the very rear. The sound is made up of *individual objects* existing within a space, just as we would hear at a live performance. Moreover, we hear the oboe's timbre coming from the oboe's position, the violin's timbre coming from the violin's position, and the hall reverberation surrounding the instruments. Our listening room vanishes, replaced by the vast space of the concert hall—all from two voltages.

Interestingly, a soundstage is created in our brains by the time and amplitude differences encoded in the two audio channels. When we hear instrumental images toward the rear right of the soundstage, the ear/brain processes the slightly different information in the two signals arriving at our ears and synthesizes that image. Our visual perception works the same way; there is no depth information present on our retinas, but the brain creates depth from the two flat images.

Audio components vary greatly in their ability to present these spatial aspects of music. Some products shrink soundstage width and shorten the impression of depth. Others reveal the glory of a fully developed soundstage. I find good soundstage performance crucial to satisfying musical reproduction. Unfortunately, many products destroy or degrade the subtle cues that provide soundstaging.

The most obvious descriptions of the soundstage are its physical dimensions—width and depth. We hear the musical presentation as existing beyond the left and right loudspeaker boundaries, and extending farther away from us than the wall behind the loudspeakers.

Terms descriptive of poor soundstage width are *narrow* and *constricted*—the music, squeezed together between the loudspeakers, does not envelop the listener. A soundstage lacking depth is called *flat, shallow,* or *foreshortened.* Ideally, the soundstage should maintain its width over its entire depth. A soundstage that narrows toward the presentation's rear robs the music of its size and space.

The illusion of soundstage depth is aided by resolution of low-level spatial cues such as hall reflections and reverberation. When listening to the reverberation decay after a loud climax followed by a rest, the reverberation defines the acoustic space. The loud signal is like a flash of light in a dark room; the space is momentarily illuminated, allowing us to see its dimensions and characteristics.

In a related aspect, the acoustic space surrounding the instruments and the reverberation should appear as separate from instrumental images. Better audio components place the image *within* the recorded acoustic, rather than *attached* to it. The reverberation and hall sound must be distinct from the image itself to produce a realistic impression of a real instrument in a real acoustic space. Poor-quality components don't resolve these spatial cues; they shorten soundstage depth, truncate reverberation decay, and fuse the reverberation into the instrumental images. When this happens, our ability to be transported to the original acoustic space is diminished.

Now that we've covered space and depth, let's discuss how the instrumental images appear within this space. Images should occupy a specific spatial position in the soundstage. The sound of the bassoon, for example, should appear to emanate from a specific point in space, not as a diffuse and borderless image. The same could be said for guitar, piano, sax, or any other instrument in any kind of music. The lead vocal should appear as a tight, compact, definable point in space exactly between the loudspeakers. Moreover, instrumental images shouldn't overlap; the vocal should be a totally separate image within the music. Some products—particularly large loudspeakers—distort image size by making every instrument seem larger than life—a classical guitar suddenly sounds ten feet wide. A playback system should reveal somewhat correct image size, from a 60'-wide symphony orchestra to a solo violin. I say "somewhat" because it is impossible to recreate the correct spatial perspective of such widely divergent sound sources through two loudspeakers spaced about 8' apart. Although image size and placement are characteristics inherent in the recording, they are dramatically affected by components in the playback system.

Terms that describe a clearly defined soundstage are *focused, tight, delineated,* and *sharp. Image specificity* also describes tight image focus and pinpoint spatial accuracy. A poorly defined soundstage is described as *homogenized, blurred, confused, congested, thick,* and lacking *focus.* A good test of image focus is background vocals on a pop recording or voices in a choir. You should hear the individual voices as existing next to each other, not smeared into a single large image.

A related issue is soundstage *layering.* This is the ability of a sound system to resolve front-to-back cues that present some images toward the soundstage front and at varying distances toward the soundstage rear. The greater the number of layers of depth gradation, the better. Poor components produce the impression of just a few layers of depth; we hear perhaps three or four discrete levels of distance within the soundstage. The best components produce a sense of distance along a continuum; very fine gradations of depth are clearly resolved. Again, the absence of these qualities constitute subconscious cues that what we're hearing is artificial. When this important spatial information is revealed, however, we can more easily forget that we're not hearing the "real thing."

Bloom—the impression that the individual instrumental images are surrounded by a halo of air—is often associated with soundstaging. Although image outlines may be clearly delineated, a soundstage with bloom has an additional sense of diffused air around the image. It is as though the instrument has a little space around it, in which it can "breathe." Bloom gives the soundstage a more natural, open, and relaxed feeling.

A product's soundstaging performance should be evaluated with a wide range of musical signals. Some products throw a superb soundstage at low levels, only to collapse when the volume increases during musical climaxes. Listen for changes in the spatial perspective with signal level.

Some products produce a crystal-clear, *see-through* soundstage that allows the listener to hear all the way back into the hall. A *transparent* soundstage has a lifelike immediacy that makes every detail clearly audible. Conversely, an *opaque* soundstage is *thick* or *murky*, with less of an illusion of "seeing" into space. *Veiling* is often used to describe lack of transparency. A good analogy is that of looking through a huge picture window on a beautiful scene. If the window is dirty, the image is less vivid and immediate. Colors are dulled, and we don't see fine detail. But when washed, the view through the window is crystal-clear, deep, and richly detailed.

Soundstaging is toward the top of my list of sonic priorities. The ability to present the music as a collection of individual images surrounded by space, rather than as one big image, is very important to the creation of musical realism. A soundstage with space, depth, focus, layering, bloom, and transparency is nothing short of spectacular.

To evaluate soundstaging and hear the characteristics I've described, you must use recordings that contain these spatial cues. Studio recordings made with multiple microphones and overdubs rarely reveal the soundstaging characteristics described. Recordings made in real acoustic spaces with stereo microphone techniques and a pure signal path are essential to hearing all aspects of soundstaging. In short, soundstaging is provided by a combination of the recording and the playback system. If soundstaging cues aren't present in the recording, you'll never know how well or how poorly the component or system under evaluation reveals them. Most audiophile recordings are made with purist techniques (usually two microphones) that naturally capture the spatial information present during the original musical event.

Finally, superb soundstaging is relatively fragile. You need to sit directly between the loudspeakers, and every component in the playback chain must be of high quality. Soundstaging is easily destroyed by low-quality components, a bad listening room, or poor loudspeaker placement. This isn't to say you have to spend a fortune to get good soundstaging; many very low-cost products do it well, but it is more of challenge to find those bargains. The next chapter has many practical suggestions for achieving the best soundstaging possible from your system.

Dynamics

The *dynamic range* of an audio system or individual component is the range between the softest and loudest sounds that system or component can reproduce. It is often specified technically as the difference in level between the component's noise level and its maximum output level. Dynamic range isn't how loudly the system will play, but the *difference* in level between loud and soft. A symphony orchestra has a dynamic range of about 100 decibels, or dB (decibels are defined in Appendix A);

a typical rock recording's dynamic range is about 10dB. The rock band is always loud; it has little dynamic range.

Dynamics are a very important part of music reproduction. It's the characteristic that propels the music forward and totally involves us in the music. Much of music's expression is conveyed by dynamic contrast, from *pp* (pianissimo) to *fff* (triple forte).

There are two distinct qualities to dynamics: macro and micro. *Macrodynamics* refers to the presentation's overall sense of slam, impact, and power—bass-drum whacks and orchestral crescendos, for examples. If the system has poor macrodynamics, we say the sound is *compressed* or *squashed*.

Microdynamics occur on a smaller scale. They don't produce a sense of impact, but are essential to providing realistic dynamic reproduction. Microdynamics describes the fine dynamic structure in music, from the attack of a triangle in the back of the soundstage to the suddenness of a plucked string on an acoustic guitar. Neither sound is very loud in level, but both have dynamic structures that require quickness and speed from the playback system. Products with good dynamics—macro and micro—make the music come alive, allowing a vibrancy and life to emerge. Dynamic changes are an important vehicle of musical expression; the more we hear the musician's intent, the greater the musical communication between performer and listener. Some otherwise excellent components fail to convey the broad range of dynamic contrast.

These characteristics are associated with *transient response*, the system's ability to quickly respond to an input signal. A drum being struck produces a waveform with a very steep attack. Attack is the way the sound begins. If any component in the playback system can't respond as quickly as the waveform changes, a distortion of the music's dynamic envelope occurs, and the steepness is slowed. Electrostatic and ribbon loudspeakers are noted for their ability to reproduce the sudden attack of transient signals. Such loudspeakers are said to be *quick* or *fast*.

But just because a component or system can reproduce loud and soft levels doesn't necessarily mean it has good dynamics. We're looking for more than a wide dynamic range. The system must be capable of expressing fine gradations of dynamics, not just loud and soft. As the music changes in level (which it's doing most of the time), we should hear loudness changes along a smooth continuum, not as abrupt jumps in levels.

Another aspect of dynamics we seek is the ability to play loudly without the sound becoming *congested*. Many products—particularly CD players and digital-to-analog converters—become thick during musical climaxes. As the music gets louder, the sound becomes harder, timbre is obscured, and the soundstage degenerates into a confused mess. The word *congeal* aptly describes the homogenization of instrumental images within the soundstage. The nice sense of space and image placement heard at moderate volume often collapses during loud passages. This produces a sense of *strain* on musical peaks, greatly detracting from our enjoyment. When a component doesn't exhibit these problems, we say it has *effortless* dynamics.

Detail

Detail refers to the small or low-level components of the musical presentation. The fine inner structure of an instrument's timbre is one kind of detail. The term is also associated with transient sounds (those with a sudden attack) at any level, such as those made by percussion instruments. A playback system with good resolution of detail will infuse music with a sense of more music happening.

Assembling a good-sounding music system or choosing between two components can often be a tradeoff between smoothness and the resolution of detail. Many audio components hype detail, giving transient signals an *etched* character. Sure, we can hear all the information, but the presentation becomes too *aggressive, analytical*, and *fatiguing*. Low-level information is brought up and thrust at us. We feel a sense of relief when the music is turned down or off—not a good sign.

Components that err in the opposite direction don't have this etched and analytical quality, but neither do they resolve all the musical information in the recording. These components are described as overly *smooth*, or of *low resolution*. They tend to make music bland by removing parts of the signal needed for realistic reproduction. These kinds of components don't rivet our attention on the music; they are *uninvolving* and bland. We aren't offended by the presentation as we are with an analytical system, but something is missing that we need for musical satisfaction. Some products are actually designed to gloss over detail to make the product more "musical." Lack of detail is often an unintended consequence of removing treble brightness or grain. The design aspects that tamed the aggressive treble also obliterated real musical information. The components are said to have low resolution. Some listeners prefer such low-resolution presentation to a more natural rendering.

It is a rare product indeed that presents a full measure of musical detail without sounding etched. The best products will reveal all the low-level cues that make music interesting and riveting, but not do so in a way that gives us listening fatigue. The music playback system must walk the very fine line between resolution of real musical information and sounding analytical. The components that provide the most long-term musical satisfaction are the ones that reveal fine detail without being etched.

Pace, Rhythm, and Timing

The British audio reviewer Martin Colloms deserves the credit for identifying and defining an important aspect of music reproduction he calls *pace, rhythm,* and *timing.* These terms refer to the system's ability to involve the listener in a physical way in the music's forward flow and drive. Pace is that quality that makes your body want to move with the beat, your foot to tap, and your head to bob—the feeling of being propelled forward on the music's beat. Good pace and rhythm in an audio system can produce a physical exhilaration from the sound.

Though the music's tempo doesn't change in an objective sense from component to component (one power amplifier to another, for example), the subjective impression of a timing difference can be profound. Some products put a drag on the rhythm, making the tempo seem slower or *sluggish.* Others are *upbeat,* conveying the music's rhythmic tautness and drive. In addition to apparently slowing the tempo, components with poor pace give the impression that the band is less tight and musically "up." The music has less vitality and energy, and the band is less locked-in to the groove.

Martin Colloms wrote this in his revelatory article on this overlooked aspect of music reproduction, published in the November, 1992 issue of *Stereophile.*

"While good rhythm is a key aspect of both live and reproduced music-making, it is not easy to analyze. It's as if the act of focusing on the details of a performance blinds one to the parameter in question. The subjective awareness of rhythm is a continuous event, registered at the whole-body level, and recognized in a state of conscious but relaxed awareness. Once you've learned that reproduced sound can impart that vital sense of music-making as an event, that the impression of an upbeat, involving drive can be reproduced again and again, you can't help but pursue this quality throughout your listening experience."

Rhythm and pace are more important in rock, jazz, blues, pop, and other forms of music than in classical. Much of the feeling of propulsion comes from the bass drum and bass guitar working together.

Martin Colloms has identified specific conditions which detract from pace and rhythm. Any random energy, such as in a power amplifier's power supply, loudspeaker cabinets—even a loosening of the bolts that secure drivers to loudspeaker baffles—can degrade pace and timing.

I'm sure that many listeners have heard examples of good pace and lack of it, but didn't recognize it as such. Instead, they may have felt an undefinable involvement in the music if the system had good timing, or a general apathy or boredom with the music if the system didn't convey pace and rhythm.

How do you listen for pace and rhythm? Forget about it, and if you find yourself wanting to dance, the component probably has it.

Coherence

Coherence describes the impression that the music is integrated into a satisfying whole, not a collection of bass, midrange, and treble. The music's harmonic tapestry is integrally woven, and not a patchwork quilt.

The term also applies to the system or component's dynamic performance, specifically the impression that all the transient edges are lined up with each other. This provides a sense of wholeness to the sound that we react to favorably. Coherence is more a feeling of musical rightness than any specific characteristic.

Musicality

Finally, we get to the most important aspect of the musical presentation—*musicality*. Unlike the previous characteristics, musicality isn't any specific quality that we can listen for, but the musical satisfaction the system provides. Our sensitivity to musicality is destroyed when we focus on a certain aspect of the presentation; i.e., when we listen critically. Instead, musicality is the *gestalt*, the whole of our reaction to the reproduced sound. We also use the term *involvement* to describe this oneness with the music. Ultimately, musicality—not dissecting the sound—is what high-end audio is all about.

The following essay grapples with the conflict between analytical listening and musicality. It first appeared as an editorial in the November, 1992 issue of *Stereophile*, and is reprinted with their permission.

Between the Ears
By Robert Harley

Audiophiles constantly seek ways to improve the experience of hearing reproduced music. Preamps are upgraded, digital processors are compared, turntables are tweaked, loudspeaker cables are auditioned, dealers are visited, and, yes, magazines are read—all in the quest to get just a little closer to the music.

These pursuits have one thing in common: they are all attempts by physical means to enjoy music more. But there's another way of achieving that goal that is far more effective than any tweak, better than any component upgrade, and more fulfilling even than having *carte blanche* in the world's finest high-end store. And it's free.

I'm talking about what goes on *between* our ears when listening, not what's impinging on them. Our ability—or lack of—to clear the mind of distractions and let the music speak to us has a huge influence on how much we enjoy music. Have you ever wondered why, on the same system and recordings, there is a vast range of involvement in the music? The only variable is our state of mind.

Because audiophiles care about sound quality, we are often more susceptible to allowing interfering thoughts to get in the music's way. These thoughts are usually concerned with aspects of the *sound's* characteristics. Does the soundstage lack depth? Does the bass have enough extension? Is the treble grainy? How does my system compare to those described in magazines?

Unfortunately, this mode of thinking is perpetuated by high-end audio magazines. The descriptions of a product's sound—its specific performance attributes—are what make it into print, not the musical and emotional satisfaction to which the product contributes. The latter is ineffable: words cannot express the bond between listener and music that some products facilitate more than others. Consequently, we are left only with descriptions of specific characteristics that can leave the impression that being an audiophile is about dissection and critical commentary, and not about more closely connecting with the music's meaning.

A few months after I became an audio reviewer (and a much more critical listener), I underwent a kind of crisis; I found myself no longer enjoying music the way I once did. Listening became a chore, an occupational necessity, rather than the deeply moving experience that made me choose a career in audio. My dilemma was precipitated by the mistaken impression that whenever I heard music I had to have an opinion about the quality of its reproduction. Music became secondary to the sound. Music was merely an assemblage of parts, something to be dismantled and studied, not something that spoke to me emotionally.

I found, however, that only after I'd turned in the month's reviews did the party begin. I stopped being a critic and was a music lover again. I played favorite records, *not* those that would tell me what the equipment was doing. The music as a whole, not the sound as an assemblage of artifacts, once again became the object of my attention. It was as though an enormous burden had been lifted. I made up for lost time in those few days before the inevitable return to reviewing as the next month's products were set up for critical auditioning.

Here I was with a custom-built listening room, racks full of the world's finest audio reproduction equipment, and a job in which I spent a good deal of my time listening, yet most of the time I wasn't enjoying the music. My cheap car stereo gave more musical satisfaction. Something was dreadfully wrong.

This experience precipitated a catharsis that forced me to reexamine what music listening—among other things—was all about. I decided to forget about the sound for the vast majority of the listening time and let the music tell me which components were better than others. Critical listening and analytical reasoning became secondary to musical enjoyment. I began listening to music I *liked*, rather than diagnostic recordings that would tell me about the product's specific characteristics. The impulse to disassemble, listen to the *sound*, and constantly form judgments gradually disappeared. The result is that I now enjoy music more than at any other time of my life. Better sound *does* result in more music, but paradoxically, *only when the sound is forgotten*. Moreover, this conversion increased my listening and reviewing skills: I now have a much better feeling for which products will produce long-term musical satisfaction.

Nevertheless, analytical listening using particularly revealing recordings must remain a vital part of the reviewing process. Similarly, conveying the specific sonic characteristics of products under review is essential—potential purchasers should know what the product sounds like and decide if it's what they're looking for. But this type of diagnostic analysis no longer dominates—it has become merely one aspect of reviewing. Moreover, I came to realize that the information gained by analytical reasoning is a lower form of knowledge and that the *feeling* about a product's quality—its ability to convey the music—is a higher form of knowledge.

These experiences point to a deeper problem of how rationality and the impulse toward dissection as the vehicle to understanding pervades Western thought. Traditional rationality views a whole as a collection of parts. The need to dissect, classify, and assign hierarchical structure is the very foundation of rationality. Our Western upbringing makes it seem so natural that any entity is merely an assemblage of component parts. Why should reproduced music be any different? Consequently, we hear in reproduced music treble, bass, midrange, soundstage, detail, and air. But how often at a live concert do you dismantle the sound the same way you do when listening to a hi-fi? I don't know about you, but I never experience live music in terms of tonal balance, depth, lack of grain, or other characteristics we assign to reproduced sound.

Consider two approaches to knowing a flower. Traditional rationality would pick it, dissect it, classify its parts, and attempt to understand and document its mechanisms. Another way to know the flower would be to just sit and look at it, appreciating its beauty, discovering subtleties in shape, color, smell, texture, and just absorbing its essence.

The first method produces one kind of knowing—an important one, to be sure—but it isn't a complete knowledge.

Moreover, doesn't the first method destroy something in the process—namely, the flower? After the dissection is finished we find ourselves left with nothing. This is why I no longer enjoyed music; the analytical dismantling consumed the very thing I was trying to know. By allowing intellectual thought to intrude, the oneness between music and listener is destroyed.

The great accomplishments of rationality—making reproduced music possible in the first place, for example—produces a hubris that tempts one to overlook the virtues of non-rational experience. Rationality can point to its achievements as "proof" of its superiority. The kind of knowing produced by nonrational experience can point to no physical manifestations of its value. Instead, the worth is completely internal and unknowable by anyone who hasn't experienced it firsthand.

But it isn't just listening analytically to the sound that interferes with musical enjoyment. *Any* intellectual activity diminishes the experience. It is the quality of the listening experience that matters—the here and now—not an assignment of value as measured against some standard promulgated by hi-fi magazines, comparisons with other systems, or anything else that distracts from the music.

I see an analogy with a hobby of mine—motorcycle touring. I bought a new Honda Gold Wing Aspencade in 1987 and have ridden it many enjoyable miles. The next year, it was completely redesigned, with a six-cylinder, 1520cc engine (instead of my four-cylinder, 1200cc motor), reverse gear, and many other features and refinements. The motorcycle magazines raved about the new Wing, particularly in comparison with the older version I had.

But when my wife and I tour the American Southwest, am I thinking how much better it would be on the new model? Does the existence of the better motorcycle diminish in any way our touring enjoyment?

Not a chance. What *would* diminish the experience, however, is allowing the immediate pleasure to be intruded upon by external and irrelevant thoughts about the past (I should have waited for the new model) or future (how can I afford one?).

It's the same with music reproduction equipment. The Krell KSA-250, for example, is a much better amplifier than the KSA-200. But if you own a KSA-200, should you enjoy music any less after the KSA-250 comes out? It's a ridiculous supposition. The KSA-200 performs no differently after the KSA-250 is introduced. It brought musical pleasure when you bought it—why should it produce any less pleasure now? It's purely a state of mind.

There's nothing wrong with being dissatisfied with your system; that's what fuels improvement. And a better system does produce a deeper musical experience. But you shouldn't enjoy music any less if your system falls short of a friend's system, or if you don't have the latest hot product, or if the sound doesn't equal that described in magazines. These things are artificial inventions *superimposed on* reality, not the reality itself. What really matters is the experience—the immediate, here-and-now existence. All other thoughts or intellectual abstractions diminish our potential for a oneness with the music.

In this way of thinking (or, more precisely, *not* thinking), musical fulfillment is no longer dependent on external means. Yes, the technology that brings music into our homes is physical and external, but satisfaction cannot be experienced purely through the equipment, no matter how good it is. Instead, getting closer to the music is a special interaction between music and listener, the equipment merely serving as intermediary. Without this state of mind, no level of equipment will provide us with what we seek. My temporary lack of musical enjoyment, despite having a custom-built room filled with topnotch products, affirmed this truism.

By all means, continue critiquing and upgrading your system—it can be a path to more musical enjoyment. But when a favorite record goes on the turntable and the lights dim, forget about cables, preamps, tweaks, and magazines. At that moment, the only thing that *really* matters is the music.

Notes on Learning Descriptive Terms

By practicing critical listening and adopting the language used here and in high-end audio magazine product reviews, you will be much better able to assess audio equipment quality and make better purchase decisions. By associating the descriptive terms with your own listening impressions, you can more tangibly characterize how good products and systems are and *why* they are good or bad.

I recommend that you write down your listening impressions during or immediately after the listening session. This will not only solidify your impressions, but force you to find words to describe what you heard. Often we remember more strongly the memory of the impression, rather than the impression itself. I'm often asked how I can remember how a specific component sounds when I haven't heard that product for a year or more. The answer is that because I record my sonic experiences when writing product reviews for *Stereophile*, I have formed a capsule impression of that product's basic character. I don't remember every detail, of course, but the mental image may be something like "slightly etched treble, very transparent and spacious soundstage, lean bass, somewhat lacking in dynamics, and analytical rather than smooth." I also associate a general value judgment with that component—would I want to listen to it for pleasure over a long period of time?

By writing down these impressions, you'll not only have a written record of your experience, but also a more tangible mental impression which you can use when making later comparisons with other components.

Critical Listening Set-up Procedures

Now that we've explored the lexicon of critical listening, let's look at the procedures required to reach valid listening judgments. These procedures are controls on the process that help ensure that our listening impressions are valid. It's easy to be fooled if we don't take certain precautions.

The following procedures are the result of my experience evaluating products professionally, and reporting those evaluations to a sizable audience. In my profession, the need to be right about products is paramount. Not only will my readers buy or not buy products based on my opinions, but the fortunes of high-end manufacturers are greatly affected by reviews, positive or negative. Accurately describing a product's sound, and reaching correct value judgments about that product, is a huge responsibility—to readers, manufacturers, and the truth. The techniques described are essential to reaching the right conclusions. I wouldn't even consider forming concrete opinions about products without these safeguards. Neither should you.

By using these controlled procedures, we can stop second-guessing what we hear and concentrate on the real musical differences between components. Removing the variables that may skew the listening impressions allows us to have greater confidence that the differences we're hearing are real musical differences between products and not the result of improper set-up. If you follow these procedures and hear differences, you can have confidence in your listening impressions.

As you go into the listening session, turn your mind into a blank slate. Forget about the brand names of the products you're about to audition, their reputation for certain sonic characteristics, the products' prices, and whom you may offend if you like product A better than product B. Be completely receptive to whatever your ears tell you. If your impressions match your preconceived ideas about what the product sounds like, suspect bias. But if you find that the listening impressions contradict your prejudices, you've developed the ability to listen without bias. Removing bias is essential to reaching accurate value judgments.

The first rule of critical listening is that only one variable must be changed at one time. If comparing preamps, use the same source components, interconnects, AC power conditioner, power amp, cables, loudspeakers, music, and room. This is obviously impossible when comparing products at different dealers with different playback systems. But changing one variable at a time is an absolute requirement for arriving at valid opinions. This is why I stress taking the competing products home over the weekend for comparison. Not only can you evaluate them under the same conditions, but you get to hear how they interact with the rest of your system.

Changing only one component at a time is vital; big differences (two different pairs of loudspeakers, for example) will often swamp small differences. You can't separate what one new component is doing from what the second new component is doing. The ultimate expression of this mistake is someone who hears a system for the first time and remarks on how good (or bad) the loudspeaker cables are. It's ridiculous; you can't isolate what the loudspeaker cable is doing within the context of a completely unknown system.

The second rule is to match volume levels between components under audition. Level matching assures that both products produce the same volume at the loudspeakers. If you're comparing two digital processors, match their output levels to within 0.2dB, preferably to within 0.1dB of each other. Level-matching should become an integral part of critical listening sessions. All it takes is an inexpensive voltmeter and a few minutes of time. You'll be well rewarded for those few minutes spent level-matching with more accurate value judgments about the products. The section at the end of this chapter explains how to match levels.

Level-matching is crucial because slight level differences between products can lead you to the wrong conclusion. As described in Appendix A ("Sound and Hearing"), the ear's sensitivity to bass and treble increases disproportionately with volume. That is, we hear more bass and treble when the music is loud. If product A is played louder than product B, product A may sound brighter, more forward, more detailed, more dynamic, and have more bass. If product A has a soft treble, lacks detail, and has a lean bass balance, you may not know it if the levels aren't precisely matched. If you *can* distinguish product A's character with mismatched levels, the degrees to which the treble is soft, the detail lacking, the dynamics missing, and the bass thin are much harder to gauge. With level matching, you'll know precisely how *much* these characteristics are present in the product you're evaluating. You can forget about trying to mentally compensate for different levels and concentrate on characterizing the sonic differences.

With the same playback system and matched levels, you're ready to compare products. The typical method is called A/B, in which you hear product A, then immediately afterward the same music through product B. One problem with A/B listening is called "The A/A Paradox." This states that when hearing two identical presentations (A/A), we tend to hear differences between them. The A/A paradox happens because music has meaning; we perceive it and react to it a little differently every time we hear it. Moreover, if the music is unfamiliar, a second hearing allows us to hear more detail. These factors combine to fool us into hearing differences that aren't there.

Fortunately, overcoming the A/A paradox is easy. When comparing products, listen to A, then B, then A again. The differences you heard between A and B are often solidified after hearing A again. After selecting another piece of music for further comparison, make the order B/A/B. This technique of hearing three presentations (or five, A/B/A/B/A) confirms or refutes first impressions. Usually, a characteristic heard in the first comparison is more apparent after hearing it the second time.

Selecting the right source material is important in fully exploring a product's character. If the source material doesn't contain certain cues, you won't know how well the product reproduces those cues. For example, if we're comparing two power amplifiers, and use only dry studio recordings of pop music, we'll never know how good the amplifiers are at resolving soundstage depth and other spatial cues. Similarly, if we listen to nothing but chamber music in evaluating loudspeakers, we can't tell how the loudspeaker conveys bass dynamics, punch, and rhythmic intensity.

Establish a repertoire of familiar music for evaluating components, with each piece selected for some sonic characteristic that will tell you how the component behaves. Remember, this is diagnostic listening, not listening for pleasure. A range of source material should include: a full-scale symphonic recording, chamber music, orchestra with choir, solo piano, popular vocal, rock, blues, or other music with electric bass and kick drum, jazz with acoustic bass, and music with cymbals. Some of the jazz and orchestral recordings should be naturally miked; that is, recorded in a way that captures the original spatial aspects of the music and concert hall. Audiophile record labels will often describe how the recordings were made, and even include a photograph of the hall and where the microphones were placed. Get to know these recordings intimately. By hearing the same recording played back on many different systems, you can quickly characterize a component's sonic signature.

Another factor that can lead us astray in critical listening is *absolute polarity* (discussed in Appendix A). If one product under comparison inverts absolute polarity and the other one doesn't, you may be led to the wrong conclusions, or, at the very least, be confused about which product is better. Many owner's manuals will state if the product inverts polarity, and *Stereophile*'s equipment reports always include the product's absolute polarity. If you know product A is non-inverting and product B is polarity inverting, reverse the positive and negative connections on *both* loudspeakers; the red wire goes to the loudspeaker's black terminal, and the black wire goes to the loudspeaker's red terminal when auditioning product B. If your preamp has a polarity inversion switch, you can just throw it instead of swapping loudspeaker leads. Fortunately, very few components invert absolute polarity.

It's also easy to be misled by a colored playback system. Say you have loudspeakers that are bright, forward, and a little rough in the treble, and you are comparing two digital processors to determine which one to buy. Processor A produces a sound through your system that is bright and forward in the treble. Processor B renders a smoother treble and is more musical in your system.

Is processor B inherently more musical? Not necessarily. It probably has colorations—an overly soft treble—that complement the loudspeaker's bright treble. Two products in the playback chain that have reciprocal flaws will often produce a musical result. And there's no reason not to buy processor B if you intend on keeping your loudspeakers. But don't make the mistake of thinking processor B is inherently better than processor A. In fact, processor A is probably more neutral and would be a much better choice with smoother loudspeakers. Although not ideal, choosing a product based on how it corrects other faults in your system is valid if the end result is a more musical presentation. Just recognize the situation when it occurs.

Single Presentation Listening—What it's all About

The type of analytical listening I've described will reveal specific sonic attributes of components in relation to each other; CD transport A has deeper bass extension, smoother treble, and a deeper soundstage, while transport B has more inner detail, quicker transients, and a more focused soundstage. This kind of analytical listening tells us a lot about the products' strengths and weaknesses, but it isn't the whole story.

What's missing from this dissection is how each product makes us *feel* about the music. Does your mind wander, thinking about what you're going to do next? Or are you riveted in the listening seat, playing record after record well into the night?

This difference in a product's ability to express the music in a way that compels us to continue listening is called musicality and involvement. Musicality and involvement are rarely revealed in A/B comparisons and can't be described in terms of specific sonic attributes. Instead, this fundamental characteristic of a product's ability to provide long-term musical satisfaction is discovered only when listening for pleasure, without level-matching, selecting music for its sonic rather than musical qualities, or analytical thinking. Dissecting the music to characterize specific sonic attributes, as in A/B comparisons, destroys our receptivity to the music's meaning. Involvement comes only when we consider music as a whole, not as a collection of sonic parts.

This is why all critical listening should include not only A/B/A comparisons, but also what's called "single-presentation listening" and listening just for pleasure. Single-presentation listening is listening to the product under evaluation over a long time period—days or weeks rather than hours—with an unconscious ear to how the product affects the music. Listening for sheer pleasure involves no such thinking about the sound, only about the music. If, after a long session, you feel exhilarated and fulfilled, you can be confident in the product's ability to convey the music's expression and meaning. In fact, this is the most important indicator of quality in an audio component.

There is a general correlation between a product's sonic performance as revealed during analytical listening and its musicality as discovered during listening for pleasure. Specific sonic flaws—grainy treble, hard textures, flat soundstage—often distract us from the music in a way that prevents deep involvement. The less the presentation sounds artificial, synthetic, or affronts our ears, the easier it is to forget the hardware and hear only the music. Indeed, making the hardware disappear is the Holy Grail of high-end audio.

Your evaluative listening should thus include a mix of analytical A/B/A comparisons with single-presentation listening (with an ear to specific sonic attributes) and pure listening for pleasure.

Critical Listening Summary

Following, I've summarized the set-up procedures for conducting critical listening that will provide valid, useful information about the product under evaluation.

- *Use the same playback system for comparisons*

- *Change only one component at a time*

- *Match levels between products under audition*

- *Listen to A/B/A, not A/B*

- *Use very familiar music*

- *Select music that reveals specific sonic characteristics; i.e., bass, midrange liquidity, dynamics, treble, and soundstaging.*

- *Listen to the product for pleasure over a long period of time*

Do I follow all these guidelines every time I listen critically? No. But I don't reach firm opinions about products unless I do. If you're listening to make a purchase decision, follow these guidelines religiously. Be suspicious of any listening impressions made under poor circumstances. And don't reach firm opinions unless all these guidelines have been followed.

By applying these techniques, you'll be more likely to reach accurate value judgments and consequently buy products that will provide the greatest long-term musical satisfaction.

Level Matching

Level-matching procedures are identical for all electronic components, whether a digital processor, preamp, or power amp. First, play music at a comfortable level through the system to set the volume. Then play a test CD that has a 1kHz sine wave recorded at a low level. Track 1 on the first *Stereophile* Test CD is ideal. Measure the voltage across the loudspeaker terminals when the tone is playing, and note the voltage. Put a piece of masking tape on the preamp's face plate around the preamp's volume control and mark the position of the volume control.

After you switch components (power amp, digital processor), play the tone again and measure the voltage across the loudspeaker terminals. Adjust the preamp's volume control so that the voltage across the loudspeaker terminals is the same you measured for the first component. Mark the volume-control position on the masking tape. By setting the volume control at the first mark for product A and at the second mark for product B, you've got matched levels.

Some preamplifiers with detented (click stop) volume controls but continuous attenuation make level matching easier and more precise by removing the need for tape. Just count the number of steps necessary to achieve the same voltage across the loudspeaker terminals. Setting the volume control between detents is surprisingly accurate and repeatable. This technique doesn't work with detented volume controls that aren't continuously adjustable between the detents.

If you're comparing preamps, you don't need the masking tape—just find the volume setting on both preamps that produces the same voltage across the loudspeaker terminals when playing the test tone and leave the volume controls in the same position.

Phono cartridge and phono preamplifier level-matching is identical, except that a test LP replaces the test CD.

Level-matching isn't required when comparing products that don't affect the volume. These include interconnects, loudspeaker cables, CD transports, CD tweaks, digital interconnects, AC line conditioners, AC power cords, spikes, cones, vibration-damping devices, and equipment stands.

Ideally, the playback level between products should be matched to within 0.2dB, preferably to within 0.1dB. To calculate the dB difference between two measured voltages, you need only a calculator with a "log" button. Here's how to do it.

First find the ratio of the two measured voltages by dividing one into the other. Then find the logarithm of that ratio by pressing the calculator's "log" button with the ratio in the display. Next, multiply the result by 20. The answer is the difference in dB between two voltages.

For example, if we measured 2.82V across the loudspeaker terminals with digital processor A, and 2.88V across the loudspeaker terminals with digital processor B after level matching, we first divide 2.88 by 2.82, giving us the ratio of the two voltages (1.0213:1). We next push the "log" button on the calculator with 1.0213 in the display, getting the answer 0.00914, which we then multiply by 20. The answer is that the levels are matched to within 0.18dB—close enough for meaningful comparisons.

4 How to Get the Best Sound from Your Room

Introduction

The room in which music is reproduced has a profound effect on sound quality. In fact, the listening room's acoustic character should be considered another component in the playback chain. Because every listening room imposes its own sonic signature on the reproduced sound, your system can only sound its best when given a good acoustical environment. A poor room can make a great system sound mediocre, and an excellent room can help get the most out of a modest system.

Fortunately, you can greatly improve a listening room with a few simple tricks and devices. The possibilities range from simply moving your loudspeakers a few inches to building a dedicated listening room from scratch. Between these two extremes are many options, including adding inexpensive and attractive acoustical treatment products.

In this chapter, we'll cover everything you need to know to get the best sound from your system, beginning with the most effective and least expensive acoustical technique of all—loudspeaker placement. And don't be intimidated by the technical information toward the end of the chapter. It's included for those wanting to know some of the theory behind the practical information presented in the beginning sections. And if you find this next section difficult, I've summarized it in "Acoustical Do's and Don'ts" later in the chapter.

Loudspeaker Placement

The most basic problem in many listening rooms is poor loudspeaker placement. Finding the right spot for your loudspeakers is the single most important factor in getting good sound in your room. Loudspeaker placement affects tonal balance, bass quantity and quality, soundstage width and depth, midrange clarity, articulation, and imaging. As you make large changes in loudspeaker placement, then fine-tune placement with smaller and smaller adjustments, you'll hear a newfound musical rightness and seamless harmonic integration to the sound. When you get it right, your system will come alive. Best of all, it costs no more than a few hours of your time.

Before getting to specific recommendations, let's cover the six fundamental factors that affect how a loudspeaker's sound will change with placement. (Later we'll look at each of these factors in detail.)

1) The relationship between the loudspeakers and the listener is of paramount importance. The listener and loudspeakers should form a triangle; without this basic setup, you'll never hear good soundstaging and imaging.

2) Proximity of loudspeakers to walls affects the amount of bass. The nearer the loudspeakers are to walls and corners, the louder the bass.

3) The loudspeaker and listener positions in the room affect the audibility of room resonant modes. When room resonant modes are less audible, the bass is better defined, and midrange clarity increases. Room resonant modes are reinforcements at certain frequencies that create peaks in the frequency response. (Room resonant modes are described in detail later in the chapter.)

4) The farther out into the room the loudspeakers are, the better the soundstaging—particularly depth.

5) Listening height affects tonal balance.

6) Toe-in (angling the loudspeakers toward the listener) affects tonal balance (particularly the amount of treble), soundstage width, and image focus.

Let's look at each of these factors in detail.

1) Relationship between the loudspeakers and the listener

The most important factor in getting good sound is the geometric relationship between the two loudspeakers and listener (we aren't concerned about the room yet). The listener should sit exactly between the two loudspeakers, at a distance away from each loudspeaker slightly greater than the distance between the loudspeakers themselves. Though this is not a hard and fast rule, you should certainly sit exactly between the loudspeakers, and the same distance from each one. If you don't have this fundamental relationship, you'll never hear good soundstaging from your system.

Fig.4-1 shows how your loudspeaker and listening positions should be arranged. The listening position—equidistant from the speakers, and slightly farther from each speaker than the speakers are from each other—is called the "sweet spot." This is roughly the listening position where the music will snap into focus and sound the best.

Fig. 4-1 The listener should sit between the loudspeakers and at the same distance from each loud-speaker.

Sweet Spot

Setting the distance between the loudspeakers is a tradeoff between a wide soundstage and a strong center image. The farther apart the loudspeakers are (assuming the same listening position), the wider the soundstage will be. As the loudspeakers are moved farther apart, however, the center image weakens, and can even disappear. If the loudspeakers are too close together, soundstage width is constricted.

The best listening angle will produce a strong center image and a wide soundstage. You can experiment with angle by simply moving your listening chair forward and backward. There will likely be a position where the center image snaps into focus, appearing as a stable, pinpoint spot exactly between the loudspeakers. A musical selection with a singer and sparse accompaniment is ideal for setting loudspeaker spacing and assuring a strong center image.

A factor to consider in setting this angle is the relationship to the room. You can have the same geometric relationship between loudspeakers and listener with the loudspeakers close together and a close listening position, or with the loudspeakers far apart and a distant listening position. At the distant listening position, the listening room's acoustic character will affect the sound more than at the close listening position. The ratio of direct to reflected sound is determined by how close you sit to the loudspeakers. Generally, the farther away you sit, the more spacious the sound. The closer you sit, the more direct and immediate the presentation. Some loudspeakers—especially those with first-order crossovers—need a significant distance between the loudspeaker and the listener to allow the loudspeakers' individual drive units to integrate. If you hear a large tonal difference just by sitting closer, you should listen from farther away.

2) *Proximity to walls affect the amount of bass*

The room boundaries have a great effect on a loudspeaker's overall tonal balance. Loudspeakers placed close to walls will exhibit a reinforcement in the bass, making the musical presentation weightier. Some loudspeakers are designed to be near a rear wall and need this reinforcement for a natural tonal balance. These loudspeakers sound thin if placed out into the room. Others sound thick and heavy if not at least 3' from the rear and side walls. Be sure which type you're buying if your placement options are limited.

When placed near a wall, bass energy from the loudspeaker is reflected back into the room essentially in phase with the loudspeaker output, reinforcing low frequencies. This bass reinforcement occurs only when the extra distance the reflected wave must travel (called the "path length difference") is short relative to the 1/4 wavelength of sound being reproduced. With a loudspeaker 2' from a rear wall, the path length difference of 4' (2' going to the rear wall, 2' coming from the rear wall) is considerably shorter than bass wavelengths. Fig.4-2 shows the difference in a loudspeaker's response when measured in an anechoic chamber (a reflection-free room) and in a normal room. As you can see in the graph, not only is the bass boosted, but the loudspeaker's low-frequency extension is also increased. Each surface near the loudspeaker (floor, rear wall, and side walls) will add to the loudspeaker's bass output. The closer to the corners the loudspeakers are placed, the more bass you will hear.

Fig. 4-2
Comparison of a loudspeaker's anechoic and in-room response (Courtesy Avalon Acoustics, Inc.)

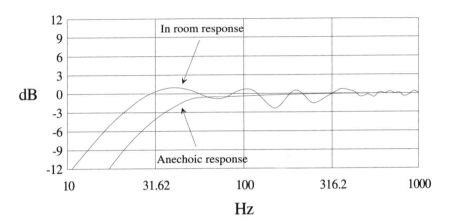

The loudspeaker's position in relation to the rear and side walls will also affect which frequencies are boosted. Correct placement can not only extend a loudspeaker's frequency response by complementing its natural rolloff, but also avoid peaks and dips in the response. Improper placement can cause frequency-response irregularities that color the bass. The graph of Fig.4-3a is a loudspeaker's in-room response when placed equidistant from the rear and side walls. Note the 10dB notch at about 200Hz and the peak centered at 60Hz. The result will be a boominess in the bass and a leanness in the midbass. By moving the loudspeaker different distances from the rear and side walls, the response is much smoother (Fig.4-3b). The same loudspeaker's response at a different room position is shown in Fig.4-4. These graphs illustrate that a loudspeaker's room position affects the bass response, and that the loudspeakers should be positioned at different distances from the rear and side walls. A rule of thumb: the two distances shouldn't be within 33% of each other. For example, if the loudspeaker is 3' from the side wall, it should also be at least 4' from the rear wall.

Many loudspeaker manufacturers will specify the correct distance from the rear and side walls. When a measurement is specified, the distance is between the woofer cone and the wall. Start with the loudspeakers in the manufacturer-recommended locations, then begin experimenting.

Fig. 4-3a Placing the loudspeakers the same distance from the rear and side walls produces peaks and dips in the bass response.

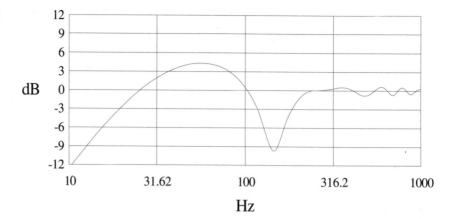

Fig. 4-3b Placing the loudspeakers different distances from the rear and side walls smooths the bass response.

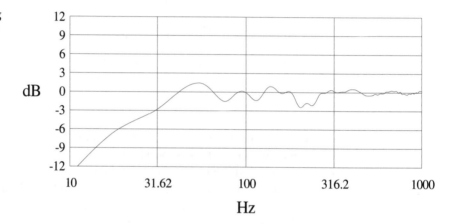

Fig. 4-4 Response of the same loudspeaker in Fig. 4-3, but in a different room position (Figs. 4-3a, 4-3b, and 4-4 Courtesy Avalon Acoustics, Inc.)

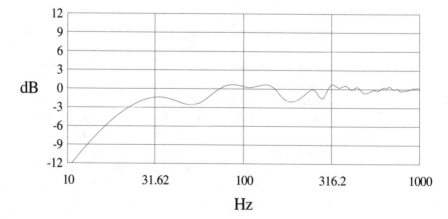

Finally, how close the loudspeakers are to the side walls affects the amplitude of the side-wall reflection. The closer the loudspeakers are to the side walls, the higher the level of the side-wall reflections reaching the listener—not a good thing. If you've treated the side walls as described later in this chapter, putting the loudspeaker closer to the side wall won't have as great an effect as if the side walls were untreated.

3) Loudspeaker and listener positions affect room-mode audibility

In addition to deepening bass extension and smoothing bass response, correct loudspeaker placement in relation to the room's walls can also reduce the audible effects of your room's *resonant modes*. Room resonant modes, described later in this chapter, are reinforcements at certain frequencies that create peaks in the frequency response. Room modes also create *standing waves*, which are stationary patterns of high- and low-pressure in the room that color the sound. The standing-wave patterns in a room are determined both by the room's dimensions and by the position of the sound source in the room. By putting the loudspeakers and listener in the best location, we can achieve smoother bass response.

A well-known rule of thumb states that, for the best bass response, the distance between the loudspeakers and the rear wall should be one-third of the length of the room. If this is impractical, try one-fifth of the room length. Both of these positions reduce the excitation of standing waves and help the loudspeaker integrate with the room. Ideally, the listening position should be two-thirds of the way into the room.

Starting with these basic configurations, move the loudspeakers and the listening chair in small increments while playing music rich in low frequencies. Listen for smoothness, extension, and how well the bass integrates with the rest of the spectrum. When you find the loudspeaker placement where the bass is the smoothest, you'll also hear an increase in midrange clarity and definition.

An excellent test signal for evaluating bass and midrange sound in a room is the Music Articulation Test Tone (MATT) developed by Acoustic Sciences Corporation (ASC). This special test signal is a series of tone bursts that rise in pitch, with silence between bursts. Ideally, you should hear the bursts and silence as separate events. When heard through headphones or with your ear near the loudspeaker, each burst is clearly articulated. But when the sound is modified by the listening room, certain frequency bands of the ascending tone bursts become smeared or garbled, indicating a problem in the listening room at those frequencies. By moving the loudspeakers and listening to the MATT, you can easily discover where your loudspeakers work best in the room. The MATT is available on the Prosonus test CD ($65), or the *Stereophile*

Test CD 2 ($8.95 Tel: 800-358-6274). (*Stereophile*'s Test CD includes more detailed information about how to use this unique test signal.)

The best way to find the right spots for your loudspeakers and listening chair with regard to reducing the influence of standing waves is a computer program called "The Listening Room," distributed by Sitting Duck Software (503-935-3982). This $47.50, IBM-compatible program asks for your room dimensions and loudspeaker and listening positions. The display shows the frequency and amplitude of room resonance modes at the listening position for that configuration. As you "move" the loudspeaker and listening positions within the program, the display shows the effect in real time so that optimum locations can be found for loudspeakers and listener. The Listening Room is highly recommended for this aspect of loudspeaker placement.

4) *Distance from rear wall affects soundstaging*

Generally, the farther away from the rear wall the loudspeakers are, the deeper the soundstage. A deep, expansive soundstage is rarely developed with the loudspeakers near the rear wall. Pulling the loudspeakers out a few feet can make the difference between poor and spectacular soundstaging. Unfortunately, many living rooms don't accommodate loudspeakers far out into the room. If the loudspeakers must be close to the rear wall, make the rear wall acoustically absorbent.

5) *Listening height and tonal balance*

Most loudspeakers exhibit changes in frequency response with changes in listening height. These changes affect the mid-band and treble, not the bass balance. Typically, the loudspeaker will be brightest (i.e., have the most treble) when your ears are at the same height as the tweeters, or on the tweeter axis. Most tweeters are positioned between 32" and 40" from the floor to coincide with typical listening heights. If you've got an adjustable office chair, you can easily hear the effects of listening axis on tonal balance.

The degree to which the sound changes with height varies greatly with the loudspeaker. Some models have a very broad range over which very little change is audible; others can exhibit large tonal changes when you merely straighten your back while listening. Choosing a listening chair that sets your ears at the optimum axis will help achieve a good treble balance.

This difference in response is easily measurable. A typical set of loudspeaker measurements will include a family of response curves measured on various axes. The on-axis response (usually on the tweeter axis) is normalized to produce a straight line; the other curves show the *difference* between the on-axis response and at various heights. Chapter 7 ("Loudspeakers") includes a full description of how to interpret these measurements.

6) Toe-in

Toe-in is pointing the loudspeakers inward toward the listener rather than facing them straight ahead (see Fig.4-5). There are no rules for toe-in; the optimum amount varies greatly with the loudspeaker and listening room. Some loudspeakers need toe-in; others work best firing straight ahead. Toe-in affects many aspects of the musical presentation, including mid- and high-frequency balance, soundstage focus, sense of spaciousness, and immediacy.

Fig. 4-5
Loudspeakers positioned with no toe-in (left diagram) and with toe-in (right diagram)

Most loudspeakers are brightest directly on-axis (directly in front of the loudspeaker). Toe-in thus increases the amount of treble heard at the listening seat. An overly bright loudspeaker can often be tamed by pointing the loudspeaker straight ahead. Some models, designed for listening without toe-in, are far too bright on-axis.

The ratio of direct to reflected sound increases with toe-in. A toed-in loudspeaker will present more direct energy to the listener and project less energy into the room, where it might reach the listener only after reflecting from room surfaces. In a listening room with reflective side walls, toeing-in the loudspeakers can be a decided advantage. Moreover, the amplitude of side-wall reflections is greatly decreased with toe-in. Conversely, less toe-in increases the amount of reflected energy heard by the listener, adding to a sense of spaciousness and air. Reducing toe-in can open up the soundstage and create a feeling of envelopment.

Similarly, toe-in often increases soundstage focus and image specificity. When toed-in, many loudspeakers provide a more focused and sharply delineated soundstage. Images are more clearly defined, compact, and tight, rather than diffuse and lacking a specific spatial position. The optimum toe-in is often a tradeoff between too much treble and a strong central image. With lots of toe-in, the soundstage snaps into focus, but the presentation is often too bright. With no toe-in, the treble balance is smoother, but the imaging is more vague.

Toe-in also affects the presentation's overall spaciousness. No toe-in produces a larger, more billowy, and less precise soundstage. Instruments are less clearly delineated, but the presentation is bigger and more spacious. Toeing-in the loudspeakers shrinks the apparent size of the soundstage, but allows more precise image localization. Again, the amount of toe-in depends on the loudspeaker, room, and personal preference. There's no substitute for listening, adjusting toe-in, and listening again.

Identical toe-in for each loudspeaker is vital. This is most easily accomplished by measuring the distances from the rear wall to each of the loudspeaker's rear edges; these distances will differ according to the degree of toe-in. Repeat this procedure on the other loudspeaker, adjusting its toe-in so that the distances match those of the first loudspeaker. Another way to assure identical toe-in is to look at the loudspeaker's inside edges while in the listening seat. You should see the same amount of the cabinet's inner side panel on both loudspeakers.

Loudspeaker Placement Summary

Loudspeaker placement is the single most important thing you can do to improve your system's sound. It's free, helps develop listening skills, and can make the difference between mediocre and spectacular sound with the same electronics and loudspeakers. Before spending money on upgrading components or acoustic treatments, be sure you've realized your system's potential with correct loudspeaker placement.

After you've found the best loudspeaker placement, install the spikes supplied by the manufacturer. Level the spikes so that the loudspeaker doesn't rock: all four (or three) spikes should carry the loudspeaker's weight.

We've seen how loudspeaker placement gives us precise and independent control over different aspects of the music presentation. We can control both the quantity and the quality of bass by changing the loudspeakers' distances from the rear and side walls. The audibility of room resonance modes can be reduced by finding the best spots for the loudspeakers and listening chair. Treble balance can be adjusted by listening height and toe-in. The balance between soundstage focus and spaciousness is easily changed just by toeing-in the loudspeakers. Soundstage depth can be increased by moving the loudspeakers farther out into the room.

Loudspeaker positioning is a powerful tool for achieving the best sound in your listening room, and it doesn't cost a cent. Take advantage of it.

Common Room Problems and How to Treat Them

Treating your listening room can range from simply hanging a rug on a wall to adding specially designed acoustic devices. Large gains in sound quality can be realized just by adding—or moving—common domestic materials such as carpets, area rugs, and drapes. This approach is inexpensive, simple, and often more aesthetically pleasing than installing less familiar acoustic products. Once the room is optimized using existing household materials, the next step is installing dedicated acoustic control devices. Here are some of the most common room problems, and how to correct them.

1) Untreated parallel surfaces

Perhaps the most common and pernicious of room problems is that of untreated parallel surfaces. If two reflective surfaces face each other, *flutter echo* will occur. Flutter echo is a "pinging" sound that remains after the direct sound has stopped. If you've ever been in an empty, uncarpeted house and clapped your hands, you've heard flutter echo. It sounds like a ringing that hangs in the air long after the clap has decayed. Flutter echo is a periodic repetition caused by the uncontrolled reflection of a sound back and forth between two surfaces. Imagine two mirrors facing each other, the reflections bouncing back and forth between the reflective surfaces to create the illusion of an infinitely receding distance. Flutter echo can blur transient attacks and decays and add a hard, metallic character to the upper midband and treble.

Try clapping your hands in various rooms of the house—particularly the bathroom or hallway. If your listening room has a pinging overhang similar to what you hear in the bathroom, you need to correct this problem.

Flutter echo is easy to prevent. Simply identify the reflective parallel surfaces and put an absorbing or diffusing material on one of them. This will break up the repeated reflections between the surfaces. The material could be a rug hung on a wall, a carpet on the floor (if the flutter echo is between a hard floor and ceiling), drapes over a window, or an acoustic absorbing material applied to a wall. Even small patches of highly absorbent acoustical foam such as Sonex (described later) will kill flutter echo.

An effective material for controlling flutter echo without making the room too dead is a very thin carpet-like material used in airports and conference rooms. (The photographs of a sample listening room later in this chapter show this material installed on the walls.) Although very expensive when sold as an acoustical treatment, this same carpet-like material is available from carpet mills for a fraction of the acoustic supply house's price. It is unobtrusive, easy to apply, available in a variety of colors, relatively inexpensive, and highly effective. Moreover, its absorption characteristics are just right for preventing flutter echo without absorbing too much energy and making the room "dead." The carpet can be glued or tacked into place; mounting it on masonite backing allows you to move it around to find its most effective placement.

Whatever solution works best for you, killing flutter echo is of utmost importance.

2) Uncontrolled floor and side-wall reflections

It is inevitable that loudspeakers will be placed next to the room's side walls and near the floor. Sound from the loudspeakers reaches the listener directly, in addition to being reflected from the side walls, floor, and ceiling. Side-wall reflections are the music signal delayed in time, colored in timbre, and spatially positioned at different locations from the direct sound. All these factors can degrade sound quality. Moreover, floor and side-wall reflections interact with the direct sound to further color the music's tonal character. Fig.4-6 shows how the sound at the listening seat is a combination of direct and reflected sound.

Fig. 4-6 The listener receives a combination of direct and reflected sound.

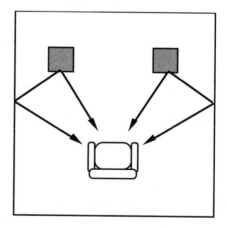

Side-wall reflections color the music's tonal balance in three ways. First, virtually all loudspeakers' *off-axis responses* (frequency response measured at the side of the loudspeaker) are much less flat (accurate) than their on-axis responses. The sound emanating from the loudspeaker sides (the signal that reflects off the side wall) may have large peaks and dips in its frequency response. When this colored signal is reflected from the side wall to the listener, we hear this tonal coloration imposed on the music.

Second, the side wall's acoustic characteristics will further color the reflection. If the wall absorbs high frequencies but not midband energy, the reflection will be rolled-off in the treble.

Finally, when the direct and reflected sounds combine, the listener hears a combination of the direct sound from the loudspeaker and a slightly delayed version of the sound reflected from the side wall. The delay is caused by the additional path-length difference between the sound source (the loudspeaker) and the listener. Because sound travels at 1130 ft/second, we can easily calculate the delay time. If the additional path-length difference in Fig.4-6 was 4', the side-wall reflection will be delayed by 35ms (35 milliseconds, or 35 thousandths of a second) in relation to the direct sound.

The result is a phenomenon called *comb filtering* (see Fig.4-7), a sequence of peaks and notches—hence its similarity to a comb—in the frequency response caused by constructive and destructive interference between the direct and reflected sounds. The phase difference between the two signals causes cancellation at certain frequencies and reinforcement at others, determined by the path-length distance. It all adds up to coloration of the signal at the listening position.

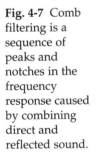

Fig. 4-7 Comb filtering is a sequence of peaks and notches in the frequency response caused by combining direct and reflected sound.

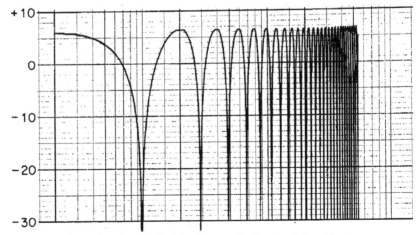

Courtesy *Audio Engineering Handbook*, K. Benson, McGraw-Hill, Inc., 1988

The result of these mechanisms is a sound with a very different tonal balance from that of the direct signal from the loudspeakers. Side-wall reflections are one reason the same loudspeakers sound different in different rooms.

Side-wall reflections not only affect the perceived spectral balance, they also destroy precise image placement within the soundstage. The reflections present "virtual" images of the loudspeakers' signal that appear on the side walls. Although some degree of side-wall reflection adds spaciousness and size, strong reflections increase the *apparent* distance between the loudspeakers. This blurs the spatial distinction between individual images and makes the soundstage less focused and precise. When we hear a center-placed image as partially emanating from positions beyond the left and right loudspeaker boundaries, the tight image focus we seek is destroyed.

Sound also reflects from the rear wall and ceiling. Reflections from the rear wall are less pernicious; they're lower in amplitude and are more delayed in time. The ceiling reflection affects the sound less than the side-wall reflections because of its greater path-length difference, but can raise the soundstage above the horizon. A sloped ceiling further reduces the ceiling's effect on the loudspeakers' sound.

Fortunately, treating side-wall reflections is simple: just put an absorbing or diffusing material on the side walls between the loudspeakers and listening position. The floor reflection is even easier to deal with: carpet or a heavy area rug on the floor will absorb most of the reflection and reduce its detrimental effects. Low frequencies, however, won't be absorbed by a carpet or rug, leading to a cancellation in the midbass caused by interference between the direct and reflected waves. This is the so-called "Allison Effect," named after loudspeaker designer Roy Allison, who first publicized the phenomenon.

Side-wall reflections should be diffused (scattered) or absorbed. Diffusion turns the single discrete reflection into many lower-amplitude reflections spread out over time and reflected in different directions (see Fig.4-8). Diffusion can be achieved with specialized acoustic diffusers such as those made by RPG Diffusors (shown in Fig.4-9a, and described later in this chapter), or an irregular surface. A open-backed bookcase full of books makes an excellent diffuser, particularly if the books are of different depths, or are arranged with their spines sticking out at different distances. Fig.4-9b shows RPG Diffusors installed behind loudspeakers. Note the rug on the floor between the loudspeakers and listening position.

Fig. 4-8 Sound striking a surface is either absorbed, reflected, or diffused (or a combination of the three).

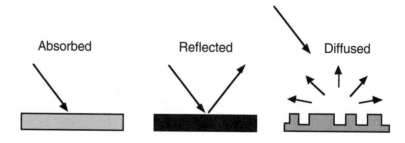

Absorbed   Reflected   Diffused

Fig. 4-9a An RPG Diffusor

Courtesy RPG Diffusor Systems, Inc.

Fig. 4-9b QRD Diffusors, a product of RPG Diffusor Systems, Inc. installed at dmp, (Digital Music Products, Inc.), Stamford, CT

The second option is to absorb the side-wall reflection with an acoustically absorbent material. The acoustical foams described later in this chapter will work, but completely absorbing the side-wall reflection

with an aggressive foam or fiberglass panel can make the room sound lifeless, and constrict the presentation's sense of size and space.

There is some debate in the high-end community over whether side-wall reflections should be absorbed or diffused. Diffusion proponents argue that the reflected energy is beneficial if converted to many lower-amplitude reflections spread out over time and space, the diffused reflections increasing the presentation's spaciousness and air. Absorption proponents suggest that any reflections within the first 20ms of the direct sound degrade the signal from the loudspeakers. Most recording-studio control rooms are designed to provide a "Reflection Free Zone" (RFZ) where the engineer sits so that he or she hears only the direct sound from the studio monitors. My experience suggests that absorbing side-wall reflections is better than diffusing them, but that diffusing materials behind the listening seat are better than absorbing materials. There is no debate, however, that uncontrolled side-wall reflections degrade a room's sonic performance.

An excellent product for controlling side-wall reflections is the Tower Trap made by the Acoustic Sciences Corporation. This is a tall, cylindrical device with absorptive and reflective (diffusive) sides. Absorption or diffusion can be selected by just turning the device. When placed near the side wall with the reflective side to the room rear, the absorptive side prevents the first reflection from reaching the listener directly. Some of the energy striking the side wall is reflected into the Tower Trap's rear (diffusive) side. Most of the side wall reflection is absorbed, and some is delayed in time, attenuated, and diffused—exactly what we want.

Note that it isn't necessary to treat a listening room's entire side-wall area; the reflections come only from small points along the wall. At mid- and high frequencies, sound waves behave more like rays of light. We can thus trace side-wall reflections to the listening seat and put the treatment in exactly the right location. As with light rays, the angle of incidence equals the angle of reflection.

The technique for tracing side-wall reflections is shown in the series of photographs and illustrations in Figs.4-10, 4-11, and 4-12. First, mount a reflective Mylar strip on the side wall between the listener and the loudspeaker. The strip's center should be at the height of your ears when you're sitting in the listening chair. Next, put light sources (two lamps with their shades removed is ideal) where the loudspeakers are normally placed, as shown in Fig.4-10. When sitting in the listening chair, you'll see the two lamps reflected in the Mylar strip (Fig.4-11). The points along the Mylar strip where you see the lamps' bulbs are exactly the points where sound is reflected from the side walls to the listening seat. This is where to put the acoustic treatment. The photograph in Fig.4-12 shows how strategically placed acoustical materials (in this case, ASC

Tower Traps) can kill side-wall reflections from both loudspeakers. Compare Fig.4-11 to Fig.4-12.

Fig. 4-10
Replace the loudspeakers with light sources and install a Mylar strip.

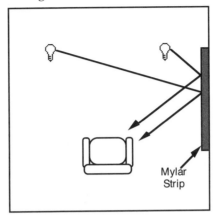

Fig. 4-11 The points of visual reflection are also the points of acoustic reflection.

Fig. 4-12 Acoustic treatments placed exactly at the reflection points kill side-wall reflections.

Repeat the process for the left side wall. If your listening room is symmetrical and the listening position is in the middle of the room, you can use this technique on only one side wall, then duplicate the acoustic treatment on the other side. Both side-wall treatments should be the same to maintain acoustical symmetry in the room.

Treating the side-wall reflections from *both* loudspeakers on *each* side wall improves imaging. The right side wall will reflect sound from both right *and* left loudspeakers. The reflection of the left loudspeaker's signal from the right side wall confuses image placement and constricts sound-stage width. This reflection can be thought of as a kind of "acoustic crosstalk"; we don't want left-channel information reflecting from the side wall into the right ear.

Note that a treatment placed away from the wall creates a larger apparent surface area than a treatment attached to the wall. The distance between the treatment and the wall causes the treatment to cast an acoustic shadow on the wall, widening the effective absorption area.

This technique can be applied to all reflections in the listening room. If you put a Mylar strip around the entire listening room, any point where you see a reflection of the light bulb itself is also a sound-reflection point. Additional absorptive or diffusive surfaces can then be placed and oriented exactly where they do the most good.

Even if you don't go to the trouble of putting up a Mylar strip and lamps, you should do something to treat side-wall reflections. Bookcases, rugs, and drapes are all better than bare walls. If you really want to get the best from your system, however, there's no substitute for professionally-designed acoustic treatments.

3) Thick, boomy bass

Thick and boomy bass is a common affliction that can be difficult to control. It often results from room resonance modes, poor loudspeaker placement, poor loudspeakers, or not enough low-frequency absorption in the listening room. As we will see in the later section on standing waves, listening-seat position can also exacerbate bass bloat.

If thick and boomy bass persists even after minimizing it with careful loudspeaker placement (the most effective method of alleviating the problem), you may want to consider different loudspeakers. If, however, the boominess is minor and you want to keep your loudspeakers, you can make the presentation leaner and tighter by adding low-frequency absorbers. These devices soak up low frequencies rather than reflecting them back into the room.

Passive low-frequency absorbers simply convert acoustic energy into another form—usually heat within a fibrous material. Low-frequency absorbers can be bought ready-made (such as ASC's Tube Traps and

Tower Traps), built from common materials, or incorporated into an existing room structure.

A very inexpensive and effective low-frequency absorber can be made in a few hours for less than $20. These devices, called *panel absorbers,* have very high absorption coefficients at low frequencies, and can be tuned to the exact frequency and bandwidth required.

Panel absorbers can stand free of or be built right into an existing wall. In a typical built-in absorber, a 4' by 8' frame of 2x4s is nailed on its edge to the existing wall. The inside is sealed with caulking where the wood meets the wall to make it airtight, then filled with fiberglass insulation. Next, a sheet of masonite or plywood is nailed over the frame. Many tiny holes are then drilled in the panel. *Voilà*—a low-frequency panel absorber. This type of perforated panel absorber is also called a Helmholtz resonator.

Some panel absorbers have no holes, instead using a very thin sheet of material that flexes when struck by sound. The structure's absorption frequency is a function of the airspace depth (2x4s, 2x8s, 2x10s, or 2x12s may be used) and panel thickness. The fiberglass inside the structure broadens the absorption peak. By changing the airspace depth and—in perforated absorbers—hole size, panel absorbers can be tuned to any low- to mid-frequency. Most rooms need broadband absorption in the bass, but panel absorbers can be narrowly tuned to absorb room resonance problems. A few panel absorbers, tuned to major resonance modes in the low-frequency spectrum, can greatly reduce bass problems in small rooms. To make these rather ugly contraptions palatable in a home, cover them with fabric. (Note that Helmholtz-type resonators shouldn't be covered directly with fabric: they need at least 1/4" of airspace to allow the holes to "breathe" freely.)

Specific details on building panel absorbers—material thickness, perforation size, spacing, etc.—can be found in the reference at the end of this chapter.

Free-standing panel absorbers are built the same way, but with a sturdy backing (3/4" particleboard, for example) instead of being attached to a wall.

Yet another way to get much-needed low-frequency absorption is by building a bass trap into an existing structure—a closet, say. Simply hanging an absorptive material such as acoustical foam or ordinary fiberglass over the closet opening provides low-frequency absorption. This type of structure is called a *quarter-wavelength trap.* The trap will have peak absorption at the frequency whose 1/4 wavelength equals the distance between the closet back wall and the absorptive material, and also at odd multiples of 1/4 wavelength. In fact, any absorptive material hung in front of a reflective surface will form a quarter-wavelength trap. Drapes in front of a window will work, but the distance between the window and drapes is so short that the lowest absorption frequency will be in the midband.

Let's calculate the absorption frequency for a 2' deep closet with absorptive material hung at the front. The formula is $F = 1130/4D$, where F is the lowest absorption peak, 1130 is the speed of sound in feet per second, and 4D is 4 times the distance between the reflective closet wall and the absorptive material. The lowest peak absorption frequency for a 2'-deep closet is 141Hz. This structure will also have peak absorption at odd multiples of a quarter wavelength: for instance, at three (423Hz), five (706Hz), and seven (989Hz) times 141Hz, and so on. Drapes hung 6" from a window will provide peak absorption at 565Hz, 1695Hz, 2825Hz, 3955Hz, and so on. Slanting the absorptive material will skew these values along a continuum, making the absorption more even with frequency.

The quarter-wavelength trap is typically limited to providing mid-bass absorption because of the large dimensions needed to achieve deep-bass absorption. I must stress, however, that proper loudspeaker placement is the easiest and most effective technique for reducing bass thickness. These acoustic treatments should be tried only *after* exhausting every possible loudspeaker placement option.

4) Reflective objects near the loudspeaker

Reflective objects near the loudspeakers—equipment racks, windows behind the loudspeakers, subwoofers or furniture between the loudspeakers, even power amplifiers on the floor—can cause poor image focus and lack of depth. The best solution is to remove the offending object. I gained a huge increase in image focus and soundstage depth in my system just by moving my equipment racks from between the loudspeakers to the side of the room. If this is impractical, move the reflective objects as far behind the loudspeakers as possible. Power amplifiers should not extend in front of the loudspeakers' front panels, for example. And don't put a big television monitor between the loudspeakers. This is one reason why a music system should be separate from a video system: you just can't get good imaging with a television between the loudspeakers.

If you can't move the offending object, cover it with an absorbing material such as Sonex. Windows behind the loudspeakers should be draped, with the drapes closed when listening. There's a large window directly behind my loudspeakers; I hear a significant increase in soundstage depth with the drapes pulled closed.

A good test of whether imaging is degraded by reflective objects near the loudspeakers is the Listening Environment Diagnostic Recording (LEDR) found on the first Chesky Test CD (Chesky JD37). The test consists of a synthetic percussion instrument processed to sound as if it is moving in an arc between and above the loudspeakers. A system and room with good imaging will make the sound appear to move smoothly and consistently in the intended direction. Any holes in the image will be characterized by the sound jumping from one spot to the next rather than smoothly moving. Such holes could be due to poor loudspeaker quality or placement, but can often be corrected just by moving reflective objects away from the loudspeakers. Best of all, a potentially large improvement in imaging and soundstaging can be had for a few hours of your time.

These, then, are the most common acoustical problems and how to fix them. Later in this chapter, we'll look at these problems and treatments with a real example of a treated listening room.

Acoustical Do's and Don'ts

I've summarized this chapter into a few simple guidelines for improving your listening room. This next section is a short course for those readers who don't want to read about absorption coefficients and off-axis response. If you just want some practical tips for getting the most out of your system, this is the section to read. More detail on each of these points can be found throughout the chapter.

1) Loudspeaker placement

Just as real estate agents name "location, location, and location" as the three most important things about the desirability of a house, the three most important ways to improve the sound in your room are "loudspeaker placement, loudspeaker placement, and loudspeaker placement." Follow the suggestions in this chapter and spend a few hours moving your loudspeakers around and listening. You'll not only end up with better sound, but become more attuned to sonic differences. All acoustic treatments should be built on a foundation of good loudspeaker placement.

2) Start with good ratios between the room's length, width, and height.

This isn't always possible, but when you're out house-hunting, take your tape measure and the table on good room ratios on page 98. If you can build a room from scratch, or convert a garage or basement into a listening room, choosing optimum dimensional ratios gives you a significant head start in getting great sound from your system.

3) Avoid untreated parallel surfaces.

If you've got bare walls facing each other, you'll have flutter echo. Kill the flutter echo by facing one wall with an absorbent material. Use one of the acoustical foams described, a pair of ASC Tower Traps, a rug, or the carpet-like material described later in this chapter.

4) Absorb or diffuse side wall and floor reflections.

Bare floors should be covered with carpet between the listening seat and the loudspeakers. Treat the side walls between the loudspeakers and the listening position with an absorbing or diffusing material. Avoid having reflective surfaces, such as bare walls and windows, next to the loudspeakers. ASC Tower Traps, the various acoustical foams, and RPG Diffusors are all effective in treating side-wall reflections. Bookcases on the side walls make good diffusers.

5) Keep reflective objects away from loudspeakers.

Equipment racks, power amplifiers, furniture, and other acoustically reflective objects near the loudspeakers will degrade imaging and soundstaging. Move them behind the loudspeakers, or cover them with an absorbing material.

6) Choose a room with a high, sloped ceiling.

This isn't always possible, but a high, sloped ceiling skews the floor-to-ceiling resonance modes and reduces the early reflections at the listening position, resulting in smoother bass and a more spacious and open presentation. The loudspeakers should be positioned in the low-ceilinged portion of the room.

7) Balance high-frequency absorbing materials with low-frequency absorbing materials.

Most rooms have lots of high-frequency absorption but little low-frequency absorption. Carpet, drapes, and soft furniture should be complemented with low-frequency absorbers (ASC Tower Traps or home-made panel absorbers) to keep the reverberation time flat across the band. Thick, slow bass results from such imbalances in reverberation.

8) Move the listening seat for best low-frequency balance.

Standing waves create stationary areas of high and low pressure in the room. Move the listening chair for best balance. Avoid sitting against the rear wall; the sound will be bass-heavy.

9) Break up standing-wave patterns with irregular surfaces or objects.

Strategically placed furniture or structures help break up standing waves. Large furniture behind the listening position diffuses waves reflected from the rear.

A Sample Listening Room

I was lucky enough to be able to build a dedicated listening room from scratch. Although I don't claim that my room is a paradigm of the form, it nevertheless illustrates many of the ideas presented in this chapter.

First, the room has good dimensional ratios. It is 21' long, 14.5' wide over most of its width (13.5' over 6' of width), and has a high, sloped ceiling. I chose the ratios based on suggestions made in acoustics books, and on my own analyses of room-mode distribution. Subsequent computer analysis confirmed the efficacy of these dimensions.

The room is rather odd-shaped, both to fit in with the design of the rest of the house, and to create a structure that skews resonant modes and breaks up standing waves. As you can see in Fig.4-13, the room actually has three lengths: 21' to the rear wall, 18' to the closet front, and 15' to the upper wall. With a larger budget and less need to make the room conform to the rest of the house, I would have splayed the walls to create an even more irregular shape.

Fig. 4-13 The listening room has three lengths to spread resonant modes. Slatted, bi-fold doors behind the listening chair provide diffusion.

The slatted bi-fold doors that close off the closet provide high-frequency diffusion behind the listening chair while being transparent to low frequencies. The closet was designed so that sheets of acoustic foam could be hung at the closet front just inside the bi-fold doors to form a quarter-wavelength bass trap. Angling the foam rather than putting it parallel to the rear wall spreads the peak absorption frequency for a smoother absorption characteristic. The closet's 3' depth gives it a peak absorption frequency of 94Hz. The ASC Tower Trap directly behind the listening chair is placed reflective-side out for maximum diffusion.

The floor covering of Berber carpet over padding provides high-frequency absorption. The carpet also prevents flutter echo between the wood ceiling and the floor, and absorbs the floor reflection from the loudspeakers. All walls in the room's front portion are covered with the thin carpet-like material described earlier. This prevents flutter echo and ringing, absorbs high frequencies, and takes the bright edge from the room without making it too dead. Drapes cover the two windows.

Two Phantom Acoustics Shadows, an active low-frequency control device, are placed in the corners behind the loudspeakers. These smooth the excessive bass energy caused by room resonance modes. The Shadows also control the room's low-frequency reverberation time and prevent the loudspeakers' rear-radiated bass energy from being reflected back into the room, where it can interact with the loudspeakers' direct output (I didn't include the Shadows in the list of acoustical treatments presented later in this chapter not only because they were expensive— $2500 a pair—but are also no longer available.)

Side-wall reflections are treated with two pairs of ASC Tower Traps, their reflective sides facing toward the rear. This takes advantage of the phenomenon described earlier under "Treating side-wall reflections" (Fig.4-14).

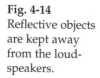

Fig. 4-14
Reflective objects are kept away from the loudspeakers.

The loudspeakers are positioned for best coupling to the room and least excitation of room modes. They are well out into the room, and at different distances from the side and rear walls. Note that no reflective objects are near the loudspeakers; the power amplifiers are well behind the plane of the loudspeakers' backs.

I'm very happy with the room's sound; many loudspeakers work well in it. The room tends to be a little lean in the midbass, but very articulate. It is the antithesis of thick, boomy, or slow. This is most likely the result of the good dimensional ratios, the bass absorbers, high ceiling, and staggered length. The room is also more tolerant of bright loudspeakers and those with poor (highly colored) off-axis responses.

A Short Course in Acoustical Theory

You don't need to know any acoustical theory to get good sound from your system. However, I've included the following survey of basic acoustical principles for those who want to take the next step in understanding how sound behaves in a room.

Listening-Room Resonance Modes

Resonance is the vibration of an object at its natural frequency, determined by the object's material and dimensions. Resonances surround us all the time—from a bell ringing at a certain pitch, to the sound made by blowing across the opening of a soda bottle. A singer breaking a glass with her voice is another example of resonance. It's not that the singer is that loud; when she hits the resonant frequency of the air in the glass, the reinforcement caused by the resonance adds energy to her voice.

As music lovers, we're interested in acoustic resonance: the reinforcement of certain frequencies within an enclosed volume of air—such as a listening room. When excited by the sound from the loudspeakers, the air in the listening room will resonate at particular frequencies, determined by the distances between the room's walls. These resonant points, called *room resonance modes*, can severely color the bass by creating large peaks and dips in the frequency response. Room resonance modes impose a sonic signature on the reproduced sound.

The room acts as an equalizer between your loudspeakers and ears, boosting certain frequencies and attenuating others. The result is degraded sound quality. In a poor room, the bass might lack specific pitch definition or sound slow and tubby, certain notes might be more prominent than others, dynamic impact could be reduced—or all of these at once.

Let's consider what happens along the length of a listening room when the air inside it is excited by sound from the loudspeakers. For now, we'll ignore the fact that the room has height and width, and consider only the resonance between the two walls that define the room's length.

A listening room's resonant frequencies are determined by the distance between the room's walls. The farther apart the walls are, the lower the resonant frequency. Specifically, the lowest resonant frequency, called the *fundamental* resonance, occurs when the room's length equals half the wavelength of sound. Put another way, a resonant mode will occur when the sound's wavelength is twice the length of the room.

Other resonant modes occur at twice this frequency, three times this frequency, and so on. Whenever the length of the room is a multiple of half of the sound's wavelength, a resonant mode will occur. This phenomenon, along with the formula for calculating resonant mode frequencies, is shown in Fig.4-15.

Fig. 4-15
Resonant modes occur when the distance between the room's walls equals half the wavelength of sound and at multiples of half a wavelength.

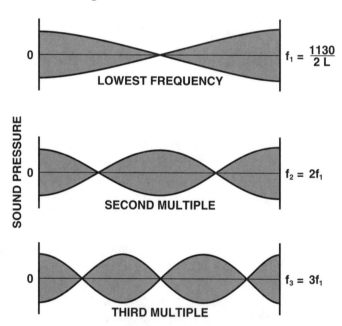

Calculating your listening room's resonant modes is easy. (But remember: we're still considering only the room's length.) The formula is F1 = 1130/2L. F1 is the first resonant mode, 1130 is the speed of sound in air (in feet per second), and 2L is two times the room's length (in feet). If the room is 21' long, its first resonant mode will be 27Hz (1130/2 x 21).

We know that the next mode will occur when the wavelength equals the room's length, at 54Hz (2 x F1), then again at the next multiple of half a wavelength (1-1/2 wavelengths) at 81Hz (3 x F1), again at 108Hz (4 x F1), and so forth. It is only necessary to consider room modes up to about 300Hz, after which they tend to become so dense that they don't cause problems.

The room's height and width will also create their own resonant modes. If we have an 8' ceiling, the resonant modes will occur at 71Hz (1130/2 x 8), 141Hz, 212Hz, and so on. If the width is 13', the resonant modes will be at 43Hz (1130/2 x 13), 87Hz, 130Hz, 174Hz, 217, 261Hz, etc.

What this means to audiophiles wanting the most accurate reproduction possible is that those frequencies will be emphasized in a 21' by 8' by 13' room because of the room's resonance modes. This emphases, or peaks, in the frequency response color the sound. In fact, room resonance modes can cause bass peaks and dips as large as 10dB. Resonance modes are a significant source of coloration in listening rooms, causing poor bass articulation, boominess, and bass thickness.

Optimizing Dimensional Ratios

We can minimize the frequency-response peaks and dips caused by room resonance modes by choosing a listening room with dimensional ratios that more evenly spread the resonant modes over the low-frequency band. Let's examine the resonance modes of two rooms of about equal volume. The first room has poor dimensional ratios, while the second room's dimensional ratios are excellent.

The first room is 24' long, 16' wide, and 8' high. If we calculate and plot the resonant modes for each distance (length, width, height), we end up with a chart that looks like this:

Mode	Length	Width	Height
	24'	16'	8'
F1	24Hz	35Hz	71Hz
F2	48Hz	70Hz	142Hz
F3	72Hz	105Hz	213Hz
F4	96Hz	140Hz	284Hz
F5	120Hz	175Hz	355Hz
F6	144Hz	210Hz	
F7	168Hz	245Hz	
F8	192Hz	280Hz	
F9	216Hz	310Hz	
F10	240Hz		
F11	264Hz		
F12	288Hz		
F13	312Hz		

Notice that the third length mode (F3) at 72Hz coincides with the second width mode (F2) and the first height mode (F1). These three modes combine, piling up at 70Hz to create a huge peak in the response at this frequency. This undesirable situation occurs again at 140Hz, 213Hz, 284Hz. The resonant modes coincide because the room's length, width, and height are multiples of each other. Actually, the three modes are perfectly coincident at 70.6Hz, 141.2Hz, etc. I've rounded them so they are slightly skewed, making the pileup more visible in Fig.4-16, following. Moreover, there are no modes between 105Hz and 140Hz which will make the pileup at 140Hz much more audible. The result will be a thick, peaky, and very colored bass reproduction.

We can also plot these modes graphically to better visualize room-mode distribution. This mode vs. frequency graph is shown in Fig.4-16.

Fig. 4-16
Plotting the
resonant modes
graphically

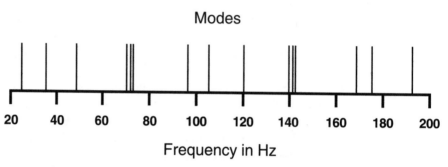

As we can see, the modes are bunched together, with large spaces between them. The "holes" between modes are just as detrimental as the coincident modes; they make the adjacent modes much more audible.

Let's see how this situation can be avoided by a room with better dimensional ratios. Our second room has approximately the same volume, but different distances between its walls. This room is 21' long, 14' wide, and has a 10' ceiling. Calculating the resonant modes for each dimension, we see that they are much better distributed:

Mode	Length	Width	Height
	21'	14'	10'
F1	27Hz	40Hz	56Hz
F2	54Hz	81Hz	113Hz
F3	81Hz	121Hz	169Hz
F4	108Hz	161Hz	226Hz
F5	135Hz	201Hz	282Hz
F6	161Hz	242Hz	339Hz
F7	188Hz	282Hz	
F8	215Hz	322Hz	
F9	242Hz		
F10	269Hz		
F11	296Hz		

These data look like this in graphical form (Fig.4-17):

Fig. 4-17 Good dimensional ratios better distribute room resonant modes.

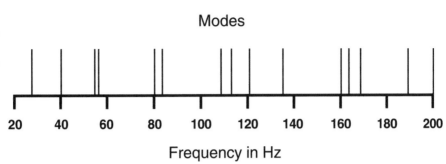

We can see by comparing Fig.4-16 to Fig.4-17 that the resonant modes are more evenly distributed in the second room. Although there is some coincidence of modes, they are much less severe than in the first room. This second room will have smoother bass response, less coloration, and a more taut, punchy low end than the first room. Note that larger rooms have inherently more modes, and that the modes will therefore be more smoothly distributed— assuming good dimensional ratios. The smaller the room, the greater the challenge in distributing room resonance modes.

A sloped ceiling helps greatly in skewing the height modes along a continuum. The resonant modes are naturally spread out rather than occurring at the same frequency as with a flat ceiling. If a ceiling starts at 8' and slopes up to 12', calculate its modes assuming a height of 10' (the average of the two heights). The sloped ceiling doesn't eliminate resonance modes, but it does help to distribute them. Similarly, splayed walls tend to skew the resonance modes, but don't eliminate them.

Room resonant modes can be made less audible by avoiding square or cubical rooms—i.e., rooms of equal width and height, or width and length, or length and height, or length and width—or rooms whose long dimensions are multiples of its short dimensions. If the ceiling is 8', we want to avoid another dimension at 8', 16', 24', etc. Note that resonance modes will always occur; good dimensional ratios merely distribute them evenly rather than allowing them to coincide. The following chart shows, in descending order of quality, the best dimensional ratios (according to acoustician M.M. Louden):

Quality	Height	X	Y
1	1	1.9	1.4
2	1	1.9	1.3
3	1	1.5	2.1
4	1	1.5	2.2
5	1	1.2	1.5
6	1	1.4	2.1
7	1	1.1	1.4
8	1	1.8	1.4
9	1	1.6	2.1
10	1	1.2	1.4
11	1	1.6	1.2
12	1	1.6	2.3
13	1	1.6	2.2
14	1	1.8	1.3
15	1	1.1	1.5
16	1	1.6	2.4
17	1	1.6	1.3
18	1	1.9	1.5
19	1	1.1	1.6
20	1	1.3	1.7

(X can be length and Y width, or vice versa)

If you don't have the luxury of choosing the dimensions of your listening room, you can use the techniques described earlier in this chapter to minimize the audibility of room resonant modes.

Computer software for calculating room resonance modes is available at a moderate price. For example: Given your room's dimensions, the "Modes for Your Abode" software will run a full modal analysis.

This explanation of room resonance modes and the examples given are greatly simplified for this book. I've just covered what are called *axial modes*—those that exist between one pair of surfaces. Other modes resulting from two surface pairs (*tangential modes*) and three surface pairs (*oblique modes*, from all six walls of a room) aren't discussed. The end of this chapter cites a reference work for those wanting to delve deeper into listening-room acoustics.

Standing Waves

If you've seen a cup of coffee sitting on a vibrating surface, you've seen standing waves. The vibration excites the liquid, causing waves to spread out from the center and reflect back from the cup's perimeter. At some points, the waves reinforce each other, while at other points, the waves cancel. The result is an apparently stationary pattern of peaks and dips in the coffee. This is exactly what happens to sound in a listening room.

Standing waves are stationary areas of high and low sound pressure in a room. They are caused by constructive and destructive interferences between the incident (direct) sound and the reflected sound from a room boundary. For example, when the reflected waveform's positive pressure phase is superimposed on the incident waveform's positive pressure phase, the two waves will reinforce each other (constructive interference), producing a *peak*. If the reflected wave's negative pressure phase meets the incident wave's positive pressure phase, the two waves will cancel (destructive interference), producing a dip or *null*. These interactions produce a particular pattern of stationary areas of more and less bass for each resonant frequency in the room.

Let's look at how a standing wave is set up along the length of a 20'-long listening room. If we excite this room at its lowest resonant frequency, the pressure maximum will occur at the room walls, the pressure minima in the center. (See Fig.4-18. This drawing is analogous to Fig.4-15, which showed how a resonant mode occurs when half a wavelength equals the room's length.)

Fig. 4-18
Maximum pressure occurs at room boundaries.

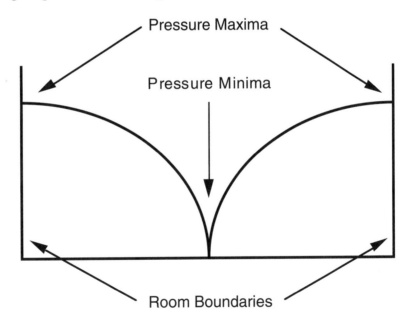

By playing a tone at the room's resonant frequency and walking around in the room, we can hear the sound get louder and softer. In practice, the model in Fig.4-18 isn't so neat; the effects of other room boundaries and objects in the room (furniture) skew this theoretical representation. In addition, the associated resonant modes at multiples of the modal frequency tend to make the pattern of standing waves more complex.

Nevertheless, standing waves create areas in the room in which the bass sounds heavier, and some in which it sounds thinner. Play music with continuous bass energy (organ music works well) and move your listening chair forward and backward; the presentation will be heavier in some areas, leaner in others.

Although this unequal pressure distribution is undesirable, we can use standing waves to our advantage. If your loudspeakers and room tend to be thick and heavy in the bass, try moving your listening chair forward or backward until the bass is a little smoother and leaner. Or use the same technique to add fullness and weight to a thin-sounding loudspeaker.

Reverberation

The sound in a room is a combination of three components: 1) direct sound from the loudspeakers, 2) discrete early reflections from the floor, ceiling, and side walls, and 3) later, more diffuse reflections, called reverberation. This concept of three components to sound is illustrated in Fig.4-19.

Fig. 4-19 Sound in a room is composed of direct sound, early reflections, and reverberation.

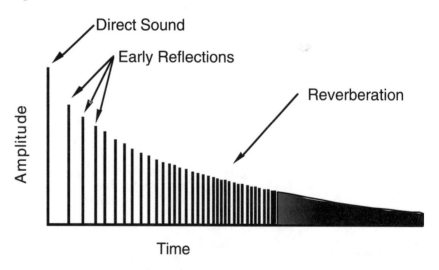

Reverberation is such a fundamental part of sound that we take it for granted. Although we don't hear it as a separate component of sound, reverberation adds warmth and space to music. If reverberation were completely missing from a sound, we would immediately identify the sound as being unusual.

Reverberation in a room takes a finite time to decay into inaudibility (as shown in Fig.4-19). The time it takes for sound to decay by 60dB is called the room's RT_{60}. A small, acoustically dead rock recording studio may have an RT_{60} of 0.1 seconds; a cathedral may have an RT_{60} of six or seven seconds. A room's RT_{60} quantifies how acoustically "live" or "dead" the room is.

Although the concept of reverberation is less applicable to small spaces such as hi-fi listening rooms than to concert halls, it is nonetheless instructive in balancing sound absorbing materials in the room. A room with reflective surfaces will have a longer reverberation time than a room with absorptive surfaces such as carpets, soft furniture, and drapes. These materials absorb sound rather than reflect it back into the room. We want to choose materials in the listening room that contribute to an optimum RT_{60}, and balance those materials so that the reverberation time is constant over the audio band.

But what is the ideal reverberation time in a music listening room? And what combination of reflective and absorptive materials will produce the optimum reverberation time?

The quick answer is that optimum reverberation time in a listening room varies with the room's volume. For a 3000-cubic-foot room, a good reverberation time is about 0.9 seconds. For a 20,000-cubic-foot room, about 1.4 seconds is ideal. A surprisingly accurate measure of a room's reverberation time can be made with a handclap or balloon pop and a stopwatch. Have someone clap their hands loudly, or pop a balloon. Start the stopwatch when you hear the sound, and stop it when the sound has completely died away. Repeat the measurement several times and average the values. The measured result in seconds is a fairly reliable indicator of a room's RT_{60}.

Unfortunately, an optimum overall reverberation time isn't enough: we must ensure that the room's reverberation time is the same at all audio frequencies. A room with thick carpet and heavy draperies—materials that absorb high frequencies, yet do nothing to low frequencies—will have a longer reverberation time at low than at high frequencies. This condition, shown in Fig.4-20, can make a hi-fi system sound slow and thick in the bass, or dead in the treble. Reverberation time is thus specified at six frequencies: 125Hz, 250Hz, 500Hz, 1kHz, 2kHz, and 4kHz. Our goal is to make the reverberation time roughly equal at these frequencies by choosing the appropriate mix of acoustical treatments. We do this by mixing different materials, each having absorption characteristics that vary with frequency. Let's look at how these surfaces affect the sound impinging on them.

Every surface in a listening room will either absorb, reflect, or diffuse (scatter) sound. We'll deal first with absorption and reflection. The degree to which a surface absorbs sound is called its *absorption coefficient*.

This is a measure of the percentage of sound it absorbs, specified at the six frequencies previously listed. An absorption coefficient of 1.0 means that 100% of the sound is absorbed; this condition is likened to an open window—no energy is reflected back into the room. An absorption coefficient of 0.1 means 10% of the sound is absorbed and 90% is reflected back into the room. Absorption coefficients of more than 1.0 are possible with a material that presents a surface area to the sound field that is greater than its area of wall contact. Absorbers placed in corners also increase their ability to absorb acoustic energy.

Fig. 4-20 Long reverberation time at low frequencies makes the sound heavy and muddy.

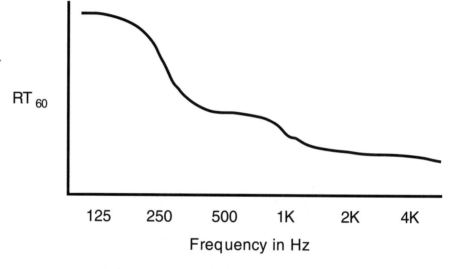

The absorption coefficients for two common materials—heavy carpet over felt, and drywall on studs (1/2″ thick on 2x4s, spaced 16″ on center—are as follows:

	125Hz	250Hz	500Hz	1kHz	2kHz	4kHz
Carpet	0.08	0.24	0.57	0.69	0.71	0.73
Drywall	0.29	0.10	0.05	0.04	0.07	0.09

We can quickly see that carpet absorbs virtually no energy in the bass, but a significant percentage of the energy in the treble—nearly 75% at 4kHz. Conversely, drywall absorbs (and leaks out of the room) a moderate amount of energy in the bass (29% at 125Hz), and reflects virtually all midband and treble energy. Drywall on studs absorbs low frequencies by diaphragmatic action: sound striking the drywall causes it to flex.

Now, suppose we built a room completely covered in thick carpeting—like a rock garage studio. The carpet would absorb nearly all the treble and reflect nearly all the bass. The result would be a very short reverberation time at high frequencies and a very long reverberation time at low frequencies. The room would sound thick, heavy, and congested in the bass, and be generally unpleasant. Moreover, the room would store energy in the bass through resonance and release that energy over time, smearing transient signals.

At the other extreme, a room of bare drywall, an uncovered concrete floor, and no high-frequency absorbing materials would sound bright, hard, and thin. The trick is to balance absorptive materials so that the amount of absorption is roughly the same at all six frequencies. In practice, it's difficult to get enough low-frequency absorption; most rooms have longer reverberation times in the bass. Fortunately, a slightly longer reverberation time at low frequencies is desirable to give the room warmth.

You can calculate your room's reverberation time. First, multiply the absorption coefficient of every surface in the room by the square footage of that surface at the six frequencies. For example, if you have 294 square feet of carpet, multiply 294 x 0.73 (absorption coefficient of carpet at 4kHz) to get 215 absorption units. (These absorption units are called "sabines," after Wallace Clement Sabine, the American physicist who founded the science of architectural acoustics. Boston Symphony Hall, designed in 1900 by Sabine, was the first concert hall to be designed using the new field of architectural acoustics.)

Multiplying each surface area's square footage by the absorption coefficients at the six frequencies gives us a chart of every material in the room and how many sabines of absorption that material provides at the six frequencies (125Hz, 250Hz, 500Hz, 1kHz, 2kHz, and 4kHz).

To convert the total sabines at each frequency into a reverberation time at that frequency, we use the following formula:

$$RT_{60} = \frac{(0.049)(V)}{(S)\ (a)}$$

where

RT_{60} = reverberation time, seconds
V = volume of room, cu ft
S = total surface area of room, sq ft
a = average sabine absorption coefficient

This method of calculating reverberation time works best with large rooms (and assumes that the materials are uniformly distributed throughout the room), but nevertheless gives us an idea of the balance between low-and high-frequency absorption. If you perform these calculations on your own room and find a large difference in the total sabines between 125Hz and 4kHz, you can add low-frequency absorbers to even out the reverberation time. The acoustical materials described earlier in this chapter can be used to achieve a smooth reverberation time with frequency. A full listing of materials and their absorption coefficients is included in the reference book cited at the end of this chapter.

Building a Listening Room from Scratch

This chapter cannot guide someone through the long and complicated process of building a dedicated listening room from the ground up. Instead, I recommend two approaches: The first is to study the subject and design the room yourself, bringing in an acoustician for consultation two or three times during the design process. You can end up with a good room without spending a fortune. This is how I designed my room.

The second approach is to commission a full-fledged design from an architectural acoustics design firm. Some acoustic treatment manufacturers, notably RPG and ASC, also offer full acoustic design services. This way is ideal for those with large budgets or a lack of time to learn acoustic design themselves. The design firm will often oversee construction, providing you with a turnkey room. This can be a *very* expensive proposition. RPG and ASC will, however, provide as much or as little help as you need. A little expert knowledge goes a long way.

Isolating the Listening Room

Many music listeners want to play music at high levels without disturbing neighbors or other family members. This brings us to a specialized area of acoustics called isolation. Acoustic isolation prevents sound in one area from escaping into another area. A good example of isolation is the midtown Manhattan recording studio that records during business hours.

Keeping sound in the listening room from getting into the rest of the house is a daunting challenge. It requires good design, precision construction, and lots of money. There are, however, a few principles and techniques that can help minimize sound transmission.

Very briefly, most sound escapes from the listening room into the rest of the house through doors, not walls. Even small openings, such as the space between the floor and door, allow large amounts of acoustic energy through. This phenomenon is called "flanking." To reduce flanking, use a solid-core door and seal its perimeter with weather-stripping or refrigerator seals.

Second, isolating a room requires lots of mass between the sound source and the area to be protected from sound. Thick walls, double walls with unbridged air cavities, lead sheeting, and double solid-core doors are all fundamental prerequisites to achieving high isolation. Most audiophiles don't need such isolation, but if you do, it's very expensive. Half-hearted attempts at isolation just don't work; it takes a serious effort to achieve adequate isolation. And remember: If you do construct very rigid walls, the room will contain bass energy, requiring more low-frequency absorption.

A Promise for the Future: DSP Room Correction

An entirely new field of audio engineering seeks to make moot most of what I've talked about in this chapter. The new area of study, called "DSP room correction," tries to remove the room's effects on reproduced sound *electronically*, before it is reproduced by the loudspeakers.

DSP stands for Digital Signal Processing, a powerful technology for manipulating audio signals in the digital domain. In DSP room correction, the audio signal is processed in the digital domain to remove listening-room problems by applying filters to remove room resonance modes. In effect, the signal is distorted in a way that counteracts the distortion imposed by the listening room. DSP room correction not only corrects frequency-response peaks and dips, but also removes the effects of reflections on the reproduced sound.

Here's how DSP room correction will apply in practice. When you buy a DSP room-correction system, your dealer will install it and measure your room at the listening position. The measured response is then sent to the DSP room-correction system manufacturer, who converts that frequency-response data into filter algorithms. These algorithms are then stored on an Erasable Programmable Read-Only Memory (EPROM) chip inserted into your DSP room-correction box. The EPROM tells the filters what correction to apply. The EPROM will work effectively only for your room, only with the loudspeakers used during the measurement, only at the loudspeaker position used during the measurement, and only from one listening position.

This is a potentially powerful new technology, though very immature at the time of this writing (late 1993). It may take years before the technique is perfected, particularly in consumer products. (There is a more detailed discussion of DSP room-correction systems in Appendix C.)

A Survey of Acoustical Treatments

Although most of the products listed are designed for professional applications such as recording studios, they are very effective in a domestic listening room. Still, they can often look more professional, even industrial, than domestic. The RPG Diffusors and ASC Tower Traps look like acoustic treatment devices, but are nicely finished. Sonex foam and Sonex ceiling tiles can also fit into many decors. Many of the following products are sold by mail through Audio Advisor (Tel: 800-942-0220). Note that all prices listed, though accurate at press time, are subject to change.

Sonex. Manufacturer: Illbruck, 3800 Washington Ave. North, Minneapolis, MN 55412-2197. Tel: (800) 662-0032. Dimensions: 4′ by 4′. Colors: charcoal, tan, blue, brown. Prices: $295 per box (2″ thick, 128 square feet per box), $288 (3″ thick, 96 square feet per box), $289 (4″ thick, 64 square feet per box).

Sonex is a popular—but expensive—acoustical foam used primarily in recording studios. It comes in three thicknesses—2,″ 3,″ and 4″—and a variety of colors. Sonex has a very high absorption coefficient, but the amount of low-frequency absorption varies with the thickness. Sonex 2″ thick has an absorption coefficient of 0.2 at 250Hz; the 4″ version has a coefficient of 0.7 at 250Hz.

Sonex comes in 4′ by 4′ squares that are usually attached to walls with panel adhesive. Sonex sheets are made in reciprocal pairs: one 4′ by 4′ sheet has wedges, the other matching indentations, but their function is identical. Sonex is also available in 2′ by 4′ sizes at the same price per square foot. A 2′ by 2′ version called "Sonex Juniors" is also available. A pair of Sonex Juniors sells for $53.99, and is available in gray, beige, blue, and brown.

Sonex Ceiling Tiles. Manufacturer: Same as previous. Dimensions: 15″ by 15″. Colors: gray, blue, beige, brown. Price: $139 per box (one box contains 28 2″-thick tiles, covers 44 square feet, and includes adhesive).

Sonex Ceiling Tiles are a better-looking alternative to Sonex foam. The tiles absorb less energy than foam, but look great. If you watch *Star Trek: The Next Generation*, you've seen Sonex Ceiling Tiles covering the walls of 10-Forward. The tiles have radiused corners and a less industrial look than Sonex foam. Sonex Ceiling Tiles are designed to attach to ceilings, but can be used anywhere. Available in five patterns. The most elegant-looking absorptive treatment.

Markerfoam. Manufacturer: Markertek, 4 High Street, Saugerties, NY 12477. Tel: (800) 522-2025. Dimensions: 54" by 54." Colors: studio gray or medium blue. Prices: $19.99 each (2" thickness), $29.99 each (3" thickness), add $4.00 per sheet for flame-retardant treatment.

Markerfoam is a lower-price alternative to Sonex. Its surface structure is less aggressive than that of Sonex, but Markertek claims very high absorption coefficients for Markerfoam (0.7 at 1kHz for 2," 0.92 at 1kHz for 3").

Markertek Blade Tiles. Manufacturer: Same as previous. Dimensions: 16" by 16". Colors: gray or blue. Price: $3.49 (2"), $4.49 (3"), or $5.49 (4") each.

Blade Tiles are made from flame-resistant polyester foam. Their 16"-square size makes them easier to install than 54" sheets of Markerfoam. Blade Tiles also have very high absorption coefficients (over 1.0 at 1kHz for all thicknesses).

Tower Trap. Manufacturer: Acoustic Sciences Corporation, P.O. Box 1189, Eugene, OR 97440. Tel: (503) 343-9727. Fax: (503) 343-9245. Dimensions: 10" diameter by 6' tall (Tower Slims), 15" diameter by 4' tall (Tower Stouts). Colors: quartz, gray, brown. Price: $395/pair (Tower Slims), $495/pair (Tower Stouts).

ASC makes a wide range of acoustic treatment devices that are used in recording studios, churches, and hi-fi listening rooms. The company's Tower Trap is a new, low-cost alternative to ASC's popular Tube Trap. A new manufacturing technique allows ASC to sell Tower Traps for about half the price of Tube Traps. Both devices are cylinders with a reflective side and an absorptive side, allowing them to be tuned to the room's needs just by rotating them. They absorb bass, kill side-wall reflections, absorb treble, or diffuse sound over a wide band. They are most effective as bass absorbers when placed in corners. Tower Traps are moderately priced, look good, and are highly effective. (Tower Traps are shown in Fig.4-12)

RPG Diffusors. Manufacturer: RPG Diffusor Systems Inc., 651-C Commerce Drive, Upper Marlboro, MD 20772. Tel: (301) 249-0044.RPG makes such a wide range of diffusing products that I can't list them all here. RPG offers professional individual acoustical components as well as complete packages designed for the home listening room. "Acoustic Tools for Audiophiles," "SoundTrac," and "Concert Hall in a Box" are a few of the complete acoustic treatment packages offered by RPG. The "SoundTrac" product includes complete acoustical consulting by RPG to achieve excellent acoustics with a visually appealing finish. RPG products are widely used in recording studios, concert halls, and auditoriums.

In addition to these specialized acoustical materials, mid- and high-frequency absorption is provided by common building materials. Standard acoustical ceiling tile, fiberglass insulation, and glass fiber boards (Owens-Corning Type 703 and Johns-Manville 1000 Series Spin-Glass, for example) are very effective absorbers.

The thin carpet described under "Untreated Parallel Surfaces" in this chapter also works well. It is much less absorbent than the foams and glass fiber panels, but that can be an advantage if you're covering a large area and want to keep the room from becoming too dead.

A Final Note

This chapter is by no means a comprehensive treatment of listening-room acoustics. Rather, it offers simple suggestions for getting the best sound in your room, and serves as an introduction to acoustics by presenting the field's fundamental principles. I strongly recommend F. Alton Everest's excellent *Acoustic Techniques for Home and Studio, Second Edition*, published by Tab Books, or Everest's more comprehensive *Master Handbook of Acoustics* (also published by Tab). The text is easily accessible to the layperson, yet contains information advanced enough to design a listening room from scratch.

5 Preamplifiers

Overview and Terminology

The preamplifier is the Grand Central Station of your hi-fi system. It receives signals from source components—turntables, CD players, tuners, tape decks—and allows you to select which of these to send to the power amplifier for listening. In addition to allowing you to switch between sources, the preamplifier performs many other useful functions, such as amplifying the signal from your phono cartridge, adjusting the balance between channels, and allowing you to set the volume level. The preamplifier is the component you will use, touch, and adjust most often. It also has a large influence on the system's overall sound quality. (Note: preamplifiers are built into, or "integrated" with, integrated amplifiers and receivers, instead of being housed in a separate chassis.)

There are many types of preamplifiers. Choosing the one best suited to your system requires you to define your needs. Listeners whose only signal source is a CD player, for example, won't need a preamplifier with a phono stage. Others will need many inputs to accommodate tape decks, tuners, and audio from a video source.

The following table lists preamplifier types, outlines their uses, and defines some common preamplifier terms.

Line-Stage Preamplifier: Accepts only *line-level* signals, which include every source component *except* a turntable. Line stages have become much more popular as listeners increasingly rely on CDs rather than LPs as their main signal source. If you don't have a turntable, you need only a line-stage preamplifier.

Phono Preamplifier: (also called a *phono stage*): Takes the very tiny signal from your phono cartridge and amplifies it to line level. It also performs *RIAA equalization* on the signal from the cartridge. RIAA equalization, named after the Recording Industry Association of America, is a bass boost and treble cut that counteract the bass cut and treble boost applied in disc mastering, thus restoring flat response.

A phono stage can be an outboard stand-alone unit in its own chassis, or a circuit section within a full-function preamplifier. If you play records, you must have a phono stage, either as a separate component or as part of a full-function preamplifier.

Pre-Preamplifier: Takes a very low level signal from a moving-coil phono cartridge and amplifies it to a level acceptable by a phono preamplifier.

Step-Up Transformer: Performs the same function as a pre-preamplifier, but uses a transformer rather than an amplifying circuit.

Full-Function Preamplifier: Combines a phono stage with a line-stage preamplifier, usually in one chassis.

Tubed Preamplifier: A tubed preamplifier uses vacuum tubes to amplify the audio signal.

Solid-state Preamplifier: A solid-state preamplifier uses transistors to amplify the audio signal.

Hybrid Preamplifier: A hybrid preamplifier uses a combination of tubes and transistors.

Audio/Video Preamplifier: A preamplifier with video switching functions, Dolby Surround decoding, or both. (A/V preamplifiers are described in Chapter 13, "Audio for Home Theater.")

Passive Level Control: Sometimes erroneously called a *passive preamp*, the passive level control can replace a line-stage preamplifier in some situations. It is inserted in the signal path between a source component and the power amplifier.

Instead of amplifying the source signals and acting as a *buffer* between source components and the power amplifier, a passive level control merely attenuates (reduces) the signal level driving the power amplifier. It doesn't plug into the wall, and cannot amplify a signal as does an active line-stage preamplifier. (Advantages and disadvantages of passive level controls are discussed in detail later in this chapter.)

No Preamplifier: If you listen to only CD as a source—no turntable, tape deck, tuner, or other source—a CD player or digital processor with a volume control can replace a preamplifier. The CD player or processor drives the power amplifier directly, with volume adjustable via its output level control.

How to Choose a Preamplifier

Once you've decided on a line-stage, a full-function preamp, or separate line and phono stages (the last are generally more expensive), it's time to define your system requirements. The first is the number of inputs you'll need. If you have only a CD player, the four or five line inputs on most preamps is more than enough. But let's say you have a turntable, CD player, tuner, two cassette decks, Hi-Fi VCR, and a laserdisc player. You'll need a phono input, four line inputs, and two tape loops—at the minimum. A tape loop is a pair of input and output jacks for driving a tape deck and receiving a signal from a tape deck. Other preamplifier features this complex system may need are the ability to copy from one tape deck to another, or listen to one source while recording another. Preamps with tape copy will usually have the legend "2–1" or "1–2" inscribed on the front panel, meaning tape deck #1 can feed tape deck #2, and vice versa. If the preamplifier has separate selector switches marked "Listen" and "Record," this means one source can be recorded while another one is listened to. An example of this is recording a cassette for the car stereo from CD while listening to the turntable.

I've included these examples for the sake of completeness; most high-end preamps have few features—and for good reason. First, the less circuitry in the signal path, the purer the signal and the better the sound. Second, the preamp designer can usually put a fixed manufacturing budget into making a preamp that either sounds superb or has lots of features—but not both. Mass-market mid-fi equipment emphasizes vast arrays of features and buttons at the expense of sound quality. Don't be surprised to find very expensive preamps with almost no features; they were designed, first and foremost, for the best musical performance. Most high-end preamps don't even have tone (bass and treble) controls. Not only do tone controls electrically degrade the signal— and thus the musical performance—but the very idea of changing the signal is antithetical to the values of high-end audio. The signal should be reproduced with the least alteration possible. Tone controls should be completely unnecessary in a high-quality system.

Another school of thought, however, holds that a playback system's goal isn't to perfectly reproduce what's on the recording, but to achieve the most enjoyable experience possible. If changing the tonal balance with tone controls enhances the pleasure of listening to music, use them. If you're comfortable with the latter philosophy, be aware that tone controls invariably degrade the preamplifier's sonic quality. (Some preamps with tone controls do allow you to switch them out of the circuit when they're not being used, a feature called "tone defeat.")

A similar debate rages over whether or not to include balance controls in a high-end preamp. A balance control lets you adjust the relative levels of the left and right channels. If the recording has slightly more signal in one channel than the other, the center image will appear to shift toward the louder channel, and the sense of soundstage layering may be reduced. A similar problem can occur if the listening room has more absorptive material on one side than the other, pulling the image off center. A small adjustment of the balance control can correct these problems. Like tone controls, balance controls can slightly degrade a preamplifier's sonic performance. It isn't unusual to find a $6000 state-of-the-art preamplifier with no tone or balance controls, and a $99 receiver with both of these features.

Some preamplifiers have balanced inputs, balanced outputs, or both. If you have a balanced source component—usually a digital processor—you'll want a balanced input on your preamplifier. Nearly all source components with balanced outputs also have unbalanced outputs. You can use either output, but you may not get the best sound quality unless you use the balanced output option. (See Chapter 8, "The Digital Front End," for the reason why.)

A preamp with unbalanced inputs and a balanced output can accept unbalanced signals but still drive a power amplifier through a balanced interconnect. If your power amplifier has balanced inputs, getting a balanced output preamplifier is a good idea. You can listen to the system through both balanced and unbalanced lines and decide which sounds better. Some products sound better through balanced connections; others perform best with unbalanced lines. (A more technical description of balanced preamplifiers is included later in this chapter.)

After you've decided on your functional needs, determine how much you can spend on a preamp using the guidelines in Chapter 2. Then put together a short list of preamps worthy of serious auditioning. Use dealer recommendations, read reviews in responsible audiophile magazines, and ask friends who have high-end systems. Look through the "Recommended Components" listings in *Stereophile* and *read the original reviews* of the products.

Now that you know what features and functions you're looking for, its time to begin listening.

What to Listen For

The preamplifier has a profound effect on the music system's overall performance. Because each of the source signals must go though the preamp, any coloration or unmusical characteristics it imposes will be constantly overlaid on the music. You can have superb source components, a topnotch power amplifier, and excellent loudspeakers, yet still have mediocre sound if the preamp isn't up to the standards set by the rest of your components. The preamplifier can establish the lowest performance level of your system; careful auditioning and wise product selection is crucial to building a first-rate playback system.

A preamplifier's price isn't always an indicator of its sonic quality. I know of one $1500 model that is musically superior to another preamp selling for nearly $8000. If you do your homework and choose carefully, you'll avoid paying too much for a poor-sounding product.

In addition to the usual listening procedures described in Chapter 3, preamplifiers offer several methods of sonic evaluation not possible with other components. We can therefore more precisely evaluate preamps and choose the best one for the money.

We'll start with the standard listening evaluation techniques. First, the same musical selection can be played on the same system, alternating between two competing preamps. Listen for the presentation differences described in Chapter 3—particularly clarity, transparency, lack of grain, low-level detail, soundstaging, and a sense of ease.

The most common sonic problems in preamplifiers are a bright and etched treble and a thickening of the soundstage. Many preamps, particularly inexpensive solid-state units, overlay the midrange and treble with a steely, metallic hardness. These preamps can give the impression of more musical detail, but quickly become fatiguing. The treble becomes drier, more forward, and etched. Cymbals lose their sheen, instead sounding like bursts of white noise. Vocal sibilants ("s" and "ch" sounds) become objectionably prominent; violins become screechy, thin, and wiry.

The preamplifier that thickens the sound makes the soundstage more opaque. The transparent quality is gone, replaced by a murkiness that obscures low-level detail and reduces resolution. Instruments and voices no longer hang in a transparent, three-dimensional space. Instead, the presentation is thick, confused, congealed, and lacking clarity. Even some expensive models impose these characteristics on the music.

Compare the preamps under audition to the very best preamp in the store. Listen for the qualities distinguishing the best preamp, and see if those characteristics are in the preamps you're considering. This will not only give you a reference point in selecting a preamplifier for yourself, but is also the best way to become a more skilled listener. The preceding description applies to both line-level and phono preamplifiers.

A useful way of evaluating preamplifiers—one not possible with other components—is the *bypass test*. This technique compares the pre-amplifier to no preamplifier, revealing the preamplifier's editorial effect on the music. This most revealing of comparisons leaves the preampli-fier's shortcomings nowhere to hide.

To conduct a bypass test, drive a power amplifier at a comfortable volume with a known high-quality preamplifier, or directly from a CD player or digital source that has an output level control. Using a volt-meter and a test CD with test tones, set the preamplifier under evalua-tion for unity gain—the volume position at which the input level is iden-tical to the output level (usually a third to half-way up on the volume control). Put the preamplifier under evaluation in the signal path between the known preamp and the power amp. Compare the system's sound with and without the preamp in the playback chain. Did the pre-amp thicken the sound? Did the treble become dry and brittle with the preamp in the system? Was the sense of space, clarity, and transparency replaced by an opaque thickness that homogenized the individual instruments? Did the preamplifier cast a common sonic characteristic over varied recordings? Most important, was the music less involving? The bypass test provides a quick and accurate assessment of the type and amount of coloration imposed by a preamplifier.

If you're comparing two preamplifiers, use preamp A to drive the power amplifier; listen, then put preamp B in the signal path at unity gain between preamp A and the power amplifier. Listen for the differ-ence between the signal path with and without preamp B in the signal path. Then reverse the roles of the two preamps, listening for preamp A's effect on the presentation. This technique, shown in Fig.5-1, quickly reveals exactly what each preamp does to the music. This method, how-ever, doesn't provide the highest resolution listening conditions; the col-orations of the first preamplifier can obscure qualities in the second pre-amplifier. It also adds another run of interconnects and terminations to the signal path. You can also conduct a bypass test by substituting a pas-sive level control for the preamplifier. Although passive level controls can reduce dynamic contrast and soften the bass in some systems, they rarely add grain and etch, or reduce soundstage depth and clarity as do most active preamplifiers.

A less analytical method is to borrow the preamp from your dealer for a weekend and just listen to it. How much more exciting and involv-ing is the music compared to using your existing preamp? Does the new preamp reveal musical information you hadn't heard before in familiar recordings? How much does the new preamp *compel* you to continue playing music? These are the best indicators of the product's ability to provide long-term musical satisfaction. Trust what your favorite music tells you about the preamplifier.

Fig. 5-1 The bypass test for evaluating pre-amplifiers

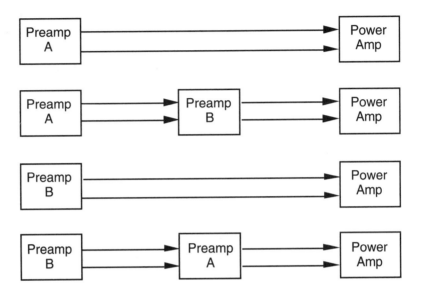

Tubes vs. Transistors

Of the many components that make up a hi-fi system, the preamplifier is the most likely to use vacuum tubes instead of solid-state devices (transistors). This is because preamplifiers handle only low-level signals, making tubes more practical and affordable than in power amplifiers. Power-amplifier tubes are large, expensive, run hot, and require replacement. Further, one theory of audio design holds that if the system is to include tubes, they are best employed closest to the signal source—such as in the preamplifier. Moreover, the qualities that have endeared many music lovers to the magic of tubes (described later) are much more affordable when used in a preamplifier. Tubed audio components are more expensive to build and maintain than solid-state units, but that cost differential is much lower in preamplifiers than in power amplifiers. If you want the special qualities of tubes but not their heat, greater expense, and higher maintenance, the tubed preamplifier is the way to go.

A preamplifier can require anywhere from one to eight tubes. Tubes generally need replacing after about 1000–2000 hours of use. Any time the preamplifier is turned on, the hour meter is ticking. This fact encourages many owners of tubed preamplifiers to turn their units off when not listening. Although this extends tube life, an electronic component doesn't sound its best until it's been on for a few hours. The best advice is to turn on the preamplifier an hour or two before a listening session, if possible. If you know you'll be listening at night after work, turn on the preamplifier in the morning and it will be at peak performance when you get home. Another alternative is to buy a mechanical AC timer (about $10) from a hardware store and set it to switch on the preamp two hours before you expect to come home. Solid-state preamplifiers, on the other hand, draw very little current and don't need tube replacement—they can be left on continuously.

Replacement tubes vary in cost from $10 for an untested generic type to $50 for a premium-grade tube that has been thoroughly tested and selected for best electrical performance. Because tube quality has a big effect on the preamplifier's sound, high-quality tubes are worth the money. Different brands of tubes equal in technical performance will also sound different, making choosing difficult. Your local dealer is the best guide in selecting the optimum replacement tubes for your preamplifier. Equipment reviews of tubed preamplifiers will sometimes include the reviewer's opinion on different tube brands used in a particular preamplifier.

Tubes are often claimed to sound sweeter, warmer, and to have a more natural treble. Many solid-state preamps tend to make the treble dry, brittle, metallic, and etched. The result is steely-sounding strings (particularly violins), unnaturally emphasized vocal sibilants ("s" and "ch" sounds), and cymbals that sound like bursts of high-frequency noise rather than a delicate brass-like shimmer. Because these unpleasant artifacts can be introduced by many components (digital sources, power amplifiers, cables, dome tweeters), a natural-sounding tubed preamplifier can tend to ameliorate the system's tendency toward the amusical characteristics described. As stated in Chapter 3, don't mistake an etched treble for increased resolution.

Be aware, however, that some tubed preamps are intentionally designed to sound very colored. Rather than present the music with the least effect on it, tubed preamps often add significant amounts of *euphonic coloration*. This form of distortion is at first pleasing to the ear, but represents a departure from the original signal. This type of "tubey" coloration is characterized by a soft treble, an overly laid-back and easygoing presentation, lack of detail, and a "syrupy" sound. Many audiophiles, in their attempts to avoid the worst characteristics of solid-state, turn to euphonically colored tubed preamps to make their systems listenable. It is a far better approach, however, to make sure that each component in the chain is as transparent as possible. If this is achieved, there will be no need for "tubey" preamps. Ideally, the listener shouldn't be aware that she is listening to tubes; instead, she should be aware of only the music. Just as poor solid-state preamps color the sound by adding grain, treble hardness, and etch, the poor tube preamp will often err in the opposite direction, obscuring detail, adding "bloom," and reducing resolution. Be equally aware of both forms of coloration.

It's a mistake to "fall in love" with either solid-state or tubes for the wrong reasons. The solid-state lover may think he is getting "more detail," and the tube aficionado may fall for the "lush sweetness." Both extremes are to be avoided in the pursuit of a truly musical playback system. The overly "sweet" preamplifier may become uninvolving over time because of its low resolution; the "etched" solid-state unit may eventually become unmusical for the fatigue it produces in the listener. Not all tube and solid-state preamps can, however, be categorized so neatly. Many tubed preamps are extremely transparent, neutral, and have very little effect on the sound.

Nor should you buy a preamp purely because it uses tubes. Certain circuits are better implemented with tubes, others with solid-state devices. There are no magic components or circuit designs that will ensure a product's musicality. Worthy—and unworthy—products have been made from both tubes and transistors.

The best advice is to choose the preamp that has the least effect on the music; you'll get much more musical satisfaction from it for a longer period of time. And remember: The perfect tubed preamp and the perfect solid-state preamp would sound identical.

The Line-Stage Preamplifier

A typical minimalist line-stage preamplifier is shown in Fig.5-2. This model, an Audio Research LS2B, has five unbalanced line inputs (labeled "Tape," "Tuner," "CD," "Video," and "Aux"), and one balanced line input (labeled "Direct"). A front-panel input selector switch selects which input is routed to the output. A mute switch shuts off the signal at the preamplifier output. (This is useful when changing records or disconnecting and connecting source components—engaging the mute switch prevents a loud thump from going through your system). Note that this preamplifier has no balance control for adjusting the relative levels between left and right channels.

The rear panel, shown in Fig.5-3, has one "Tape Out" for driving a tape deck input, an unbalanced "Main Out," and two balanced "Main Out" pairs. One of the pairs of "Main Out" jacks would be connected to the power amplifier through a pair of interconnects. Whether to use the balanced or unbalanced outputs depends on whether the power amplifier has balanced or unbalanced inputs. The tape outputs are *buffered*, meaning that there is a separate amplifier for driving the tape recorder's inputs. The front-panel "Defeat" switch turns off this buffer amplifier.

Fig. 5-2 A line-stage preampli-fier's front panel

Courtesy Audio Research Corporation

Fig. 5-3 A line-stage preampli-fier's rear panel connections

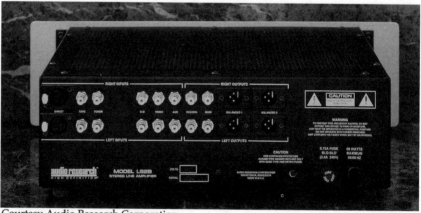

Courtesy Audio Research Corporation

The "Direct" input has a shorter signal path, bypassing the input selector switch for maximum sonic purity. Though this is a small refine-ment, such details are audible at the very top levels of performance.

Some preamplifiers let you completely bypass all the active electron-ics in the unit. The preamp then becomes a passive level control, with the preamp's volume control the only function that works. All the limita-tions of passive level controls—described later in this chapter—come into play with this feature.

The Phono Stage Preamplifier

The phono stage amplifies the very tiny signal (between a few tens of microvolts and a few millivolts) from the phono cartridge to a line-level (about one volt) signal. This line-level signal can then drive a line-stage preamplifier, just as any other source component would. A phono stage can be an integral part of a full-function preamplifier, an optional board that plugs into some line-stage preamplifiers, or an outboard unit in its own chassis. Outboard phono stages have no volume controls; they usually feed a line input on a line-stage preamplifier.

In the days before CD, virtually all preamplifiers included integral phono stages. In many of today's preamplifiers, however, a phono stage is an option (usually about $200–$400) for those listeners who play LPs. The phono stage is a small circuit board that plugs into the preamplifier. This arrangement reduces the preamplifier's price for those needing only a line-stage preamplifier.

Not all line stages accept a phono board; if you think you'll want to play records in the future, be certain the line-stage preamp you buy will accept a phono board. If the preamp's rear panel has an input marked "phono," a ground lug, and a front-panel input selection position marked "phono," you can be confident that the preamp has a built-in phono stage, or will accept a phono board. Note, however, that some line-stage preamps have a line-level input marked "phono" but no phono stage. Look for the ground lug on the rear panel, a post for connecting a ground wire between the preamplifier and the turntable. If it has a ground lug, the preamplifier probably has provisions for accepting phono signals.

RIAA Equalization

In addition to amplifying the cartridge's tiny output voltage, the phono stage performs RIAA equalization on the signal. RIAA stands for Recording Industry Association of America, the body that standardized the equalization curve. Phono-stage RIAA equalization boosts the bass and attenuates the treble. This equalization counteracts the bass cut and treble boost applied to the signal during disc mastering. By combining exactly opposite curves in disc mastering and playback, a flat response is achieved. RIAA equalization curves are shown in Fig.5-4. The dotted trace is the curve applied when the lacquer master is cut; the solid trace is the curve applied in the phono preamplifier to restore flat response.

Attenuating bass and boosting treble when the disc is cut allows more signal to be cut into the record groove, improving the signal-to-noise ratio. In addition, the treble boost in disc cutting and subsequent treble cut on playback act as a noise-reduction system: attenuating treble on playback also attenuates record-surface noise. Attenuating bass in the record provides longer playing time; low frequencies take up much more room in the grooves. Because a phono stage applies RIAA equalization, you can't plug a line-level source into a preamplifier input marked "phono." Similarly, a phono cartridge can't be plugged into a line input.

Fig. 5-4 RIAA equalization curves

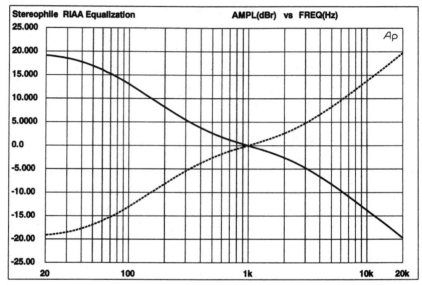

Courtesy *Stereophile*

One aspect of a phono preamp's technical performance is its *RIAA accuracy*. This measurement or specification indicates how closely the phono stage's RIAA equalization circuit matches the standard curve used in disc mastering. Typical performance is 20Hz–20kHz, ±0.5dB. RIAA errors are essentially frequency-response errors, and can greatly affect the phono stage's sound. A positive RIAA error in the treble can make the phono stage bright and etched; a negative error in the treble can make the sound dull and lifeless. Examples of RIAA errors are shown later in this chapter under "Specifications and Measurements."

Note that European audio equipment often has a low-frequency rolloff curve built into the phono stage's RIAA circuit. This prevents very low frequencies (below about 30Hz) generated by warped records from getting into the rest of the system, but can also reduce bass extension on playback systems capable of reproducing frequencies down to 20Hz.

Phono-Stage Gain

The amount of amplification provided by a phono stage (or any other amplifier) is called its *gain*. Gain is specified either in decibels (dB), or as a number expressing the ratio between input and output voltages. Phono stages have much more gain than line stages. Where a line stage may have 10 to 20dB of gain, a phono stage typically amplifies the signal by 30 to 60dB.

The amount of phono-stage gain required depends on the type of phono cartridge driving the phono preamplifier. Phono stages are of two varieties, each named for the type of cartridge with which it is designed to work. The first is the *moving-magnet* phono stage. Moving-magnet phono stages have their gain optimized to work with the relatively high output voltages from moving-magnet cartridges. Moving-magnet cartridges have a relatively high output voltage, on the order of two to eight millivolts (2–8mV). Consequently, the moving-magnet phono stage's gain is toward the lower end of the range, typically about 35dB.

Moving-coil cartridges have much lower output voltages due to their different method of generating a signal. Moving-coil output levels range from 0.15mV to 2.5mV. Consequently, they need more amplification (gain) in the phono preamplifier to reach line level than do moving-magnet cartridge signals. Moving-coil phono preamplifiers have about 40–60dB of gain. Note that moving-coil output voltages vary greatly with the cartridge design, with some so-called "high-output" models reaching moving-magnet levels.

Because of this wide variation in cartridge output level, a gain mismatch can occur between the cartridge and phono stage: The phono stage can have either too much or too little gain for a specific cartridge output voltage. If the phono preamp doesn't have enough gain, the volume control must be turned up very high for sufficient playback levels. This raises the noise floor (heard as a loud background hiss), often to the point of becoming objectionable. Conversely, a high-output cartridge can overload a moving-coil phono stage's input circuitry, causing distortion on peaks. A high-output cartridge driving a high-gain phono preamplifier can also make the preamplifier's volume control too insensitive. A moderate listening level may be achieved with the volume control barely cracked open; this makes small volume adjustments difficult.

Correctly matching the cartridge output voltage to the phono-stage gain avoids excessive noise and the possibility of input overload. A moving-coil cartridge specified at 0.18mV output needs about 55dB of gain. A typical moving-magnet output of 3mV should drive a phono stage that has about 35dB of gain. Some phono stages and full-function preamps have internal switches that adjust the gain between moving-magnet and moving-coil levels.

A pre-preamplifier is a small stand-alone component that can boost a moving-coil signal up to moving-magnet levels. If you have a moving-magnet phono input and upgrade to a moving-coil cartridge, you can add a pre-preamplifier instead of getting a new phono stage. Similarly, a step-up transformer increases a moving-coil's output voltage to a higher level. A transformer can improve the phono system's signal-to-noise ratio, or allow a moving-coil cartridge to drive a moving-magnet phono input.

High phono-stage gain carries the penalty of increased noise. Although phono stages in general have poorer signal-to-noise specifications than other components, very-high-gain phono preamps can be objectionably noisy. All other factors being equal, the greater the gain, the higher the noise. Select a phono preamp with just enough gain for your cartridge.

Cartridge Loading

Cartridge loading is the impedance and capacitance the phono cartridge "sees" when driving the phono input. Cartridge loading, specified in both impedance and capacitance, has a large effect on how the cartridge sounds, particularly moving-magnet types. Improper loading can cause frequency-response tilts, ringing, and other undesirable conditions. Many preamps allow you to adjust the input impedance and input capacitance to match the phono cartridge by adding resistors and capacitors to the phono stage's input circuit. These adjustments usually require a soldering iron, however, and should be done by your dealer. Some preamps have tiny internal switches to adjust cartridge loading, while others provide front-panel adjustments. With the tiny output signals from phono cartridges, soldering-in resistors is a better method. Note that the tonearm cable's capacitance must be added to the phono preamplifier's input capacitance to find the total capacitance loading the cartridge. More discussion of cartridge loading is included in Chapter 9 ("The LP Playback System").

Passive Level Controls: Are They Right for Your System?

A passive level control replaces a line-stage preamplifier with a simple volume control. On the plus side, passive level controls introduce the fewest electronics into the signal path between the source and power amplifier. A passive level control usually consists of only a continuously variable potentiometer (volume control), or a stepped knob that switch-es-in one of many discrete resistors. Fig.5-5 shows a high-quality stepped-resistor passive level control.

Fig. 5-5 A stepped-resistor passive level control

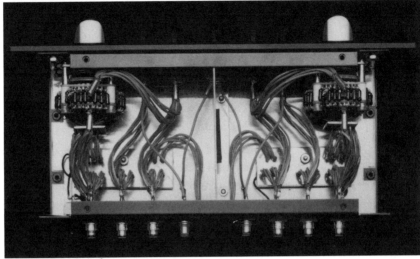

Courtesy First Sound

Removing the capacitors, transistors (or vacuum tubes), circuit-board traces, and wiring found inside a line-stage preamplifier reduces the likelihood of degrading the signal passing through the passive level control. I've found passive controls extremely transparent, with very lit-tle effect on the signal passing through them. Only the best active line-stages have the passive level control's lack of coloration and degradation of the music. In addition, passive level controls are less expensive than active preamplifiers, making them attractive to the purist on a budget.

There are, however, many factors to consider when deciding if a passive level control will work in your system. Because the passive level control cannot amplify or *buffer* the source signal, the burden of driving the power amplifier and interconnects falls on the source component.

Most source components are designed to drive the relatively high input impedance of preamplifiers (usually 47k ohms), not the low input impedance of passive level controls. The source component's output impedance must be added to the passive control's output impedance to find the total output impedance driving the interconnects and power amplifier. This high output impedance can cause high-frequency rolloff, particularly if high-capacitance interconnects run between the passive level control and the power amplifier. (A full explanation of how and why this high-frequency rolloff occurs is included in Appendix B.)

Finally, a passive level control has no buffer to drive the tape output jacks. The source component must therefore drive both the power-amplifier and tape-deck inputs when recording, a condition that can degrade sound quality.

Passive level controls aren't the answer for all systems. They're often limited in functions, have only one or two inputs, and tricky to match to the rest of your system. But replacing a colored line-stage preamplifier with a passive level control can greatly improve your system's sound. Listen to the passive level control in your system before you buy.

How a Preamplifier Works

A preamplifier consists of several *stages*, each performing a different function. The *input stage* is the first circuit element in the signal path. It acts as a buffer between the preamp's internal circuitry and the components driving it. The input stage presents a high input impedance to source components driving the preamp, and a low output impedance to the next preamplifier stage. Input stages are often built from FETs (Field Effect Transistors) for low noise and high input impedance.

The next circuit stage provides gain, amplifying the input signal. The last stage is the *output stage,* the circuit block that serves as a buffer between the gain stage and the power amplifier connected to the preamp. The output stage has a high input impedance, low output impedance, and is designed to drive interconnects and a power amplifier input. These circuit blocks are shown in Fig.5-6. Each of these stages can be transistors, vacuum tubes, integrated circuits (operational amplifiers, or *op-amps*), or a combination of devices.

Fig. 5-6
Preamplifier
block diagram

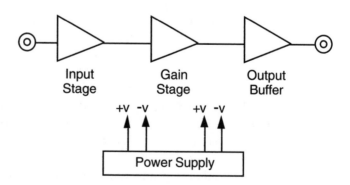

As with all components, a power supply delivers a supply of direct current (DC) to power the preamplifier's circuits. To prevent this DC from appearing at the preamplifier output along with the audio signal, *DC blocking capacitors* are often placed between stages, or at the preamplifier output. Some preamps avoid capacitors in the signal path by using a *DC servo* circuit that also prevents DC from appearing at the output jacks. A preamplifier without capacitors in the audio signal path is said to be *direct-coupled*.

Class-A refers to a type of transistor operation in which the transistor is always biased on, meaning that it always conducts current. A *discrete* preamplifier is one that uses no integrated circuits (op-amps), only separate transistors or vacuum tubes. Discrete preamps are more expensive than op-amp-based designs. Virtually all state-of-the-art preamps are discrete class-A designs. (Descriptions of class-A operation are included in Appendix B and Chapter 6, "Power Amplifiers.")

Fig.5-7 is a schematic of a discrete class-A preamplifier using a combination of solid-state devices (FETs) and vacuum tubes. The input stage is Q5, the FET at the diagram's top left. The gain stage is the 6DJ8 vacuum tube. The three devices next to the 6DJ8 aren't directly in the audio signal path, but are part of the power supply, serving as a constant current source for the tube. The output stage is Q9, seen at the diagram's top right. A single blocking capacitor (C40) prevents DC from appearing at the output.

Fig. 5-7 Hybrid preamplifier schematic (input, gain, and output stages)

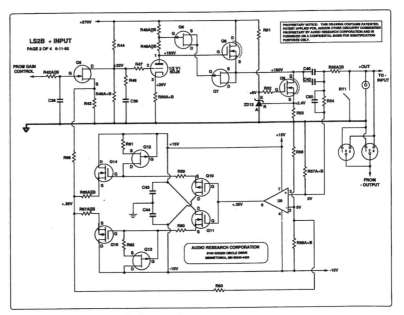

Courtesy Audio Research Corporation

The entire circuit block below the ground line running horizontally through the diagram's middle is the *feedback* circuit. Feedback is the part of an amplifier's output signal that is returned to the input. This makes the circuit more linear, and lowers distortion.

Because this preamp accepts balanced input signals and has unbalanced outputs (in addition to balanced outputs), a *differential amplifier* converts the balanced signal to an unbalanced signal. The two halves of the balanced signal are input to the differential amplifier, which outputs an unbalanced signal. (Differential amplifiers are explained in more detail in Appendix B.) A *phase splitter* converts the unbalanced signal back to balanced at the output.

The power supply, shown in Fig.5-8, is quite elaborate—in sharp contrast to the audio circuit's apparent simplicity. This supply generates +270V for the tube's plate, and ±15V for the solid-state circuits.

Fig. 5-8 A pre-amplifier power-supply schematic

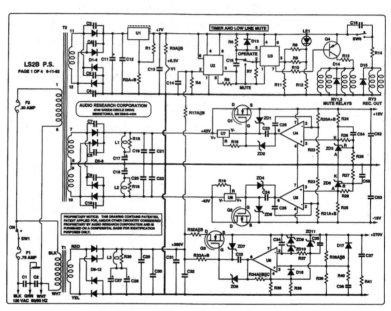

Courtesy Audio Research Corporation

This preamplifier is the company's mid-level model. The top-of-the-line unit, a pure tubed design, is fully balanced from input to output (no differential amplifier at the input, and no phase splitter at output).

Balanced and Unbalanced Preamplifiers

As described earlier in this chapter, preamplifiers can have balanced inputs, balanced outputs, or both. Although all balanced preamps have XLR jacks, not all balanced preamplifiers are created equal. Two preamps that have balanced inputs and outputs can be very different in how they treat the signal.

Most preamps accepting a balanced signal immediately convert it to an unbalanced signal, perform the usual preamplifier functions (provide gain and volume adjustment) on the unbalanced signal, then convert the signal back to balanced just before the main output. The preamp with balanced inputs and outputs, but unbalanced internal topology, often adds two active stages to the signal path: the differential amplifier at the input and the phase splitter at the output. This kind of preamplifier is shown in block form in Fig.5-9.

Fig. 5-9 Some "balanced" preamplifiers convert a balanced input to unbalanced, then back to balanced.

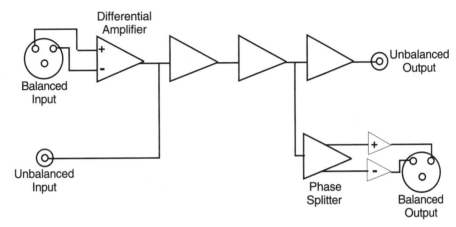

The preferred, but much more expensive, method is to keep the signal balanced throughout the preamplifier. This technique requires double the audio circuitry; each portion of the balanced signal is amplified separately. Moreover, very close tolerances between halves of the balanced signal are required. The two signal halves must have identical gain and noise characteristics. Further, the four-element volume control must maintain precise tracking at all positions. Although the fully balanced circuit has more active devices in the signal path, the signal isn't subjected to a differential amplifier or a phase splitter. A fully balanced preamplifier is shown in block form in Fig.5-10.

Fig. 5-10 A fully balanced preamplifier keeps the signal balanced from input to output.

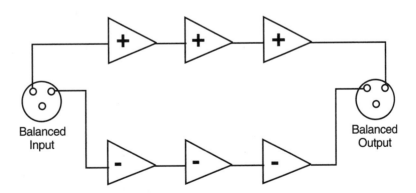

One way to tell if a preamplifier is fully balanced, or if it converts a balanced signal to single-ended, then back to balanced, is to look at the volume control. If it has two elements (left and right channels), it has single-ended internal circuitry. If the volume control has four elements (left +, left –, right +, right –), the preamp is fully balanced.

Preamplifier Specifications and Measurements

An important specification is a line-stage's gain: the amount of amplification the preamp provides. Gain is expressed either in decibels (dB), or as a number representing the ratio between the input and output voltages.

A preamplifier's gain can be expressed indirectly as *input sensitivity*. This is the voltage required to produce some reference level (usually 0.5V) at the preamplifier output with the volume turned all the way up. A preamplifier with an input sensitivity of 0.05V has a gain of ten (which can also be expressed as 20dB, because 20dB represents a ten-to-one voltage ratio).

The preamp's gain is important to consider in relation to the output voltage of source components. If you have a very high output CD player or digital processor feeding a high-gain preamplifier, you'll barely crack open the volume control before you get loud listening levels. This has several disadvantages. First, it makes setting a "just right" volume difficult. The volume control is so insensitive that even small adjustments make large differences in listening level. Second, volume controls are often less well matched between channels at the low end of their range. This means that one channel becomes louder than the other when the volume control is turned down. The effect is the same as if you'd turned a balance control off-center. This difference can be as much as 3dB—enough to shift the image to one side. A digital processor putting out, say, 5V RMS at full-scale and driving a line-stage preamp with 25dB of gain would produce this problem.

Conversely, high gain can be an advantage when using a line-stage preamplifier with an external phono stage. Many phono stages have just enough gain of their own to feed a line-stage, but no more. It therefore requires a fair amount of gain in the line-stage to adequately drive the power amplifier.

Line-stage gain varies between 5dB and 25dB. The 5dB figure is very low—perhaps too low for some outboard phono stages, and even tuners and tape decks. This will be especially true if the power amplifier has low gain or the system has insensitive loudspeakers, and could require using the volume control near the maximum setting. For most CD sources, about 10dB to 15dB of gain is ideal.

Phono-stage gain should be matched to your phono cartridge. Moving-magnet cartridges need about 35dB of gain, while moving-coil types require up to 60dB. If the phono preamp has less than adequate gain, a line-stage preamp with high gain can further amplify the phono signal for adequate listening levels.

A preamplifier's *input impedance* specification describes the electrical resistance to current flow "seen" by the source component (such as a CD player) driving the preamp. Most preamps have input impedances between 10 and 50 thousand ohms (10–50k ohms). The preamp's input impedance is the *load* the source component drives. The higher the input impedance, the easier it is for the source to drive. As the input impedance increases, however, current flow though the interconnects and preamplifier input stage decreases. Some designers believe moderate rather than very high input impedance results in the best sonic performance. If the preamplifier's input impedance is too low, it can *load down* the source component, resulting in poor technical and sonic performance.

A preamplifier is also specified according to its *output impedance*. Output impedance is best thought of as a resistor inside the preamplifier that couples its output stage to the rear panel jacks. Output impedance describes the preamplifier's ability to deliver current into a load (the power amplifier). A preamplifier's output impedance is much lower than its input impedance; where input impedance may be 50k ohms or more, output impedance may be less than a thousandth of that value.

By having a high input impedance and a low output impedance, the preamplifier acts as a buffer between the source components and the power amplifier. The sources drive a high input impedance—which is very easy for them—and the preamp takes on the burden of driving the interconnects and power amplifier. The preamplifier's low output impedance makes it ideal for this job. (The advantages of low output impedance are discussed in more detail in the section on passive level controls earlier in this chapter.)

A preamplifier's *input overload* specification refers to the maximum input voltage the preamp can accept without distorting (with distortion defined as 1% THD). The higher the input overload figure, the better. A full-function preamplifier will have two input overload specifications: one for the line-level inputs (typically more than 10V RMS), and one for the phono inputs (typically several hundred millivolts).

Maximum output level is the maximum output voltage the preamplifier can swing from its output stage. Maximum output level is often as much as 50V—far higher than any audio signal. Because most power amplifiers have an *input sensitivity* (the input voltage required to produce maximum power output) of under 1.5V, virtually any preamp will drive any power amplifier.

Signal-to-noise ratio is a measurement of how quiet the preamplifier is. It expresses in decibels the ratio between a signal level of 0.5V output and the residual noise floor. The higher the signal-to-noise ratio, the quieter the preamp. Because the ear isn't equally sensitive to noise at all frequencies, a *weighting curve* is sometimes applied to the noise spectrum to more closely approximate the noise's audibility. (Weighting curves are described in more detail in Appendix A.) A signal-to-noise ratio of 90dB unweighted is good, a figure that will increase if "A"-weighted. A preamp with lots of 60Hz hum in the audio signal will exhibit a very large increase in signal-to-noise ratio (as much as 25dB) when "A"-weighted. If the preamplifier's signal-to-noise ratio is referenced to 1V output instead of 0.5V, subtract 6dB from the signal-to-noise ratio to find the equivalent 0.5V figure.

Preamps rarely have frequency-response errors; virtually all modern preamps have flat response from below 20Hz to above 50kHz. Phono stages, however, often have errors in their RIAA response, producing the equivalents of frequency-response errors. These errors are caused primarily by capacitor tolerances in the RIAA circuit. An example of a preamp with RIAA errors is shown in Fig.5-11a. The solid line is the left channel, the dotted line is the right channel. A phono preamplifier with no RIAA errors would produce a perfectly flat line. The rolloff in the upper midrange and treble seen in Fig.5-11a will make this phono stage sound dark, closed-in, and lacking immediacy. A phono preamp with more accurate RIAA equalization is shown in Fig.5-11b.

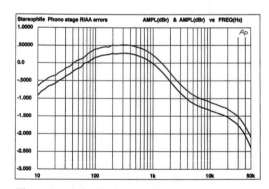 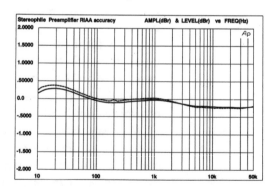

Fig. 5-11a & b Examples of poor (left) and typical (right) RIAA accuracy (Courtesy *Stereophile*)

A preamplifier's *Total Harmonic Distortion* (THD) is often measured and expressed as *THD+N* (Plus Noise). This name reflects the technique that measures the sum of harmonic distortion and noise. Here's how THD+N is measured: The preamp under test is driven by a swept sinewave signal, a band-reject filter removes the test signal, and whatever is left (distortion and noise) is plotted as function of frequency. Note that very low distortion preamps can have a higher THD+N figure than their intrinsic harmonic distortion; the noise, rather than distortion, dominates the measurement.

A typical preamplifier THD+N vs. frequency plot is shown in Fig.5–12. The vertical scale is THD+N in percent. The upper pair of traces is measured through the phono inputs, the lower pair through the line inputs. The apparently higher distortion through the phono inputs is undoubtedly caused by its higher noise level, not increased distortion.

Fig. 5-12 A typical preamplifier THD+N measurement

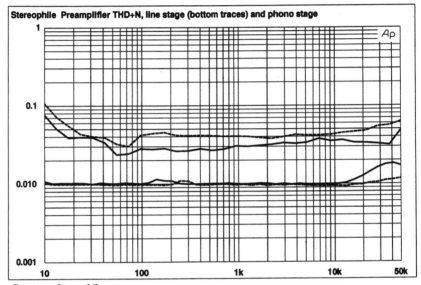

Courtesy *Stereophile*

Interchannel crosstalk, also called *channel separation*, is a measure of how much the signal in one channel leaks into the other channel. The higher the number, the better, with 100dB being excellent and 50dB being on the poor side. A crosstalk specification should include the measurement frequency; crosstalk usually increases as frequency rises. Crosstalk will generally increase at the rate of 6dB per octave, due to capacitive coupling between channels.

When expressing this phenomenon as *crosstalk*, the *lower* the specified crosstalk the better; it indicates how much signal has leaked into the other channel. Conversely, when expressing *channel separation*, the *higher* the figure the better; the number indicates the degree of isolation between channels.

Fig.5-13a shows mediocre crosstalk performance; Fig.5-13b shows excellent crosstalk performance. The measurement is made by driving one channel of the preamplifier with a swept sine wave at a reference output level (which is made the 0dB reference on the graph's vertical scale), then plotting the undriven channel's output signal as a function of frequency. The measurement is repeated with the channels switched, and both traces are combined on the same graph. In the example of poor crosstalk performance, the signal (crosstalk) in the undriven left channel was 60dB below that of the driven right channel at 1kHz. In Fig.5-13b, the signal in the undriven channel was down by 100dB at 1kHz.

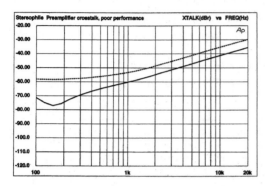
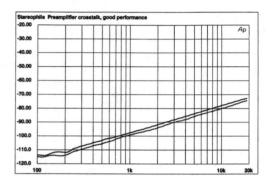

Fig. 5-13a & b Examples of poor (left) and excellent (right) crosstalk (Courtesy *Stereophile*)

Channel balance is a measure of how closely in level the two channels are matched. Some preamplifiers have slightly more gain in one channel than the other, creating a channel imbalance. Volume controls can also introduce channel imbalance, particularly at the low end (counterclockwise) of their range. Channel balance is often measured at three volume-control positions, and should be within 0.2dB at any volume setting. Large channel imbalances can cause the center image to shift to one side. Tubed preamps sharing a single dual tube for left and right channels are particularly susceptible to channel imbalances; the two elements within the tube may have slightly different gains. Fortunately, the problem can be corrected simply by changing the tube to one with matched gain.

Preamplifier specifications should be used to ensure electrical compatibility with other components, not as indicators of sound quality. Many superb-sounding preamps measure poorly, and some preamps that look great on paper disappoint in the listening room. Let your ears—not the specification sheet—be your guide to choosing a preamplifier.

The Preamplifier of the Future

In the not-too-distant future, the preamplifier we know today may be considered an archaic holdover from a bygone era. As audio systems become more and more digital, the preamplifier's role will need to be rethought. We can already see trends toward audio systems without pre-amplifiers, as well as preamplifiers radically different from today's products.

In one scenario, the preamp of the future is no preamplifier at all. Volume control, input selection, and signal routing will all be performed in the digital domain, and controlled by a remote handset. Similarly, loudspeakers accepting digital inputs will simply incorporate the preamplifier's traditional functions within them.

A power amplifier could be configured to accept several line-level sources, with remote control of switching and volume. The preamplifier as we know it, with knobs and switches, would become superfluous.

Another, perhaps more realistic, scenario is that of preamplifier functions becoming part of the digital-to-analog converter. Several products now on the market hint at such a future. In these new products, the digital processor incorporates volume control, balance adjustment, source selection, and other preamplifier functions, all performed in the digital domain. Such a "preamp" accepts analog signals from a tuner or an analog cassette deck, for example, and converts these signals to digital form with an on-board analog-to-digital (A/D) converter. Both analog and digital tape loops are included. Once all the signals are in the digital domain, signal control and processing is performed by Digital Signal Processing (DSP) chips. The digital signal is then converted to analog with the product's integral D/A converter. This component's analog output then drives a conventional power amplifier. Alternately, the device's digital output could drive digital-input loudspeakers.

This product is a reality today. Two examples of forward-thinking digital processor/preamplifiers are the PS Audio Reference Link and the Meridian Multimedia Controller. The Reference Link has an on-board A/D, analog and digital inputs, selection between input sources, digital and analog tape loops, and full remote control. The Multimedia Controller functions similarly, but also provides video switching.

But no matter what the preamplifier's future may be, you'll still need to select one that fits your functional needs, and most important, choose one that provides the greatest musical satisfaction.

6 Power Amplifiers

Overview and Terminology

The power amplifier is the workhorse of a hi-fi system. It takes the low-level signal from the preamplifier and converts it to a powerful signal to drive the loudspeakers. It has a line-level input to receive the signal from the preamplifier, and terminals for connecting loudspeaker cables. The power amplifier is the last component in the signal chain before the loudspeakers.

Because of the power amplifier's unique function, it differs from other components in size, weight, and use. High-quality power amplifiers are usually large and heavy. Moreover, the power amplifier is the component you don't need to touch and adjust. Consequently, power amplifiers are often placed on the floor near the loudspeakers rather than in an equipment rack.

Here are definitions of some of the terms associated with power amplifiers.

Stereo Power Amplifier: A power amplifier with two audio channels (left and right) in one chassis.

Monoblock Power Amplifier: A power amplifier with only one audio channel per chassis. Two monoblocks are required for stereo reproduction.

Watt: A unit of electrical power. Power is the ability to do work, in this case, the ability of the amplifier to make a loudspeaker's diaphragm move.

Power Output: The maximum amount of power the amplifier can deliver to the loudspeaker; measured in watts.

Load: In power-amplifier terminology, a load is the loudspeaker the power amplifier must drive.

Tubed: A tubed power amplifier uses vacuum tubes to amplify the audio signal.

Solid-State: A solid-state power amplifier uses transistors to amplify the audio signal.

Hybrid: A power amplifier combining vacuum tubes and solid-state devices. The input and driver stages are usually tubed, the output stage is usually solid-state.

Bridging: Converting a stereo power amplifier into a monoblock power amplifier. Some power amplifiers have a rear-panel bridging switch. Also called "strapping" into mono.

Bi-amping: Driving a loudspeaker's midrange and treble units with one amplifier, the woofer with a second amplifier.

How to Choose a Power Amplifier

Unlike most of the other components in your system, power amplifiers vary greatly in their electrical performances. Consequently, choosing a power amplifier requires careful system matching for electrical compatibility, not just musical compatibility. While any CD player or digital processor will function in a system (even though it may not be musically ideal), some power amplifiers just won't work well with certain loudspeakers on a technical level. Choosing a power amplifier thus requires careful attention to system matching. We'll discuss these technical factors throughout this chapter.

Power amplifiers range from $300 solid-state stereo units to $20,000 tubed monoblocks. Choosing the right one for you begins with narrowing the range of possibilities. Start by defining your requirements and setting your budget; the vast range of products will be quickly reduced to a more manageable number of contenders. Because a power amplifier's cost is often proportional to its output power, read this chapter's "How Much Power do You Need?" to select just the right power rating for your needs. Whatever your budget, the power amplifier should consume about 20 to 25% of your total system budget.

The first division of power amplifiers—a stereo unit or a pair of monoblocks—will be decided by your budget. Monoblocks generally *start* at about $2500 per pair. At this price level, a single stereo unit may make more sense; with only one chassis, power cord, and shipping carton, the manufacturer can put more of the manufacturing cost into better parts and performance. I advise against monoblocks if your amplifier budget is less than about $4000. There may be exceptions to this figure, but it nonetheless offers a broad guideline. There are, for example, many excellent stereo units costing upward of $6000. A very popular price range for high-quality power amplifiers is $800–$2000, with the $2000 models sometimes offering musical performance close to that of the most expensive amplifiers.

Monoblocks generally perform better than a single stereo unit for several reasons. First, because the two amplifier channels are separate chassis, there is no chance of interaction between channels. Consequently, monoblocks typically have better soundstage performance than stereo units. Second, monoblocks have completely separate power supplies, including power transformers; the left- and right-channel amplifier circuits don't have to share their current source. This gives monoblocks the ability to provide more instantaneous current to the loudspeaker, all other factors being equal. Finally, most manufacturers put their cost-no-object effort into monoblocks, which are often the flagships of their lines. If you want all-out performance and can afford them, monoblocks are the way to go.

At the other end of the scale from monoblocks is the *integrated amplifier*. An integrated amplifier combines a preamplifier and power amplifier in the same chassis. The power output from integrated amplifiers is generally much lower than that of power amplifiers, but they are much less expensive. An integrated amplifier is ideal for budget systems, or those listeners who don't need much power. Integrated amplifiers cost between $300 and $1000.

With that introduction, let's look at the specifics of how to choose a power amplifier.

How Much Power do You Need?

The first question to answer when shopping for a power amplifier is how much output power you need. Power output, measured in watts into a specified loudspeaker impedance, varies from about 20 watts per channel (Wpc) in a very small amplifier to about 800Wpc. Most high-end power amplifiers put out between 40 and 250Wpc.

Choosing an appropriate amplifier power-output range for your loudspeakers, listening tastes, room, and budget is essential to getting the best sound for your money. If the amplifier is under-powered for your needs, you'll never hear the system at its full potential. The sound will be constricted, fatiguing, lack dynamics, and the music will have a sense of strain on climaxes. Conversely, if you spend too much of your budget on a bigger amplifier than you need, you may be shortchanging other components. Choosing just the right amplifier power is of paramount importance.

The amount of power needed varies greatly according to loudspeaker sensitivity, loudspeaker impedance, room size, room acoustics, and how loudly you like to play music. Loudspeaker sensitivity is by far the biggest determining factor in choosing an appropriate power output. Loudspeaker sensitivity specifies how high a sound pressure level the loudspeaker will produce when driven by a certain power input. A typical sensitivity specification will read "88dB SPL, 1W/1m." This means this loudspeaker will produce a sound pressure level (SPL) of 88dB with one watt of input power when measured at a distance of one meter. Although 88dB is a moderate listening volume, a closer look at how power relates to listening level reveals that we need much more than one watt for music playback.

Each increase in sound pressure level of 3dB requires a doubling of amplifier output power. Thus, our loudspeaker with a sensitivity of 88dB at 1W would produce 91dB with 2W, 94dB with 4W, 97dB with 8W, and so on. For this loudspeaker to produce musical peaks of 109dB, we would need an amplifier with 256Wpc of output power.

Now, say we had a loudspeaker rated at 91dB at 1W/1m, only 3dB more sensitive than the first loudspeaker. We can quickly see that we would need only *half* the amplifier power (128W) to produce the same volume of 109dB SPL.

This relationship between amplifier power output and loudspeaker sensitivity was dramatically illustrated in an unusual demonstration nearly 50 years ago. In 1948, loudspeaker pioneer Paul Klipsch conducted a live vs. reproduced demonstration with a symphony orchestra and his Klipschorn loudspeakers. His amplifier power: 5W. The Klipschorns are so sensitive (an astounding 105dB SPL, 1W/1m) that they will produce very high volume with very low amplifier power.

This example illustrates how loudspeaker sensitivity greatly affects the amount of amplifier power you need. Even small differences in loudspeaker sensitivity—2dB, say—changes your amplifier power requirements.

We've seen that every doubling of amplifier power yields an increase of 3dB. Consequently, there is a 3dB difference between a 10W amplifier and a 20W amplifier, but also between a 500W amplifier and a 1000W amplifier. Although the output power is vastly greater between 500W and 1000W than between 10W and 20W, the difference is still 3dB.

When comparing amplifier power ratings, consider the *ratio* of output powers, not the number of watts.

The dBW Power Rating

Fortunately, there is a way of expressing amplifier power that takes into account this exponential relationship between dB and power, a rating called the "dBW." The "W" after dB means that 0dB is referenced to 1W. A 10W amplifier has a dBW rating of 10dBW, a 20W amplifier has a dBW rating of 13dBW—twice the power, or the ability to play 3dB louder than a 10W amplifier. One hundred watts equals 20dBW, and a 1000W amplifier is said to have 30dBW of output power. The dBW rating conveys the ratio of amplifier output powers, referenced to 1W of output power. The relationship between power output (into an 8-ohm load) and dBW is shown in the following table.

Watts	dBW	Watts	dBW	Watts	dBW
1.0	0	10.0	10	100	20
1.25	1	12.5	11	125	21
1.6	2	16	12	160	22
2.0	3	20	13	200	23
2.5	4	25	14	250	24
3.2	5	32	15	320	25
4.0	6	40	16	400	26
5.0	7	50	17	500	27
6.3	8	63	18	630	28
8.0	9	80	19	800	29

Most manufacturers don't include the dBW rating on their amplifiers. You can, however, perform this conversion yourself with a pocket calculator that has a "log" button. Punch in the number of watts you want to convert to dBW, find the logarithm of that number by pressing the "log" key, then multiply by 10. This will give you the dBW value when driving an 8-ohm load. To find the dBW rating with a 4-ohm load, subtract 3dB from the result. To calculate for 2 ohms, subtract 6dB from the result.

For example, if an amplifier puts out 150W into 8 ohms, enter "150" into the calculator and press the "log" key; 2.176 will appear in the display. Then press "x" and "10" to multiply the log by 10, to get the dBW rating of 21.76dBW.

If this same amplifier puts out 225W into 4 ohms, enter "225" into the calculator, press "log" to get 2.352, then multiply by 10 to get the intermediate result of 23.52dBW. But this is a 4 ohm power rating; subtracting 3 from the result will give us the final dBW rating of 20.52W into 4 ohms.

If you're choosing between 60Wpc and 110Wpc amplifiers, you can calculate the difference in dB between them. Converting 60W (at 8 ohms) into dBW gives us 17.78dBW. Converting 110W (at 8 ohms) into dBW works out to 20.41dBW. The difference is a little less than 3dB. Note that the same dB difference exists between a 600W amplifier and a 1100W amplifier, or between a 6W amplifier and a 11W amplifier.

The concept of dBW becomes even more useful when we take a closer look at amplifier output ratings. Most of the power figures we've discussed are with the amplifier driving an 8-ohm load. But most loudspeakers have an impedance of less than 8 ohms, and some have impedance dips below 2 ohms. How does our power amplifier behave when asked to drive low impedances?

Instead of just considering the amplifier's 8 ohm power rating, look at how the power output changes into 4- and 2-ohm loads. An amplifier acting as a perfect *voltage source* will double its power every time the load impedance is cut in half; this amplifier would be capable of driving 100W into 8 ohms, could deliver 200W into 4 ohms, 400W into 2 ohms, and 800W into 1 ohm. (A more technical discussion of this aspect of amplifier performance appears later in this chapter.)

Some amplifiers barely increase their output power when driving 4 ohms; others can double it. This means that not all "100Wpc" amplifiers are created equal. One "100Wpc" amplifier might put out 150W into 2 ohms, while another might deliver 350Wpc into 2 ohms. This ability to drive low impedance loads (specifically, to deliver lots of current) has a large influence on an amplifier's sound and subjective power capability.

This is where our dBW rating comes into play again. When calculating dBW, subtract 3dBW from the 8-ohm dBW rating when the amplifier is driving 4 ohms, and subtract 6dBW when the amplifier is driving 2 ohms. In the example of the two "100Wpc" amplifiers in the preceding paragraph, each is rated at 100Wpc into 8 ohms, or 20dBW. But the first amplifier puts out only 150W into 2 ohms, while the second puts out 350W into 2 ohms. Converting the 2 ohm power ratings into dBW, we see that the first amplifier has a dBW rating of 15.76dBW at 2 ohms, while the second has a dBW rating of 19.44dBW into 2 ohms. Quite a difference—nearly 4dB—between two "100Wpc" amplifiers.

Why Amplifier Output Current Matters

This difference has real-world consequences. The ability to increase output power into low impedances indicates how much current the amplifier can deliver to the loudspeaker. It is current flow through the loudspeakers' voice coils (in dynamic loudspeakers) that creates the electromagnetic force that causes the cones and domes to move, producing sound. If current flow through the voice coil is constrained, so is the music.

The problem is exacerbated by low-impedance loudspeakers; The low impedance demands more current from the power amplifier. The musical result is strain—or even distortion—on musical peaks, weak bass, loss of dynamics, hardening of timbre, and a collapsing sound-stage. In short, we can hear the amplifier give up as it runs out of power. Conversely, amplifiers that can continue increasing their output power as the impedance drops generally have very deep, extended, and power-ful bass, unlimited dynamics, a sense of ease and grace during musical peaks, and the ability to maintain correct timbre and soundstaging, even during loud passages. If you have relatively high-impedance loudspeak-ers with no severe impedance dips, you are much less likely to encounter these sonic problems, even with modest power amplifiers; the loudspeaker simply demands less current from the power amplifier.

Amplifiers with high current capability (indicated by their ability to increase output power into low impedances) are often large and expen-sive. Their current capability comes from massive power transformers, huge power supplies, and lots of output transistors—all expensive items. Fig.6-1a and b show such power amplifiers. The massive power trans-former and filter capacitors seen in the middle of the amplifier can sup-ply large amounts of current to the circuits. The output stage has many output transistors in parallel for increased current capacity. These tran-sistors are mounted to huge heat sinks to keep the transistors running relatively cool.

Fig. 6-1a Power amplifiers that can deliver high current into low impedance loads are massive.

Courtesy Madrigal Audio Laboratories, Inc.

Fig. 6-1b Inside a high-current power amplifier

Courtesy Krell Industries

In the measurements section of this chapter, we'll look at how to evaluate a power amplifier's ability to deliver current into low-impedance loads.

What to Look For when Comparing Power Ratings

When comparing power ratings, make sure the specified power is *continuous* or *RMS* rather than peak. Some manufacturers will claim a power output of 200W, for example, but not specify whether that power output is available only during brief peaks, or if the amplifier can deliver that power continuously into a load. RMS stands for "Root Mean

Square," a mathematical calculation expressing the effective, or average, power output. Very few amplifiers are specified by peak power.

Another way manufacturers exaggerate power ratings is by not specifying the *power bandwidth*. A power amplifier delivering 200W at 1kHz is a far cry from one that can deliver 200W over the full audio bandwidth of 20Hz to 20kHz. Further, stereo power amplifiers can deliver more power with only one channel driven—look for the words "both channels driven." The maximum power output should also be specified at a certain distortion level.

We can see the potential for misleading power-amplifier output claims. The abuses were so bad the Federal Trade Commission (FTC) stepped in to regulate power claims—the only example of an audio specification being regulated by a governmental body. The FTC mandate for power ratings requires that the power rating be continuous (not peak), that the load impedance and bandwidth be specified, and that the Total Harmonic Distortion (THD) be given at full power and measured over the audio bandwidth. We may see a power specification that reads "50W per channel continuous (or RMS) power into 8 ohms, both channels driven, from 20Hz-20kHz, with less than 0.1% THD." A power specification including all these conditions is called an "FTC power rating."

When you're amplifier-shopping, look a little closer at the power-output specifications into low impedances. Make sure you see the words "continuous" or "average" in the power rating. See if the bandwidth and distortion are specified. These figures don't tell us everything we need to know about the amplifier's musical qualities, but nevertheless indicate good technical performance.

Why Amplifier Power Isn't Everything

We've seen how loudspeaker sensitivity greatly affects how much amplifier power you need, and how power amplifiers with the same 8 ohm power rating can differ radically in their abilities to drive loudspeakers. Now let's look at some other factors influencing how much amplifier power you need.

The first is room size. The bigger the room, the more amplifier power you'll need. A rough guide suggests that increasing the room volume by four times requires a doubling of amplifier power to achieve the same sound pressure level.

How acoustically reflective or absorptive your listening room is will also affect how much amplifier power you need. If we put the same-sensitivity loudspeakers in two rooms of the same size, one room acoustically dead (absorptive) and the other acoustically live (reflective), we would need roughly double the amplifier power to achieve the same sound pressure level as in the live room.

Fig. 6-2 The relationship between loud-speaker sensitivity, room size, room acoustics, and power amplifier output power (after *High Fidelity*)

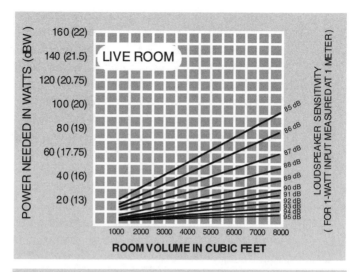

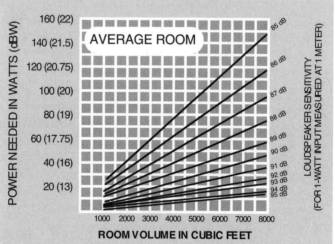

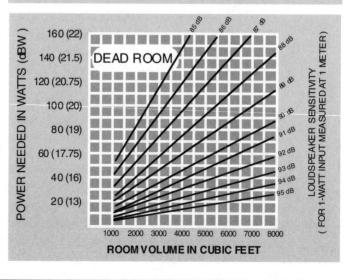

Finally, how loudly you listen to music greatly affects how much amplifier power you need. Chamber music played softly requires much less amplifier power than rock or orchestral music.

The relationships between loudspeaker sensitivity, room size, room acoustics, and amplifier power are shown in Fig.6-2.

We can see that a low-sensitivity loudspeaker in a large, acoustically dead room, driven by rock music, by someone who likes high playback levels, may require hundreds of times the amplifier power as someone listening to chamber music at moderate listening levels through high-sensitivity loudspeakers in a small, live room. A 30Wpc amplifier may be sufficient for the second listener, but 750Wpc may be needed by the first listener.

Other Power-Amplifier Considerations

Tubes vs. Transistors

The perennial tubes vs. transistors debate arises when choosing a power amplifier. Tubed units can offer stunning musical performance, but they have their drawbacks. Here are the advantages and disadvantages of tubed power amplifiers.

Tubed power amplifiers are more expensive than their similarly powered solid-state counterparts. The cost of tubes, transformers, and more extensive power supplies all make owning a tubed power amplifier a more expensive proposition than owning a solid-state one. Moreover, the tubes will need replacing every few years, further adding to the real cost of ownership. A set of sixteen EL34 output tubes, for example, can cost from $200 to $400.

In terms of bass performance, tubed power amplifiers can't compete with good solid-state units. Tubes have less control in the bass, making the presentation less punchy, taut, and extended. Further, tubed power amplifiers often have limited current delivery into low-impedance loads, making them a poor choice for current-hungry loudspeakers. Tubes also require monthly biasing to maintain top performance. Biasing is very easy, but some music lovers are understandably reluctant to take a voltmeter and screwdriver to their amplifiers.

Power-amp tubes can fail suddenly, sometimes in smoke and (momentary) flames. Such dramatic failure is rare, however; I've used a pair of tubed monoblocks almost continuously for the past four years and have had two tube failures out of 16 tubes over that time. Both tubes failed uneventfully.

Finally, there is the possibility of small children getting burned by hot tubes. Many, but not all, tubed power amplifiers have exposed output tubes.

Given these drawbacks, why would anyone want to own a tubed power amplifier? It's simple: tubes can sound magical. When matched with an appropriate loudspeaker, tubed power amplifiers offer unequaled musicality, in my experience. Even small, moderately priced tubed amplifiers have more than a taste of tube magic.

Many important aspects of music reproduction seem to come naturally to tubed amplifiers. They generally have superb presentation of instrumental timbre, smooth and unfatiguing treble, and spectacular soundstaging. The hard, brittle, and edgy midrange and treble presentation of many solid-state amplifiers is contrasted with the lush liquidity and ease of a good tubed amp. Music has a warmth, ease, and natural musicality when reproduced with many tubed designs. This isn't to say there aren't good-sounding solid-state power amplifiers; only that tubes seem to more consistently deliver the musical goods. A tubed amplifier's softer bass is often willingly sacrificed for its magical midrange, treble, and soundstaging.

Solid-state amplifiers have, however, some decided sonic and technical advantages. Tubed units are no match for solid-state amplifiers in bass performance. Transistor power amplifiers have tighter, deeper, and much more solid bass than tubed units. The feeling of bass tautness, kick, extension, and power are all better conveyed by solid-state amplifiers, regardless of how good the tubed amplifier is. On a technical level, solid-state amplifiers have a greater ability to deliver current into low-impedance loudspeakers.

No one but you can decide if a tubed power amplifier is ideal for your system. I strongly suggest, however, that you audition at least one tubed amplifier before making a purchasing decision. You may get hooked.

Balanced Inputs

If your preamp has balanced outputs, you may want to consider a power amplifier with balanced inputs. Most power amps with balanced inputs also provide unbalanced inputs, allowing you to choose later which connection to use. Some preamplifier/power amplifier combinations sound better via balanced connection, others via the unbalanced jacks. The best way to discover which method is better is by listening to both. (See Chapter 5 for a discussion of why some preamplifiers may sound better from their unbalanced outputs).

If you have a power amplifier with both balanced and unbalanced inputs, but use the unbalanced inputs, be sure you have a *shorting plug* in the amplifier's XLR input jacks. This is a small "U"-shaped plug that shorts pin 3 of the XLR jack to ground, preventing noise from getting into the amplifier.

Bridging

Some stereo power amplifiers can be "bridged" to function as monoblocks. The amplifier will have a switch on the rear panel to convert the amplifier to bridged operation. Note that two such amplifiers are needed for stereo. If you have a stereo amplifier that can be bridged and you want more power, simply buy a second identical amplifier and bridge them for double the power.

Bridging changes the amplifier's internal connections so that one channel amplifies the positive half of the waveform and the other channel amplifies the negative half. The loudspeaker is connected as the "bridge" between the two amplifier channels instead of between one channel's output and ground.

Bi-Amping

Any loudspeaker with two sets of input terminals is a candidate for bi- amping. In a bi-amped setup, two power amplifiers are used to drive one loudspeaker. One amplifier drives the woofer, the other drives the midrange and tweeter.

Let's first consider *passive bi-amping*. The preamplifier output is split into two left-channel signals and two right-channel signals. (Many pre-amps have two stereo output pairs for this purpose.) The left-channel preamp output drives the left-channel inputs on both power amps. The right-channel preamp output drives the right-channel inputs on both power amps. One power amp drives the bass input on both loudspeakers, the other power amp drives the midrange and tweeter input on both loudspeakers. Note that the loudspeaker's crossover still operates; both amplifiers receive and amplify a full-bandwidth signal. This is called passive bi-amping; the frequency division into bass and midrange/treble is performed by passive components (capacitors, resistors, and inductors) in the loudspeaker's crossover.

In *active bi-amping*, rather than allow the loudspeaker's crossover to split the frequency spectrum, an *electronic crossover* between the preamp and power amps does the job. Active bi-amping divides the frequency spectrum *before* the power amplifiers, not after, as in passive bi-amping. The losses and problems inherent in any passive crossover are eliminated by active bi-amping. Moreover, each power amplifier receives only the portion of the frequency band it will amplify. Active bi-amping is more efficient than passive bi-amping, but requires bypassing the loudspeaker crossovers and adding an electronic crossover.

Bi-amping not only increases the total power delivered to the loudspeaker, but allows each amplifier to work over a narrower frequency range. We can thus choose a bass amplifier for its superior bottom-end performance regardless of how it sounds in the mids and treble, and a midrange/treble amplifier without concern for its bass. An ideal combination may include a large, solid-state amplifier for the bass and a sweet-sounding tubed amplifier for the top end. The small tubed amplifier is relieved of the burden of driving the bass, allowing it to do what it does best. Bi-amping is one way of getting the best of both the solid-state and tubed worlds.

Another advantage of (active) bi-amping is that the woofer amplifier can be connected directly to the woofer's voice coil rather than through a passive crossover network, particularly the series inductor found in most woofer crossovers. This provides much tighter damping (the ability of the amplifier to control woofer motion) and results in tighter, deeper bass reproduction.

When bi-amping, the two amplifiers' *gains* (the amount of amplification) must be exactly matched. If you're using identical amplifiers, the gain will be inherently matched. But with different amplifiers, a gain mismatch will produce too much or too little bass. Amplifiers can be *padded down* at the input with an *attenuator* to reduce the input level and match its output to the second amplifier. If you're using an active external crossover, the crossover may include independent output-level controls to balance the level between woofer and midrange/tweeter amplifiers.

Bi-amping can be tricky. I don't recommend it for most systems unless you fully understand what's happening, or unless your dealer helps you. A few manufacturers—Linn Products, for example—have designed easy bi-amping upgradability into their products; bi-amping is just a matter of installing active crossover boards in the company's power amplifiers and adding a second amplifier.

Incidentally, adding an active subwoofer (see Chapter 7) automatically makes your system actively bi-amped. The subwoofer's internal amplifier drives the low bass, and your main amplifier handles only the upper bass, mids, and treble. Installing an active subwoofer is one way of getting the benefits of bi-amping without changing amplifiers or adding an additional electronic crossover.

What to Listen For

How can you tell if the power amplifier you're considering will work well with your loudspeakers? Simple: Borrow the amplifier from your dealer for the weekend and listen to it. This is the best way of not only assessing its musical qualities, but determining how well it drives your loudspeakers. In addition, listening to the power amplifier at home will let you hear if the product's sonic signature complements the rest of your system. The next best choice is if the dealer sells the same loudspeakers you own, allowing you to audition the combination in the store. Finally, you could bring your loudspeakers into the store for a final audition.

All the sonic and musical characteristics described in Chapter 3 apply to power amplifiers. However, some sonic characteristics are more influenced by the power amplifier than by other components.

The first thing to listen for is whether the amplifier is driving the loudspeakers adequately. The most obvious indicator is bass performance. If the bass is soggy, slow, or lacks punch, the amplifier probably isn't up to the job of driving your loudspeakers. Other telltale signs that the amplifier is running out of current include loss of dynamics, a sense of strain on musical peaks, hardening of timbre, reduced pace and rhythm, and soundstage collapse or congestion. Let's look at each of these individually.

First, play the system at a moderate volume. Select music with a wide dynamic range—either full orchestral music with a loud climax accompanied by bass drum, or music with a powerful rhythmic drive from bass guitar and kick drum working together. Audiophile recordings typically have much wider dynamic ranges than general-release discs, making them a better source for evaluation. Music that has been highly compressed to play over the radio on a 3" car speaker will tell you less about what the system is doing.

After you've become used to the sound at a moderate level, increase the volume—you want to push the amplifier to find its limits. Does the bass seem to give out when you turn it up, or does the amplifier keep on delivering? Listen to the dynamic impact of kick drum on a recording with lots of bottom-end punch. It should maintain its tightness, punch, quickness, and depth at high volume. If it starts to sound soggy, slow, or loses its power, you've gone beyond the amplifier's comfortable operating point. After a while, you can get a feel for when the amplifier gets into trouble. Is the sound strained on peaks, or effortless?

NOTE: When performing this experiment, be sure not to overdrive your loudspeakers. Turn down the volume at the first sign of loudspeaker overload (distortion or a popping sound.)

Compare the amplifier's sound at high and low volumes. Listen for brass instruments becoming hard and edgy at high volumes. See if the soundstage degenerates into a confused mess during climaxes. Does the bass drum lose its power and impact? An excellent power amplifier operating below its maximum power capability will preserve the sense of space, depth, and focus, while maintaining liquid instrumental timbre. Moreover, adequate power will produce a sense of ease; lack of power often creates listener fatigue. Music is much more enjoyable through a power amplifier with plenty of reserve power.

All the problems I've just described are largely the result of the amplifier running out of current. Just where this happens is a function of the amplifier's output power, its ability to deliver current into the loudspeaker, the loudspeaker's sensitivity, the loudspeaker's impedance, room size, and how loudly you expect your hi-fi system to play. Even when not pushed to maximum output, a more powerful amplifier will often have a greater sense of ease, grace, and dynamics than a less powerful amplifier.

Assuming that the power amplifier can drive your loudspeakers, let's evaluate its musical characteristics.

First, listen for its overall perspective. Determine if it's forward or laid-back, then decide if the amplifier is too "up front" or too recessed for your system or tastes. A *forward* perspective seems to put you in Row C of the concert hall; a *laid-back* perspective puts you in Row W. Forwardness gives the impression of presence and immediacy, but can quickly become fatiguing. A presentation that's too laid-back is less exciting and compelling. If the amplifier's overall perspective isn't right, nothing else it does well may matter.

Next, listen for brightness, hardness, treble grain, and treble etch. If you feel a sense of relief when the volume is turned down, you can be pretty sure that the treble is at fault. Listen to midrange timbre, particularly voice, violin, piano, and flute. Midrange textures should be sweet, liquid, and devoid of grain, hardness, or a glassy edge. Many power amplifiers—particularly inexpensive solid-state units—make the treble dry, forward, and unpleasant. Any hint of these characteristics during a few hours' listening will only grow more annoying over time. Many moderately priced amplifiers don't add these unmusical characteristics—keep shopping.

Power amplifiers vary greatly in their ability to throw a convincing soundstage. With naturally miked recordings, the soundstage should be deep, transparent, and focused, the loudspeakers and listening room seeming to disappear. Instruments should hang in space within the recorded acoustic. The presentation should provide a transparent, picture-window view into the music. If the sound is flat, veiled, or homogenized, you haven't found the right amplifier.

Bass performance is also largely influenced by the power amplifier. It should sound taut, deep, quick, dynamic, and effortless. The music should be propelled forward, involving your body in the music's rhythmic drive. Kick drum should have depth, power, and a feeling of suddenness. The bass guitar and kick drum should provide a tight, solid, and powerful musical foundation.

The best way to find out which power amplifiers sound good and are well made is by reading product reviews in reputable high-end magazines. Responsibly written reviews can save you from spending time and trouble on unworthy contenders, and point you toward products that offer promise. Further, thorough reviews will include a full set of measurements, with commentary on the amplifier's technical performance. If the amplifier has technical characteristics that make it questionable or unsuitable for a particular type of loudspeaker, the review will reveal this fact. A review's technical section may state that, "Although the Symphonic Bombast 101 power amplifier sounded terrific with the Dominator 1 loudspeakers, its high output impedance and limited current delivery make it a poor choice with low-sensitivity loudspeakers (below 86dB 1W/1m), or those with an impedance below 5 ohms." This kind of technical commentary can point you toward the best amplifiers for your loudspeakers.

In short, read lots of product reviews before drawing up a list of candidates to audition. Restrict candidates to those that fall within your budget, and take the few contenders home for an evening's listen. And don't be in a hurry to buy the first amplifier you audition—listen to several before choosing. Your effort and patience will be rewarded with a more musical amplifier, and one better suited to your system.

How a Power Amplifier Works

A power amplifier converts the 60Hz AC power from your wall outlet into direct current (DC), which is then converted into an audio signal. The small input signal from a preamplifier controls a very large signal at the power amplifier output, which is then delivered to the loudspeakers.

At its most basic level, a power amplifier consists of a power supply, an input stage, a driver stage, and an output stage. Fig.6-3a and b shows a photograph of a power amplifier's circuitry and a power amplifier block diagram. Let's look at each of these sections of the block diagram in more detail.

Fig. 6-3a A
solid-state power
amplifier

Courtesy McCormack

Fig. 6-3b A
solid-state power
amplifier block
diagram

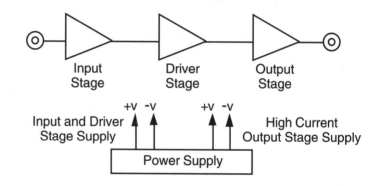

The Power Supply

The power supply converts 60Hz 120V AC (Alternating Current)
into the DC (Direct Current) the audio circuits need. Power-amplifier
power supplies differ greatly from those for other audio components. (A
close reading of Appendix B will be helpful in understanding the rest of
this explanation.) Power-amplifier supplies must be able to provide large
amounts of current, operate at much higher voltages, and have much

larger storage capacities. Parts sizes and ratings are thus much higher in a power amplifier than in the power supply of a preamp or CD player.

The power transformer *steps down* the 120V AC line voltage to a lower value, perhaps 80V. The power transformer can be seen at the front center of the amplifier shown in Fig.6-3a. You can get a pretty good idea of how powerful the amplifier is by the power transformer's size and rating. Transformers are rated in "VA" or "kVA" (x 1000); i.e., voltage ("V") multiplied by the maximum current in amperes ("A") they can supply. A transformer with a VA rating of 1kVA can deliver 8.34 amperes of current (1000 divided by the AC line voltage of 120V) to the amplifier's circuits (assuming a 1:1 turns ratio). Because most power transformers step-down the voltage to 80V, a 1kVA transformer could deliver 12A.

Note that the amplifier's overall continuous output current for both channels combined can never exceed the power transformer's current rating. The amplifier can, however, deliver short bursts of higher current (such as on musical transients like bass-drum whacks) because of the energy stored in the capacitors—provided the output transistors can handle the current. One very large power amplifier's transformer, with a VA rating of 4.5kVA, weighs 85 of the amplifier's total 147 pounds. A more moderate-sized power amplifier may have a power transformer with a rating of 300VA.

This stepped-down AC voltage from the power transformer is then *rectified* (turned into DC) by a bridge rectifier and filtered by very large electrolytic capacitors. The filter capacitors also smooth the DC by removing any trace of *ripple* (the AC frequency appearing on the DC supply). The filter capacitors are also called *reservoir* capacitors because they store large amounts of electrical energy. A reservoir of electrical energy is needed because the power supply cannot pull current from the wall outlet fast enough to deliver instantaneous surges of high current to the loudspeakers. The reservoir capacitors act as a temporary storage area, or buffer, between the AC wall outlet and the power-supply output. Some of these capacitors are the size of soda cans, and can store huge amounts of electrical energy. Power-supply reservoir capacitors are typically between 30,000μF (microfarad) and 500,000μF—very large values. If you turn off a power amplifier when music is playing, you'll hear music for a few seconds or nearly a minute. The power to run the amplifier comes from the reservoir capacitors.

This high-energy supply is the power source for the output stage; the stored energy is converted by the output-stage transistors into the audio signal that drives the loudspeakers. The amplifier shown in Fig.6-3a is unusual in that it uses many smaller reservoir caps, each placed next to the transistor it supplies, rather than a few very large capacitors.

The ideal power supply would maintain its voltage no matter how much current the output devices demanded. In practice, the output supply voltages are *pulled down* when the output transistors suddenly draw current (as during a musical peak). This drop in power-supply output voltage is called *droop*. If your lights have ever dimmed momentarily when the refrigerator motor turned on, you've seen power-supply droop. The refrigerator motor draws a large amount of current when it starts, pulling down the voltage available to power the lights. A power supply that resists drooping is called a *stiff* supply.

The fuses on the backs of many power amplifiers are in series with the output stage's power-supply. If the output stage draws too much current, the fuse blows. If a fuse blows once, replace it with one of identical rating. If it blows again, the amplifier probably needs service. *Under no circumstances should you replace a fuse with one of a higher rating*. The fuse is there for a reason: to protect the output stage and the power supply. Defeating the fuse, or replacing a lower-value fuse with a higher-value one, can cause catastrophic damage to the amplifier. Moreover, there's a reason the fuse blew a second time: something was wrong in the amplifier. Have it serviced by a qualified technician.

Input and Driver Stages

The audio input signal driving the power amplifier is first buffered and amplified by the *input stage*. The input stage has a high input impedance and a low output impedance, buffering later stages from the preamplifier driving the power amplifier. It is here, at the input stage, that the amplifier's *input impedance* is determined. Input impedance, specified in ohms, is the resistance to current flow from the preamplifier's drive signal. An input impedance of 47k ohms is fairly standard for an unbalanced input. The input stage is followed by the *driver stage*, the circuit that amplifies the signal and drives the final *output stage*. The input and driver stages are located on the large flat circuit board in the middle of the amplifier shown in Fig.6-3a. The left and right channel output stages are mounted vertically along the amplifier's left and right sides. In class-A/B amplifiers (explained later in this chapter), the driver stage also acts as a *phase splitter*, converting the AC audio signal into positive and negative halves for presentation to the output stage. The need for a phase splitter will be apparent later in the discussion of output stages.

Many amplifiers have *coupling capacitors* between these stages. A coupling capacitor, also called a "DC blocking capacitor", stops direct current (DC) and passes the alternating current (AC) audio signal to the next stage. But the fact that these capacitors can degrade the amplifier's musical performance leads some designers to omit them from the signal path. An amplifier without coupling capacitors is called *direct-coupled*. Direct-coupled amplifiers can present a danger: any DC at the input will be amplified and sent to your loudspeakers. Because even small amounts of DC can destroy a loudspeaker, some amplifiers have a *DC servo* to prevent this DC from appearing at the output terminals. A DC servo monitors the DC level and adjusts the circuitry for minimum DC. You can easily measure how much DC appears at a power amplifier's outputs: just put a DC voltmeter across the loudspeaker terminals. Values below 200mV are typical.

Most high-quality power amplifiers use *discrete* circuitry in the input and driver stages. A discrete circuit is made from individual transistors rather than integrated-circuit operational amplifiers (op-amps). Discrete circuits are generally better than op-amp-based designs. Field Effect Transistors (FETs) are often used in the input stages of power amplifiers for their intrinsically high input impedance and low noise. Their low power capability, however, limits their use to the low-level signals of the input stage.

Nearly all power amplifiers use *feedback*, a technique that takes part of the output signal and returns it to the input. This makes the circuit more linear and lowers distortion. Too much feedback, however, results in poor sound. Many power amplifiers are touted as "low-feedback" designs. These amplifiers will probably have higher distortion figures, but may sound better as a result of less feedback. Two types of feedback are *local* and *global*. Local feedback is feedback around one stage within an amplifier; global feedback is feedback from the final output stage back to the input stage.

Finally, the input and driver stages are almost always class-A operation, meaning that one transistor amplifies the entire audio signal. The following discussion of output stages explains class-A operation in more detail.

The Output Stage

When discussing power amplifiers, the most common topic is the output stage. The output stage comprises many transistors, usually *bipolar* types, and less frequently, *MOSFETs*, another type of transistor. These transistors are the workhorses of a power amplifier; the current that makes the loudspeaker cones move is driven by the output transistors. Consequently, adding more transistors to the output stage increases the amplifier's output current capability. More transistors, however, require a bigger power supply. In addition, these output transistors produce very high temperatures that must be dissipated by *heat sinks*, the large black fins protruding from the sides of many power amplifiers.

When the output stage is asked to deliver more power than it is capable of, the top and bottom of the waveform are flattened, or *clipped*. When a power amplifier goes into *clipping*, the output is severely and audibly distorted. If clipping occurs only briefly on a few musical peaks, we may not notice it. An amplifier driven into *hard clipping* will, however, quickly destroy loudspeakers. Loudspeakers can handle surprising amounts of power, provided that the power amplifier driving them isn't itself driven into clipping.

Power-amplifier output stages are often described as being of *class-A* or *class-A/B* operation. In class-A/B, the most common and economical operation, the output transistors are arranged in *complementary* pairs. A complementary pair consists of one PNP-type transistor and one NPN-type. One transistor handles the signal during the positive-going portion of the signal, the other handles the negative-going signal half. When one is working, the other is resting (and getting some needed cooling). A complementary output pair (driven by a class-A driver stage) is shown in Fig.6-4. This circuit is also called *push-pull* output because one transistor "pushes" current through the loudspeaker while the other "pulls" it, shown by the arrows indicating current flow direction in Fig.6-4. As we discussed earlier, the power amplifier's driver stage also functions as a phase splitter to divide the AC audio signal into positive and negative halves. One phase drives the PNP transistor, the other phase drives the NPN.

Fig. 6-4 A complementary output pair driven by a class-A driver stage (Copied with permission from *Audio Technology Fundamentals* by Alan A. Cohen)

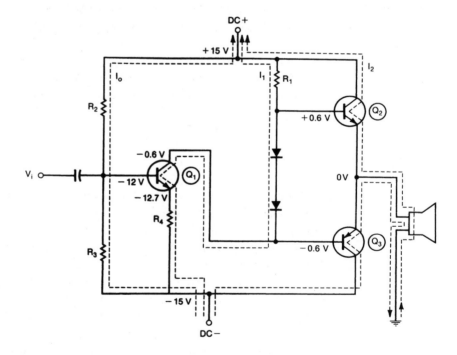

Pure class-A operation works differently. Instead of splitting the signal into positive and negative phases and using a transistor on each signal half, class-A operation forces the output transistors to handle both positive- and negative-going signal halves. This places much greater demands on the output transistors; they are conducting current all the time instead of half the time. Transistors operating in class-A are always turned on, instead of half on and half off as in class-B operation. Class-A amplifiers are very inefficient, produce *lots* of heat, require huge heat sinks, have lower power output for their size, and are expensive.

Class-A has many advantages, however. Because the transistors are always conducting, they are more *linear*; the output signal more closely resembles the input signal. Moreover, class-A avoids a problem with class-B amplifiers: *crossover distortion*. Crossover distortion can occur at the *zero crossing*, where one transistor turns off and the other turns on. A waveform discontinuity can occur at this transition. Crossover distortion can't occur in class-A operation because both the "upper" and "lower" transistors of the pair are always turned on.

Class-A also has the advantage of keeping the output transistors in thermal stability (a constant temperature). This makes their operating characteristics more uniform, and less subject to changes resulting from the signal characteristics the transistors are amplifying. In other words, if the transistors have just delivered a surge of current to the loudspeakers, they won't behave differently—and thus *sound* different—immediately afterward because they are momentarily hotter.

Class-A/B power amplifiers operate in class-A at very low power outputs, then switch to class-B operation at higher power outputs. A 100Wpc amplifier may put out 5W of class-A power, then switch to class-B above that level. Even the heftiest class-A/B amplifiers can put out only about 15% of their rated power in class-A. A more typical value is about 5%.

Pure class-A amplifiers are rare. Although many manufacturers claim "class- A" operation, a closer examination reveals they are actually class-A/B designs operating in class-A at lower power outputs. Class-A input and driver stages, however, are common. At the low signal levels present in the first stages, class-A operation is more easily achieved.

How much of an amplifier's output is class-A is determined by the amount of *bias* applied to the output transistors. Bias is a small DC current that makes the transistors conduct a larger current. The higher the bias, the more current flows through the transistors, even when they aren't amplifying a signal. The current through a transistor when not amplifying a signal, called *quiescent current*, is determined by the amount of bias. More bias results in a higher *operating point* and more class-A output power. Increasing the bias, however, makes the transistors run hotter. If the heat-sinking is inadequate, the transistors will overheat.

Because the quiescent current determines how much class-A power the amplifier will deliver, we can calculate the point at which the amplifier switches from class-A to class-B operation by measuring its quiescent current. First, we measure the voltage across one output transistor's emitter resistor. From that, and using Ohm's law, we calculate the quiescent current flowing through that transistor. We then multiply the quiescent current by the number of output devices to find the total quiescent current. If the amplifier has a fuse on its power supply output, the total quiescent current can be measured by putting an ammeter (a current meter) in series with the fuse. This is the absolute maximum current that can be delivered to the loudspeaker in class-A operation. Again, using Ohm's law, the output supply voltage, and quiescent current, we can calculate the maximum power output in class-A operation into a given load impedance.

Class-A power amplifiers can sound extremely good. They have a sweetness and liquidity that sets them apart from class-A/B amps. True class-A amplifiers are, however, massive, very heavy, and expensive. Moreover, they consume large amounts of power, even when not amplifying music. They draw the same current from the wall at idle as at full power output. Because they also need a long warm-up time to sound their best, class-A amplifiers can easily double your electric bill. Fortunately, class-A/B amplifiers offer many of the benefits of full class-A operation, putting out a significant portion (even 15% is excellent) of their rated output in class-A.

A unique solution to the problems of class-A power amplifiers has been devised by designer Dan D'Agostino of Krell Industries. At low power output, less bias is needed to keep the transistors operating in class-A. As the input signal level increases, more bias is required. "S"-series Krell amplifiers use a technique called "Sustained Plateau Biasing" that changes the bias current according to the input signal level. If the amplifier is driven hard, the bias is increased to maintain class-A operation. When the signal level drops, so does the bias, allowing the output stage to cool. Moreover, with no or very low input signals, the bias is so low the amplifier runs very cool and consumes very little electricity. Front-panel LEDs indicate the bias level. Incidentally, high-level transient signals—drums, for example—are reproduced in class-A; the input signal sensor and bias-adjust circuit are fast enough to ramp up the output stage bias before the transient reaches full level at the output stage. The result is full class-A output operation with less expense, size, and power consumption than conventional class-A power amplifiers.

Some power amplifiers use MOSFET output devices instead of bipolar transistors. MOSFET stands for Metal Oxide Semiconductor Field Effect Transistor. These devices operate differently; they are turned on (biased) by voltage rather than by current, as are bipolar devices. In this respect, they operate like vacuum tubes. MOSFETs have other technical attributes, and MOSFET amplifiers often have a characteristic sound.

How a Tubed Power Amplifier Works

The basic functions of tubed and solid-state power amplifiers are almost identical. Instead of using transistors in the input, driver, and output stages, tubed power amplifiers use vacuum tubes. A tubed power amplifier may use one tube in the input stage, another in the driver stage, and perhaps eight in a push-pull configuration in the output stage. Some amplifiers use tubes at the input and driver stages, then use solid-state devices in the output stage. Such amplifiers are called *hybrid* power amplifiers.

Fig.6-5a shows a tubed power amplifier; Fig.6-5b is a tubed power-amplifier block diagram. The most obvious difference between a tubed power amplifier and a solid-state unit is that the tubed amplifier has an *output transformer*. We can clearly see the output transformers (one per channel) at the amplifier rear, a feature not found in solid-state amplifiers. The output transformer functions as an impedance-matching device between the amplifier's output stage and the loudspeaker. The tubed amplifier's output stage thus "sees" the transformer's high input impedance rather than the loudspeaker's low input impedance. The transformer also cancels harmonic distortion by mixing the plate currents from both halves of the push-pull output stage. Finally, the output transformer prevents DC from appearing at the amplifier output terminals.

Fig. 6-5a A stereo tubed power amplifier

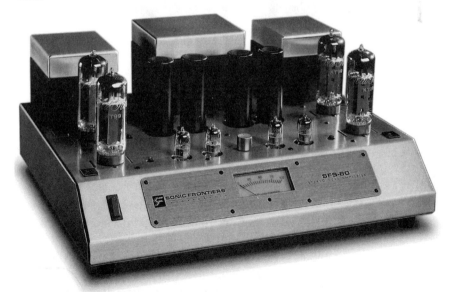

Courtesy Sonic Frontiers, Inc.

Fig. 6-5b A tubed power amplifier block diagram

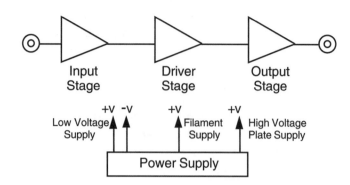

The output transformer must be large enough not to *saturate* at low frequencies. If saturation occurs, the bass become soft and "woolly." Some tubed power amplifiers have selectable *taps* on their transformers (see Fig.6-6), for loudspeakers of different impedances. These outputs are additional transformer *secondary windings*, providing the optimum impedance match between the transformer secondary windings and the loudspeaker.

Fig. 6-6 Some tubed power amplifiers provide different impedance taps from the output transformer.

Courtesy Audio Research Corporation

A few tubed amplifiers have *no* output transformer. They are called "OTL," for *Output TransformerLess*. OTLs generally aren't very powerful and don't work well with low-impedance loudspeakers. They are huge, have *lots* of output tubes, and are idiosyncratic in loudspeaker matching. The OTL amps I've heard have poor bass and not much in the way of dynamics, but spectacular soundstaging and beautiful rendering of timbre. OTLs aren't for everyone, but with the right loudspeaker, they can be magical.

Because a tube's operating characteristics change with age, all output tubes need to have their biases adjusted periodically. Bias is a small amount of current (typically between 20mA and 70mA) applied to the tube's grid to turn on the tube. Its transistor counterpart is the bias current we talked about in solid-state output stages. A tubed amplifier will often have test points and *trim pots* (trimmer potentiometers, tiny variable resistors adjustable with a small screwdriver) readily accessible on the front panel or chassis for bias adjustment.

To set an output tube's bias, put a DC voltmeter probe in the test point, ground the other test lead, and turn the trim pot until the voltage reading matches the manufacturer's bias specification. Bias is especially important in amplifiers having many output tubes; we want the tubes to operate identically. Not only do tubes age differently, but they need different amounts of bias when new due to manufacturing variability. When an output tube approaches the end of its useful life, the bias trim pots may be turned all the way up without reaching the specified bias voltage. When that happens, it's time for a new tube. Bias should be checked about once a month, or whenever changing tubes. (Fig.6-7 shows an amplifier being biased.)

Fig. 6-7 Biasing a tubed power amplifier

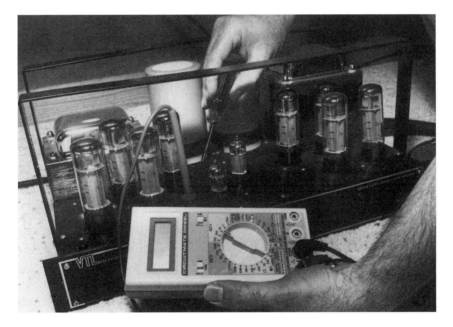

When you buy replacement output tubes, you can specify matched pairs or matched quartets of tubes. These are tubes with matched electrical characteristics for better performance. An amplifier with a single push-pull pair per channel will benefit from matched pairs, and an amplifier with four output tubes per channel needs matched quartets. Expect to pay a premium for tube matching, however.

Tubed amplifiers are often referred to by the operating principle of their output stage: *triode* or *pentode*. A triode is the simplest of all tubes, having just three elements: the plate, cathode, and grid (these are described in detail in Appendix B). Triode power amplifiers generally sound the best, but aren't very powerful, and are much more expensive "per watt" than other tubed designs. An output tube functioning in pentode mode engages another tube element—the screen grid—increasing power output for the same tube. Many tubed amplifiers have a switch to select between triode and pentode mode.

Note that tubed amplifiers don't increase their power outputs as the load impedance drops, as do solid-state units. The output transformer acts as a current source rather than as a voltage source, decreasing the available output voltage when the load impedance drops. This is one reason why tubed amplifiers have less tight and extended bass than solid-state power amplifiers.

Finally, tubed power-amplifier power supplies are different from their solid-state counterparts. The voltage to the output-stage supply rail is many hundreds of volts, not ±60V to ±100V as in a solid-state amplifier's power supplies. Because of this very high voltage, the reservoir capacitors generally store vastly more energy than the reservoir caps in a solid-state amp. This so-called "B+" voltage is lethal—the voltage is very high, and the capacitors can deliver lots of current through your body. Energy storage is measured in Joules, and is a function of the capacitance in Farads (a unit of stored charge) multiplied by the voltage. Given the same capacitance (same number of microfarads), but ten times the voltage, power supplies for a tubed amplifier may have ten times the energy storage of a solid-state amplifier. This factor may account for tube amplifiers' subjectively greater power output for the same rated power compared to a solid-state amplifier.

Tubed amplifiers must also supply the tube filaments (the part that glows) with a low DC voltage. In low-signal-level tubes, the number beginning the tube's designation (6DJ8, 12AX7, for examples) indicates the filament voltage, usually 6V or 12V.

From a design standpoint, tubed power amplifiers have several inherent advantages. First, they're simple. Comparing the schematics of solid-state and tubed amplifiers reveals many more parts in the transistor design, most of them in the signal path. Fewer parts in the signal path generally results in better sound. When overdriven, tubes *soft-clip*, meaning that the waveform gently rounds off rather than immediately flattening. Moreover, a tubed amplifier in clipping produces primarily second- and third-harmonic distortion, which is fairly benign sonically. A transistor amplifier driven into clipping immediately produces a whole series of very objectionable upper-order odd harmonics (fifth, seventh, ninth). In fact, 10% second-harmonic distortion is less annoying than 0.5% seventh-harmonic distortion.

Power Amplifier Specifications and Measurements

Power amplifiers share many specifications with other components (signal-to-noise ratio, crosstalk, etc.), yet have some unique specifications and measurements.

Power amplifiers typically have input impedances of between 20 and 150k ohms, with 47k ohms being a standard for unbalanced inputs. This is a high enough value to ensure the power amplifier's input stage won't *load* the preamplifier's output and put a strain on the preamplifier's output stage.

Power-amplifier *output impedance* is usually a very low value, between 0.05 and 0.5 ohms for solid-state amplifiers. Tubed power amplifiers have a higher output impedance—about 0.5 ohms to as high as 2 ohms. Think of output impedance as a resistor in series with the output transistors (or output transformer in a tubed amplifier) connected to the load. Low output impedance is a desirable design goal; when the power amplifier's output impedance becomes a significant fraction of the loudspeaker's input impedance, the two might interact. The result can be peaks and dips in the amplifier's frequency response caused by the loudspeaker's impedance change with frequency. A high output impedance is also characterized by soft bass, lack of bass extension and dynamics, and less bass control. A power amplifier with a high output impedance is less able to control woofer motion. Output impedance is related to an amplifier's *damping factor*—the ability to control cone motion in the loudspeaker. The higher the damping factor, the better. Note that damping factor is specified at the amplifier's output terminals; resistance in loudspeaker cables can dramatically decrease the effective damping factor, particularly in long cable runs.

Gain refers to the ratio between the input and output voltages. Gain can be specified as the ratio between the voltages, or in decibels (dB). Typical gain is about 26dB, or a ratio of 20:1 (i.e., an input voltage of 1V will produce 20V at the output).

Input sensitivity is the input voltage required to drive the amplifier to clipping. A typical value is between 0.775V and 2V, with about 1.2V being standard. If the power amplifier has a very high input sensitivity (less than 0.5V), the preamplifier's volume control will be extremely insensitive—you'll get plenty of volume with the knob barely turned up. Conversely, a low-output preamp driving a low sensitivity power amplifier (2V, say), will require the preamp's volume control to be turned up very high to get adequate volume.

We've talked a lot about maximum output power; now let's see how it's measured. With a dummy load (a huge power resistor) connected to the amplifier's output, we drive the power-amplifier input with a gradually increasing voltage. Distortion in the output is monitored and plotted as a function of output power. When the amplifier clips, the distortion shoots up instantaneously. The clipping point, defined as 1% THD, is the amplifier's maximum output power. This test is performed with the amplifier driving 8-ohm, 4-ohm, and 2-ohm loads. The results are combined and plotted on a single graph (Fig.6-8a). The farther to the right the "knee" in the distortion trace, the higher the output power at clipping. Note that some THD vs. output power plots have only two traces, at 8 ohms and 4 ohms. These amplifiers cannot be tested into 2 ohms at full output power: the power supply fuses blow, or the amplifier simply shuts down.

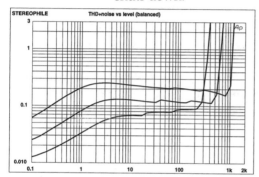 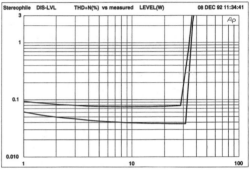

Fig. 6-8a and b The power output vs. THD curves show an amplifier's maximum output power, and how well it can increase its power into low-impedance loads. (Courtesy *Stereophile*)

By combining the three traces on one graph, we can quickly assess the amplifier's ability to increase its output power into low impedances. The greater the distance between the curves' knees, the greater the amplifier's ability to drive current into low-impedance loads. Fig.6-8b is an amplifier with very little ability to deliver current into a 4-ohm load. It produced 15.6dBW at 8 ohms, and 12.5dBW at 4 ohms.

By contrast, Fig.6-8a is an amplifier behaving as a virtually perfect voltage source, maintaining its voltage and doubling its current output each time the load impedance is halved. This graph, the result of an actual measurement, reveals exemplary—and extraordinary—performance. The performance would have been even better if the AC line voltage had not drooped under the heavy load, decreasing the raw power available to the amplifier. The amplifier pulled so much current out of the wall that the AC line voltage dropped from 118V to 106V. This amplifier put out 325W into 8 ohms (25.1dBW), 635W into 4 ohms (25dBW), 1066W into 2 ohms (24.3dBW), and 1548W into 1 ohm (22.9dBW). Moreover, it was perfectly stable driving this tremendous amount of current into such a low impedance.

Another way to look at a power amplifier's output capability is the *power-bandwidth* test. The amplifier is driven to just below clipping, and the output power is plotted against frequency. We're looking for the widest bandwidth over which the amplifier can maintain full output power.

How much peak power an amplifier can deliver on transient signals (musical peaks) above its continuous power rating is called its *dynamic headroom*, expressed in dB. A power amplifier rated at 100Wpc (RMS) that can deliver 200Wpc for brief periods (measured in milliseconds) without severe distortion is said to have 3dB of dynamic headroom (double the RMS rating). An amplifier's dynamic headroom says a lot about its subjective ability to play loudly.

In addition to plotting THD against output level to find the clipping point, a power amplifier's distortion can be measured at low signal levels and plotted as a function of frequency. Fig.6-9 is such a graph. The lower trace is THD+N (THD plus Noise) measured at 1W into 8 ohms. The next higher trace is at 2W into 4 ohms, and the upper trace (highest distortion) is with 4W driving a 2-ohm load. The lower the distortion and noise, the better, with less than 0.2% constituting good performance.

Fig. 6-9 THD vs. frequency measurements show how the amplifier's distortion changes into low-impedance loads.

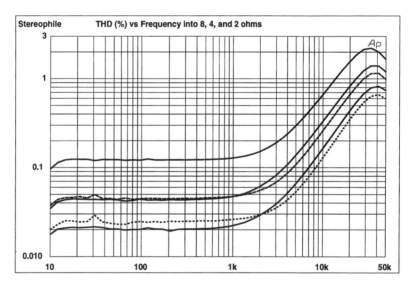

Courtesy *Stereophile*

Although knowing how much *total* distortion a power amplifier generates is important, an examination of the harmonic distortion *spectrum* is more instructive. We want to know *which* harmonics are present; some harmonic products are much more audible and annoying than others. As stated earlier in the discussion of tubed power amplifiers, 10% second-harmonic distortion is less musically objectionable than 0.5% seventh-harmonic distortion. We thus need to characterize the distortion spectrum rather than use a single THD figure.

To do this, we drive the power amplifier at two-thirds rated power with a 50Hz sinewave and perform an FFT (Fast Fourier Transform) on the output signal. The FFT captures the amplifier's output signal and transforms it into its constituent parts. (Specifically, the FFT can convert a time-domain signal into the frequency domain.) An FFT produces a plot showing energy vs. frequency, shown in Fig.6-10a. We can see that this particular amplifier generates an entire series of harmonic-distortion products. The distortion spectra of Fig.6-10b, however, shows a much lower level of distortion products.

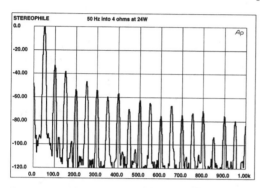 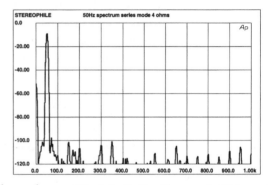

Fig. 6-10a and b An FFT of an amplifier's output shows the amplifier's individual harmonic-distortion components. (Courtesy *Stereophile*)

Note that harmonic distortion in itself isn't that significant a criterion in the evaluation of power amplifiers. This specification has been touted as the definitive performance parameter of power amplifiers and receivers. Many amplifiers with 0.5% distortion sound just fine, while others with 0.01% sound awful. As described in Chapter 1, THD can be reduced by increasing the amount of negative feedback in the amplifier. Unfortunately, negative feedback introduces other problems that make the amplifier sound worse. Although it's interesting to know how much harmonic distortion an amplifier produces and the spectral distribution of those distortion products, I wouldn't let THD figures influence my purchasing decision.

Intermodulation Distortion (IMD) is distortion that occurs when two signals of different frequencies are amplified simultaneously—something that happens all the time in music. IMD creates *sum-and-difference* signals of the signals being amplified. For example, if we drive a power amplifier with 10kHz and 1kHz sinewaves, the amplifier produces an output signal containing the original test tones at 10kHz and 1kHz, but also *intermodulation products* at 11kHz (the sum of the two signals) and at 9kHz (the difference between the two signals). Though the 9kHz and 11kHz sum-and-difference IMD products are usually the highest in amplitude, IMD creates an infinite series of distortion products.

Intermodulation distortion is expressed as a percentage of the test signals and the intermodulation products, with typical values falling between 0.01% and 0.2%. IMD test signals are often 60Hz and 7kHz (combined at equal amplitude, or with the higher-frequency tone at one-quarter the amplitude (-12.04dB), or 19kHz and 20kHz (at equal amplitude). To test with the latter signals, the amplifier is driven at two-thirds rated power and an FFT is performed on the amplifier's output. We look for the 1kHz difference signal (20kHz minus 19kHz); the lower its amplitude, the better. This 1kHz intermodulation product is usually between 55dB down (55dB below the test signal amplitude) and 75dB down. We also sometimes see a family of sideband signals around the test tones.

Some of these measurements are unique to power amplifiers. Other, more universal measurements include those of frequency response, crosstalk, and signal-to-noise ratio. It's rare, however, for a modern amplifier to depart from flat frequency response. Note that the sonic characteristics of bright, extended, forward, etc. are not functions of the amplifier's frequency response.

Finally, a power amplifier is said to be *inverting* if it reverses absolute polarity between its input and output. A *non-inverting* amplifier maintains the same polarity between input and output. Because most gain stages invert absolute polarity, an inverting amplifier usually has an odd number of gain stages, while a non-inverting amplifier has an even number; one isn't necessarily better than the other. (See "Absolute Polarity" in Appendix A.)

7 Loudspeakers

Introduction and Overview

Of all the components in your audio system, the loudspeaker's job is by far the most difficult. The loudspeaker is expected to reproduce the sound of a pipe organ, the human voice, and a violin through the same electro-mechanical device—all at the same levels of believability, and all at the same time. The tonal range of virtually every instrument in the orchestra is to be reproduced from a relatively tiny box. This frequency span of ten octaves represents a sound wavelength difference of 60 feet in the bass to about half an inch in the treble.

It's no wonder that loudspeaker designers often spend their lives battling the laws of physics to produce musical and practical loudspeakers. Unlike other high-end designers who create a variety of products, the loudspeaker designer is singular in focus, dedicated in intent, and deeply committed to the unique blend of science and art that is loudspeaker design.

Although even the best loudspeakers can't convince us that we're hearing live music, they nonetheless are miraculous in what they *can* do. Think about this: a pair of loudspeakers converts two two-dimensional electrical signals into a three-dimensional "soundspace" spread out before the listener. Instruments seem to exist as *objects* in space; we hear the violin here, the brass over there, and the percussion behind the other instruments. A vocalist appears as a palpable, tangible image exactly between the two loudspeakers. The front of the listening room seems to disappear, replaced by the music. It's so easy to close our eyes and be transported into the musical event.

To achieve this experience in your home, however, you must carefully choose the best loudspeakers from among the literally thousands of models on the market. As we'll see, choosing loudspeakers is a challenging job.

How to Choose a Loudspeaker

The world abounds in poor-quality, even dreadful, loudspeakers. What's more, some very bad loudspeakers are expensive, while superlative models may sell for a fraction of an inferior model's price. There is often little relationship between price and musical performance.

This situation offers the loudspeaker shopper both promise and peril. The promise is finding an excellent loudspeaker for a reasonable price. The peril is sorting through mediocre models to find the rare gems that offer either high absolute performance, or sound quality far above what their price would indicate.

This is where reviews come in handy. Reviewers who write for audio magazines hear lots of loudspeakers (at dealers, trade shows, and consumer shows), but review only those that sound promising. This weeds out the vast majority of underachievers. Of the loudspeakers that *are* reviewed, some are found to be unacceptably flawed, others are good for the money, while a select few are star overachievers that clearly outperform their similarly priced rivals.

The place to start loudspeaker shopping, therefore, is in the pages of a reputable magazine with high standards for what constitutes good loudspeaker performance. Be wary of magazines that end every review with a "competent for the money" recommendation. Not all loudspeakers are good; therefore, not all reviews should be positive. The tone of the reviews—positive or negative—should reflect the wide variation in performance and value found in the marketplace.

After you've read lots of loudspeaker reviews, make up your short list of products to audition from the *crème de la crème*. There are several criteria to apply in making this short list to ensure that you get the best loudspeaker for your individual needs. As you apply each criterion described, the list of candidate loudspeakers will get shorter and shorter, thus easing your decision-making process. If you find yourself with too few choices at the end of the process, go back and revise your criteria. For example, if you find a loudspeaker that's perfect in all ways but size, you may want to find the extra space in your living room. Similarly, an ideal loudspeaker costing a little more than you intended on paying may suggest a budget revision. As you go through this selection process, remember that the perfect loudspeaker for you is probably out there. Be selective and have high standards. You'll be rewarded by a much higher level of musical performance than you thought you could afford.

1) Size, Appearance, and Integration in the Home

After you've designated a place for your loudspeakers, determine the optimum loudspeaker size for your room—the urban apartment dweller will likely have tighter size constraints than the suburban audiophile. Some listeners will want the loudspeakers to be discreet and blend into the room; others will make the hi-fi system the room's center of activity and won't mind large loudspeakers. When choosing a place for your loudspeakers, keep in mind that their placement is a critical factor in how your system sounds. (Chapter 4 includes an in-depth treatment of loudspeaker positioning.)

The loudspeaker's appearance is also a factor to consider. An inexpensive, vinyl-covered box would be out of place in an elegantly furnished home. Many high-end loudspeakers are finished in beautiful cabinetry that will complement any decor. This level of finish can, however, add greatly to the loudspeaker's price.

Note that many small loudspeakers must be mounted on high-quality stands to achieve top performance. The term "bookshelf" loudspeaker shouldn't be used in the same breath as "high-end"; you can never get good performance from a loudspeaker put in a bookshelf. Small loudspeakers mounted on stands, however, often provide terrific imaging, great clarity in midband and treble, and can easily "disappear" into the music. On the down side, small loudspeakers have restricted dynamics, no low bass, and won't play as loudly as their floorstanding counterparts.

2) Match the Loudspeaker to Your Electronics

The loudspeaker should be matched to the rest of your system, both electrically and musically. A loudspeaker that may work well in one system may not be ideal for another system—or another listener.

Let's start with the loudspeaker's electrical characteristics. The power amplifier and loudspeaker should be thought of as an interactive combination; the power amplifier will behave differently when driving different loudspeakers. Consequently, the loudspeaker should be chosen for the amplifier that will drive it.

The first electrical consideration is the loudspeaker's sensitivity—how much sound the loudspeaker will produce for a given amount of amplifier power. Loudspeakers are rated for sensitivity by measuring their sound pressure level (SPL) from one meter away while they are being fed 1 watt (1W) of power. For example, a sensitivity specification of "88dB 1W/1m" indicates that this particular loudspeaker will produce a sound pressure level of 88dB when driven with an input power of 1 watt, measured at a distance of 1 meter. High-end loudspeakers vary in sensitivity between 80dB 1W/1m and 93dB 1W/1m.

A loudspeaker's sensitivity is a significant factor in determining how well it will work with a given power-amplifier output wattage. To produce a loud sound (100dB), a loudspeaker rated at 80dB sensitivity would require 100W. A loudspeaker with a sensitivity of 95dB would require only 3W to produce the same sound pressure level. Each 3dB decrease in sensitivity requires double the amplifier power to produce the same SPL. (This topic is discussed in greater technical detail in Chapter 6, "Power Amplifiers.")

Another electrical factor to consider is the loudspeaker's load impedance. This is the electrical resistance the power amp meets when driving the loudspeaker. The lower the loudspeaker's impedance, the more demand is placed on the power amp. If you choose low-impedance loudspeakers, be certain the power amp will drive them adequately. (See Chapter 6 for a full technical discussion of loudspeaker impedance as it relates to amplifier power.)

On a musical level, you should select as sonically neutral a loudspeaker as possible. If you have a bright-sounding CD player or power amp, it's a big mistake to buy a loudspeaker that sounds soft and rolled-off in the treble to compensate. Instead, change your CD player or amplifier.

Another mistake is to drive high-quality loudspeakers with poor amplification or source components. The high-quality loudspeakers will resolve much more information than lesser loudspeakers—including imperfections in the electronics and source components. Match the loudspeaker quality to the rest of your system. (Use the guidelines in Chapter 2 to set a loudspeaker budget within the context of the cost of your entire system.)

3) Musical Preference and Listening Habits

If the perfect loudspeaker existed, it would work equally well for chamber music or heavy metal. But because the perfect loudspeaker remains a mythical beast, musical preferences must play a part in choosing a loudspeaker. If you listen to mostly small-scale classical music, choral works, or classical guitar, a small mini-monitor would probably be your best choice. Conversely, rock listeners need the dynamics, low-frequency extension, and bass power of a large full-range system. Different loudspeakers have strengths and weaknesses in different areas; by matching your listening tastes to the loudspeaker, you'll get the best performance in the areas that matter most to you.

Other Guidelines in Choosing Loudspeakers

In addition to these specific recommendations, there are some general guidelines you should follow in order to get the most loudspeaker for the money.

First, buy from a specialty audio retailer who can properly demonstrate the loudspeaker, advise you on system matching, and tell you the pros and cons of each candidate. Many high-end audio dealers will let you try the loudspeaker in your home with your own electronics and music before you buy.

Take advantage of the dealer's knowledge—and reward him with the sale. It's not only unfair to the dealer to use his expensive showroom and knowledgeable salespeople to find out which product to buy, then look for the loudspeaker elsewhere at a lower price, but it prevents you from establishing a mutually beneficial relationship with him (or her).

In general, loudspeakers made by companies who make *only* loudspeakers are better than those from companies who also make a full line of electronics. Loudspeaker design may be an afterthought to the electronics manufacturer—something to fill out the line. Conversely, many high-end loudspeaker companies have an almost obsessive dedication to the art of loudspeaker design. Their products' superior performance often reflects this commitment.

Don't buy a loudspeaker based on technical claims. Some products claiming superiority in one aspect of their performance may overlook other, more important aspects. Loudspeaker design requires a balanced approach, not reliance on some new "wonder" technology that may have been invented by the loudspeaker manufacturer's marketing department. Forget about the technical hype and listen to how the loudspeaker reproduces *music*. You'll know if the loudspeaker is any good or not.

Don't base your loudspeaker purchases on brand loyalty or longevity. Many well-known and respected names in loudspeaker design of ten or twenty years ago are no longer competitive. The companies may still produce loudspeakers, but the recent products' inferior performance only throws into relief the extent of the manufacturer's decline. The brands the general public thinks represent the state of the art are actually among the worst-sounding loudspeakers available. These companies were either bought by multinational business conglomerates who didn't care about quality and just wanted to exploit the brand name, or the company has forsaken high performance for mass-market sales. Ironically, the companies with the biggest advertising spreads in the mainstream magazines often offer the lowest-performance loudspeakers.

The general public also believes that the larger the loudspeaker and the more drivers it has, the better it is. Given the same retail price, there is often an *inverse* relationship between size/driver count and sonic performance. A good two-way loudspeaker with a 6" woofer/midrange and a tweeter in a small cabinet is likely to be vastly better than a similarly priced four-way in a large, floorstanding enclosure. Two high-quality drivers are much better than four mediocre ones. Further, the larger the cabinet, the more difficult—and expensive—it is to make it free from vibrations that degrade the sound. The four-way's more extensive crossover will require more parts; the two-way can use just a few higher-quality crossover parts. The large loudspeaker will probably be unlistenable; the small two-way may be superbly musical.

If both of these loudspeakers were shown in a catalog and offered at the same price, however, the large, inferior system would outsell the high-quality two-way by at least ten times. The perceived value is much higher.

The bottom line is that you can't tell anything about a loudspeaker until you listen to it. In the next section, we'll examine common problems in loudspeakers and how to choose one that provides the highest level of musical performance.

Finding the Right Loudspeaker—Before You Buy

You've done your homework, read reviews, and narrowed down your list of candidate loudspeakers based on the criteria described earlier—you know what you want. Now it's time to go out and listen. This is a critical part of shopping for a loudspeaker, and one that should be approached carefully. Rather than buying a pair of speakers on your first visit to a dealer, consider this initial audition to be simply the next step. Don't be in a hurry to buy the first loudspeaker you like. Even if it sounds very good to you, you won't know *how* good it is until you've auditioned several products.

Audition the loudspeaker with a wide range of familiar recordings *of your own choosing*. Remember that a dealer's strategic selection of music can highlight a loudspeaker's best qualities and conceal its weaknesses—after all, his job is to present his products in the best light. Further, auditioning with only audiophile-quality recordings won't tell you much about how the loudspeaker will perform with the music you'll be playing at home, most of which was likely *not* recorded to high audiophile standards. Still, audiophile recordings are excellent for discovering specific performance aspects of a loudspeaker. The music selected for auditioning should therefore be a combination of your favorite music, and diagnostic recordings chosen to reveal different aspects of the loudspeaker's performance. When listening to your favorite music, forget about specific sonic characteristics and pay attention to how much you're enjoying the sound. Shift into the analytical mode only when playing the diagnostic recordings. Characterize the sound quality according to the sonic criteria described in Chapter 3, and later in this chapter.

Visit the dealer when business is slow so you can spend at least an hour with the loudspeaker. Some loudspeakers are appealing at first, then lose their luster as their flaws begin to emerge over time. The time to lose patience with the speakers is in the dealer's showroom, not a week after you've bought them. And don't try to audition more than two loudspeakers in a single dealer visit. If you must choose between three models, select between the first two on one visit, then return to compare the winner of the first audition with the third contender. Finally, you should choose how long to listen to each candidate.

Some loudspeakers have different tonal balances at different listening heights. Be sure to audition the loudspeaker at the same listening height as your listening chair at home. A typical listening height is 36", measured from the floor to your ears. Further, some loudspeakers with first-order crossovers sound different if you sit too close to them. When in the showroom, move back and forth a few feet to be certain the loudspeaker will sound the same as it should at your listening distance at home.

Make sure the loudspeakers are driven by electronics and source components of comparable quality to your components. It's easy to become infatuated with a delicious sound in a dealer's showroom, only to be disappointed when you connect the loudspeakers to less good electronics. Ideally, you should drive the loudspeakers under audition with at least the same power amp as you have at home, or as you intend to buy with the loudspeakers.

Of course, the best way to audition loudspeakers is in your own home—you're under no pressure, you can listen for as long as you like, and you can hear how the loudspeaker performs with your electronics and in your listening room. Home audition removes much of the guesswork from choosing a loudspeaker. But because it's impractical to take every contender home, and because many dealers will not allow this, save your home auditioning for only those loudspeakers you are seriously considering.

What to Listen For

There are several common flaws in loudspeaker performance that you should listen for. Though some of these flaws are unavoidable in the lower price ranges, a loudspeaker exhibiting too many of them should be quickly passed over.

Listen for thick, slow, and tubby bass. One of the most annoying characteristics of poor loudspeakers is colored, peaky, and pitchless bass. You should hear distinct pitches in bass notes, not a low-frequency, "one-note" growling away under the music.

Certain bass notes shouldn't sound louder than others. Listen to solo piano with descending or ascending lines played evenly in the instrument's left-hand, or lower, registers. Each note should be clearly articulated, and even in tone and volume. If one note sounds different from the others, it's an indication that the loudspeaker may have a problem at that frequency.

The bottom end should be tight, clean, and "quick." When it comes to bass, quality is more important than quantity. Poor-quality bass is a constant reminder that the music is being artificially reproduced, making it that much harder to hear only the music and not the loudspeakers. The paradigm of what bass should *not* sound like is a "boom truck." Those car stereos are designed for maximum output at a single frequency, not articulate and tuneful bass. Unfortunately, *more* bass is generally an indicator of *worse* bass performance in low- to moderately-priced loudspeakers. A lean, tight, and articulate bass is preferable in the long run to the plodding boominess that characterizes some loudspeakers.

Listen to kick drum and bass guitar working together. You should hear the bass drum's dynamic envelope through the bass guitar. The drum should lock in rhythmically rather than seem to lag slightly behind the bass guitar. A loudspeaker that gets this wrong dilutes rhythmic power, making the rhythm sound sluggish, even slower. But when you listen to a loudspeaker that gets this right, you'll find your foot tapping and hear a more "upbeat" and involving quality to the music.

Midrange coloration is a particularly annoying problem with some loudspeakers. Fortunately, coloration levels are vastly lower in today's loudspeakers than they were even ten years ago. Still, there are lots of colored loudspeakers out there. These can be identified by their "cupped hands" coloration on vocals, a nasal quality, or an emphasis on certain vowel sounds. A problem a little higher in frequency is manifested as a "clangy" piano sound. A good loudspeaker will present vocals as pure, open, and seeming to exist independently of the loudspeakers. Midrange problems will also make the music sound as though it is coming out of boxes rather than existing in space.

Poor treble performance is characterized by grainy or dirty sound to violins, cymbals, and vocal sibilants ("s" and "ch" sounds). Cymbals should not splash across the soundstage, sounding like bursts of undifferentiated white noise. Instead, the treble should be integrated with the rest of the music and not call attention to itself. The treble shouldn't sound hard and metallic; instead, cymbals should have some delicacy, texture, and pitch. If you find that a pair of speakers is making you aware of the treble as a separate component of the music, keep looking.

Another thing to listen for in loudspeakers is their ability to play loudly without congestion. The sounds of some loudspeakers will be fine at low levels, but will congeal and produce a giant roar when pushed to high volumes. Listen to orchestral music with crescendos—the sound should not collapse and coarsen during loud, complex passages.

Finally, the loudspeakers should "disappear" into the soundstage. A good pair of loudspeakers will unfold the music in space before you, giving no clue that the sound is coming from two boxes placed at opposite sides of the room. Singers should be heard as pinpoint, palpable images directly between the loudspeakers (if that's how they've been recorded). The sonic image of an instrument should not "pull" to one side or another when the instrument moves between registers. The music should sound open and transparent, not thick, murky, or opaque. Overall, the less you're aware of the loudspeakers, the better.

Some loudspeakers with less than high-end aspirations have colorations intentionally designed into them. The bass is made to be big and fat, the treble excessively bright to give the illusion of "clarity." Such speakers are usually extremely sensitive, so that they'll play loudly in comparisons made without level matching. These loudspeakers may impress the unwary in a two-minute demonstration, but will become extremely annoying not long after you've brought them home.

Finally, the surest sign that a loudspeaker will provide long-term musical satisfaction at home is if, during the audition, you find yourself greatly enjoying the music and not thinking about loudspeakers at all.

The flaws described here are only the most obvious loudspeaker problems; a full description of what to listen for in reproduced music in general is found in Chapter 3.

Loudspeaker Types and How They Work

Many mechanisms for making air move in response to an electrical signal have been tried over the years. Three methods of creating sound work well enough—and are practical enough—to be used in commercially available products. These are the dynamic driver, the ribbon transducer, and the electrostatic panel. A loudspeaker using dynamic drivers is often called a *box* loudspeaker because the drivers are mounted in a box-like enclosure. Ribbon and electrostatic loudspeakers are called *planar* loudspeakers because they're often mounted in flat, open panels.

The Dynamic Driver

The most popular loudspeaker technology is without question the *dynamic driver*. Loudspeakers using dynamic drivers are identifiable by their familiar cones and domes. The dynamic driver's popularity is due to its many advantages: good dynamic range, high power handling, high sensitivity, relatively simple design, and ruggedness. Dynamic drivers are also called *point-source* transducers because the sound is produced from a point in space.

Dynamic loudspeakers use a combination of different-sized dynamic drivers. The low frequencies are reproduced by a paper or plastic cone *woofer*. High frequencies are generated by a *tweeter*, usually employing a small metal or fabric dome. Some loudspeakers use a third dynamic driver, the *midrange*, to reproduce frequencies in the middle of the audio band.

Despite the very different designs of these drivers, they all operate on the same principle (Fig.7-1). The *voice coil* is a length of wire wound around a thin cylinder called the voice-coil former. The former is attached to the diaphragm, either a cone or dome. Electrical current from the amplifier flows through the voice coil, which is mounted in a permanent magnetic field whose magnetic lines of flux cross the gap between two permanent magnets. According to the "right-hand rule" of physics, the circular flow of current through the voice-coil windings generates magnetic forces that are directed along the voice-coil's axis. The interaction between the fluctuating field of voice coil and the fixed magnetic field in the gap produces axial forces that move the voice coil back and forth, carrying the diaphragm with it. The faster the audio signal alternates, the faster the diaphragm moves and the higher the frequency produced. The amount of diaphragm movement is called *excursion*. Dynamic drivers are also called *moving-coil* drivers, for obvious reasons.

Other elements of the dynamic driver include a *spider* that suspends the voice coil in place as it moves back and forth. The *basket* is a stamped metal or cast structure holding the entire assembly together. A ring of compliant material, called the *surround*, attaches the cone to the basket rim.

Fig. 7-1
Dynamic driver
cutaway (Courtesy
Thiel) and cross
section

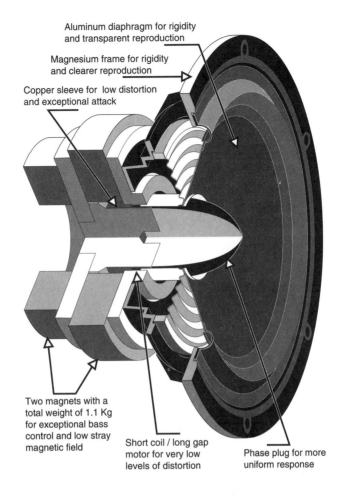

Aluminum diaphragm for rigidity
and transparent reproduction

Magnesium frame for rigidity
and clearer reproduction

Copper sleeve for low distortion
and exceptional attack

Two magnets with a
total weight of 1.1 Kg
for exceptional bass
control and low stray
magnetic field

Short coil / long gap
motor for very low
levels of distortion

Phase plug for more
uniform response

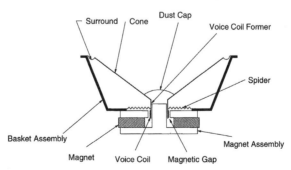

Surround   Cone   Dust Cap   Voice Coil Former

Spider

Basket Assembly   Magnet Assembly

Magnet   Voice Coil   Magnetic Gap

Common cone materials include paper, paper impregnated with a
stiffening agent, a form of plastic such as polypropylene, or exotic
materials such as Kevlar. Metal has also been used in woofer cones, as
have sandwiched layers of different materials. Designers use these
materials to prevent a form of distortion called *breakup*. Breakup occurs
when the cone material flexes instead of moving as a perfect piston.

Because the cone is driven at a small area at the inside (an area the size of the voice coil), the cone tends to flex and produce non-linear distortion. Stiff cone materials help prevent breakup.

The cone should also be lightweight. A lighter cone will respond faster to transient signals and have less mass that would make the cone continue to move after the drive signal has ceased. Loudspeaker designers therefore search for cone materials that combine high stiffness with low mass.

Tweeters work on the same principle, but typically use a dome instead of a cone. Common dome materials include plastic, woven fiber coated with a rubbery material, aluminum, titanium, aluminum alloys, and gold-plated aluminum. Unlike cone drivers that are driven at the cone apex, dome diaphragms are driven at the dome's outer perimeter. Most dome tweeters use Ferrofluid to cool the tweeter's small voice coil. The first breakup mode of modern dome tweeters is above 25kHz, well out of the audible range.

Midrange drivers are smaller versions of the cone woofer. Some, however, use dome diaphragms instead of cones.

The Planar Magnetic Transducer

The next popular driver technology is the *planar magnetic* transducer, also known as a *ribbon driver*. Although the term "ribbon" and "planar magnetic" are often used interchangeably, a true ribbon driver is actually a sub-class of the planar magnetic driver. Let's look at a true ribbon first.

Instead of using a cone attached to a voice coil suspended in a magnetic field, a ribbon driver uses a strip of material (usually aluminum) as a diaphragm suspended between the north-south poles of two magnets (as shown in Fig.7-2). The ribbon is often pleated for additional strength. The audio signal travels through the electrically conductive ribbon, creating a magnetic field around the ribbon that interacts with the permanent magnetic field. This causes the ribbon to move back and forth, creating sound. In effect, the ribbon functions as both the voice coil and the diaphragm. The ribbon can be thought of as the voice coil stretched out over the ribbon's length.

In all other planar magnetic transducers, a flat or slightly curved diaphragm is driven by an electromagnetic conductor like a voice coil that is stretched out in straight-line segments. In most designs, the diaphragm is a sheet of plastic, with the electrical conductors bonded to the surface, operating in the magnetic field mounted on the frame. The flat metal conductor provides the driving force, but it occupies only a portion of the diaphragm area.

Fig. 7-2 A true
ribbon driver

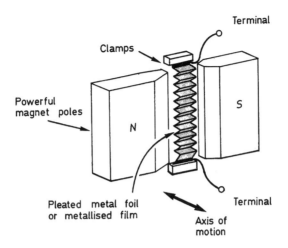

Courtesy Martin Colloms, *High Performance Loudspeakers*

A planar driver is a true ribbon only if the diaphragm is conductive, and the audio signal flows directly through the diaphragm, rather than through conductors bonded to a diaphragm, as in planar magnetic drivers. (Despite this semantic distinction, I'll use the term "ribbon" throughout the rest of this section, with the understanding that it covers both true ribbons and planar magnetic drivers.)

Ribbon drivers like the one in Fig.7-2 are called *line-source* transducers because they produce sound over a line rather than from a point, as does a dynamic loudspeaker. Moreover, a ribbon's radiation pattern changes dramatically with frequency. At low frequencies, when the ribbon's length is short compared to the wavelength of sound, the ribbon will act as a point source and produce sound in a sphere around the ribbon—just like a point-source woofer. As the frequency increases and the wavelength of sound approaches the ribbon's dimensions, the radiation pattern becomes more narrow, like a cylinder around the ribbon instead of a sphere. At very high frequencies, the ribbon radiates horizontally but not vertically. This can be an advantage in the listening room: the listener hears more direct sound from the loudspeaker and less reflection from the sidewalls and ceiling. Pinpoint imaging and the ability to hear a concert hall's acoustic signature are hallmarks of good ribbon loudspeakers.

The main technical advantage of a ribbon over a moving-coil driver is the ribbon's vastly lower mass. Instead of using a heavy cone, voice coil, and voice-coil former to move air, the only thing moving in a ribbon is a very thin strip of aluminum. A ribbon tweeter may have one quarter the mass and ten times the radiating area of a dome tweeter's diaphragm. Low mass is a high design goal: the diaphragm can respond more quickly to transient signals. In addition, a low-mass diaphragm will stop moving immediately after the input signal has ceased. The ribbon starts and stops faster than a dynamic driver, allowing it to more faithfully reproduce transient musical information.

Another great advantage enjoyed by ribbons is the lack of a box. As we'll see in the section of this chapter on loudspeaker enclosures, the enclosure can greatly degrade a loudspeaker's performance. The ribbon driver is usually mounted in a flat, open-air panel, that radiates sound to the rear as well as to the front. A loudspeaker that radiates sound to the front and rear is called a *di-pole*. Not having to compensate for an enclosure makes it easier for a ribbon loudspeaker to achieve stunning clarity and lifelike musical timbres.

A full-range ribbon loudspeaker is illustrated in Fig.7-3. The large area is the low-frequency ribbon driver, the thin strip is the mid- and high-frequency ribbon driver. Note that the panel is tapered to smooth out the bass response. The large panel extends the system's bass response: when the average baffle dimension approaches half the wavelength, front-to-rear cancellation reduces bass output. Thus, the larger the panel, the deeper the low-frequency extension.

Fig. 7-3 A full-range ribbon loudspeaker

Courtesy Apogee Acoustics, Inc.

Ribbon loudspeakers are characterized by a remarkable ability to produce extremely clean and quick transients—such as those of plucked acoustic guitar strings. The sound seems to start and stop suddenly, just as one hears from the live instrument. In addition, the sound has an openness, clarity, and transparency often unmatched by dynamic drivers. Finally, the ribbon's di-polar nature produces a huge sense of space, air, and soundstage depth (provided this spatial information was captured in the recording). Some argue, however, that this sense of depth is artificially *produced* by ribbon loudspeakers, rather than being a *re*production of the actual recording.

Despite their often stunning sound quality, ribbon drivers have several disadvantages. The first is low sensitivity; it takes lots of amplifier power to drive them. Second, ribbons inherently have a very low impedance, often a fraction of an ohm. Most ribbon drivers therefore have an impedance matching transformer in the crossover to present a higher impedance to the power amp. Design of the transformer is therefore critical to prevent it from degrading the sound quality.

From a practical standpoint, ribbon-based loudspeakers are more difficult to position in a room. Small variations in placement can greatly change the sound, due primarily to their di-polar radiating pattern. This di-polar pattern requires that the ribbon loudspeakers be placed well away from the rear wall, and that the rear wall be acoustically benign.

Low-profile, ribbon-based loudspeakers with the ribbon top at the same height as the listener's ears will have a radically different treble balance if the listener moves up or down a few inches. Some ribbon loudspeakers have a tilt adjustment to allow the user to set the correct treble balance for her listening height.

Ribbons also have a resonant frequency which, if excited, produces the horrible sound of crinkling aluminum foil. Consequently, the ribbon must be used within strict frequency-band limits. Still, a properly set up ribbon loudspeaker can be nothing short of magical.

Ribbon drivers don't necessarily have to be long and thin. Variations on ribbon technology have produced drivers having many of the desirable characteristics of ribbons, but few of the disadvantages. The superb 1″ ribbon tweeter developed by Genesis Technologies is a good example. The device is a 2.5μm thick (one tenth of one thousandth of an inch) layer of Kapton with a voice coil etched on it that sits in a magnetic field. The diaphragm is of extremely low mass (it has less mass than the air in front of it), and its point-source radiation pattern allows it to be used like a conventional dome tweeter. Because the voice coil is etched onto the diaphragm, the Genesis tweeter (Fig.7-4) is technically a planar magnetic driver, not a ribbon. Infinity's EMIT (Electromotive Induction Tweeter) is another example of a planar magnetic driver.

Fig. 7-4 A planar tweeter

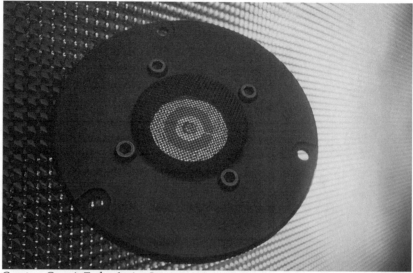

Courtesy Genesis Technologies, Inc.

Fig. 7-5 "Hybrid" loudspeakers combine dynamic woofers with ribbon midrange/tweeters.

Courtesy Apogee Acoustics, Inc.

Finally, some loudspeakers use a combination of dynamic and ribbon transducers to take advantage of both technologies. These so-called *hybrid* loudspeakers typically use a dynamic woofer in an enclosure to reproduce bass, and a ribbon midrange/tweeter. The hybrid technique brings the advantages of ribbon drivers to a lower price level (ribbon woofers are big and expensive), and exploits the advantages of each technology while avoiding the drawbacks. A ribbon/dynamic hybrid loudspeaker range is illustrated in Fig.7-5.

The Electrostatic Driver

Like the ribbon transducer, an electrostatic driver uses a thin membrane to make air move. But that's where the similarities end. While both dynamic and ribbon loudspeakers are electromagnetic transducers—they operate by electrically-induced magnetic interaction—the electrostatic loudspeaker operates on the completely different principle of electrostatic interaction.

The electrostatic driver is like a giant capacitor. One element is a thin moveable membrane—sometimes made of Mylar—stretched between two static elements called *stators* (Fig.7-6). The membrane is charged to a very high voltage with respect to the stators. The audio signal is applied to the stators, which create electrostatic fields around them that vary in response to the audio signal. The varying electrostatic fields generated around the stators interact with the membrane's fixed electrostatic field, pushing and pulling the membrane to produce sound. One stator pulls the membrane, the other pushes it.

Fig. 7-6 An electrostatic driver

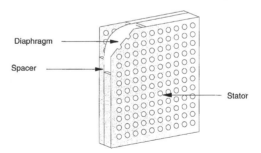

Diaphragm

Spacer

Stator

Courtesy Martin-Logan, Ltd.

The voltages involved in an electrostatic loudspeaker are very high. The polarizing voltage applied to the diaphragm may be as high as ten thousand volts (10kV). In addition, the audio signal is stepped up from several tens of volts to several thousand volts by a *step-up transformer* inside the electrostatic loudspeaker. These high voltages are necessary to produce the electrostatic fields around the diaphragm and stators.

To prevent arcing—the electrical charge jumping between elements—the stators are often coated with an insulating material. Still, if an electrostatic loudspeaker is overdriven, the electrostatic field strips free electrons from the oxygen in the air, making it *ionized*; this provides a conductive path for the charge. Large diaphragm excursions—i.e., a loud playing level—put the diaphragm closer to the stators and also encourage arcing. Arcing can destroy electrostatic panels by punching small holes in the membrane.

Electrostatic panels are often divided into several smaller panels to reduce the effects of diaphragm resonances. Some panels are curved to reduce the *lobing* effect (uneven radiation pattern) at high frequencies. Lobing occurs when the wavelength of sound is small compared to the diaphragm.

Electrostatic panels are of even lighter weight than planar magnetic transducers. Unlike the ribbon driver, in which the diaphragm carries the audio signal current, the electrostatic panel has no conductor attached to it. The diaphragm can therefore be very thin, often less than 0.001". Such a low mass allows the diaphragm to start and stop very quickly, improving transient response. And because the electrostatic panel is driven uniformly over its entire area, the panel is less prone to breakup. Both the electromagnetic planar loudspeaker (a ribbon) and the electrostatic planar loudspeaker enjoy the benefits of limited dispersion, and thus less reflected sound arriving at the listener. Like ribbon loudspeakers, electrostatic loudspeakers also have no enclosure to degrade the sound.

In the debit column, electrostatic loudspeakers must be plugged into an AC outlet to generate the polarizing voltage. Their unusual high-frequency dispersion pattern can also create what *Stereophile* magazine founder J. Gordon Holt calls the "vertical venetian-blind effect," in which the tonal balance changes rapidly and repeatedly as you move your head from side to side. Because the electrostatic is naturally a di-polar radiator, room placement is more critical. Electrostatics also tend to be insensitive, requiring large power amplifiers. The load impedance they present to the amplifier is also more reactive than that of dynamic loudspeakers, further taxing the power amp. Nor will they play as loudly as dynamic loudspeakers; they aren't noted for their dynamic impact, power, or deep bass. Instead, electrostatics excel in transparency, delicacy, transient response, resolution of detail, stunning imaging, and overall musical coherence. (A full-range electrostatic loudspeaker is illustrated in Fig.7-7.)

Electrostatic loudspeakers can be augmented with separate dynamic woofers or a subwoofer to extend the low-frequency response and provide some dynamic impact. Other electrostatics achieve the same result in a more convenient package: dynamic woofers in enclosures

Fig. 7-7 A full-range electrostatic loudspeaker

Courtesy Martin-Logan, Ltd.

mated to the electrostatic panels. Some of these designs achieve the best qualities of both the dynamic driver and electrostatic panel. (An example of a hybrid electrostatic/dynamic loudspeaker is illustrated in Fig.7-8.)

One great benefit of full-range ribbons and full-range electrostatics is the absence of a crossover; the diaphragm is driven by the entire audio signal. This prevents any discontinuities in the sound as different frequencies are reproduced by different drivers. In addition, removing the resistors, capacitors, and inductors found in crossovers greatly increases the full-range planar's transparency and harmonic coherence.

Even hybrid planars put the crossover frequency between the dynamic woofer and the planar panel very low (below 700Hz), so there's no discontinuity between drivers through most of the audible spectrum.

Fig. 7-8 An electrostatic/ dynamic hybrid loudspeaker

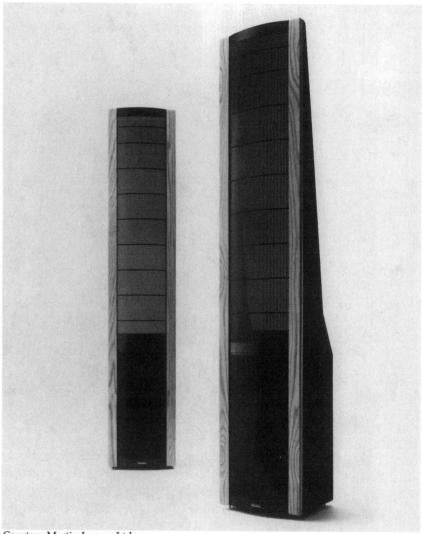

Courtesy Martin-Logan, Ltd.

The Di-polar Radiation Patterns of Ribbons and Electrostatics

Because planar loudspeakers (ribbons and electrostatics) are mounted in an open frame rather than an enclosed box, they radiate sound equally from the front and back. The term "di-polar" describes this radiation pattern. This is contrasted with *point source* loudspeakers, whose drivers are mounted on the front of a box. Point-source loudspeakers are usually associated with dynamic drivers, but any type of driver in an enclosed cabinet qualifies as a point-source loudspeaker.

The di-polar radiation patterns of ribbons and electrostatics make using them very different from point-source loudspeakers. Because they launch just as much energy to the rear as they do to the front, positioning a di-pole is more critical, particularly their distance from the rear wall. Di-poles need a significant space behind them to work well. In addition, the rear wall's acoustic properties have a much greater influence over the sound. A few attempts have been made to absorb a ribbon's rear energy and thus make placement easier, but these have been largely unsuccessful.

Ribbons and electrostatics also tend to have much narrower radiation patterns than point-source loudspeakers. Consequently, the listener hears much more of the loudspeaker's direct sound and much less sound reflected from the floor, ceiling, and sidewalls. This is particularly true in the midrange and treble, where the radiation pattern becomes cylindrical. The result is often a greatly improved transparency and more natural timbre. (The effects of these reflections are discussed in Chapter 4.) The negative effects of this tendency for planar loudspeakers to "beam" at high frequencies is a disturbing shift in the tonal balance with small side-to-side head motions, the "vertical-venetian blind effect" described earlier. This tendency can be minimized with a curved diaphragm (seen in the earlier photographs of an electrostatic loudspeaker) or by electrically segmenting the diaphragm.

Loudspeaker Enclosures

The enclosure in which a set of drivers is mounted has an enormous effect on its reproduced sound quality; in fact, the enclosure is as important as the drive units themselves. The ideal enclosure would produce no sound of its own, and would thus not interfere with the sound produced by the drivers. One of the factors that makes current high-end loudspeakers so much better than mass-produced products is the extreme length to which some manufacturers go to prevent the enclosure from degrading the sound. Mass-market manufacturers generally skimp on the enclosure because it adds very little to the perceived value to the uninformed consumer.

Let's look at why a loudspeaker needs an enclosure, and survey the most popular enclosure types.

An enclosure around a woofer is required to prevent the woofer's rear-radiated wave from combining with the woofer's front-radiated wave. When the woofer moves forward, a compression wave is launched at the front, and a rarefaction (negative pressure) wave of equal intensity is launched to the rear. Because low frequencies can refract (bend) around small objects such as a woofer, the rear wave will combine with the front wave and cancel the sound. The result is reduced bass output. Putting an enclosure around the woofer prevents this cancellation and allows the loudspeaker to generate low frequencies.

In addition to preventing this front-to-back cancellation, the enclosure should also present the optimum environment for the drivers, particularly the woofer. This is called *loading*. Various loading techniques have evolved to optimize the way the woofer operates in the cabinet. The most common techniques are the *infinite baffle* (also called air suspension in smaller enclosures), *reflex* (also called a ported enclosure), and *transmission line*.

Infinite Baffle

The infinite baffle simply seals the enclosure around the driver rear to prevent the two waves from meeting. In theory, such an enclosure approximates a baffle of "infinite" size; in fact, it wraps around the driver. The air inside the sealed enclosure acts as a spring, compressing when the woofer moves in and creating some resistance to woofer motion. The sealed enclosure has a low-frequency rolloff slope of 12dB per octave; this means that, one octave below the system's resonant frequency, the output will be reduced by 12dB.

Reflex Loading

A reflex enclosure extends the low-frequency cutoff point by venting some of the energy inside the enclosure to the outside. The duct in a reflex system delays the inside wave so it emerges in-phase with the front-firing wave. The rear wave from the port thus reinforces rather than cancels the front wave. A loading material such as long-hair wool or fiberglass batting is sometimes put in the duct to smooth response peaks.

Reflex loading has three main advantages. First, it increases a loudspeaker's maximum acoustic output level—it will play louder. Second, it can make a loudspeaker more sensitive—it needs less amplifier power to achieve the same volume. Third, it can lower a loudspeaker's cutoff frequency—the bass goes deeper. Note that these benefits are not available simultaneously; the acoustic gain of a bass-reflex system can be used either to increase a loudspeaker's sensitivity or to extend its cutoff frequency, but not both.

Although, given the same woofer and enclosure volume, a reflex system's low-frequency cutoff point is lower than that of a sealed system; the reflex system's bass rolls off at a much faster rate—24dB per octave—compared to the sealed enclosure's 12dB per octave rolloff. Subjectively, a higher cutoff frequency with a more gradual rolloff provides a more satisfying feeling of bass fullness than a lower cutoff frequency and steeper rolloff. Reflex loading is more often used in small enclosures, which trade low-frequency extension and sensitivity for compactness. However, a small reflex enclosure can still achieve some of the extension and sensitivity of a larger cabinet. A comparison of low-frequency cutoff points and rolloff slopes is illustrated in Fig.7-9.

Fig. 7-9
Frequency response characteristics of vented and sealed enclosures

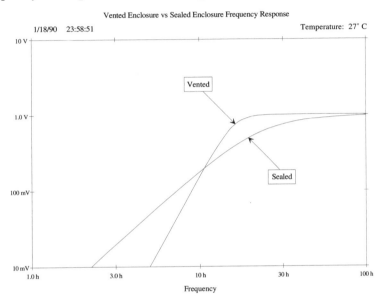

Fig. 7-10
Transient response comparison between vented and sealed enclosures

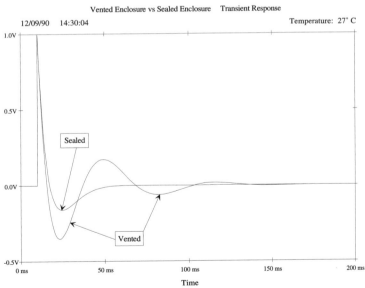

Fig. 7-9 and Fig. 7-10 courtesy Avalon Acoustics, Inc.

Reflex systems have gotten a bad name, both because of inherent limitations and poor implementation in certain products. Reflex systems tend to be boomy, slow, fat, and poorly defined in the bass. They often have an annoying thumpy quality. Transient response is also poor, making kick drum sound sluggish rather than taut and fast. A sealed enclosure generally will have much better transient response and better bass definition, at the cost of lower sensitivity and less deep bass extension. (Fig.7-10 shows the difference in transient response between a reflex system and a sealed enclosure.)

Passive Radiators

A variation on the reflex system is the *passive radiator*, also called an auxiliary bass radiator, or *ABR*. This is usually a flat diaphragm not electrically connected. Instead, the diaphragm covers what would have been the port in the reflex system. The passive radiator smoothes out any response peaks, and eliminates a ported system's wind noise and port resonances. Fig.7-11 shows a loudspeaker using a passive radiator (the flat diaphragm between the woofer and midrange drivers). This particular design has exploited the advantages of reflex loading while minimizing the drawbacks.

Transmission Line Loading

Another loading technique is the transmission line. In a transmission line, the rear wave from the woofer is channeled through a folded labyrinth or duct—the transmission line—filled with absorbent material such as wool. The end of the transmission line appears at the outside of the enclosure, just as in a reflex system. The acoustic energy traveling down the transmission line is absorbed, with the goal of no acoustic output at the end of the transmission line. In theory, the woofer's rear wave is dissipated in the line. This isn't the case in practice: most transmission lines have some output at the end of the line, causing them to function partially as reflex systems. Because the line must be at least as long as the lowest wavelength to be absorbed, transmission-line enclosures are usually very large. Proponents of transmission lines argue that the springiness of sealed enclosures is not the ideal environment for the woofer.

Transmission-line loudspeakers have extremely deep extension and the ability to deliver very loud and very clean bass with an effortless quality not heard from other loading designs.

Fig. 7-11 A dynamic loudspeaker using a passive radiator

Courtesy Thiel

Isobarik Loading

A fourth type of loading, used by Linn Products, is called Isobarik (Linn's trade name), or by the more descriptive generic term *constant pressure chamber*. In the Isobarik system, a second woofer is mounted directly behind the first woofer and driven in parallel with it. As the front woofer moves back, so does the second, maintaining a constant pressure inside the chamber separating the two woofers. This technique offers deeper low-frequency extension, higher power handling, greater linearity, and reduced standing-wave reflections inside the enclosure. Isobarik loading reduces sensitivity because the amplifier must drive two woofers, although only one produces acoustic output. Two woofers mounted in an Isobarik configuration can be modeled as a single woofer whose greater mass and compliance delivers useful deep bass in an enclosure half the usual size. (Isobarik loading is illustrated in Fig.7-12.)

Fig. 7-12
Isobarik loading

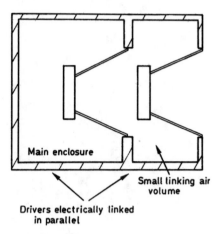

Courtesy Martin Colloms, *High Performance Loudspeakers*

The Finite Baffle

The only examples of the finite-baffle, or open-panel, loading technique are planar loudspeakers such as the full-range ribbon system illustrated in Fig.7-3. The finite baffle has a rolloff of only 6dB per octave until the driver's free-air resonance frequency, then drops at the rate of 18dB per octave.

System Q

A critical factor in each of these loading techniques is the system's low-frequency alignment, or steepness. This is called its "quality," or "Q" factor. Specifically, a loudspeaker's Q equals the resonant peak's center frequency divided by the peak's bandwidth. The steeper the resonance, the higher the Q.

The woofer has its own resonant Q, which is modified by the enclosure's Q to reach some optimum figure, usually a Q of 0.7. A "critically damped" system having a Q of 0.5 provides perfect transient response, with no detectable hangover. A Q of less than 1 is considered *overdamped*, while a Q of more than 1 is *underdamped*. These terms refer to the system's anechoic response—whether the response is up or down at the resonant frequency—and not the loudspeaker's response as modified by a listening room.

Fig.7-13 shows a comparison of different alignments. Subjectively, an underdamped alignment has lots of bass, but lacks tightness, has poor pitch definition, and tends to produce a "one note" bass. An overdamped alignment produces a very tight, clean, but decidedly lean bass response. An overdamped loudspeaker has less bass, but that bass is of higher quality than the bass from an underdamped system. Most loudspeaker designers aim for a Q of 0.7 to reach a compromise between frequency response (down only 3dB at resonance) and good transient response (very slight hangover.) Some designers maintain that a Q of 0.5 is ideal, and that a higher Q produces poorer quality bass.

Fig. 7-13 A comparison of system Qs

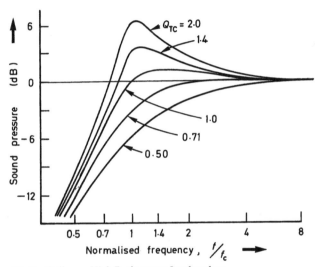

Courtesy Martin Colloms, *High Performance Loudspeakers*

Enclosure Resonances

One mechanism by which a loudspeaker enclosure colors the sound is cabinet vibration. When excited by the sound from the driver (primarily the woofer), the enclosure resonates at its natural resonant frequencies. This causes the enclosure panels to move, producing sound. The enclosure thus becomes an acoustic source: we hear music not only from the drivers, but also from the enclosure. The sound produced by enclosure vibration covers only a narrow band centered on the panel's resonant frequency. The loudspeaker thus has greater acoustical output at that frequency. Consequently, cabinet resonances change the timbre of instruments that have most of their energy in the bass and lower midrange. You can easily hear cabinet resonances on a double bass or cello as changes in timbre occur at certain notes. Some musical instruments exhibit a similar phenomenon, producing "wolf notes."

Enclosure resonances not only color the sound spectrally (changing the timbre), they smear the time relationships in music. The enclosure stores energy and releases that energy slowly over time. When the next note is sounded, the cabinet is still producing energy from the previous note. Loudspeakers with severe cabinet resonances produce smeared, blurred bass instead of a taut, quick, clean, and articulate foundation for the music.

The acoustic output of a vibrating surface such as a loudspeaker enclosure panel is a function of the excursion of the panel and the panel's surface area. A large panel excited enough that you can feel it vibrating when you play music will color the sound of that loudspeaker.

Enclosure resonances can be measured and displayed in a way that lets you intuitively see how bad the resonances are. (This technique is discussed later in this chapter under loudspeaker measurements.) An easier way of judging an enclosure's inertness is the "knuckle rap" test. Simply knock on the enclosure and listen to the resulting sound. A relatively resonance-free enclosure will produce a dull thud, while a poorly damped enclosure will generate a ringing tone. You can also drive the loudspeaker with a swept sinewave with your hand on the enclosure. When the sinewave reaches the enclosure's resonant frequencies, the enclosure will vibrate and you will hear a change in the tone's sound. The less the enclosure vibrates and the fewer the resonant modes, the better.

Designers use thick, vibration-resistant material for loudspeaker enclosures. Generally, the thicker the material, the better. Most loudspeakers use 3/4" Medium Density Fiberboard (MDF). MDF 1" thick is better; some manufacturers use 3/4" on the side panels and top, and 1" MDF for the front baffle, which is more prone to vibration. Braces are also used to reduce the area of unsupported panels and make the enclosure more rigid. (A heavily braced enclosure is illustrated in Fig.7-14.)

The enclosure can also degrade a loudspeaker's performance by creating diffraction from the cabinet edges, grille frame, and even the drivers' mounting bolts. Diffraction is a re-radiation of energy when the sound encounters a discontinuity in the cabinet, such as at the enclosure edge. (Diffraction is illustrated conceptually in Fig.7-15.) Diffracted energy combines with the direct sound to produce ripples in the frequency response; i.e., colorations. Rounded baffles, recessed drivers and mounting bolts, and low-profile grille frames all contribute to reduced diffraction.

Fig. 7-14 A
heavily braced
loudspeaker
enclosure
(Courtesy Thiel)

Fig. 7-15
Diffraction
causes re-radia-
tion of the sound
from cabinet
edges

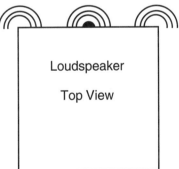

Some loudspeaker enclosures are tilted back to align the drivers in
time. This tilt aligns the acoustic centers of all the drivers so that their
outputs arrive at the listener at the same time (see Fig.7-16). Fig.7-11
shown earlier illustrates an aligned cabinet, as well as the diffraction-

reducing techniques described in the previous paragraph. Although many loudspeaker manufacturers use the words "time-aligned", the term is actually a trademarked name of loudspeaker designer Ed Long.

Fig. 7-16 A sloped baffle causes the sound from each driver to reach the listener simultaneously. (Courtesy Thiel)

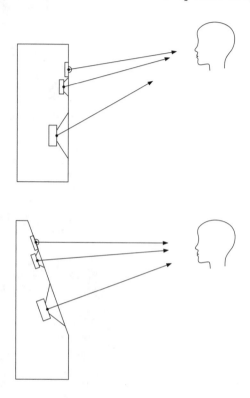

Crossovers

A loudspeaker crossover is an electronic circuit inside the loudspeaker that separates the frequency spectrum into different ranges and sends each to the appropriate drive unit: bass to the woofer, mid-band frequencies to the midrange, and treble to the tweeter (in a 3-way loudspeaker). (Fig.7-17 illustrates this process.)

A crossover is made up of capacitors, inductors, and resistors. These elements selectively filter the wide-band signal driving the loudspeaker, creating the appropriate filter characteristics for the particular drivers used in the loudspeaker. A crossover can be seen in the photograph of Fig.7-14 shown earlier.

A crossover is described by its *cutoff frequency* and *slope*. The cutoff frequency is the frequency at which the transition from one drive unit to the next occurs—between the woofer and midrange, for example. The crossover's slope refers to the rolloff's steepness. A slope's steepness describes how rapidly the response is attenuated above or below the cutoff frequency. For example, a *first-order* crossover has a slope of 6dB per octave, meaning that the signal to the drive unit is halved (a reduction of 6dB) one octave above the cutoff frequency. If the woofer crossover circuit produces a cutoff frequency of 1kHz, the signal will be rolled off by 6dB one octave higher, at 2kHz. In other words, the woofer will receive energy at 2kHz, but will be down in level by 6dB. A first-order filter producing a 6dB per octave slope is the slowest and most gentle rolloff used.

Fig. 7-17 A crossover divides the frequency spectrum.

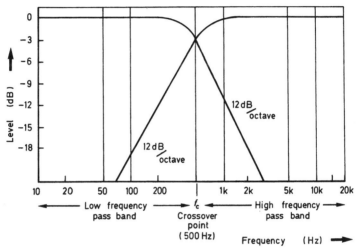

Courtesy Martin Colloms, *High Performance Loudspeakers*

The next-steeper filter is the *second-order* filter, which produces a rolloff of 12dB per octave. Using the preceding example, a woofer crossed over at 1kHz would still receive energy at 2kHz, but that energy would be reduced by 12dB at 2kHz. A *third-order* crossover has a slope of 18dB per octave, and a *fourth-order* crossover produces the very steep slope of 24dB per octave. Using the previous example , the fourth-order filter would still pass 2kHz to the woofer, but the amplitude would be down by 24dB (1/16th the amplitude). Fig.7-18 compares crossover slopes.

Typical crossover points for a two-way loudspeaker are between 800Hz and 2.5kHz. A three-way system may have crossover frequencies of 800Hz and 3kHz. The woofer reproduces frequencies up to 800Hz, the midrange driver handles the band between 800Hz and 3kHz, and the tweeter reproduces frequencies above 3kHz.

Note that the actual *acoustic* crossover slope—the drive unit's acoustical output—may be different from the *electrical* slope produced by the crossover. If a drive unit is operated close to its own rolloff, this inherent rolloff is added to the electrical rolloff. For example, a woofer rolling off naturally at 1kHz at 6dB per octave will produce an acoustic rolloff of 12dB per octave when crossed over at 1kHz with an electrical 6dB per octave filter.

Fig. 7-18 A comparison of crossover slopes

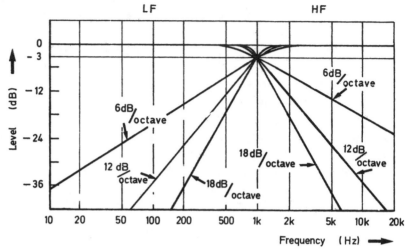

Courtesy Martin Colloms, *High Performance Loudspeakers*

The crossover slope chosen has a large effect on the loudspeaker's performance. A shallow first-order slope produces the least phase error in the crossover region between the two drive units. The two drive units operate in-phase at both the crossover point and outside the crossover region. A fourth-order filter, by contrast, can cause a phase lag of 360° between drivers. Loudspeakers with second-order crossovers usually have their tweeters wired in inverse polarity to provide correct acoustic polarity.

Simple first-order crossovers have inherently better time behavior than more complex crossovers. First-order crossovers, however, produce considerable overlap between drive units. There is a relatively wide band over which both the woofer and midrange produce the same frequency, and over which the midrange and tweeter overlap. This can cause dips in the frequency response if the listener's ears aren't exactly the same distance from each drive unit. The outputs of the two drivers can combine, causing destructive interference and irregular amplitude response. The listener should also sit farther away from a loudspeaker with first-order crossovers to give the individual drive units more time to integrate.

In addition, first-order crossovers can allow the tweeter to be overdriven by midrange frequencies in the octaves below the nominal cutoff frequency. A tweeter's excursion quadruples with each halving of frequency, moving four times farther at 1kHz than at 2kHz, given the same drive level. At 500Hz its motion quadruples again, if it isn't rolled off by the tweeter's fundamental resonance. Although a 6dB per octave crossover slope halves the drive signal with each halving of frequency, that's not enough to offset the tweeter's natural quadrupling of excursion. Proponents of high-order crossovers suggest that any phase advantages of first-order slopes are more than offset by the inherent overlap between drivers, and concomitant potential for driver overload.

A factor in choosing crossover points is the individual drivers' directivity—their dispersion of sound with frequency. As the frequency a driver is producing increases, the dispersion pattern becomes narrower. In other words, bass is omnidirectional and high frequencies tend to beam. Driver size and crossover points are chosen so that there is no discontinuity in directivity between drivers. This is why you don't see a 10" woofer mated to a 1" tweeter.

Some loudspeakers can be connected to a power amp with two runs of loudspeaker cable, a technique called *bi-wiring*. A loudspeaker with provision for bi-wiring has separate high-pass and low-pass crossover sections, along with two pairs of input terminals. You should always take advantage of this feature by running two pairs of loudspeaker cables. Bi-wiring can significantly improve a loudspeaker's sound. (Bi-wiring is discussed in more detail in Chapter 11.)

Crossovers vary greatly in the quality of parts used. Budget loudspeakers will likely use *iron-core* inductors rather than the preferable *air-core* types. Air-core inductors are larger and more expensive than iron-core coils, but are immune to saturation. Similarly, lower-cost loudspeakers use *electrolytic* capacitors rather than the more expensive *plastic-film* types. Electrolytic capacitors are sometimes *bypassed* with small-value polypropylene or other similar high-quality capacitors. Bypassing is putting a smaller-value, higher-quality capacitor in parallel with the larger-value capacitor. Some of the sonic virtues of high-quality capacitors are retained, accompanied by the cost and size advantages of an electrolytic capacitor. Some loudspeakers are wired internally with high-end cable rather than generic cable.

Finally, a few loudspeakers, notably those designed and made by Meridian Audio, accept a digital input signal and implement the crossover in the digital domain with Digital Signal Processing (DSP) chips. Instead of subjecting the audio signal to resistors, capacitors, and inductors, DSP crossovers separate the frequency spectrum by performing mathematical processing on the digital audio data. DSP crossovers can have perfect time behavior, any slope and frequency the designer wants without regard for component limitations or tolerances, and employ equalization to the individual drive units. These so-called "digital loudspeakers" must incorporate a digital-to-analog converter and a power amp for each drive unit inside the loudspeaker cabinet.

Subwoofers

A subwoofer is a loudspeaker that produces low frequencies that augment and extend the bass output of a full-range loudspeaker system. The term "subwoofer" is grossly misused to describe any low-frequency driver system in its own enclosure. But "subwoofer" actually means "below the woofer," and should be reserved for those products extending bass response to below 20Hz. A low-frequency driver in an enclosure extending to 40Hz and used with small satellite speakers is more properly called a woofer.

Subwoofers come in two varieties: *passive* and *active*. A passive subwoofer is just a woofer or woofers in an enclosure that must be driven by an external amplifier. In one variation of the passive woofer, the same stereo amplifier driving the main loudspeakers also powers the woofer. This is the least desirable subwoofer connection method. The full-range output from a power amp is input to the subwoofer. A crossover in the subwoofer removes low frequencies from the signal and outputs the filtered signal to the main loudspeakers. This technique puts an additional crossover in the signal path that filters speaker-level signals.

A better way of driving the subwoofer is with an *electronic crossover* and separate power amp. This method separates the bass from the signal driving the main loudspeakers at line-level, which is much less harmful to the signal than speaker-level filtering. Moreover, adding a separate power amp for the subwoofer greatly increases the system's dynamic range and frees the main loudspeaker amplifier from the burden of driving the subwoofer. Adding a line-level crossover and power amp turns the passive subwoofer into an active subwoofer.

A self-contained active subwoofer combines a subwoofer with a line-level crossover and power amp in one cabinet, eliminating the need for separate boxes and amplifiers. Fig.7-19 shows an active subwoofer input panel. As you can see in the photo, the subwoofer has line-level inputs (which are fed from the preamplifier), line-level outputs (which drive the power amp), and a volume control for the subwoofer level. The line-level output is filtered to roll off low-frequency energy to the main loudspeakers. This crossover frequency is often adjustable on subwoofers to allow the user to select the frequency that provides the best integration with the main loudspeakers (more on this later).

Adding an actively powered subwoofer to your system can greatly increase its dynamic range, bass extension, midrange clarity, and ability to play louder without strain. The additional amplifier power and low-frequency driver allow the system to reproduce musical peaks at higher levels. Moreover, removing low frequencies from the signal driving the main loudspeakers lets the main loudspeakers play louder because they don't have to reproduce low frequencies. In addition, the midrange often becomes clearer because the woofer cone isn't moving back and forth trying to reproduce low bass.

Fig. 7-19 An active subwoofer input and control panel

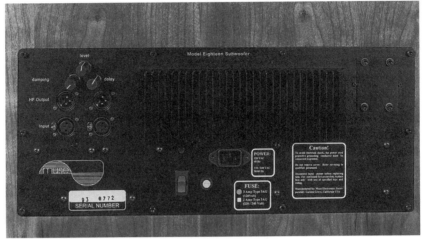

Courtesy Muse Electronics, Inc.

Now for the bad news. More often than not, subwoofers degrade a playback system's musical performance. Either the subwoofer is poorly engineered (and many are), or the subwoofer is set up incorrectly.

Let's first look at the theoretical problems of subwoofers. First, most subwoofers—passive or active—add electronics to the signal path. The active subwoofer's internal crossover may not be of the highest quality. Even well-executed crossovers can still degrade the purity of very high-quality source components, preamplifiers, and power amps. This drawback can be avoided by running the main loudspeakers full-range (no rolloff), but you lose the dynamic advantages and additional midrange clarity conferred by keeping low frequencies out of the main loudspeakers.

Second, the subwoofer's bass quality may be poor. The subwoofer may move lots of air and provide deep extension, but a poorly executed subwoofer often adds a booming thumpiness to the low end. Rather than increasing our ability to hear what's going on in the bass, a subwoofer often obscures musical information.

Third, a subwoofer can fail to integrate musically with the main loudspeakers. Very low frequencies reproduced by the subwoofer sound different from the midbass produced by the main loudspeakers. The result is an extremely distracting discontinuity in the musical fabric. This discontinuity is manifested as a change in the sound of acoustic bass in different registers. Ascending and descending lines should flow past the crossover point with no perceptible change in timbre or dynamics.

Another factor that can make integrating a subwoofer difficult is matching a slow and heavy subwoofer to taut, lean, and articulate main loudspeakers. Put another way, an underdamped subwoofer won't work very well with an overdamped loudspeaker. This condition makes it even harder for the subwoofer to integrate.

Fourth, subwoofers often trade tight control, pitch resolution, and lack of overhang for greater sensitivity or deeper extension. Consequently, many subwoofers are fat, slow, and completely lacking detail. Finally, a subwoofer can fill the listening room with lots of low-frequency energy, exciting room-resonance modes that may not have been that bothersome without the subwoofer. Placement is therefore critical—you can't just put a subwoofer in the corner out of the way and expect musical results. This problem of room-mode excitation can be ameliorated by two subwoofers; they excite different room modes, substantially smoothing the room's low-frequency response.

All of these problems are exacerbated by a tendency to set subwoofer levels way too high. The reasoning is that if you pay good money for something, you want to hear what it does. But if you're *aware* of the subwoofer's presence, either its level is set too high, it isn't positioned correctly, or the subwoofer has been poorly designed. The highest compliment one can pay a subwoofer is that its contribution can't be heard directly. It should blend seamlessly into the musical fabric, not call attention to itself.

It's a rare subwoofer that doesn't degrade the signal driving the main loudspeakers, integrates well with main loudspeakers, has tight and controlled bass, and can improve a playback system. You should therefore approach the purchase of a subwoofer with great caution. I can think of only a few true subwoofers worth owning. Further, most well-engineered, full-range loudspeakers go deep enough in the bass for most listeners. Very little program material requires 16Hz extension; most analog recordings have very little energy below about 30Hz.

Subwoofer Technical Overview

Subwoofer designers face the same low-frequency loading choices that full-range loudspeaker designers do. The woofer or woofers can be loaded into an infinite baffle (sealed box), reflex enclosure (ported), or a transmission line. Transmission-line subwoofers are rare because of the large cabinet required for such a design. Instead, the sealed box and reflex are the most popular.

The simplest subwoofer is a single driver—usually a 10" or 12" unit—in a reflex enclosure. The choice of a reflex design keeps the cabinet down to a moderate size and maintains reasonable sensitivity. A larger enclosure extends the subwoofer's bass response, but is more expensive to manufacture, particularly if the enclosure is properly constructed (well braced).

The sealed-box subwoofer is less common due to its inherently higher cutoff frequency. A sealed subwoofer would have to be enormous to achieve sub-20Hz extension. Most sealed-box units are actually woofers, not subwoofers. They trade extension for higher-quality bass: better control, faster transient response, and excellent pitch definition, for example.

Some subwoofers are mounted in *bandpass* enclosures that limit the system's bandwidth with both electrical and acoustical filtering. In a bandpass enclosure (illustrated in Fig.7-20), the woofer drives a chamber which is vented through a port or slot. The woofer is often loaded in a smaller rear chamber. This version is called a *second-order* bandpass alignment. Porting the smaller chamber results in a *fourth-order* alignment, producing steeper filter slopes. Advantages of bandpass enclosures include greater low-frequency extension, lower distortion, greater sensitivity, and higher power handling. In the sixth-order bandpass subwoofer illustrated in Fig.7-21, two 10" woofers fire into a slot running down the center of the enclosure.

Fig. 7-20 A bandpass enclosure

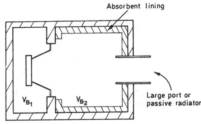

Courtesy Martin Colloms, *High Performance Loudspeakers*

Fig. 7-21 A sixth-order bandpass subwoofer (top view)

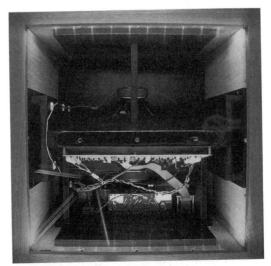

Courtesy Muse Electronics, Inc.

Subwoofers usually offer a choice of crossover frequencies, typically 80Hz, 120Hz, and 180Hz. A higher crossover frequency would be selected for mini-monitors than for a full-range loudspeaker. Generally, the lower the crossover frequency, the better; the main loudspeaker's bass is probably better than the subwoofer's, and a low crossover frequency moves any crossover discontinuity lower in frequency, where it will be less audible. Too low a crossover frequency will, however, burden small loudspeakers with excessive bass and reduce the system's power handling and maximum listening level.

Another variable in subwoofer crossovers is the slope. Most use second-order filters (12dB per octave) or higher. Ideally, the crossover frequency and slope would be tailored to the particular loudspeaker used with the subwoofer. But because the subwoofer manufacturer doesn't know which loudspeakers will be used with the subwoofer, these parameters are compromised for good performance with a variety of loudspeakers.

The subwoofer illustrated earlier, in Figs.7-19 and 7-21, presents a unique solution to this quandary. The subwoofer accepts small circuit boards that vary the crossover's slope and frequency to match specific loudspeakers. Several dozen such boards—called "personality cards"—are available for this subwoofer. The user orders the appropriate personality card for her loudspeakers, plugs it in, and has a crossover specially tailored to her particular loudspeakers.

Some subwoofers have a "delay" control that lets you align in time the subwoofer's wavefront with that of the main loudspeakers. You can accomplish the same thing by moving the subwoofer forward or backward in relation to the main loudspeakers—a much less practical approach than the delay control.

If the subwoofer has a delay control, there's a simple trick for aligning the subwoofer with the main loudspeakers. Drive the system with a sinewave at exactly the crossover frequency. This causes the main loudspeakers and the subwoofer to reproduce the same signal. Now invert the polarity of the main loudspeakers relative to the subwoofer by reversing the red and black leads going to the loudspeakers. Sit in the listening chair and have an assistant slowly vary the delay control until you hear the least sound. Return the loudspeaker leads to their former polarity. The delay control is now set optimally. Here's why. When the main loudspeakers' and subwoofer's wavefronts are 180° out of phase with each other, the greatest cancellation (the least sound heard) will occur. When the loudspeaker leads are returned to the correct position (removing the 180° phase shift), the subwoofer and loudspeaker outputs are maximally in-phase.

When positioning a subwoofer, follow the guidelines on loudspeaker placement outlined in Chapter 4. Avoid putting the subwoofer in a corner. If the subwoofer is between the loudspeakers, it should be as far behind them as possible to avoid degrading the soundstage created by the main loudspeakers.

Loudspeaker Stands

Small loudspeakers should be mounted on stands for best performance. In fact, the stands' quality can greatly affect the reproduced sound. Flimsy, lightweight stands should be avoided in favor of solid, rigid models. The stands should include spikes on their bottoms to better couple the stand and loudspeaker to the floor. Some loudspeaker stands can be filled with sand or lead shot for *mass loading*, making them more inert and less prone to vibrating. A great loudspeaker on a poor stand will significantly degrade the loudspeaker's performance. Plan to spend several hundred dollars on stands. Consider the stands' cost when comparing a floorstanding loudspeaker to one requiring stand mounting.

The interface between the loudspeaker and stand also deserves attention. Spikes, cones, and other isolation devices (see Chapter 12) can allow the loudspeaker to perform at its best. In a series of experiments attempting to quantify the effects of different materials installed between stand and loudspeaker, an accelerometer was attached to the loudspeaker's side panel and its vibration measured with the different interface materials. The loudspeaker's resonant "signature" was changed considerably with the stand, and again with the material or device between the stand and loudspeaker. Most effective was a small ball of Bostik Blue-Tak placed at each corner of the speaker stand. This very effective yet inexpensive interface is a sticky, gum-like material available at hardware stores (a lifetime supply costs about $2). John Atkinson of *Stereophile* magazine pioneered this technique of examining the loudspeaker/stand interface; his full report can be found in the September, 1992 issue.

Loudspeaker Specifications and Measurements

There is more correlation between a loudspeaker's measured performance and its sound quality than with any other component in an audio system. A loudspeaker that measures as having a treble rolloff will likely sound dull and rolled off; a loudspeaker with a measured rising top end will likely sound bright and forward. Having said that however, I must stress that you can't judge a loudspeaker's performance by reading its measurements. Although good measured performance is valued, the loudspeaker's musical abilities in the listening room are what count.

Following is an explanation of each of the measurements found in a thorough loudspeaker review or manufacturer's specification sheet.

Impedance is the electrical resistance the loudspeaker presents to the power amp. As described in detail in Appendix B, a loudspeaker's impedance is a combination of its simple DC resistance, inductive reactance, and capacitive reactance. The higher the impedance, the easier it is for the amplifier to drive. A low-impedance loudspeaker requires the amplifier to drive more current through the loudspeaker, which puts more stress on the amplifier.

Even though a loudspeaker may be specified as "6 ohms," the actual impedance almost always varies with frequency. Fig.7-22a shows an impedance curve (the solid line) for a rather low-impedance loudspeaker. The impedance dips to less than 4 ohms (the "40.0m" horizontal division) through the bass and most of the midrange. The impedance minima is just over 1 ohm at 30Hz—an extremely low value.

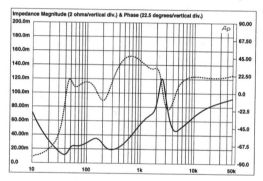 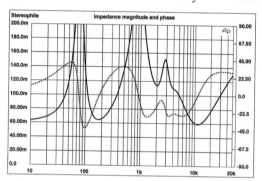

Fig. 7-22a and b A loudspeaker's impedance magnitude (solid line) and phase angle (dotted line) indicate how easy or difficult it is for a power amplifier to drive. (Courtesy *Stereophile*)

The dotted trace in the impedance plot shows the loudspeaker's *phase angle*, which indicates how inductive or capacitive the loudspeaker looks to the amplifier. If the loudspeaker presented a pure resistance (no capacitance or inductance), the phase-angle plot would be a straight line. The farther away from the center line, the more reactive the loudspeaker is at that frequency. (Phase angle is discussed in detail in Appendix B.)

A combination of high reactance and low impedance is especially difficult for a power amp to drive. The severe phase angle swings seen in Fig.7-22a, coupled with its low impedance, make this loudspeaker difficult to drive. This doesn't mean that the loudspeaker won't work, only that it will work better with a power amp that can deliver current into low-impedance loads. For example, a power amp that nearly doubles its power into a 4 ohm load compared to an 8 ohm load would be a better choice than one that barely increases its power into 4 ohms.

A much easier load to drive is illustrated in Fig.7-22b. The impedance is much higher over a wider band, and the phase-angle swings are less severe. The impedance never dips below 6 ohms, and is well above that figure over wide bands. This loudspeaker will demand much less current from the power amplifier.

A loudspeaker's impedance magnitude and phase angle must be considered in relation to its sensitivity. A loudspeaker with a high sensitivity is much less demanding on a power amp than one with a low sensitivity, regardless of the loudspeaker's impedance. The combination of low sensitivity, low impedance, and severe phase angle requires an amplifier of the highest quality to achieve musically acceptable results.

Sensitivity can be expressed as a sound pressure level with 1W input measured 1 meter away. A loudspeaker's sensitivity may be expressed as 88dB 1W/1m. High sensitivity is generally considered any value above 88dB 1W/1m, while low sensitivity is a value below 84dB 1W/1m.

Note that sensitivity can also be expressed with a drive signal of 2.83V, which corresponds to 1W into an 8 ohm load. Loudspeaker manufacturers can cheat on sensitivity figures by using the 2.83V figure into a 4 ohm loudspeaker, which increases the loudspeaker's sensitivity rating by 3dB. The loudspeaker isn't 3dB more sensitive, it's just drawing twice as much current from the power amp at the same 2.83V. If you see the 2.83V figure, make sure the impedance is 8 ohms.

Note that the term "efficiency" is often used incorrectly in place of sensitivity. Technically, efficiency is the percentage of electrical power converted by the loudspeaker into acoustical power.

Measuring a loudspeaker's impedance can be done electrically on a test bench. Measuring a loudspeaker's acoustical characteristics, however, requires putting a microphone in front of the loudspeaker and driving the loudspeaker with test signals. Consequently, the measured response will be not the loudspeaker's intrinsic characteristics, but the loudspeaker's response as modified by the room in which the measurements are taken. As we know, a loudspeaker's performance is greatly dependent on the room in which it is used. We could end up measuring more of the room's characteristics than the loudspeaker's.

One way of solving this problem is to measure the loudspeaker in an *anechoic chamber*, a room whose six surfaces are covered with highly absorbent material. This material absorbs virtually all the sound energy striking it, reflecting no energy back into the room. Consequently, the measurement microphone "sees" only the loudspeaker's response.

Anechoic chambers are expensive to build and consume lots of real estate. Engineers have therefore developed methods of measuring loudspeakers in a normal room to exclude the room's influence from the measured results. One of these techniques, invented by the late Richard Heyser, is called *Time Delay Spectrometry* (TDS). In TDS measurements, the loudspeaker under test is driven by a swept sinewave. The signal picked up by the measurement microphone is filtered by a narrow swept-bandpass filter that tracks the swept sinewave driving the loudspeaker, but is delayed in time by a few milliseconds. The filter's delay is exactly the amount of time it takes for sound from the loudspeaker to reach the measurement microphone. The sound reaching the measurement microphone is the loudspeaker's direct acoustic output, followed a few milliseconds later by room reflections. This is where the swept bandpass filter comes in. The filter tracks the sinewave stimulus so that when a reflection reaches the microphone, the filter has already moved past the reflection's frequency and rejects it. The result is the loudspeaker's intrinsic response unmodified by the room.

A second, more popular, technique is implemented in a personal-computer–based hardware and software package called Maximum Length Sequence System Analyzer (MLSSA). The loudspeaker under test is driven by a stimulus containing a specific pattern of noise sequences. The measurement microphone in front of the loudspeaker picks up this signal, which is compared to the noise-sequence pattern stored in memory. From the way the loudspeaker alters this sequence, the system computes the loudspeaker's impulse response. The period between the impulse and the first reflection is free from reflections and is indistin-guishable from an anechoic measurement. The impulse response is then "windowed" to remove the information from the first reflection onward, leaving only the anechoic window.

The impulse response, which is a time-domain signal, is transformed into the frequency domain using Fourier analysis. From this impulse response we can derive the system's amplitude response (frequency response) and other information. The result is the loudspeaker's response without the room's contribution. Note, however, that the anechoic window's length determines the low-frequency resolution of the measurement. The longer the anechoic portion of the impulse response transformed into the frequency domain, the lower the frequency that can be accurately measured. When measuring loudspeak-ers with this technique, the loudspeaker is placed on a tall stand so that it is halfway between the floor and ceiling, maximizing the anechoic window. The room should also be as large as possible.

Despite these measures, the low-frequency resolution of MLSSA measurements isn't satisfactory unless you have a huge room (a long anechoic window). To better measure the loudspeaker's low-frequency performance, a measurement microphone is placed so that it nearly touches the woofer cone. At this position, the room's contribution is negligible. This separately measured *nearfield* woofer response is appended to the MLSSA-derived response to provide an accurate wideband measurement.

With that background, let's go through the measurements in a loudspeaker review and examine what they mean.

A loudspeaker's impulse response reveals its time behavior, including how time coherent the loudspeaker system is, how much the drivers exhibit overshoot and ringing, and whether the drivers are connected in the same polarity. From the time-domain impulse response, the loudspeaker's frequency-domain behavior can be extracted using the Fourier Transform.

Fig.7-23a is the impulse response of a loudspeaker that has poor time coherence. Notice the negative-going spike (the tweeter's output), indicating that the tweeter's output occurs before the other drivers, and that it is connected in the opposite polarity. The impulse response in Fig.7-23b is much more coherent; all the drivers respond to the impulse in an identical manner. Ideally, the impulse response should have a fast rise-time (indicated by a steepness of the impulse) and minimal driver ringing after the impulse has stopped (ringing can be seen as squiggles after the impulse).

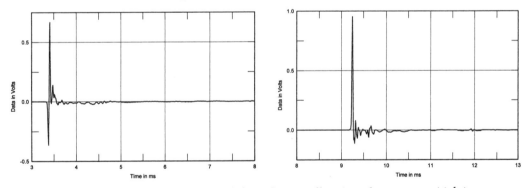

Fig. 7-23a and b A poor impulse response (left) and an excellent impulse response (right). (Courtesy *Stereophile*)

Another way of looking at a loudspeaker's time behavior is the *step response*, or how the loudspeaker behaves when presented with direct current (DC). The step response, which is derived from the impulse response, plots the loudspeaker's output vs. time. Fig.7-24a is the step response of the same loudspeaker whose impulse response we saw in Fig.7-23a. The lag between the tweeter (the negative-going spike) and the other drivers is apparent, as well as a slow rise time, indicated by the rounding of the step. For contrast, Fig.7-24b is a virtually perfect step response. The drivers are time coherent, and the rise time is extremely fast (the step is a straight vertical line). This step response was derived from the impulse response in Fig.7-23b.

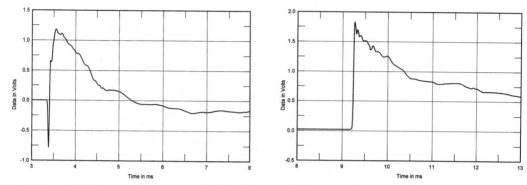

Fig. 7-24a and b A poor step response (left) and an excellent step response (right). (Courtesy *Stereophile*)

Fig.7-25 is a loudspeaker's overall frequency response as measured over a 30° horizontal window. This simply means that the frequency response was measured at various angles from the loudspeaker front baffle and averaged to produce the curve. Averaging the response gives a better representation of the listener's subjective response to the loudspeaker; some of that side energy will reach the listener after being reflected from the listening room's sidewalls. This particular loudspeaker has some excess treble energy between 5kHz and 15kHz, which may make it sound tizzy in the treble. Notice how the response drops rapidly above 15kHz. The broad dip between 500Hz and 5kHz may give the loudspeaker a distant, rather than present, perspective. The rising bass indicates the low-frequency alignment may be underdamped, giving the bass a generous, but fat quality. In short, these deviations from a flat line indicate colorations in the loudspeaker.

Fig. 7-25
Frequency
response
averaged over a
30° horizontal
window

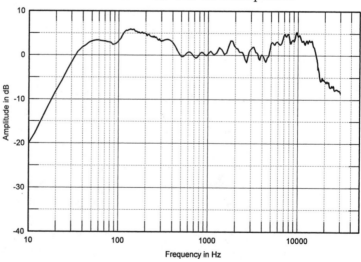

Courtesy *Stereophile*

Fig.7-26 is a loudspeaker's "horizontal family" of response curves. These show how a loudspeaker's response changes as the measurement microphone is moved around the loudspeaker. The frequency response measurement just described is an average of these individual curves.

The trace representing the frequency response directly in front of the loudspeaker (on-axis) has been normalized to be a straight line so that the other curves show only the *difference* from the on-axis response. The horizontal family shows the loudspeaker's dispersion, or how the loudspeaker radiates acoustical energy into the room as a function of frequency. This particular loudspeaker shows a typical treble rolloff as the microphone is moved to the sides of the cabinet, but also excess treble energy on-axis. These curves suggest that this loudspeaker should be listened to without toe-in; the excess treble on-axis will be reduced if the listener sits slightly off-axis (no toe-in). A loudspeaker that exhibits radical changes in off-axis response can sound colored, even though the on-axis response may be fairly flat.

Fig. 7-26 A horizontal response family

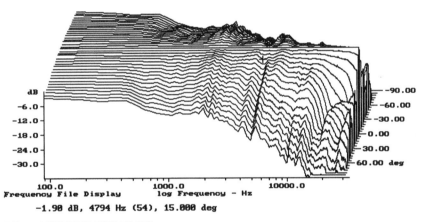

Files: \WAVEFORM\F220-??.FRQ

Courtesy *Stereophile*

The next measurement (Fig.7-27) shows how the loudspeaker's response changes with listening height. Again, the flat line has been normalized so that only the differences from vertical on-axis response are shown. The on-axis point is usually the tweeter axis, or a typical listening axis (the text accompanying the measurement will indicate which). As you can see, the frequency response changes radically with listening height. The loudspeaker has severe peaks and dips in the response (caused by interference effects) above and below the optimum listening axis. This means the loudspeaker will sound very different depending on listening height. This example is extreme; most loudspeakers don't exhibit such radical response changes with the vertical axis. All loudspeakers, however, have some change in tonal balance with listening axis. This measured response underscores the importance of listening height when auditioning a loudspeaker.

Fig. 7-27 A vertical response family

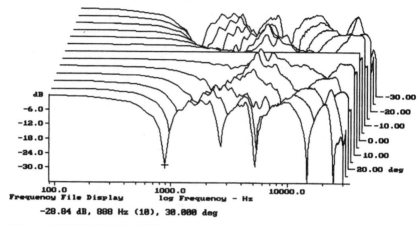

Files: \WAVEFORM\S500C-??.FRQ

Courtesy *Stereophile*

The ideal loudspeaker would stop generating acoustical energy as soon as the drive signal stopped. In practice, some acoustical energy, however small the amount, is always stored in the drivers and enclosure. This energy is radiated over time, like a bell ringing. To look at a loudspeaker's response over time, its frequency response is plotted in discrete slices of time. As described previously, the frequency response is derived from the impulse response using the Fast Fourier Transform (FFT). By moving the window in the impulse response on which the FFT is performed, the loudspeaker's frequency response can be derived at different points in time. Specifically, the FFT-derived frequency response is calculated perhaps one hundred times over 4ms to create the plots of Fig.7-28a and b. This graph is properly called a *cumulative spectral-decay*, but is more commonly called a *waterfall plot* because of its similarity to cascades of falling water. It shows how the loudspeaker's output changes over time and with frequency. The topmost curve is the loudspeaker's frequency response at time zero. The next lower line is the frequency response 40 microseconds (40μs) later. The next lower line 40μs after that, and so forth. By plotting the response over time, we can easily see cabinet resonances, driver ringing, driver breakup, and other problems. A driver resonance is seen as a vertical ridge in the plot; the loudspeaker continues to radiate energy at the ridge's frequency long after the impulse has stopped. The perfect loudspeaker would produce a flat line at the top, and instantly decay to no energy output.

Examples of poor and excellent performance on the cumulative spectral-decay test are illustrated in Figs.7-28a and b. In Fig.7-28a, we can see a ridge at 3729Hz, indicating that the loudspeaker continues to produce acoustic energy at this frequency for two milliseconds (2ms) after drive signal has ceased—a long time in loudspeaker terms. By contrast, Fig.7-28b shows exemplary behavior; the acoustic output drops very quickly (the white space between the top few traces and the lower traces) and almost no ridges are apparent. There is one minor resonance at 2963Hz, but is minuscule compared to the resonances seen in Fig.7-28a. The resonances seen in Fig.7-28a will be audible as a change in timbre when this frequency is excited by the music.

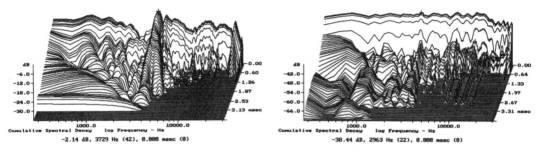

Fig. 7-28a and b Poor (left) and excellent (right) cumulative spectral-decays. (Courtesy *Stereophile*)

Fig. 7-29
Cumulative spectral-decay of an accelerometer output attached to a loudspeaker cabinet

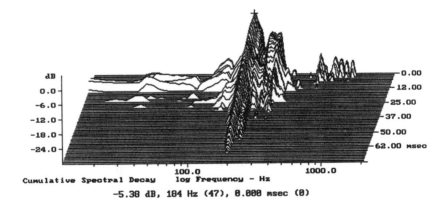

Courtesy *Stereophile*

The same technique can be used to examine the behavior of loudspeaker cabinets. An accelerometer is attached to the loudspeaker, which is driven by the MLS signal. The accelerometer output is drawn in a waterfall plot, showing the frequency and amplitude of cabinet vibrations. For example, Fig.7-29 shows an enclosure with a severe resonance at 187Hz, seen as the narrow ridge at that frequency. This loudspeaker stores, then slowly releases, energy at 187Hz. This will undoubtedly make the bass colored when the loudspeaker is excited by music with energy at this frequency.

Problems with Loudspeakers

Of all the components in your system, the loudspeaker is the most likely to develop trouble. The most common problem is a blown driver—usually the tweeter—which simply stops working. Tweeters are often destroyed by too much current flowing through their voice coils. The tweeter can't dissipate the resultant heat quickly enough, and its voice coil is burned open.

Another common cause of speaker failure is the buzzing sound produced by a loose voice coil. Too much current through the voice coil melts the glue holding the coil to the former (the bobbin around which wire is wound to make the coil), loosening turns of wire which rub against the magnet and cause the buzzing sound.

Driver mounting bolts can become loose over time and degrade a loudspeaker's performance by allowing the entire driver to vibrate rather than just its diaphragm. Gently tightening these bolts from time to time—particularly when a loudspeaker is new—can improve its sound. Be careful not to overtighten and strip the bolts.

A Final Note

Those readers wanting to delve deeper into loudspeaker design are directed to Martin Colloms's *High Performance Loudspeakers* (Halsted Press, ISBN 0-470-21721-9). *High Performance Loudspeakers* is the definitive reference book on the subject.

8 The Digital Front End: CD Players, Digital Processors, and CD Transports

Overview and Terminology

A hi-fi system's digital front end is any component or combination of components that plays music from a digital source (primarily the compact disc). A digital front end can be as simple as a CD player or as complex as a separate CD transport and multi-box digital processor. Whatever the configuration, your system's digital front end is a vital link in the audio reproduction chain, and the source you'll probably spend the most time listening to.

The digital front end reads information from a digital medium such as a CD and converts that information (which as been stored digitally; i.e., as binary "ones" and "zeros") into an analog signal to drive the rest of your playback system. The digital front end must not only retrieve the digital data representing the music, but also convert it to analog form. This is a very exacting process. Consequently, the musical differences between digital components can be vast.

Before describing how to choose the digital components best for you, let's survey the components that make up a digital front end.

CD Player: The CD player is a self-contained component which plays CDs. The CD player's analog line-level output feeds a line-level input on your preamplifier. Every CD player includes in the same chassis a transport mechanism (which spins and reads the CD) and a digital-to-analog converter.

Digital-to-Analog Converter: Also called a "digital processor" or "D/A converter," the digital-to-analog converter receives digital audio data (usually from a CD transport) and converts it to an analog signal. The digital processor has a digital input and analog output, the latter feeding one of your preamplifier's line-level inputs.

CD Transport: The CD transport reads the digitally encoded information from a CD and sends it to the D/A converter for conversion to analog. Unlike a CD player, a transport has no digital-to-analog converter built into it. A CD player with a digital output can, however, serve as a transport.

Digital Output: A jack on all CD transports and some CD players that provides access to the digital datastream. A digital output allows a CD player to send digital data to a separate digital processor via the S/PDIF interface.

S/PDIF Interface: The S/PDIF interface is a standard format for transmitting digital audio, primarily between a CD transport and digital processor. S/PDIF stands for "Sony/Philips Digital Interface Format," after the two companies who invented the compact disc. The S/PDIF signal can be transmitted on a variety of interface types such as ST-Type optical or coaxial, described in detail later in this chapter. All consumer digital audio products—transports, digital processors, and digital recorders—use the S/PDIF interface. A professional version of S/PDIF, called AES/EBU (Audio Engineering Society/European Broadcast Union), is sometimes included on consumer digital audio products.

How to Choose a Digital Front End

Since its introduction in 1983, CD playback technology has advanced more rapidly than has any other field of audio. The sound quality of the first CD players was a far cry from the musical performance available from today's high-end CD players, or even today's budget machines. Moreover, the musical and technical performance of current state-of-the-art transports and digital processors was unthinkable to the designers of first-generation CD players.

This rapidly changing technology can make choosing a digital front end more difficult than selecting other components. Although the digital source is an important factor in the system's overall sound quality, digital components continually improve in musical performance. The audiophile is thus faced with the choice of spending a significant amount of money on components that are likely to be bettered in a year (and at a lower price), or spend very little now and wait until the products have more fully evolved. Of all the components that comprise a high-end system, the digital front end is the most likely to be left behind in technology's inexorable progress.

But these factors can also work *in favor* of today's consumer. These technological advances have resulted in superb musical performance from today's moderately priced digital products—your purchase today reflects more than ten years of progress. Further, your investment will be protected if you keep your digital front end for many years. The secret to enjoying your digital source in the long run is choosing the one that best suits your system and musical taste today so it won't be obsolete tomorrow. Choose your digital source carefully; you'll enjoy music more now, and be less inclined to replace it in a few years.

The first decision in choosing a digital front end is whether to buy a CD player, or a separate transport and digital processor. There are advantages and disadvantages to each approach. Let's first look at who should buy a CD player, and why.

Those on modest budgets should opt for CD players; they offer more performance for the money than do separates. By combining the transport and processor in one chassis, with one power supply, one front panel, one shipping carton, and one AC cord, the manufacturer can put more of the manufacturing budget into better sound. Moreover, there is a very good technical reason for having the transport and processor in the same chassis—there is no S/PDIF interface between transport and processor. (The S/PDIF's detrimental effect on musical performance is described later in this chapter.)

Many excellent CD players are available for under $1000, including some legitimate "high-end" machines that sell for as little as $300. This is, however, the lower limit of true high-end CD players. Below this level you're entering the realm of mass-market products designed for maximum features and minimum manufacturing cost, not musical performance.

If you opt for a CD player, look for one that has a coaxial digital output on an RCA jack. This will let you use the CD player as a transport if you upgrade to a separate digital processor in the future. Notice that I said a *coaxial* digital output on an RCA jack. Nearly all recently made mass-market CD players use a vastly inferior optical connector called *TosLink*. If you drive an outboard digital processor with TosLink, you won't be getting the sound you paid for. Insist on a CD player with a coaxial digital output. That way, you can be assured of a clear upgrade path in the future.

Those with more ambitious digital budgets—say, over $1300— should choose separate transports and digital processors. This isn't a hard-and-fast figure, but a general guideline. I can think of some superb $2000 CD players, and a few mediocre transport/processor combinations at that price. If your budget is greater than $2000, however, the separate transport and processor are the way to go.

There are many advantages to separates. First, by separating the disc playback mechanism from the D/A converter, each portion can be optimized for its specific job. Second, isolating the two sections keeps electrical noise from the transport away from the critical D/A and analog output stages in the processor. The result is better sound. Third, a separate transport and processor allow you to more easily take advantage of improvements in digital processors. With separates, you can upgrade the processor while keeping your transport. Finally, the cutting edge in state-of-the-art digital playback is all taking place in separates.

Once you've decided on separates, you must allocate the digital front-end budget to a transport, processor, and digital interconnect. If you plan on keeping the components you select for a long time, get a transport and processor of equal quality, spending about 35% of the digital front-end budget on the transport and 65% on the processor. If, however, you expect to be constantly upgrading components, you may think about buying a state-of-the-art transport and a lesser-quality processor. This will allow you to take full advantage of the rapidly improving sound quality of processors. Then, when you've found a processor that suits you and your system, you'll have a first-class digital front end. Later sections in this chapter, on transports and digital processors, outline their features and differences.

When shopping for a digital front end, remember that technical performance is secondary to sound quality. Manufacturers will often tout their products on the basis of some technical innovation, or because it uses the latest parts. Although interesting, such descriptions don't tell you how the product *sounds*. Many technical factors influence the component's musical performance; the parts it uses are only one of these. Don't buy a product just because it uses a particular DAC or digital filter. Many digital processors with excellent parts pedigrees just don't measure up in the listening room. Listen to the product and decide for yourself if it sounds good. Just as you wouldn't consider buying an amplifier based on how little THD it has, you shouldn't choose a digital component because it features parts used successfully in other designs.

Another claim you should ignore is a processor's clock-jitter specification. Clock jitter (explained in Appendix C) degrades the sound of CD players and digital processors. Some manufacturers make unverifiable jitter claims, sometimes even picking a jitter number out of the air. Not only are there no standards for jitter specifications, but jitter is very difficult to measure—conditions that lead to the current confusion in the marketplace. When shopping for digital components, forget the marketing hype—just listen.

What to Listen For

Perhaps more than any other components, digital products come in the most "flavors"; their sonic and musical characteristics vary greatly between brands and models. This variability has its drawbacks ("Which one is *right*?"), but also offers the music lover the chance to select one that best complements her playback system's characteristics and suits her musical tastes. The different types of musical presentations heard in CD players, transports, and digital processors tend to reflect their designers' musical priorities. If the designer's parts budget—or skill—is limited, certain areas of musical reproduction will be poorer than others. The trick is to find the processor that, *in the context of your system*, excels in the areas you find most important musically.

Selecting a digital source specifically tailored for the rest of your playback system can sometimes ameliorate some of the playback system's shortcomings. For example, don't choose a bright-sounding digital processor for a system that is already on the bright side of reality. Instead, you may want to select a processor whose main attribute is a smooth, unfatiguing treble.

Each digital product has its particular strengths and weaknesses. Only by careful auditioning—preferably in your own system—can you choose the product best for you. To illustrate this, I've invented two hypothetical listeners—each with different systems and tastes—and two hypothetical digital processors. I've used a digital processor in the example, but CD transports and CD players could be easily substituted. Although the following discussion could apply to all audio components, it is particularly true of digital: Not only are there wide variations in sonic characteristics between processors, but a poor-sounding digital processor at the front end of a superb system will ruin the overall performance.

Listener A likes classical music, particularly early music, Baroque, and choral performances. She rarely listens to full-scale orchestral works, and never plays rock, jazz, or pop. Her system uses inexpensive solid-state electronics and somewhat bright loudspeakers, both of which combine for a detailed, forward, and somewhat aggressive treble.

Listener B wouldn't know a cello from a viola, preferring instead electric blues, rock, and pop. He likes to feel the power of a kick drum and bass guitar working together to drive the rhythm. His system is a little soft in the top octave, and not as dynamic as he'd like.

Now, let's look at the sonic differences between two inexpensive and similarly priced digital processors and see how each would—or wouldn't—fit in the two systems.

Processor #1 has terrific bass: it is tight, deep, driving, and rhythmically exciting. Unfortunately, its treble is a little etched, grainy, and overly prominent.

Processor #2's best characteristics are a sweet, silky-smooth treble. The processor has a complete lack of hardness, grain, etch, and fatigue. Its weakness, however, is a soft bass and limited dynamics. It doesn't have a driving punch and dynamic impact on drums compared to Processor #1.

I think you can guess which processor would be best for each system and listener. Putting Processor #1 in Listener A's system would only exacerbate the brightness in her system. Moreover, the additional grain would be more objectionable on violins and voices. Processor #2, however, would tend to soften the treble presentation in Listener A's system, providing much-needed relief from the relentless treble. Moreover, the sonic qualities of processor #1—dynamics and tight bass—are less important musically to Listener A.

Conversely, Listener B would be better off with Processor #1. Not only are its musical characteristics better suited to the type of music he likes, but the system could use a little more sparkle in the treble and punch in the bass. Processor #1's better dynamics and tighter bass not only better serve the kind of music Listener B prefers, but also complement his system.

So which processor is "better"? Ask Listener A after she's auditioned both products in her system; she'll think Processor #2 is vastly superior and wonder how anyone could like Processor #1. But Listener B will find her choice lacking rhythmic power, treble detail, and dynamic impact. To him, there's no comparison; Processor #1 is the better product.

This example is exaggerated for clarity, but shows how personal taste, musical preference, and system matching can greatly influence which digital products are best for you. The only way to make the right purchasing decision is to *audition the products for yourself*. Use product reviews in magazines to narrow your choice of what to audition. Read reviewers' descriptions of a particular product and see if the type of presentation described is what you're looking for. But don't buy a product solely on the basis of a product review. A reviewer's system and musical tastes may be very different from yours. You could be Listener A and be reading a review written by someone with Listener B's system and tastes.

Use the review as a guide to products to audition yourself, not as absolute truth. You're going to spend many hours with your decision; listen carefully before you buy. It's well worth the investment in time. Moreover, the more products you evaluate and the more careful your listening, the sharper your listening skills will become.

It's important to realize that the specific sonic signatures described in the example are much more pronounced at lower price levels. Two "perfect" digital processors would sound identical. At the very highest levels of digital playback, these sonic tradeoffs are much less acute. Instead, the best products have very few shortcomings, making them ideal for all types of music. The better the processor, the fewer and less extreme the tradeoffs.

A significant factor in how good a processor or CD player sounds is the designer's technical skill and musical sensitivity. Given the same parts, two designers of different talents will produce two very different-sounding products. Consequently, it is possible to find skillfully designed but inexpensive products that outperform more expensive products from less talented designers. Higher-priced products are not necessarily better. Don't get stuck on a specific budget and audition only products within a narrow price range. If an inexpensive product has received a rave review from a reviewer you've grown to trust, and the sonic description matches your taste, audition it. You could save yourself a lot of money. If you decide not to buy the product, at least you've added to your database, and can compare your impressions with those of the reviewer.

In addition to determining which digital products let you enjoy music more, there are specific sonic attributes you should listen for that contribute to a good-sounding digital front end. How high a priority you place on each of these characteristics is a matter of personal taste. In the following sections, I've outlined the musical and sonic qualities I look for in digital playback.

The first quality I listen for in characterizing how a digital component sounds is its overall perspective. Is it laid-back, smooth, and unaggressive? Or is it forward, bright, and "in my face"? Does the product make me want to "lean into" the music and "open my ears" wider to hear the music's subtlety? Or do my ears tense up and try to shut out some of the sound? Am I relaxed or agitated?

A digital product's overall perspective is a fundamental characteristic that defines the product's ability to provide long-term musical satisfaction. If you feel assaulted by the music, you'll tend to listen less often and for shorter sessions. If the product's fundamental musical perspective is flawed, it doesn't matter what else it does right.

Key words in product reviews that describe an easy-to-listen-to digital product include *ease, smooth, laid-back, sweet, polite,* and *unaggressive.* Descriptions of *bright, vivid, etched, forward, aggressive, analytical, immediate,* and *incisive* all point toward the opposite type of presentation.

There is a fundamental conflict between these extremes of presentation. Processors that are smooth, laid-back, and polite may not offend, but they often lack detail and resolution. The absence of aggressiveness is often at the expense of obscuring low-level musical information. This missing musical information could be the inner detail in an instrument's timbre that makes the instrument sound more lifelike. It could be the transient nature of percussion instruments; a slight rounding of the attack gives the impression of smoothness, but doesn't accurately convey the instrument's dynamic structure. Very smooth-sounding digital products often have lower resolution than more forward ones.

The other extreme is the digital product that is "ruthlessly revealing" of the music's every detail. Rather than smoothing transients, these products hype them. In a side-by-side comparison, the ruthlessly revealing product will appear to present much more detail and musical information. They are more upbeat, exciting, and appeal to some listeners. This presentation, however, quickly becomes fatiguing. The listener feels a sense of relief when the music is turned down—or off. The worst thing a product can do is make you want to turn down the volume or stop listening.

This conflict between lack of detail and ruthlessly revealing can be resolved by buying a higher-priced processor. I've found a few models that can present all the music, yet are completely unaggressive and unfatiguing. This is a rare quality, and one that I find musically important. The digital front end must walk a fine line between resolving real musical information and sounding etched and analytical.

Digital reproduction also has a tendency to homogenize individual instruments within the soundstage. This tendency to blur the distinction between individual instruments occurs on two levels: the instruments' timbral signatures and spatial specificity.

On the first level, digital products can overlay music with a common synthetic character that diffuses the unique texture of different instruments, burying the subtle tonal differences between instruments. The music sounds as if it is composed of one big instrument rather than many individual ones. Instead of hearing separate and distinct objects (instruments and voices) hanging in three-dimensional space before the listener, the presentation is a synthetic continuum of sound. There is a "sameness" to instrumental textures that prevents their individual characteristics from being heard.

The second way in which digital playback can diffuse the separateness of individual instruments is by presenting images as flat "cardboard cutouts" pasted on top of each other. The instruments aren't surrounded by an envelope of air and space; the soundstage is flat and congested; and you can't clearly hear where one image ends and the next begins. Good digital playback should present a collection of individual images hanging in three-dimensional space, with the unique tonal colors of each instrument intact and a sense of space and air between the instrumental images. This is easy for analog to accomplish, but quite difficult for digital. A recording with excellent portrayal of timbre and space will help you identify which digital products preserve these characteristics.

Another important quality in digital playback is soundstage transparency. This is the impression that the space in which the music is presented is crystal-clear, open, transparent. The opposite of this is opaque, thick, and congested. Soundstage transparency is analogous to looking at a city skyline on a perfectly clear day. Just as smog or haze will reduce the skyline's immediacy, vibrancy, and resolution of detail in the buildings, so too will soundstage opacity detract from the musical presentation.

I've focused on these aspects of the presentation for evaluating digital products because they vary so greatly between products. You should also listen for other aspects—treble grain, rhythm, dynamics—described in Chapter 3.

Beyond these specifics, a good question to ask yourself is, How long can I listen without wanting to turn the music down—or off? Conversely, the desire—or even compulsion—to bring out CD after CD is the sign of a good digital front end. Some components just won't let you turn off your system; others make you want to do something else.

This ability to musically engage the listener is the essence of high-end audio. It should be the highest criterion when judging digital front ends.

The CD Transport

The CD transport can be thought of as a CD player without a digital-to-analog converter. Instead of generating an analog audio signal as does a CD player, the transport outputs a digital datastream that must be converted to analog by another component, the digital processor. A transport-and-processor combination is essentially a CD player in two components. Fig.8-1 shows the three digital front-end connection methods: a CD player, a transport/digital processor combination, and a CD player used as a CD transport.

Many CD players have digital output jacks that enable them to function as transports. A digital interconnect cable runs from the CD player's digital output jack to a digital processor's digital input, bypassing the CD player's analog circuits and outputs. This connection method, shown in Fig.8-1, merely replaces the CD player's digital-to-analog converter with the (usually) higher-quality D/A in a separate unit. Many audiophiles upgrade their digital front ends by adding separate digital processors to their existing CD players.

Fig. 8-1 A digital front end can be a CD player (top), a CD transport and digital processor (center), or a CD player driving a digital processor (bottom).

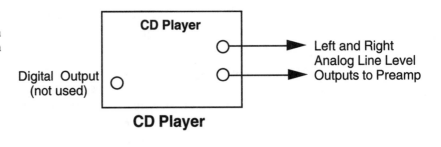

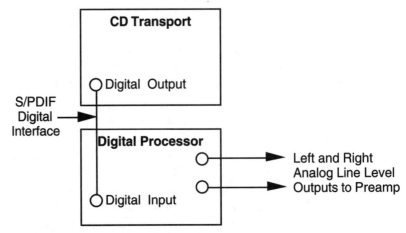

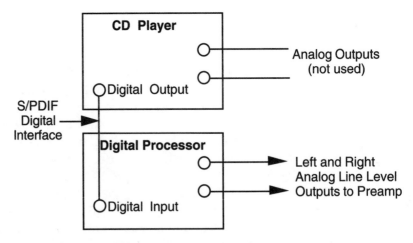

Transports have a variety of output connections. The four main types are coaxial (RCA jack), TosLink optical, AES/EBU (XLR connector) and AT&T ST-type glass fiber optical. (These interfaces are described in detail later in this chapter under "The Digital Interface.") Virtually all high-end transports have coaxial output at the minimum, and some offer all four outputs. A transport will often include coaxial output as standard, and offer AES/EBU or ST-type optical as an option. These output options usually cost between $200 and $400 each. To use ST-type glass fiber output or AES/EBU output, however, your processor must accept these interfaces.

The only way to choose a transport is by listening to several models within your price range. It's a good idea to audition transports with the processor you'll be driving with the transport. All transports have sonic strengths and weaknesses; listening to candidate transports with the digital processor you'll be using will allow you to get the best musical match. Moreover, the digital processor can affect the transport's sound. The digital front end's sound is determined not just by the transport and processor, but how they work together.

Transports will sound different depending on the processor they drive because all digital processors respond differently to *transport jitter*. Transport jitter is timing variations in the digital datastream output from the transport. This datastream jitter is either passed along to the digital processor's clock (where it degrades the sound), or is rejected by the digital processor and is less sonically detrimental. Consequently, transports make much more of an audible difference with some processors than with others. If you choose a digital processor that's relatively immune to transport jitter, you can spend less on a CD transport and still get great sound.

The interface between transport and processor will also affect the sound. Sonic difference exist not only between types of interface (coaxial, ST-type optical, AES/EBU, and TosLink), but between cables within the same interface family. Two coaxial cables may sound nearly as different as two transports. A top-end coaxial digital interconnect costs about $200. If you're on a budget, try a 75-ohm video cable, available from your local Radio Shack for about $5. Using a unique jitter-analysis instrument, I measured the jitter introduced by a variety of digital interconnects. Those designed for analog audio had the highest jitter, and those made specifically for digital data transfer had the lowest jitter. The $5 Radio Shack video cable's jitter was almost as low as that of the $200 high-end digital interconnects—and it sounded nearly as good as well. (See the November, 1993 issue of *Stereophile* for a full report.)

Incidentally, evaluating transports and digital interconnects is much easier than comparing other components: the levels are automatically and precisely matched. All transports and interconnects will produce the same listening volume when driving the same processor—the transport or interconnect doesn't change the ones and zeros in the digital code.

Transports generally cost less than digital processors. You should therefore allocate about 65% of your digital front end budget to the processor and 35% to the transport. Save some for a good digital interconnect: it can make the difference between good and great sound from your digital front end. These are very rough guidelines; the best combination of transport and processor is best decided by listening, not by an arbitrary price. The transport purchaser should be aware, however, that future breakthroughs in transport design could make superb-sounding transports available at very low cost. It may soon be possible to make a perfectly jitter-free transport using an inexpensive electronic output circuit.

Sonic differences between transports are almost certainly solely the result of jitter in their S/PDIF outputs. Recovering the correct ones and zeros from the disc is relatively straightforward; the digital output from a transport is an identical copy, bit for-bit, of the source data. The timing of those bits, however, can greatly affect playback quality. A recently devised measurement provides a means of measuring and quantifying transport jitter and revealing the jitter's spectral distribution. (See "Specifications and Measurements" later in this chapter.)

When evaluating transports, listen for the same artifacts we talked about in judging digital front ends in general. Transports vary greatly in their low-frequency dynamics, treble smoothness, overall perspective, and soundstaging. Choose one that complements your processor and playback system.

Because one company—Philips of Holland—supplies most of the transport mechanisms to high-end audio manufacturers, CD transports tend to have very similar features and functions. Many even share the same remote control. Virtually all transports have track-skip forward and back, audible search, and a time display. Other features include index search, index readout, and a variety of time-display options. This last feature allows you to switch the display between elapsed time of the track, elapsed time of the disc, remaining track time, and remaining disc time. This feature is useful when making cassette tapes for your car stereo. Transports also vary in their ease of use. Some have small buttons bunched together, making it hard to find the one you want. Others have large, clearly marked buttons. Although ergonomics take second place to sound quality, consider a transport's ease of use when deciding whether or not to buy it.

Another factor to consider is the transport's loading method. Some are top-loading, in which a lid or top opens to accept the disc. The second method is drawer-loading, with a drawer that recesses into the front panel. A top-loading transport usually requires a top shelf of an equipment rack, while a drawer-loading unit can fit on a lower shelf.

How a CD Transport Works

A CD transport has four main sections: the transport mechanism, the servo systems, decoding electronics, and output driver stage. The transport mechanism spins the CD, reads the CD's pits with a laser, and outputs a signal to the decoding electronics. The decoding circuits, usually on one integrated circuit (IC), demodulate the data stream, perform error correction, and convert the data into a form that can be transmitted from the transport to a digital processor. The servo systems maintain correct disc speed (the rotational servo), keep the laser on the spiral track of pits (tracking servo), and maintain laser focus on the spinning disc (focus servo). The output stage is a digital line driver—sometimes including a small transformer called a *pulse transformer*—to drive the cable and digital processor input.

Let's look at each of these subsystems in more detail.

The compact disc and laser pickup mechanism are a remarkable engineering feat. The CD has a spiral track of alternating *pits* and *land,* recorded from the inside of the disc to the outside. Pits are indentations in the disc surface, land is the disc surface itself. The space between adjacent tracks of pits is 1.6μm (micrometer), or 1.6 millionths of a meter. The pits vary in length from 0.8μm to 2.8μm, and are 0.56μm wide. To put these numbers into perspective, a human hair has a diameter of about 75μm. Fig.8-2 shows a CD surface photographed by a scanning electron microscope. In the scale of this photograph, a human hair would be as big around as a medium-sized tree trunk.

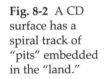

Fig. 8-2 A CD surface has a spiral track of "pits" embedded in the "land."

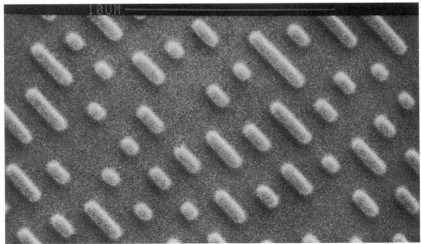

Courtesy Disc Manufacturing, Inc.

The laser beam is reflected from the disc surface to a photodetector, a device that converts light into an electrical signal. When the beam strikes either land or pit bottom, it is reflected to the photodetector at full-strength. This condition represents binary "zero." But when the laser beam strikes the transition from land-to-pit or pit-to-land, part of the beam is reflected from the land and part is reflected from the pit bottom. Because the pit depth is one quarter the wavelength of the laser light, the beam portion reflected from the pit bottom is 180° out of phase with the beam reflected from the land, as shown in Fig.8-3. The two beam portions—now out of phase with each other—cancel each other, producing reduced output from the photodetector. This reduced output, caused by a transition from pit-to-land or land-to-pit, represents binary "1."

Fig. 8-3 A pit-to-land, or land-to-pit transition produces a 180° phase reversal in part of the reflected beam reducing the beam's intensity.

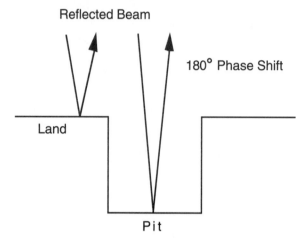

The pits thus produce a reflected beam of varying intensity, which produces a varying voltage at the photodetector output. The output signal is a series of sinewaves, the peaks representing land or pit bottom, and the zero crossing transitions the pit edges. Because the pits have nine discrete lengths, the recovered signal is composed of nine discrete-frequency sinewaves. The recovered signal is called an "eye pattern" or "RF" signal, shown in Fig.8-4. Although the eye pattern looks like an analog signal, the digital data are encoded in the zero-crossing transitions. The shortest pit or land length represents the digital data 1001; the ones are the pit edges and the zeros are the pit bottoms or land. The longest pit length represents the digital data 100000000001. The shortest pit produces a frequency (in the eye pattern) of 720kHz, and the longest pit produces a frequency of 196kHz.

Fig. 8-4 A signal reflected from the disc is composed of nine discrete-frequency sinewaves.

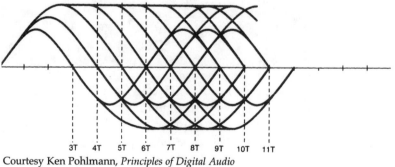

Courtesy Ken Pohlmann, *Principles of Digital Audio*

The data read from the disc don't directly represent digital audio data. Instead, a coding method is used to increase the disc's storage density and provide a clock signal within the data. The coding method is called Eight-to-Fourteen Modulation, or EFM. EFM coding takes a block of 8 bits and assigns it a unique 14-bit word. These 14-bit words are joined together by three "merging" bits to form the data pattern recorded on the CD. EFM coding inserts a minimum of two zeros between successive ones (remember, the shortest pits represent the data 1001), and a maximum of ten zeros between ones. The result a pit and land pattern of nine discrete lengths. Fig.8-5 shows the relationship between the original data, EFM-coded data, and pit structure.

Fig. 8-5 The relationship between original data, EFM-coded data, pit structure, and the RF signal.

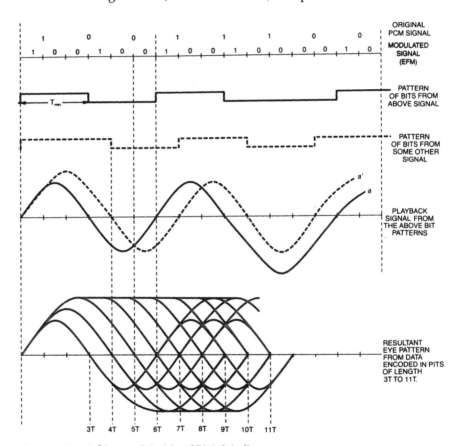

Courtesy Ken Pohlmann, *Principles of Digital Audio*

Although it is counterintuitive to think that increasing the number of bits by EFM coding stores data more efficiently, that's exactly what it does. Moreover, the specific pattern of ones and zeros creates a clock signal at the data rate read from the disc, 4.3218 million bits per second. Of these 4.3218 million bits per second, only 1.41 million are audio data.

The rest are error correction, subcode, and the result of EFM coding. EFM coding also inherently makes the signal self-clocking.

Subcode is non-audio data recorded on the disc. It contains track time, track number, whether the CD has been recorded with pre-emphasis, and other such "housekeeping" information. When the de-emphasis circuit in your CD player or digital processor is activated, it has been triggered by a bit in the subcode. (De-emphasis is described later in this chapter.)

The EFM signal is input to the decoding electronics, which convert the 14-bit words back into the original 8-bit data. These chips also perform error correction and strip out the subcode (a general description of error correction is included in Appendix C). The Cross Interleaved Reed-Solomon Code (CIRC) error-correcting system used in the CD has two levels, called "C1" and "C2." The first decoder (C1) corrects as many errors as it can before sending the data to the C2 decoder. The C2 decoder deinterleaves the data (puts it back in its original order), thereby converting a long-burst error into many shorter errors, which are more easily corrected.

The rotational servo uses an *elastic buffer* between the disc motor and the decoding electronics. Data are fed into the buffer at one end and clocked out at the other end. When the buffer is more than half full, a signal tells the rotational motor to slow down, decreasing the rate at which data are read from the disc. When the buffer is less than half full, the motor speed is increased to fill up the buffer faster. This servo mechanism always keeps the buffer half full. Data can be read in at an irregular speed, but are clocked out at a precise rate.

The focus servo system maintains the laser's objective lens at a precise distance from the spinning disc. The tracking servo keeps the laser centered on one track of the spinning disc.

A transport's output stage takes the S/PDIF signal from the S/PDIF encoder circuit and presents it to the final output jack. The job of driving the interface cable and digital processor input falls on the output stage. Some transports have a reclocking circuit at the output stage to reduce jitter in the datastream. The output stage determines the transport's output impedance, which should be 75 ohms. Most transports use a pulse transformer at the output to couple the S/PDIF signal to the outside world.

(For more information on how the CD works, I recommend *The Compact Disc: A Handbook of Theory and Use* by Ken Pohlmann, published by A-R Editions, ISBN 0-89579-228-1.)

The Digital Processor

Digital processors convert the S/PDIF digital output from a transport or other digital source to an analog signal which is fed to your preamplifier. They range in price from $200 to $14,000. Many good-sounding units can be had for under $1000. The most basic processor has one digital input on an RCA jack and one pair of unbalanced analog outputs. More complex processors have multiple digital inputs, digital outputs, balanced analog outputs, polarity inversion switching, and sometimes even a volume control.

Digital Processor Features

Let's take a closer look at the features and options available on digital processors.

Multiple Digital Inputs: An essential feature if you have more than one digital source (transport, digital recorder, videodisc player). Multiple digital inputs let you change digital sources with a push of a front-panel button instead of rerouting digital interconnects. An LED often accompanies the input selector switch to indicate which input the processor has locked to.

Various Input Types: Most processors offer different types of input connections. Virtually all processors include coaxial input on an RCA jack; some offer ST-Type glass fiber optical, AES/EBU, and TosLink optical. ST-Type optical and AES/EBU are often options, adding between $200 and $400 each to the processor's price. To use these input options, you must have a source (CD transport) with the same output options. For example, if you want to use the ST-Type optical interface, both the transport and processor must be fitted with ST-Type optical jacks.

Balanced Outputs: Balanced outputs come standard on many processors, but are sometimes an option that adds between $200 and $1000 to the price. Balanced outputs allow you to run balanced lines between your digital processor and preamp. Note that a preamp with balanced inputs is required to use this option. (See the section on balanced outputs later in this chapter for a description of different methods of creating a balanced signal.)

Digital Output: This feature allows you to send the digital signal to a digital recording device such as a DAT machine, DCC recorder, or MD. Some processors allow you to record from one digital source while listening to another. A digital output is an important feature if you own a digital recording device. Without a digital output, you'll need to unplug the digital signal going into your digital processor and run it to the digital recorder every time you want to record through the recorder's digital input. A transport with multiple digital outputs will also drive a digital processor and digital recorder simultaneously.

Polarity Inversion Switch: This front-panel switch inverts the *absolute polarity* of the signal to match its original polarity. To find correct absolute polarity, simply throw the switch back and forth to find the position that sounds the best (if there is an audible difference). A polarity-inversion switch is often marked "180°" to indicate polarity reversal. See Appendix A for a description of absolute polarity.

Volume Control: For those who listen only to CD (no tuner, tape deck, or turntable), the processor with a volume control is ideal. This feature allows you to bypass the preamplifier and drive a power amplifier directly. This saves money—on both the preamp and an additional pair of interconnects—and has the potential to sound better because fewer electronic components are in the signal path. Note, however, that some processors performing digital-domain volume control can degrade the sound. Similarly, analog volume control can also lower sound quality by adding an additional active stage to the signal path. Because a CD player or digital processor with a volume control won't accept other input signals, it isn't for everyone. This approach is highly recommended for those who listen only to CD.

If you want the most sound for the money, avoid processors with features you won't use (balanced outputs, multiple digital inputs, digital outputs). Some excellent products have only a coaxial input and unbalanced analog output. You should, however, choose a processor to accommodate your system as it grows. If you plan to get a balanced-input preamplifier, spend the money now for a balanced-output processor.

How a Digital Processor Works

Fig.8-6 shows a digital processor block diagram along with a photograph illustrating how those blocks are implemented in an actual product. The main components are a power supply, input receiver, digital filter, digital-to-analog conversion stage, current-to-voltage converter, and analog output section.

The *input receiver* takes the S/PDIF signal from a digital source and converts the serial datastream into raw digital audio data. It also generates a clock signal based on the clock embedded in the datastream (this is discussed in more detail later in this chapter). A Phase Locked Loop (PLL) compares the input signal frequency (the clock) with a reference frequency (usually generated by a crystal oscillator) and creates a new clock locked to the incoming datastream's clock. This so-called "recovered" clock becomes the master clock for the processor. The input receiver is a significant source of clock jitter and can have a large effect on how the processor sounds. Recent attempts to minimize jitter created by the input receiver include dual PLLs and custom low-jitter modules.

Fig. 8-6 A digital processor circuit and block diagram

Courtesy PS Audio

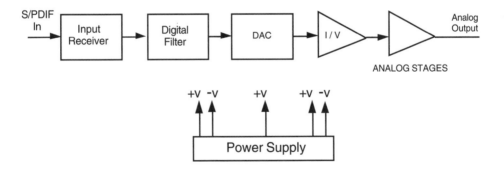

The digital data from the input receiver is sent to the *digital filter*, typically an eight times (8x) oversampling type such as the ubiquitous NPC (Nippon Precision Components) 5813 or 5803. A filter is required to remove the spurious images of the signal that appear at multiples of the sampling rate (see Fig.8-7). In the first CD players, a *brickwall* analog filter just above the audioband removed this unwanted noise. Analog filters were a significant source of unmusical sound in first-generation CD players, introducing severe phase shift, ringing, passband ripple, and often upper-treble attenuation. They were necessary, however, to remove the spurious images at multiples of the sampling frequency and smooth the stairstep waveform created by the sampling process.

Fig. 8-7 Spurious images are created at multiples of the sampling frequency (top). An oversampling digital filter shifts the first image to a higher frequency that is more easily filtered (bottom).

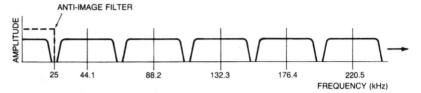

Courtesy Ken Pohlmann, *Principles of Digital Audio*

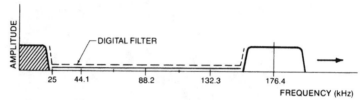

Courtesy Ken Pohlmann, *Principles of Digital Audio*

The advent of digital filters allowed designers to remove this sonically degrading analog filter. Instead of putting a steep analog filter after the DAC, the digital filter performs the same function by executing mathematical operations on the digital signal within a chip. With filtering performed *before* the digital-to-analog conversion process, designers could get rid of steep analog output filters and their sonic problems.

Digital filtering has other advantages. The filter can generate new sample points *between* the original audio samples, thus multiplying the sampling frequency. This process, called *oversampling,* shifts the effective sampling rate from 44.1kHz to a multiple of 44.1kHz. An 8x-oversampling digital filter, for example, would interpolate seven new samples for each input sample, bringing the sampling frequency to 352.8kHz (8 x 44.1kHz). The spurious images at multiples of the sampling frequency still appear, but are now shifted well away from the audio band, where they can be easily filtered with a gradual filter (even a gentle 6dB per octave slope) that won't interfere with the audio signal. In addition to increasing the effective sampling rate, oversampling digital filters also increase the output word length from 16 bits to (typically) 20 bits. Note that no new information is generated by the filter when outputting longer words. Instead, the longer words reduce errors resulting from the filter's internal calculations. The audio data being filtered may temporarily have very long word lengths—perhaps 30 bits—that need to be reduced before being output from the filter. Simply truncating (cutting off) all but the 16 needed bits results in audible distortion; some filters apply noise shaping and redithering schemes instead of truncation. These techniques only attempt to compensate for errors introduced in the filter, and cannot improve incoming data.

After digital filtering, the 8x-oversampled data are input to the *digital-to-analog converter* or *DAC*. The DAC converts digital data at its input to an analog output signal. The most common type of DAC is the "ladder," or "R/2R" DAC. Both names describe the same operating principle. Ladder DACs have "rungs" of resistors, each rung corresponding to one bit in the digital code. A 16-bit DAC will thus have 16 resistor rungs, which allow 65,536 (2^{16}) possible input codes. The input data act as switches on the rungs; a binary "1" closes the switch at that particular bit and allows current to flow through the resistor, while a binary "0" opens the switch and no current flows. The DAC's output current is thus determined by the digital input code. Each rung has an effective resistor value half that of the adjacent rung; the resistor determines how much "weight" the bit has by determining how much current flows through the "switch." The LSB (Least Significant Bit) has the lowest weight, the MSB (Most Significant Bit) has the highest. Each bit upward from the LSB should produce an exact doubling of current, in the progression 1, 2, 4, 8, 16, 32, 64, 128, 256, and so on, up to 524,288 in a 20-bit DAC. The LSB has a value of 1, the MSB a value of 524,288 (in a 20-bit DAC). When the MSB value of 524,288 is combined with the 19 lower bits, a 20-bit DAC can accommodate up to 1,048,576 input codes. (An R/2R resistor ladder DAC is shown in Fig.8-8.)

Fig. 8-8 An R/2R resistor ladder digital-to-analog converter

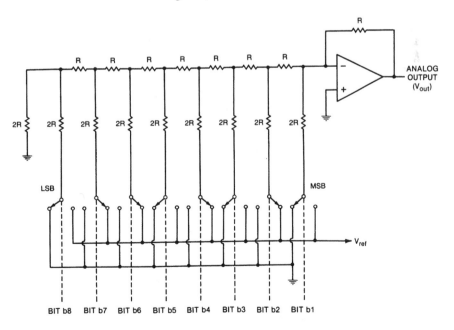

Courtesy Ken Pohlmann, *Principles of Digital Audio*

The precision of these resistor values is critical: Any deviation from a doubling of resistance causes that bit to have more or less value than it should. These *bit weighting errors* result in poor *linearity*. That is, the analog output level doesn't track the digital input code. A perfectly linear DAC will produce an analog output at exactly the same level as the digital input. For example, if the DAC is driven by the code representing a –90dB dithered sinewave, the analog output should be exactly 90dB below full scale. A non-linear DAC would produce an output level of perhaps –93dB or –86dB. Linearity errors are most significant at low signal levels.

Another factor that influences DAC linearity is the value of the MSB. The MSB should be equal in value to all the other bits combined, plus one; when this transition occurs, the 19 LSBs switch from all ones to all zeros, and the MSB toggles from zero to one. Ideally, this single quantization step should be identical in amplitude to every other quantization step. Unfortunately, making the MSB have exactly the value of the 19 LSBs plus one is difficult. Consequently, the MSB's value can be *trimmed* by an external potentiometer located on the circuit board next to the DAC. After the digital processor has been assembled, a technician measures the processor's low-level linearity and adjusts the *MSB trimmer* for least linearity error. The MSB value is adjusted so that it is exactly one quantization step above the 19 LSBs.

If the MSB is misadjusted or goes out of calibration over time and with temperature variations, a distortion called *zero-crossing distortion* results. Because the MSB represents half the signal amplitude, the MSB transition occurs at the point the waveform crosses the zero threshold. Any discontinuity produces a distortion of the waveform at the zero crossing point. This is absolutely the worst place for distortion: small amplitude signals—such as reverberation decay—move around the zero crossing point. Moreover, the zero-crossing distortion is very large in relation to the low signal amplitude. Consequently, zero-crossing distortion can cause significant distortion of low-level waveforms.

Some DACs don't need MSB trimming: they are either factory-calibrated to have no MSB error, or they shift the zero-crossing transition to a large-signal amplitude, where an MSB error is less significant. Both these techniques assure good linearity without trimming, and these DACs are not subject to misadjustment or going out of calibration over time. The UltraAnalog family of DACs is an example of converters that have been precision-calibrated at the factory and need no MSB trimmer. This is accomplished by measuring the quantization step amplitudes, then hand soldering the appropriate precision resistors on the ladder rungs so that the resistor values are perfectly matched. This procedure is performed on each DAC. Conversely, the Burr-Brown PCM63 DAC shifts the MSB transition away from the zero crossing.

Some DAC chips come in different grades, sorted according to their linearity or distortion. The Philips TDA1541, for example, comes in three grades: "R" for "relaxed," "S" for "standard," and "S1"—the so-called "Crown" version. The Burr-Brown PCM63 is available in three grades, with the "PK" designation being the highest quality. Although all the DACs of a given part number are made the same way, manufacturing tolerances produce variations within a production run.

Another problem in digital-to-analog conversion is clock jitter. The DAC is told *when* to convert the digital input word to an analog output by a timing signal called the *word clock*. Timing variations (jitter) in the word clock cause the audio samples to be converted to analog at the wrong time. The result is degraded audio quality. (Appendix C contains a full discussion of clock jitter in digital processors.)

The DAC's output is a series of currents at varying levels. This current output must be converted into a voltage that can be amplified by the processor's analog output stage. This is the next step after the DAC, called *current-to-voltage conversion*, or *I/V conversion* (*I* is the electronic symbol for current, *V* the symbol for voltage). The I/V converter takes the DAC's current output and converts it to a voltage. Virtually all digital processors use an op-amp for I/V conversion: In addition to being easier and cheaper to implement, they are generally faster than a discrete I/V stage. This is because the circuitry is on a single silicon chip rather than spread out in discrete components on a circuit board. Speed is essential in the I/V converter in order to prevent *slew-rate limiting*. Slew-rate limiting is a distortion-producing phenomenon that occurs when the input signal's slew rate is faster than the amplifier's slewing speed. Note that the DAC's current output is a rectangular waveform, with almost square leading edges. This steep input signal requires very fast I/V converters to avoid slew-induced distortion.

After I/V conversion, the analog voltage is put through an analog output stage. This circuit has several functions. First, it can provide gain to bring the final output level to the CD standard of 2V RMS (with a full-scale input signal). Second, the output stage incorporates an output filter to remove high-frequency noise above the audioband. Because the oversampling filter shifts the spurious images to a very high frequency, this filter is often a gentle first-order type. The output filter can be an elaborate active circuit, or as simple as a capacitor put across the analog output jacks. Finally, the output stage acts as a buffer between the I/V converter and the final analog output. The output stage generally has a low output impedance and is designed to drive cables and a preamplifier. The analog output stage can be a single active gain stage, or several intermediate stages followed by an output driver stage. A direct-coupled output stage has no capacitors in the signal path to block direct current (DC) from getting into the audio signal. Most direct-coupled output stages use a *DC servo* to prevent DC from appearing on the analog output jacks.

The processor's de-emphasis circuit is often built into the analog output stage. De-emphasis is a treble rolloff (with a 50/15µS characteristic) circuit that restores flat response to discs that have had their treble boosted (emphasized) during recording or mastering. Very few discs—about 2%—have been emphasized. Emphasized discs carry a flag in the subcode within the digital data stream that triggers the processor's de-emphasis circuit to engage. On some processors, a front-panel LED identifies emphasized discs.

The de-emphasis circuit can be an active stage built around an op-amp or discrete circuit, or simply an RC network (resistor and capacitor) connected to ground. Because of component tolerances (a capacitor's actual value varies from its specified value, for example), de-emphasis circuits don't always produce a perfectly flat response. Some digital filters (the NPC 5803, for example) perform de-emphasis in the digital domain. This eliminates the need for an analog de-emphasis circuit, and assures that no de-emphasis errors can occur. But because an analog de-emphasis circuit appears after the DAC, it can attenuate DAC noise and help the processor achieve a lower noise floor.

Balanced Outputs: Why They're Not All Created Equal

Balanced output has become a popular feature on digital processors. A balanced-output processor can drive a balanced-input preamplifier, often with better sound quality than is possible with unbalanced operation.

Not all balanced outputs are created equal; there are vast differences between the two techniques of creating a balanced output signal. The easiest way to make a balanced output is to simply put a phase splitter in the analog output stage. A phase splitter generates a second signal of opposite polarity to the input signal. These two signals are then connected to an XLR jack on the processor's rear panel. This technique, shown in block form in Fig.8-9, is the inexpensive and easy way to create a balanced signal.

Some processors, however, use a much more elaborate scheme. Rather than create the balanced signal in the analog domain with an additional active device (the phase splitter), these processors create a balanced signal in the digital domain *before* digital-to-analog conversion. The left and right audio-channel digital datastreams are split into a balanced signal (left +, left –, right +, right –) which are processed and converted to analog separately. Consequently, four DACs, four current-to-voltage converters, four analog output stages, and four de-emphasis circuits are needed. A digitally balanced DAC is shown in block form in Fig.8-10.

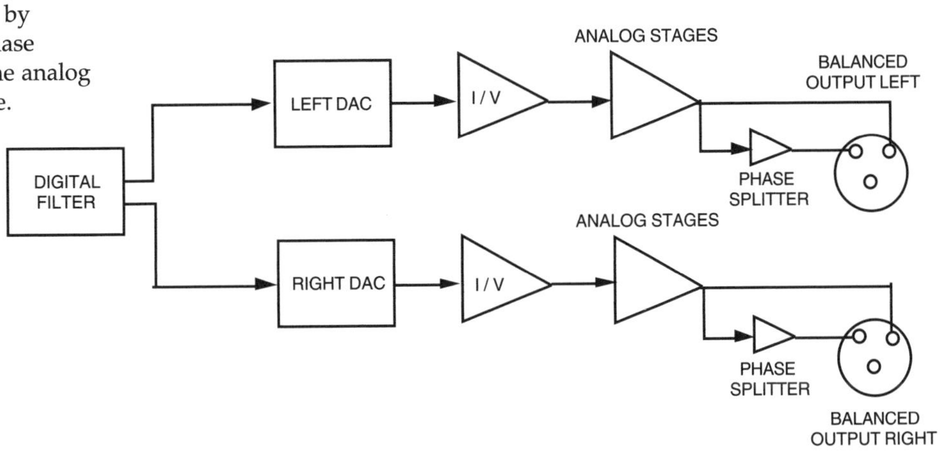

Fig. 8-9 A balanced output can be created simply by adding a phase splitter to the analog output stage.

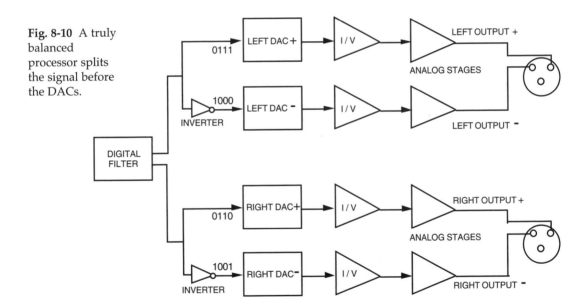

Fig. 8-10 A truly balanced processor splits the signal before the DACs.

This method is vastly more expensive than a simple phase splitter in the analog stage, but has many advantages. When the balanced signal is eventually summed (either in the preamplifier or power amplifier), any noise or distortion common to both channels will be rejected. This phenomenon, called *common-mode rejection*, is described in Chapter 11, "Cables and Interconnects." Any artifacts or spurious signals introduced by the DACs will thus cancel. Moreover, balanced DACs yield a 3dB increase in signal-to-noise ratio. Finally, a fully balanced DAC doesn't add an additional active device (the phase splitter) to the signal path.

A final consideration with fully balanced DACs is how the single-ended signal is derived. Some products merely connect half the balanced circuit (the left and right channel + signals) to the rear panel RCA jack. Others sum the + and – signals with a differential amplifier to drive the unbalanced RCA output jacks. The latter approach provides the benefits of balanced DACs even for those users who don't use the balanced XLR outputs. Conversely, taking half the balanced signal at the single-ended output obviates the advantages of fully balanced DACs. A comparison of these two techniques is shown in Fig.8-11.

Fig. 8-11 A comparison of how single-ended outputs are derived from a balanced processor

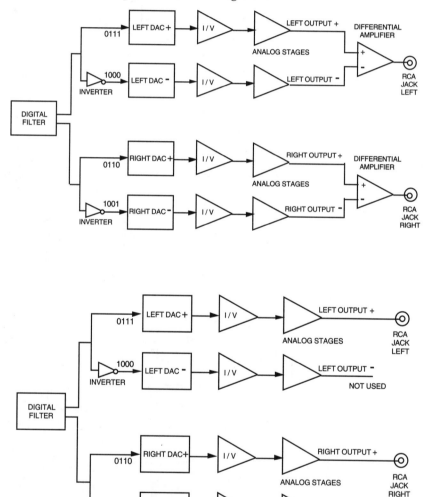

The S/PDIF Digital Interface

As described earlier, transports and processors come fitted with a variety of connection methods—AES/EBU, coaxial, TosLink, or ST-type optical. All are based on the S/PDIF (Sony/Philips Digital Interface Format) interface standard. S/PDIF is the consumer version of the AES/EBU interface used in professional equipment. Because the interface has been standardized, components made by one manufacturer will work with those made by another.

Digital Interconnects

Before looking at the interface in depth, let's survey the digital interface interconnects used in high-end digital products. Fig.8-12 shows the four common interconnect types: coaxial, TosLink, ST-Type optical, and AES/EBU. Note that all transmit the same S/PDIF signal, but in different ways.

Fig. 8-12 The four digital interface types.

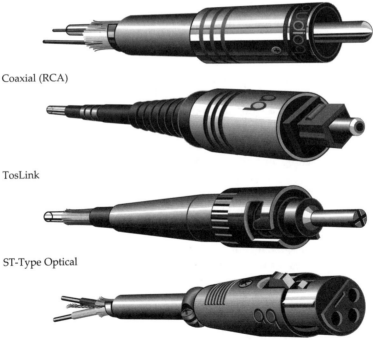

Coaxial (RCA)

TosLink

ST-Type Optical

AES/EBU
Courtesy AudioQuest

The two main interface categories are electrical and optical. In an electrical interconnect, electrons carry the signal down copper or silver wire. An optical interface transmits light down a plastic or glass tube.

The most common type of connection is called coaxial, carried on an RCA cable. This is the electrical output found on virtually all CD transports, most good CD players, and other consumer digital audio products (DAT, DCC, MD). A variation on the coaxial connection is the BNC cable, which is used in only a few products. Though BNC is better than RCA—mechanically, electrically, and sonically—it never caught on, and is consequently nonstandard.

TosLink is the low-cost optical interface promoted by mass-market audio manufacturers as an alternative to coaxial connection. TosLink, which is a trademarked name of the Toshiba Corporation, is more properly called "EIAJ Optical," named after the Electronics Industries Association of Japan. The major electronics companies had two good reasons for trying to convert the world to TosLink. First, TosLink jacks and cables are cheaper than coaxial jacks and cables. Second, TosLink connection makes it easier for the components to meet FCC (Federal Communications Commission) requirements for radiated noise. An electrical signal traveling down copper (such as the S/PDIF signal in a coax connection) throws off RF (radio frequency) noise that could interfere with radio and television transmission. The FCC will simply ban products that don't meet its criteria for radiated noise. Because TosLink sends the signal as light down glass or plastic fiber, it produces no radiated noise.

The most popular high-end interface is called *ST-Type Optical*. This interface, developed by AT&T for telecommunications, has become very popular in high-end digital processors and transports. ST-Type connection transmits the optical signal down glass fiber instead of TosLink's plastic light path (some higher-quality TosLink cables also use glass). ST's locking bayonet connector ensures a good junction between the cable and optical transmitter and receiver. ST-Type is generally considered a very good-sounding interface.

The professional AES/EBU digital interface is becoming more accepted in high-end products, and has even challenged ST-Type for highest sound quality. AES/EBU is carried on a balanced line terminated with three-pin XLR connectors. Of the three conductors in a balanced signal, one is ground, one is the digital signal, and the third is the digital signal inverted. AES/EBU benefits from all the advantages of balanced lines (described in Chapter 11). Moreover, the AES/EBU signal is 5V, compared to S/PDIF's 0.5V.

Virtually all transports and processors have RCA jacks, and most include TosLink for compatibility. ST-Type optical and AES/EBU are usually found on only the more expensive components, or are offered as options on mid-priced digital equipment. The ST-Type option can add between $200 and $400 to the product's price. Note that both the transport and processor must have the same interface. This increases ST's cost to between $400 and $800 if it is included on both the transport and processor.

Is ST worth the extra money? In most components, the answer is a definite yes. Here's why. The electrical interfaces (coax and AES/EBU) are very difficult to implement correctly. There are many variables which affect the sound quality, not all of which the designers get right. The result is less than optimum performance. By contrast, ST is a "turnkey" system that works perfectly right out of the box. The designer need only put it on the circuit board and he has an optimized system. There are no variables to affect sound quality. The best possible implementation of an electrical connection has, however, the potential of sounding better than any optical system.

TosLink is by far the worst interface, both mechanically (the physical connection between cable and jack), electrically (it has the lowest bandwidth), and sonically. TosLink connection tends to blur the separation between individual instrumental images, adds a layer of grunge over instrumental textures, softens the bass, and doesn't have the same sense of black silence between notes. Better results can be achieved with a high-end glass-fiber TosLink cable, but my advice is to forget about TosLink unless you have a laserdisc player that only has TosLink output and are forced to use it.

Some digital front ends will benefit from an optical interface because there is no ground connection between the transport and processor, as exists with an electrical interconnect. Sonically degrading high-frequency noise on a transport's ground can contaminate the digital processor's ground through an electrical connection. Because an optical interface transmits the signal without an electrical connection, there is no chance for coupling ground noise between the two components.

In theory, the electrical interfaces will work best because they have the widest bandwidth. The transmission of digital data from a source to a digital processor should be over the widest possible bandwidth link for low jitter. TosLink has a bandwidth of 6MHz (6,000,000Hz), ST-Type optical is between 50MHz and 150MHz, and electrical interfaces have a potential of 500MHz bandwidth (if implemented correctly).

The best way to choose an interface is by listening to the various types. When comparing an electrical interface to an optical interface, be sure to disconnect the electrical interface from the processor when listening to the optical interface. The advantage of keeping the transport ground isolated from the processor ground is lost if the electrical cable is still connected between the transport and processor, even though it may not be active.

A primary reason for poor-sounding transports and interfaces in electrical connections is an impedance mismatch between the transport's output impedance, the cable's characteristic impedance, and the digital processor's input impedance. The specification is 75 ohms (±5%) for S/PDIF format, and 110 ohms (±20%) for AES/EBU format. An impedance mismatch causes reflections of the signal in the cable, introducing jitter in the data stream. Manufacturers of digital products should strictly adhere to these impedance standards.

How the S/PDIF Interface Works

For those with a technical bent, let's take a closer look at the S/PDIF datastream. The S/PDIF signal contains audio data for both audio channels, as well as a synchronization signal called a clock. This clock is recovered in the digital processor, locking the transport and processor to the same timing reference. The "Lock" light or sampling-frequency indicator on the front panel of many digital processors indicates that the clock has been recovered and the two components are locked together.

S/PDIF and AES/EBU use a type of coding called "bi-phase mark," a form of self-clocking Manchester code. Fig.8-13 shows how the audio data and clock signal are combined to produce the S/PDIF datastream. Each audio data bit is represented by a two-cell doublet, each of which begins and ends with a transition. These doublets are clearly visible in the signal of Fig.8-13. A data bit "1" produces a transition within the doublet. A data bit "0" generates a doublet with no transition within the doublet. Thus, audio data and a clock signal are combined into a single datastream.

Fig. 8-13 The S/PDIF datastream uses "bi-phase mark" coding.

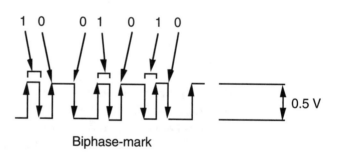

Biphase-mark

The S/PDIF datastream carries not just audio data, but housekeeping information as well, including some of the CD's subcode. This includes the sampling frequency, whether the data has had pre-emphasis applied, and whether the signal is professional AES/EBU or consumer S/PDIF. The subcode data also includes all the track number and timing information displayed on a CD player or transport.

Audio and subcode data are combined to form 32-bit subframes, shown in Fig.8-14. Each subframe begins with a preamble, a 4-bit pattern that violates the rules of bi-phase mark coding. The preamble acts as a synchronization signal to indicate the beginning of a new subframe. The preamble is followed by 4 bits of auxiliary data, then 20 bits of audio data. If 16-bit data are being transmitted, the four additional bits are not used (coded as all zeros). The 4-bit auxiliary data area can be used for audio, bringing the total audio word-length capacity to 24 bits. Four additional bits (audio sample validity, user bit data, audio channel status, and subframe parity) complete the subframe.

Fig. 8-14 S/PDIF subframe structure

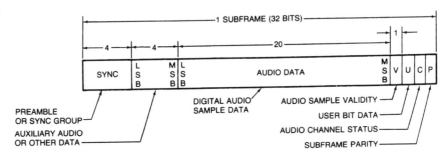

Courtesy Ken Pohlmann, *Principles of Digital Audio*

Left and right audio-channel subframes are identified by slightly different preambles. They are interleaved, making a single bitstream from both audio channels. Subframes are combined to form blocks, each of which is 192 bits long. The overall bit rate is 2.8224 million bits per second for a sampling rate of 44.1kHz.

Jitter in the S/PDIF Interface

Despite the elegance of having left- and right-channel audio data and a clock carried in the same digital channel, there are some sonic compromises inherent in the S/PDIF interface format. The digital processor's input receiver "recovers" the clock from the S/PDIF data stream, generating a new clock that becomes the timing reference for the digital processor. Virtually all input receivers pass interface jitter to the clock that controls the DAC timing. As explained in Appendix C ("Digital Audio Basics"), jitter at the DAC can introduce audible problems.

This interface-induced jitter isn't random in nature; it is directly correlated with the audio signal being transmitted. In other words, the clock is modulated by the music carried by the interface. The recovered clock is jittered at exactly the same frequency as the audio signal traveling down the interface. Using the UltraAnalog jitter-analysis instrument described later in this chapter, it's possible to *listen* to only the jitter component of the S/PDIF signal. Just from hearing the jitter, the piece of music being transmitted is readily discernible. This audio-correlated jitter ends up at the DAC's word clock, where it degrades the processor sound quality.

A solution to this problem has been adopted by a few high-end manufacturers. Linn, Krell, Sumo, Bitwise, Arcam, and DPA, for examples, use a second clock cable between the transport and processor. This additional cable works in one of two methods. In the first technique, the extra cable carries the master clock from the processor to the transport, forcing the transport to lock to the processor's master clock. The second technique transmits the clock on a separate line, removing the input-receiver PLL and obviating the need for recovering a clock. The high-precision clock in the transport is input directly to the processor. This technique eliminates interface-induced clock jitter provided the clock line is well executed. Fig.8-15 shows a processor and transport connected with a separate clock line (the clock line is the upper cable in the photograph).

Fig. 8-15 A separate clock line between a transport and processor reduces jitter.

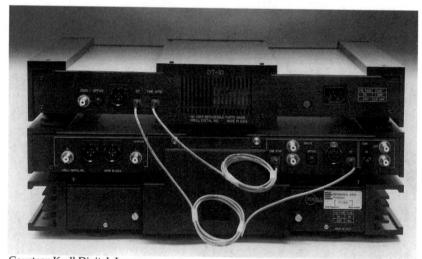

Courtesy Krell Digital, Inc.

High-end digital processors using a separate clock line also have a conventional input receiver and PLL to recover the clock. This makes them compatible with transports lacking a clock input (or output). It is thus possible to compare the standard clock-recovery technique with using a separate clock just by disconnecting the clock cable. In listening tests, I've found this additional link greatly improves sound quality. Moreover, processors and transports having a separate clock signal should be immune to sonic differences between interfaces (coax, ST-Type, TosLink, AES/EBU) and different cables within an interface family.

Despite the sonic benefits, using a second clock line between a transport and processor has been adopted by very few manufacturers. This is because there is no standard format for the clock signal, making the feature useful only on transport/processor pairs from the same company. With few transport manufacturers offering a clock input—and a lack of standardization among those who do—most digital processor manufacturers simply don't include a separate clock line on their products.

Manufacturers have recently started using newer, more sophisticated input receivers that provide low jitter without a separate clock line. The processor shown in Fig.8-6 uses one of these low-jitter input receiver modules.

There is another way to eliminate interface-induced jitter: get a CD player. Because a one-box CD player doesn't need to transmit audio data and a clock, it doesn't need the S/PDIF interface. And with no interface, there is no interface-induced clock jitter. CD players thus have an inherent advantage over separate processors and transports.

Jitter-Reduction Devices

Jitter-reduction devices are a whole new component category launched in 1993. The jitter-reduction device is inserted in the digital signal path between a CD transport (or any other digital source) and a digital processor. In theory, the jitter-reduction device takes in a jittered S/PDIF digital signal and outputs a less jittered digital signal. A problem arises when the jitter-reduction device's output jitter is higher than the transport's jitter, a condition which will degrade rather than improve sound quality. Jitter-reduction devices can improve high-jitter transports, but can also degrade low-jitter transports. These devices should therefore be auditioned in your own system before buying. Further, many jitter-reduction devices claim some low level of output jitter ("less than 50ps," for example), but the manufacturer has no way of verifying the claim of low jitter. Never buy a jitter-reduction device on the basis of a specification; instead, listen to it in your own system.

Alternative Digital Technologies

Most of the processors on the market fit this chapter's generic description of how a digital processor works. Some products, however, use different technologies, either in their digital filters or DACs. Following, I've outlined these alternative processor technologies.

1-Bit DACs

Some digital processors use so-called *1-bit* DACs. They are more correctly called *noise-shaping* DACs, *Delta-Sigma* DACs, or *oversampling* DACs. These converters are also known by their trade names: "Bitstream" (Philips), "MASH" (Matsushita's process, developed by Nippon Telephone and Telegraph), and "PEM" (Pulse Edge Modulation, developed by JVC). All of these converters work on the same principle: instead of using a resistor ladder with different bit weightings to convert a binary code into analog, 1-bit DACs operate in only two states—zero and one. The 1-bit code is a series of varying-length pulses with a single amplitude. The pulse width determines the analog output voltage. This is why 1-bit coding is also called *Pulse Width Modulation*.

The single-bit code is of a high enough frequency (typically between 64x- and 256x-oversampling) that the audio signal can be reconstructed from these two logic states with a switched capacitor network. Consequently, 1-bit DACs don't require the amplitude precision of ladder DACs. Oversampling DACs trade resolution in amplitude for resolution in time. They have inherently good linearity without the need of an MSB trimmer (they have no MSB to trim). Further, oversampling DACs don't require a current-to-voltage (I/V) converter.

Because oversampling DACs operate at such a high frequency, noise shaping can be used to shift quantization noise from the audio band to just above the audio band. The effect of noise shaping can be seen in Fig.8-20 later in this chapter.

A block diagram of an oversampling DAC is shown in Fig.8-16. The DAC has an integral digital filter that oversamples the data at a 4x (176.4kHz) rate. The audio data are then oversampled using linear interpolation at 32x the 4x rate, then oversampled again at 2x. The result is 256x-oversampling. The 17-bit–wide digital code is then converted to a 1-bit *Pulse Density Modulation* signal. A switched capacitor network converts the very fast, single-bit code into an analog signal.

Many 1-bit DACs incorporate an analog output stage and analog filter in addition to their integral digital filter. Consequently, a single 1-bit DAC can take the place of a digital filter, dual ladder DACs, dual I/V converters, dual MSB trimmers, and two analog output stages. This makes 1-bit technology much cheaper to implement than multi-bit DACs.

My listening experience suggests, however, that digital processors based on multi-bit DACs sound better than those using 1-bit technology. Processors employing 1-bit DACs tend to lack bass tautness, dynamics, and pace. They may have a smooth and transparent presentation, but often don't have rhythmic intensity and "slam" of multi-bit designs.

There are, however, some excellent-sounding 1-bit–based digital processors on the market.

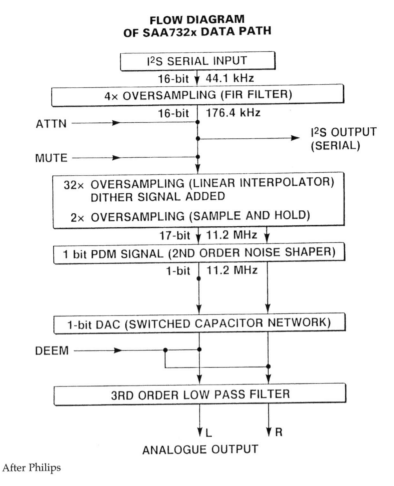

After Philips

Custom Digital Filters

A few digital processors use custom digital filters instead of off-the-shelf filter chips. Proponents of this approach—notably Krell, Theta, Wadia, and Museatex—believe their custom filtering software is better than that found in conventional integrated circuit chips. Custom filters are based on Digital Signal Processing (DSP) chips, usually the Motorola DSP56001. These sophisticated chips process the digital audio data according to software instructions contained in one or more Erasable Programmable Read-Only Memory (EPROM) chips. This software, which contains the filtering algorithm (a specific set of instruction on how to process the digital audio data) is easily changed. DSP-based filter designers can thus tailor the processor's sound by changing the EPROM containing the filtering algorithm.

Specifically, most custom digital filters are optimized for time-domain performance rather than frequency-domain performance. The Wadia processors, for example, have superb time-domain behavior, seen as near perfect reconstruction of squarewaves and no pre- or post-echo in the impulse response (the Meitner IDAT is another example). This excellent time-domain performance is sometimes achieved at the price of a steep rolloff in the audioband. One particular processor, for example, is down a full 3dB at 20kHz.

The I²S Bus

One feature found on a few digital products is a small jack labeled "I²S Bus" (pronounced "I squared S"). This rear-panel port provides access to the digital signal inside the component in a format used by the component's internal chips. With an I²S bus, external digital signal-processing devices which also have I²S bus ports can be connected to the component's internal signals. Very few manufacturers provide the I²S bus input/output jack.

Digital Recorders: Digital Audio Tape (DAT), MiniDisc (MD), Digital Compact Cassette (DCC), CD Recordable (CDR), and CD Erasable (CDE).

In addition to the most common digital products just discussed—transports and processors—an array of digital recording devices allow the consumer to make digital copies of CDs or make digital recordings from an analog source. I've outlined the various digital recording formats available to the audiophile.

Digital Audio Tape

By far the most popular digital recording format for consumer and semi-professional use is Digital Audio Tape (DAT). Although DAT never became the mass-market digital recording standard its inventors had hoped for, the format has revolutionized the professional and semi-professional recording world. It's easy to see why: DAT provides up to two hours of recording time on a small, moderately priced tape. Moreover, the recording quality is determined by the A/D and D/A converters used with a DAT machine. By adding external A/D and D/A converters (using DAT as a data-storage medium), extremely high-quality recording is possible.

DAT is the best choice for high-quality digital recording at home. First, the blank media costs are the lowest of the digital recording formats. A two-hour DAT costs about $10, in contrast to $40 for Compact Disc Recordable (two 60-minute discs at $20 each), $28 for MD (again, two 60-minute discs), and $24 for DCC (two 60-minute tapes). In addition to low tape costs, the DAT format's acceptance by the professional recording industry assures a long-term tape supply, service availability, and replacement machines well into the future. Finally, DAT records linear 16-bit PCM audio data, instead of a reduced bit-rate representation—as in MD and DCC—that reduces fidelity.

MiniDisc

The MiniDisc is a recordable/erasable optical disc format designed by Sony to replace the analog cassette. It uses a 3" optical disc encased in a plastic caddy, much like a smaller version of a 3.5" computer diskette. MD is extremely portable, easy to use, and has instant track access like CD. The price for this small size is lower sound quality, a result of a reduced–bit-rate coding scheme called ATRAC (Adaptive Transform Acoustic Coding). ATRAC produces a bit rate of 128 kilobits per channel (128 thousand bits per second), in contrast to CD's 705kbs per channel data rate. Another drawback is the high cost of blank media—about $15 for a 60-minute disc.

Digital Compact Cassette

Philips's DCC is a digital version of the venerable Compact Cassette, the most popular carrier of recorded music. DCC is a cassette identical in size to the analog cassette. Like MD, DCC uses a low–bit-rate coding scheme. DCC's low–bit-rate coder is called PASC (Precision Adaptive Sub-band Coding), and produces a data stream with a rate of 196kbs—50% greater than MD's ATRAC, but still only a quarter the data rate of CD-coded digital audio.

Philips touts DCC as being backward-compatible: analog cassettes will play back on DCC machines. Advantages of DCC include higher sound quality than MD, and lower blank media price. Disadvantage are the fact that DCC is a tape-based medium, subject to the problems of tape, primarily wear and slow access time—problems that don't afflict MD.

As of this writing, it is unclear if DCC or MD will replace the analog cassette, or, indeed, if either of them will even survive.

Compact Disc Recordable

The Compact Disc Recordable (CDR) format allows the user to record her own compact disc and play that disc on any conventional CD player. The advantage of CDR is compatibility with the huge base of CD players around the world. The big drawback to CDR is that the disc can be recorded only once. If you make a mistake in recording, or want to record something else on the disc, you're stuck. This disadvantage is further compounded by the high blank disc price—about $20 for a 60 minute disc.

Compact Disc Erasable

Compact Disc Erasable (CDE) may bring practical, high-quality digital recording to the home. CDE should have all the benefits of CDR without the drawbacks of a write-once system. Although not a reality at the time of this writing, sources indicate that a moderately priced CDE machine will be available by 1996. If the blank discs are reasonably priced, CDE will be the ideal format for the home recordist.

Digital Specifications and Measurements

Many tests and measurements exist to quantify a digital processor's technical performance, but few—if any—measurements tell us how the processor sounds. Nonetheless, good technical performance indicates that the processor is well engineered, and is more likely to have good sonic performance as well. The following set of measurements are included in the processor reviews I have written for *Stereophile*.

Let's start with a digital processor's maximum output level. (I'll use the term digital processor, although I'm also referring to CD players—the measurements are the same.) The standard analog output voltage is 2VRMS, with units varying between 1.75V and a whopping 7.2V. Most CD players and processors put out between 2.2V and 3.5V. Note that this value is the highest RMS output voltage possible from the player, measured by playing a full-scale, 1kHz sinewave.

Knowledge of a processor's output level is useful in several ways. First, a very high output processor wouldn't be ideal for driving a preamplifier that had lots of gain. Although it is unlikely that the processor would overload the preamplifier's input, you would end up using the preamp's volume control at the very low end of its range. Most volume controls exhibit their greatest channel imbalances (i.e., one channel is louder than the other) when turned down. In addition, setting a "just right" volume is more difficult with high-output processors and high-gain line-stage preamplifiers; the volume control becomes overly touchy to small movements. This is particularly true of preamps with detent level steps instead of a continuously variable volume control. A high output level is an asset when driving a passive level control, but a drawback with a high-gain line-stage preamplifier.

Another important measurement to consider when determining if a particular processor or CD player is a good candidate for a passive level control is output impedance. If a passive level control is used between a digital processor and power amplifier, the burden of driving the cables and power amplifier falls on the digital processor's output stage. If the processor has a high output impedance, dynamics can become compressed and the bass may get mushy. In extreme cases, a processor with a very high output impedance can even become current-limited and flatten the waveform peaks if it is asked to drive a low-input impedance preamplifier. Processors with the highest output impedances have an impedance of nearly 2k ohms at 20kHz and 1.5k ohms at 1kHz. This high output impedance causes the processor's output stage to clip when asked to drive impedances of less than about 15k ohms.

Further, the output impedance of the passive level control itself must be added to the equation. The passive control's output impedance (which varies depending on which resistor is switched in, or the position of the potentiometer) must be *added* to the driving component's source impedance to find the total source impedance driving the power amplifier.

Digital-processor output impedances vary from less than 1 ohm to 5.6k ohms (the highest value I've measured in a product). Generally, if the output impedance is less than a few hundred ohms, the processor should have no trouble driving a passive level control. Between 50 and 500 ohms is a typical value.

Bottom line: Don't drive a low-input-impedance power amplifier (less than about 20k ohms) with a passive level control through long, high-capacitance interconnect, with a high-output-impedance (greater than about 800 ohms) digital processor. These aren't hard and fast numbers, but general guidelines. Appendix B includes a full analysis of what can happen with a passive level control and high-output impedance sources.

The next measurement, frequency response, doesn't reveal a processor's overall tonal balance as it often does with loudspeakers, but is included in specifications and measurements for the sake of completeness. Most processors are down a few tenths of a dB at 20kHz, the result of rolloff in the digital filter.

More revealing, however, is a CD player's or processor's *de-emphasis error*. As previously described, some CDs have had their trebles boosted (emphasized) during recording, and carry a flag that tells the CD player to switch in its de-emphasis circuit to restore flat response. These de-emphasis circuits are often inaccurate (due to resistor and capacitor tolerances), producing frequency-response irregularities when the player is decoding emphasized discs. De-emphasis error should be less than ±0.1dB across the band. De-emphasis errors can cause tonal-balance irregularities (tizzy upper treble, for example) when playing pre-emphasized CDs. De-emphasis errors of 0.2dB over an octave of bandwidth are audible. Poor and good de-emphasis accuracy is shown in Fig.8-17a and b. Both these measurements were made on digital processors using analog de-emphasis circuits; processors with digital-domain de-emphasis have no errors. The positive error in Fig.8-17a will make the processor sound bright when playing pre-emphasized CDs.

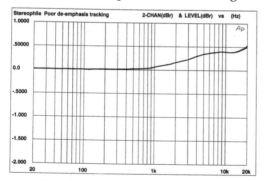 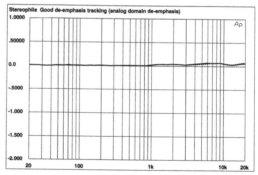

Fig. 8-17a and b De-emphasis errors (left) and accurate de-emphasis tracking (right) (Courtesy *Stereophile*)

Interchannel crosstalk, also called channel separation, is a measurement of how well the left and right channels are isolated from one another. Ideally, when a digital processor is fed a right-channel signal, that signal should not appear in the left channel, and vice versa. The lower the crosstalk (or, put another way, the greater the channel separation), the better. Many processors (and other products) have decreasing channel separation as frequency increases, a result of capacitive coupling between channels. Typical CD players and digital processors have about 90dB of channel separation at 1kHz, this decreasing to about 70dB at

20kHz. Although there is no correlation between low crosstalk and soundstage width (an intuitive link), high channel separation indicates good overall engineering. Mediocre and good crosstalk performance are shown in Fig.8-18a and b. At 1kHz, the processor shown in Fig.8-18a has 67dB of channel separation, compared with the 112dB of channel separation at 1kHz measured in the processor shown in Fig.8-18b.

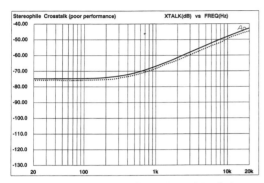 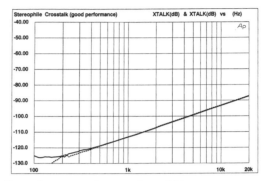

Fig. 8-18a and b Poor (left) and good (right) crosstalk performance (Courtesy *Stereophile*)

A very revealing test of a processor's ability to re-create low-level signals looks at the processor's output vs. frequency (*spectral analysis*) when the processor under test is driven with the digital code representing a –90dB, dithered 1kHz sinewave. A spectral analysis plots energy level vs. frequency. Peaks in the trace at 60Hz, 120Hz, 180Hz, and related frequencies indicate that power-supply noise is getting into the audio circuitry. A spectral analysis can also hint at how well the unit's DACs (digital-to-analog converters) are performing; the signal should peak at the –90dB horizontal division, and the left and right traces should overlap. This indicates that the DACs are linear and have similar performance between channels. The spectral analysis also shows the processor's noise level, and reveals if there is any spurious energy in the audioband. Fig.8-19a and b show very poor and excellent performance on this test respectively. In the poor-performing processor, we can see power-supply noise in the audio signal at 60Hz and harmonics of 60Hz, linearity error (the traces don't peak at the –90dB horizontal division), no overlap of the traces (indicated the DACs are not well matched between channels), and a higher overall noise level. The performance shown in Fig.8-19b is exemplary.

The same type of spectral analysis, but with the processor driven by "digital silence" (all zeros), is also performed and plotted to 200kHz. This test can reveal the presence of spurious junk in or above the audioband, and DAC artifacts such as idle tones (seen as a peak in the trace). Ideally, the trace should be a smooth line, sloping gently upward, with no peaks at the power-line frequencies and no spikes in the audioband. The effects of noise shaping in 1-bit–type converters can also be seen in this measurement. As described earlier in this chapter, noise shaping is a technique that pushes noise from the audioband into the ultrasonic band. Fig.8-20 shows the effects of noise shaping as revealed by this wideband 1/3-octave spectral analysis; The noise floor rises sharply above 10kHz. We can also see some peaks in the left channel trace (the solid line) at 18kHz and 25kHz, which may be DAC artifacts.

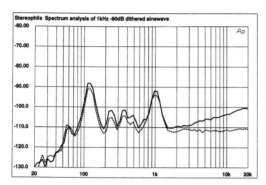 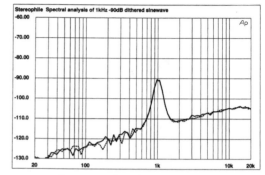

Fig. 8-19a and b Poor (left) and good (right) performance on the spectral analysis test (Courtesy *Stereophile*)

Fig. 8-20 A wideband spectral analysis reveals the effects of noise shaping in 1-bit converters.

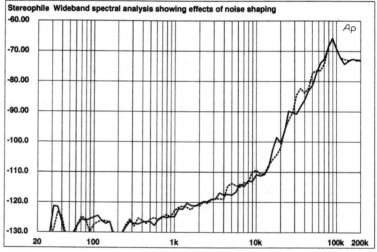

Courtesy *Stereophile*

Low-level linearity was touted a few years back as the definitive measurement in digital processors. While good linearity is a high engineering goal, it doesn't guarantee good sound.

Understanding linearity is easy: it's how well the processor's analog output level tracks the digital input level. If we put in the code representing a –88dBFS signal, for example, the analog output of the test tone should be exactly –88dB (88dB below full scale). Any deviation between digital input level and analog output level is linearity error. Linearity error occurs in all DACs, and is compensated for in many processors with an MSB (Most Significant Bit) trimmer at the factory.

Linearity error is expressed as the dB difference between the digital input level and the analog output level at a specific digital level (with any gain error normalized out of the measurement). For example, we may say that a particular converter has a 3dB positive error at –90dBFS. This means that when the processor is driven by the digital code representing a –90dBFS signal, the processor's analog output is actually –87dB, or 3dB higher than the digital input level. Note that the digital input level refers to the signal levels represented by the value of the ones and zeros in the binary code, not the input voltage to the processor's digital input, which remains constant.

A comparison of poor and good linearity is shown in Fig.8-21. A perfect processor would produce a ruler-flat line, with no deviation above or below the zero horizontal division. The linearity measurement in Fig.8-21b comes very close to this ideal. Conversely, the measurement in Fig.8-21a has a 2.6dB negative error in the right channel (dotted trace) and a 4dB negative error in the left channel (solid trace) at a signal level of –90dB.

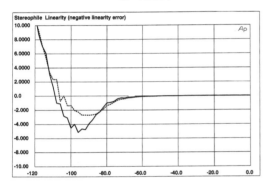 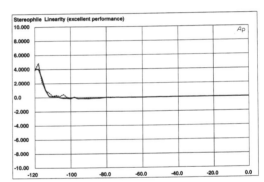

Fig. 8-21a and b Mediocre (left) and excellent (right) linearity (Courtesy *Stereophile*)

If the linearity trace dips below the center line, this indicates a negative linearity error. If it rises above the center line, the processor has a positive linearity error (the analog output is higher than it should be). The digital input level is read across the bottom, with the highest level at the graph's right-hand side. Some processors with excellent low-level linearity appear to have a positive error at very low signal levels (–115dB). This is actually noise swamping the DAC's output. The practical lower limit of measuring linearity is about –112dBFS (in quiet processors). Linearity is determined by the DAC (digital-to-analog converter) chip inside the processor.

A recently developed digital processor test, called "noise modulation," looks at how a digital processor's noise-floor shifts, or modulates, with changing input level. Not only does the noise-floor shift, but the noise-floor's spectral balance can be very different at different input levels.

In the noise modulation test, the processor is driven by the code representing a 41Hz sinewave at –60dBFS. The processor's output is high-pass–filtered to remove the test signal, and the residual noise is plotted vs. frequency. Ten samples are taken at each data point, and the average of those samples is plotted. The low-frequency test signal exercises the DAC, and the resulting noise is measured and plotted. The test is repeated at four additional levels (–70dB, –80dB, –90dB, –100dB), and the plots are combined on a single graph. This makes comparing noise-floor levels and spectral balance between input levels easier.

In a perfect processor, the five traces would overlap, indicating that there was no change in the noise level or spectral content as a function of signal level. All processors, however, exhibit some deviation between the traces. The tighter the traces, the better. Any time one trace crosses another, the noise-floor's spectral balance has shifted. The amount of this shift can be calculated by looking at the deviation between traces, using the horizontal division scale on the far-left side of the graph. Examples of poor and good noise-modulation performance are shown in Fig.8-22a and b.

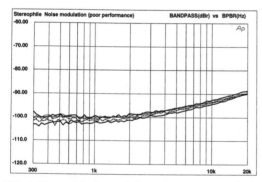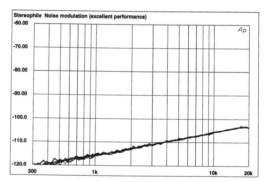

Fig. 8-22a and b Poor (left) and excellent (right) performance on the noise modulation test (Courtesy *Stereophile*)

Another test in which there may be a correlation with sound quality is the FFT-derived spectral analysis of the processor's output when decoding a full-scale mix of 19kHz and 20kHz. This test reveals inter-modulation components such as the 1kHz difference tone (20kHz minus 19kHz), and interactions between the sampling frequency (44.1kHz) and the test signals.

As with the spectral analysis we saw earlier of the –90dB, 1kHz sinewave, this spectral analysis also plots energy against frequency. But this technique does it a little differently. In an FFT-derived spectral analysis, the processor's output is captured in the time domain, creating a waveform, and transformed into the frequency domain using the Fast Fourier Transform (FFT).

The result of this technique is shown in Fig.8-23a and b, the FFT-derived spectral analysis of two processors' outputs when decoding this unusual test signal. Ideally, there should be no spikes in the noise-floor; Fig.8-23b shows exemplary performance on this test. Note the greater number of spikes in Fig.8-23a. The higher the spikes' amplitude, and the greater their number, the worse the intermodulation distortion performance. The trace in Fig.8-23b reveals a 1kHz difference component, but very few other intermodulation products.

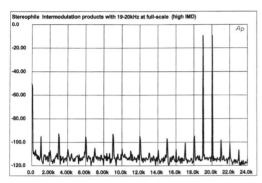 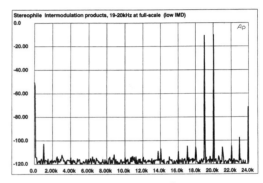

Fig. 8-23a and b Some processors produce high intermodulation distortion (left); others generate very little IMD (right). (Courtesy *Stereophile*)

Digital processors run into problems when converting very low level signals to analog. One way to examine a DAC's behavior on small signals is to capture its analog output waveform when reproducing a –90dB, undithered 1kHz sinewave. This test signal produces three quantization steps: 0, +1, and –1. The three levels should be of equal amplitude, and the signal should be symmetrical around the center horizontal division. A poor-quality reproduction of this signal is shown in Fig.8-24a, a high-quality one in Fig.8-24b. Note the absence of noise in Fig.8-24b, and the three clearly defined quantization steps. By contrast, Fig.8-24a is so noisy it's difficult to make out the wave's shape.

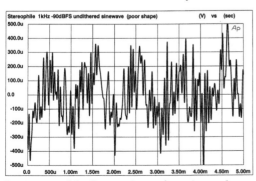 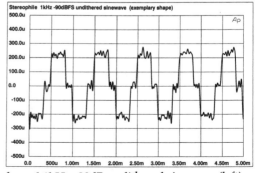

Fig. 8-24a and b Comparison of a noisy and poorly-shaped 1kHz -90dB undithered sinewave (left), and nearly perfect reproduction (right) (Courtesy *Stereophile*)

A processor's reproduction of a 1kHz, full-scale squarewave (not shown) reveals its time-domain behavior. Most measurements show the overshoot and ringing typical of the digital filters used in most processors and CD players. The digital filter determines the waveform shape; the time distortion occurs in the digital filter. Some digital processors with custom DSP-based filters don't suffer from this type of distortion.

The amount of DC at the digital processor's analog outputs is measured and noted. The lower the DC level, the better. DC may cause a thump through the system when the preamplifier's input selector is switched to select the processor's output. If the preamplifier and power amplifier are both direct-coupled (no DC blocking capacitors in the signal path) and use no DC servo correction, the DC from the processor could be amplified and appear at the loudspeaker terminals—not a good condition. Low DC—less than, say, 20mV—is therefore desirable.

The measurements section of a digital product review will often include a mention that the processor is polarity-inverting or non-inverting. A non-inverting processor's analog output will be of the same absolute polarity as the digital data on the CD. Most processors don't invert polarity, but if one does, that's no reason for concern. Without knowing the absolute polarity of the recording and the rest of your system, it's a fifty-fifty chance that the absolute polarity will be wrong. Knowing that a processor inverts absolute polarity is useful when comparing processors: all processors under audition should maintain the same polarity for the listening comparisons to be valid.

Measuring a digital processor's word-clock jitter (inaccuracy in the critical timing signal) was first made possible in 1992 by an instrument called the "LIM Detector," developed by Ed Meitner of Museatex. Although other designers have looked at word-clock jitter, the LIM Detector was the first commercially available jitter analysis tool. When used with an FFT machine and RMS-reading voltmeter, the LIM detector provides the digital processor's overall RMS jitter level (over a specified bandwidth) and a spectral analysis of that jitter.

To use the LIM Detector, the word-clock pin on the DAC is found, and a probe is connected between the word clock and the LIM Detector. The LIM Detector output is only the jitter component of that word clock. A wide range of word-clock frequencies are accommodated. The LIM Detector output is fed to the input of an Audio Precision System One, which performs an FFT on the jitter to analyze and display its spectral content. The System One's RMS reading meter displays an overall RMS voltage, which is converted to jitter in picoseconds (ps). We thus end up with a number indicating the overall amount of jitter on the digital processor's word clock, and FFTs showing the jitter's spectral distribution.

The FFT of Fig.8-25a shows a jitter spectrum in which the jitter is periodic; that is, the jitter energy is concentrated at specific frequencies, seen as spikes in the plot. Where you see a spike, it means the digital processor's word clock is being jittered at that frequency. Note that the spikes occur at 1kHz and multiples of 1kHz; the test tone driving the digital processor is a 1kHz sinewave. As described earlier in this chapter, jitter is often correlated with the audio signal—something we can readily see in Fig.8-25a. The RMS jitter level, measured over a 400Hz-20kHz bandwidth, is 350ps.

For contrast, Fig.8-25b is the jitter spectrum of a very low jitter digital processor. Not only is the overall RMS level lower (less than 80ps), but the jitter spectrum is nearly free from signal-correlated jitter.

In short, the lower the trace on the FFT, and the smoother the line (lack of spikes), the better the processor's jitter performance.

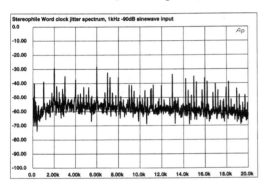 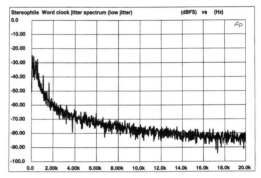

Fig. 8-25a and b High word-clock jitter in a digital processor (left), and low jitter with few periodic jitter components (right) (Courtesy *Stereophile*)

There are few measurements available that even attempt to characterize a transport's performance. One of them, however, can be made by anyone, and gauges how well the transport's tracking and error correction systems work. All you need is the Pierre Verany *Digital Test* CD (Pierre Verany PV.788031/788032). Disc 2 of the two-CD set contains a section in which the spiral track of pits is interrupted by blank areas (no pits). This simulates data dropouts caused by poor-quality CDs, dirt, scratches, or other media contamination. A continuous tone is recorded on the tracks. The blank areas gradually increase in length, and each increase is represented by a different track number. The higher the track number in this series, the longer the dropout. By listening for when the test tone is interrupted and noting the track number, the dropout length the player can track and correct can be determined. The higher the track number the transport will play flawlessly, the better. Most transports will play up to track 33. Skip-free reproduction of track 37 or higher is excellent.

A recently-devised method of characterizing transport quality measures the amount of jitter in the transport's output signal. The test instrument, developed by UltraAnalog, takes a transport's S/PDIF or AES/EBU signal and separates the jitter component from the data. The jitter signal is then plotted as a function of frequency so that we can examine the jitter's spectral content. The best transports have about 30 picoseconds (ps) of broadband jitter, the worst about 500ps of jitter. Fig.8-26a shows very high transport jitter; Fig.8-26b shows very low transport jitter. The three traces are made with different test signals: the solid trace is with the transport outputting a full-scale, 1kHz sine wave; the heavy dotted trace is with a -90dB 1kHz tone; and the light trace is measured with a signal of all zeros output from the transport. The peaks in the trace at 1kHz indicate that transport jitter is correlated with the audio signal. The peak at 7.35kHz in Fig.8-26b is the CD's 7.35kHz subcode data rate.

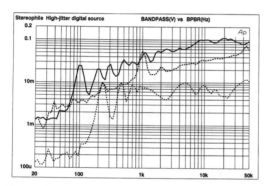 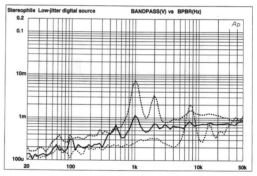

Fig. 8-26a and b Comparison of high jitter in the S/PDIF signal (right) and low jitter (left) (Courtesy *Stereophile*)

Finally, good bench performance from a digital processor or transport doesn't guarantee high sound quality. Moreover, there is no way to predict a component's musical character from looking at test results. Nevertheless, a product that sounds good and measures well inspires more confidence than one that performs poorly on the test bench.

9 Turntables, Tonearms, and Cartridges: The LP Playback System

Overview

The long-playing (LP) record playback system is a combination of a turntable, tonearm, and phono cartridge that converts the mechanical information encoded on vinyl records into an electrical signal that can be amplified by the rest of your playback system. The turntable spins the record, the tonearm holds the cartridge in place, and the cartridge converts the wiggles in the record's groove into an electrical signal. Each of these elements, and how they interact with each other, plays a pivotal role in getting good sound from your system.

The LP record playback system has been the mainstay of the audio and music industries since the early years of this century. If you wanted recorded music, you bought records. The advent of the compact disc has, however, severely restricted the availability of LPs. As the world abandons LPs in favor of the more convenient CD format, the audiophile is left with difficult choices about how much to invest in the competing LP and CD playback hardware.

This quandary—LP vs. CD—emerges from the fact that even today's state-of-the-art digital audio doesn't approach the sound quality offered by a good LP playback system. At the very highest level of music reproduction, there's not even a debate: LP is musically superior to CD.

I must qualify that last statement: a high-quality, properly set-up LP playback system, playing a record in good condition, will sound better than any CD. If, however, the record is played on a low-quality or poorly set-up system, the CD will usually offer higher sonic performance. The general public's perception that CD is vastly superior to LP (remember the "Perfect Sound Forever" marketing campaign for CD?) is perpetuated because very few listeners have heard high-quality LP play-back. When done right, LP playback has an openness, transparency, dynamic expression, and musicality not matched by CD. There's just a fundamental musical rightness to a pure analog source (one that has never been digitized) that seems to better convey the music's expression.

This isn't to say that LPs are perfect. They suffer from a variety of distortions such as mistracking, ticks and pops, speed instability, surface noise, cartridge frequency-response variations, inner-groove distortion, wear, and susceptibility to damage. But for many listeners, these prob-lems are less musically objectionable than the distortion imposed by digitally encoding and decoding an audio signal. Some listeners can hear past the LP's flaws and enjoy the medium's overall musicality. Other listeners can't stand the ritual of handling and cleaning records—not to mention keeping the turntable properly adjusted—and think CD is just fine. If you're inclined to think CD is without fault, and you've never heard a properly played LP, give yourself a treat and visit a specialty audio dealer with a high-end turntable. Listen to what vinyl can do before you write off the possibility of owning a high-quality turntable.

This state of affairs—an archaic medium nearly 100 years old surpassing the quality of today's digital wonder technology—is almost certainly temporary. Digital audio is improving at a rapid rate, and some wholesale advances in the technology are under way. It's only a matter of time before CDs finally live up to their promise and make the entire analog vs. digital debate moot.

But until then, many of us will continue enjoying our records.

System Hierarchy: Why the LP Front End Is So Important

My suggestion later in this chapter that some audiophiles spend as much as 40% of their total system budget on an LP front end may strike some as excessive. After all, how much effect can the cartridge, tonearm—and especially the turntable—have on the reproduced sound compared to the contribution of amplifiers and loudspeakers?

The answer is that the components at the front of the playback chain should be of at least as good a quality as those at the end of the chain (loudspeakers). The LP playback system's job is to extract as much musical information from the LP grooves as possible, and with the greatest fidelity to the signal cut into the LP. *Any musical information not recovered at the front end of the playback system cannot be restored later in the chain*. It doesn't do any good to have superlative electronics and loud-speakers if you're feeding them a poor-quality, low-resolution signal from an inadequate LP front end. If the music isn't there at the start, it won't be there at the end.

The importance of the turntable was first brought to the world's attention by Ivor Tiefenbrun of Linn in the early 1970s. He sold his turntable by walking into audio dealerships unannounced with the turntable under his arm, and asking the store owner to listen with him to the best system in the store with the store's turntable. Then they listened to the store's least expensive system hooked up to the Linn LP12 turntable. When the store owners heard their most modest system outperform their most expensive system, many became convinced of the turntable's importance. It took years of these kinds of demonstrations to convince the audio community that the turntable was a significant variable in a system's sound quality. Today, no debate exists over the turntable's importance in achieving good sound. (To date, more than 100,000 Linn LP12s have been sold worldwide.)

How to Choose an LP Playback System

Because there are many more variables to account for in LP play-back, how much of your audio budget you should spend on this part of your system is a more complicated decision than setting a budget for, say, a power amplifier.

Let's look at two hypothetical audiophiles, one of whom should spend much more on a turntable, tonearm, and cartridge than the other audiophile.

Our first audiophile has a huge record collection that represents a lifetime of collecting music. Her record collection is a treasure trove of intimately known music that she plays daily. Conversely, she has very few CDs, buying them only when her favorite music isn't available on vinyl. She much prefers the sound of LPs, and doesn't mind the greater effort required by LPs: record and stylus cleaning, turning over the record, lack of random access.

The second audiophile's record assortment represents a small percentage of his music collection—most of his favorite music is on CD. His LP listening time is a fraction of the time spent listening to CD. He likes the convenience of CD, and can happily live with the sound of his excellent digital processor and CD transport.

The first audiophile should commit a significant portion of her overall system budget to a topnotch LP front end—perhaps 40%. The second will want to spend much less—say, 10 to 15%—and put the savings into the components he spends more time listening to.

If you're more like the first audiophile and are about to upgrade your turntable, I suggest you stretch your budget and get a really topnotch turntable, tonearm, and cartridge. Here's why: Superlative turntables won't be around forever. With LPs continuing to decline in availability, fewer and fewer manufacturers will offer high-end turntables. If you buy a turntable good enough to keep you going for a few years with the idea of upgrading later, your upgrade options may be severely limited. By buying an excellent system now, you can probably keep it for the rest of your life. The turntable you buy now may be the last turntable you'll ever need. Make it a good one.

Further, today's turntables, tonearms, and cartridges are at the pinnacle of technical and musical achievement. They are vastly superior to the products of even the middle 1980s, and provide you with a means of hearing your LP collection with a quality you may not have thought possible. It's ironic that LP playback hardware's great progress has coincided with the LP's demise.

There's another way of getting a superb analog front end: Buy a used one from someone who's abandoned LPs in favor of CDs. (While you're at it, you can also pick up the owner's record collection.)

A decent entry-level turntable and integral tonearm runs about $450, with an appropriate cartridge adding from $30 to $150 to the price. A mid-level turntable and arm costs $800 to $1500; the cartridge price range for this level of turntable is from $200 to $700.

There are roughly two quality and price levels above the $2000 mark. The first is occupied by a wide selection of turntables and arms costing between $3000 and $6000. At this price, you can achieve very nearly state-of-the-art performance. Plan to spend at least $1000 for a phono cartridge appropriate for these turntables.

The very highest price level is established by turntables costing between $10,000 and $20,000. A topflight phono cartridge can add as much as $5000 to the price. These systems are characterized by extraordinary and elaborate construction techniques such as vacuum hold-down systems to keep the record in intimate contact with the platter, massive vibration-resistant bases, an extraordinary vibration isolation system, lots of high-precision machining, and a high-gloss finish. Although many of these turntables are sonically superlative, some turntables in the $8000 to $12,000 range are equal (or even superior) to the costliest units in construction quality, finish elegance, reliability, and sonic performance.

Once you've decided on an LP front-end budget, allocate a percentage of that budget to the turntable, tonearm, and cartridge. Many lower-priced turntables come with an arm—or an arm and cartridge—

already fitted and included in the price. At the other end of the scale, the megabuck turntables also include a tonearm. In the middle range, you should expect to spend about 50% of your budget on the turntable, 25% on a tonearm, and 25% on a cartridge. These aren't hard figures, but an approximation of how your LP front end budget should be allocated. As usual, a local audio retailer with whom you've established a relationship is your best source of advice on assembling the best LP playback system for your budget.

An item of utmost importance in achieving good sound from your records is a good turntable stand or equipment rack, particularly if the turntable has a less than adequate suspension. (Turntable suspensions are described later in this chapter.) I cannot overstate how vital a solid, vibration-resistant stand is in getting the most from your analog front end. Save some of your budget for a solid equipment rack or you're wasting your money on a good turntable, arm, and cartridge. (The very best turntables have extraordinary mechanical systems to isolate the turntable from vibration, and thus don't benefit as much from a solid stand. These turntables are rare, and occupy the upper end of the price range.)

The importance of a good rack was underscored for me recently while I was reviewing a turntable isolation system. I moved the turntable (a model that lacked a suspension) from its usual place on a 350-pound sand-filled and spiked turntable stand (the Merrill Stable Table) to a generic wooden "stereo rack" to test the effectiveness of the turntable isolation system. The difference was like night and day—and far greater than you'd expect. I'll talk more about turntable stands later in this chapter, under "LP System Setup," and also in Chapter 12.

I'll also go into some detail about how turntables, tonearms, and cartridges are built, and what to look for when choosing each element of the LP front end. You can use this information to assemble your own turntable system, or just brush up on the subject so you can talk confidently with your dealer who puts together your LP playback system. Whichever route you choose, you'll still want to listen and evaluate the turntable system's sonic merits.

What to Listen For

Judging the sonic and musical performance of an LP playback system is more difficult than evaluating any other component. If you want to audition a phono cartridge, for example, you cannot do so without also hearing the turntable, tonearm, and how the cartridge interacts with the rest of the LP playback system. The same situation applies to each of the elements that make up an analog front end; you can never hear them in isolation. Further, how those three components are set up greatly affects the overall performance. Other variables include the turntable stand, where it's located in the room, the phono preamp, and the load the preamp presents to the cartridge. Nonetheless, each turntable, tonearm, and cartridge has its own sonic signature. The better products have less of a sonic signature than lower-quality ones; i.e., they more closely approach sonic neutrality.

A high-quality LP front end is characterized by a lack of rumble (or low-frequency noise), greatly reduced record-surface noise, and the impression that the music emerges from a black background. Low-quality LP front ends tend to add a layer of sonic grunge below the music that imposes a grayish opacity on the sound. When you switch to a high-quality front end, it's like washing a grimy film off of a picture window—the view suddenly becomes more transparent, vivid, and alive.

Even if the LP front end doesn't have any obvious rumble, it can still add this layer of low-level noise to the music. The noise not only adds a murkiness to the sound, it also obscures low-level musical detail. A better turntable and tonearm strips away this film and lets you hear much deeper into the music. It can be difficult to identify this layer of noise unless you've heard the same music reproduced on a topnotch front end. Once you've heard a good LP playback system, however, the difference is startling. To use a visual analogy, hearing your records on a good analog front end for the first time is like looking at the stars on a cloudless, moonless night in the country after living in the city all your life. A wealth of subtle musical detail is revealed, and with it, a much greater involvement in the music.

Another important characteristic you'll hear on a superlative system is the impression that the music is made up of individual instruments existing in space. Each instrument will occupy a specific point in space, and be surrounded a halo of air that keeps it separate from the other instruments. The music sounds as if it is made up of individual elements, rather than sounding homogenized, blurred, congested, and confused. There's a certain realness, life, and immediacy to records played on a high-quality turntable system.

A related aspect is soundstage transparency—the impression that the musical presentation is crystal-clear rather than slightly opaque. A transparent soundstage lets you hear deep into the concert hall, with instruments toward the rear maintaining their clarity and immediacy, yet still sounding far back in the stage. The ability to "see" deep into the soundstage provides a feeling of a vast expanse of space before you in which the instruments can exist (if, of course, the recording engineers have captured these qualities in the first place). Reverberation decay hangs in space longer, further conveying the impression of space and depth.

Conversely, a lower-quality LP front end will tend to obscure sounds emanating from the stage rear, making them sound undifferentiated and lacking life. The presentation is clouded by an opaque haze that dulls the music's sense of immediacy, prevents you from hearing low-level detail, and tends to shrink your sense of the hall's size. The differences between superb and mediocre LP reproduction are much like those described Chapter 1's Grand Canyon analogy.

Other important musical qualities greatly affected by the LP front end are dynamic contrast and transient speed. A topnotch LP replay system has a much wider dynamic expression than a mediocre one; the difference between loud and soft is greater. In addition to having wider dynamic range, musical transients have an increased sense of suddenness, zip, and sharpness of attack. The attack of an acoustic guitar string, for example, is quick, sharp, and vivid. Many mediocre turntables and arms slow these transient signals, making them sound synthetic and lifeless. A good LP front end will also have a coherence that makes the transients sound as if they are all lined up in time with each other. The result is more powerful rhythmic expression.

Just as we want the LP front end to portray the steep attack of a note, we want the note to decay with equal rapidity. A first-rate LP front end is characterized by its ability to clearly articulate each note with a sense of silence between the notes, rather than blurring them together. A good test for an LP front end's transient characteristics is intricate percussion music. Any blurring of the music's dynamic structure—attack and decay—will be immediately obvious as a smearing of the sound, lack of immediacy, and the impression that you're hearing a replica of the instruments rather than the instruments themselves. Hearing live, unamplified musical instruments periodically really sharpens your hearing acuity for judging reproduced sound.

All turntables, tonearms, and cartridges influence the sound's overall perspective and tonal balance. Even high-quality components can have distinctive sonic signatures. Careful matching is therefore required between the turntable, arm, cartridge to achieve a musical result. Matching a bright, forward cartridge on an arm with the same characteristics, and mounting both on a somewhat aggressive-sounding turntable, could be a recipe for unmusical sound. Those same individual components may, however, be eminently musical when mixed with other components that tend to complement each other.

The very best turntables, tonearms, and cartridges are more sonically neutral than lesser products. System matching is therefore less critical as you go up in quality. State-of-the-art turntables and tonearms tend to be so neutral that you can put together nearly any combination and get superlative sound.

You should listen for two other aspects of turntable performance: *speed accuracy* and *speed stability*. Speed accuracy is how close the turntable's speed is compared to 33 1/3rpm. You need to worry about speed accuracy only if you have absolute pitch (the ability to identify a pitch in isolation). Speed instability, however, is easily audible by anyone, and is particularly annoying. Speed stability is how smoothly the platter rotates. Poor speed stability causes *wow and flutter*. Wow is a very slow speed variation that shifts the pitch slowly up and down. It is most audible on solo piano with sustained notes. Flutter is a rapid speed fluctuation that almost sounds like tremolo. Together, wow and flutter make the sound unstable and blurred rather than solidly anchored. A good turntable with no obvious flutter can still suffer from speed instability. Instead of hearing flutter overtly, you may hear a reduction in timbral accuracy—an oboe, for example, will sound less like an oboe and more like an undifferentiated sound.

Technical Aspects of Choosing an LP Front End

Matching a turntable, tonearm, and cartridge involves some technical decisions, not just aesthetic choices about which combinations sound the most musical.

First, the tonearm must be able to fit the turntable's arm-mounting area. Many turntables have an *arm-mounting board* on which the tonearm is fastened. The arm-mounting board must be at least as big as the arm's base, and be able to securely hold the arm. Any looseness here will seriously degrade the sound. When mounted to the arm board, the tonearm's cartridge end should be positioned within a range that allows the cartridge to be positioned at exactly the correct distance from the tonearm's pivot point, a parameter called *overhang*. Overhang can be set using the turntable manufacturer's template, or a third-party alignment protractor.

The turntable's suspension should be stiff enough to support the tonearm's weight. If the tonearm is too heavy for the turntable's suspension, the turntable won't be level. Turntable manufacturers will specify a range of tonearm weights appropriate for their turntables.

Next, the tonearm's *effective mass* must be matched to the cartridge's *compliance*. Let's define these terms before examining how they interact.

An arm's effective mass isn't the tonearm's weight, but the mass of the moving parts, and where along the tonearm's length that mass is distributed. Any body has a certain amount of inertia: a body at rest tends to stay at rest, and a body in motion tends to stay in motion. The amount of a body's inertia is its mass. If this body is rotated, however, the amount of its inertia in the rotational direction is called its *moment of inertia*. The effective mass of a rotating or pivoting object is the amount of mass that object would have if all of its mass were located at its "center of mass."

For example, adding one gram to the arm tube near the pivot point would only slightly increase the effective mass; adding that same gram to the cartridge end of the arm tube would greatly increase the effective mass. If you imagine pushing down on the counterweight side of the tonearm to lift the cartridge end of the arm, you can see how that one gram would require more force to lift when it is far away from the pivot point.

Less than ten grams of effective mass is considered low mass; eleven to 20 grams is considered mid-mass, and more than 20 grams is high mass.

A cartridge's compliance describes how stiffly or loosely the suspension holds the *cantilever*. The cantilever is the thin tube that emerges from the cartridge *body* and holds the *stylus*. If the cantilever is easily moved, the cartridge is *high-compliance*. If the cantilever is stiffly mounted, the cartridge is said to have *low compliance*.

Compliance is expressed as a number indicating how far the cantilever moves when a force is applied. Specifically, a force of 10^{-6} dynes is applied, and the cantilever's movement in millionths of a centimeter is the cartridge's compliance. For example, a low-compliance cartridge (a stiff suspension) may move only ten millionths of a centimeter; we say the cartridge has a compliance of 10. Because this method of expressing compliance is standardized, the reference to millionths of a centimeter is dropped, leaving only the value 10. Moderately compliant cartridges have compliances of 12 to 20, and high-compliance cartridges are of any value above 20.

A cartridge's compliance and the tonearm's effective mass form a resonant system. That is, the combination will vibrate much more easily at a particular frequency than at other frequencies. When a bell is struck, it rings at the bell's resonant frequency. Similarly, a tonearm and cartridge will resonate when put into motion. Energy is imparted to the tonearm and cartridge by record warp, turntable rumble, the turntable's resonance, record eccentricity (the center hole isn't exactly centered), and footfalls (the vibrations of someone's footsteps transmitted from the floor to the turntable). These energy sources are all of very low frequencies, perhaps below 8Hz. Higher in frequency, the tonearm and cartridge can be set in motion by the musical signal in the grooves, with the lowest frequency being about 20Hz. Although we can't avoid resonance in the tonearm and cartridge, we can adjust it so that their resonant frequency falls *above* the very low frequency of rumble and record warp, but *below* the lowest musical pitch recorded in the record grooves. By matching the arm's effective mass to the cartridge's compliance, we can tune the resonant frequency to fall between the sources of vibration. (Fig.9-1 shows the resonant frequencies of different values of arm mass and cartridge compliance.)

Fig. 9-1 The relationship between a tonearm's effective mass, cartridge compliance, and resonant frequency

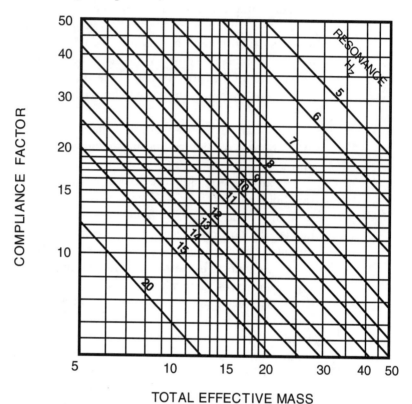

After Merrill

Preventing the tonearm and cartridge from resonating is of utmost importance. The audio signal is generated in the phono cartridge by the motion of the cantilever relative to the cartridge. If the arm and cartridge are vibrating even slightly, that vibration is converted into an electrical signal by the cartridge. Because the cartridge can't distinguish between groove modulation (the musical information) and tonearm resonance, distortion is mixed in with the music. Tonearm resonance distorts the music's tonal balance, colors instrumental timbre, changes the music's dynamic structure (the way notes start and stop), and destroys the sense of space and imaging on the recording.

The Turntable

It's easy to think of the turntable as having a minor role in a playback system's sound quality. After all, the turntable only spins the record and holds the tonearm; how much sonic influence could it have?

The answer is surprising: a high-quality turntable is absolutely essential to getting the best performance from the rest of your system. A good turntable presents a solid, vibration-free platform for the record and tonearm, allowing the cartridge to recover the maximum amount of information in the grooves and allow the minimum of interference with the audio signal.

The turntable is composed of a base, platter, platter bearing, plinth, drive system, and often a sub-chassis. The *base* is the turntable's main structure; it holds all the components, and is usually finished in black or natural wood. The *platter* is the heavy disc that supports the record; it rests on the *bearing assembly*. The *plinth* is the top of the turntable beneath the platter. The *drive system* conveys the motor's rotation to the platter. Some turntables have a *sub-chassis* suspended within the base on which the platter and tonearm are mounted. Every turntable will also have an *armboard* for mounting a tonearm. Many turntables have no base or plinth, instead suspending the sub-chassis in open air.

Let's look at how each of these components is assembled into the modern turntable.

The Base and Plinth

A turntable's base and plinth play important roles in sound quality. The base must be a rigid, vibration-resistant structure on which the other turntable components can be mounted. If the base is flimsy, it will vibrate and transmit that vibration to the platter and tonearm, thus degrading the sound.

A turntable system can be set vibrating by four forces: 1) acoustic energy impinging on the turntable (called *feedback*); 2) structure-borne vibration traveling through the turntable stand (primarily when the stand is located on a suspended floor); 3) the turntable's mechanical systems, such as the platter bearing and motor vibration; and 4) the motion imparted to the tonearm by groove modulations.

This vibration creates relative motion between the stylus and the cartridge. Because the cartridge can't distinguish between groove modulation and turntable resonance, this vibration is converted to an electrical signal and amplified by your system. This is why turntable designers go to elaborate measures to prevent vibration.

Let's first take the case of acoustic energy impinging on the turntable. If the base and plinth aren't rigid, they're more likely to be set in motion by sound striking the turntable. In extreme cases, the loudspeakers and turntable create an *acoustic feedback* loop in which sound from the loudspeakers is converted into an electrical signal in the cartridge through vibration, which is amplified by the loudspeakers, which causes even more feedback to be produced by the cartridge, and so forth. This acoustic feedback can muddy the music, or even make it impossible to play records at a moderately high playback level. You can hear this phenomenon by putting the stylus on the lead-in groove without the record spinning, then gradually turning up the volume. You'll start to hear a howling sound as the acoustic feedback loop grows strong enough to feed on itself, and a "runaway" condition develops in which the sound keeps getting louder. If you try this, keep your hand on the volume control and be ready to turn down the volume as soon as you hear the howl—if you don't turn down the volume *immediately*, the system could be damaged. The more vibration-resistant the turntable, the less severe this phenomenon. You might try this with and without the turntable's dustcover in place. A turntable's dustcover can catch acoustic energy and feed it into the base and plinth, degrading the sound. Other dustcovers protect the turntable from vibration.

Turntable bases and plinths are designed to resist vibration by making them very massive (so it's hard to put them in motion), and by *damping* any vibrations that do exist. Inert materials such as Medium Density Fiberboard (MDF) and Fountainhead are often used in turntable bases. Very high-quality turntables are made from machined acrylic. Vibration damping is achieved with layers of material applied to or within the base so that the vibration stops rather than being allowed to ring. An example of vibration damping is putting a wet rag on a steel plate before striking the plate. Instead of hearing the plate ring, you hear a dull thud—the vibrational energy is dissipated more quickly. In practice, damping materials are often exotic compounds (one turntable use the same sound-deadening material that lines a submarine's hull). One technique, called *constrained layer damping*, puts layers of soft damping material between layers of harder materials to more effectively dissipate vibrational energy. When vibration encounters a discontinuity in the material, shear forces between layers produce shear strain, which causes frictional losses. The mechanical energy is converted into a minute amount of heat. Another technique distributes lead inserts throughout the base and platter.

The armboard should have vibration resistance and damping properties similar to those of the base. Some armboards, made from acrylic and lead, weigh up to six pounds.

Another theory of turntable design suggests that the *less* massive the base and plinth, the better. This belief argues that a very rigid, low-mass base is ideal because there's less mass to resonate. This theory, used in only a few turntable models, has been discredited by proponents of high-mass turntables.

So much for the problem of acoustic energy putting the turntable in motion. Now let's look at how turntable design addresses the problems of structure-borne vibration. Vibration entering the turntable through the stand or rack can be greatly reduced by mechanically isolating the turntable's key components (platter, armboard, and tonearm/cartridge) with a suspension system—the sprung turntable.

Sprung and Unsprung Turntables

Most turntables are *sprung*, meaning that the platter and armboard are mounted on a sub-chassis which floats within the base on springs. The terms *suspended* and *floating* describe the same construction.

Sprung turntables can be one of three designs. In one method, the sub-chassis sits on springs attached to the base bottom. In the second method, the sub-chassis hangs down from the plinth on springs. (Fig.9-2 shows the latter of these two techniques.) The third technique dispenses with the base entirely and hangs the sub-chassis in open air on pillars (Fig.9-3). The turntable is suspended on the four pillars at each corner of the turntable.

Fig. 9-2 The sub-chassis can be hung from the plinth.

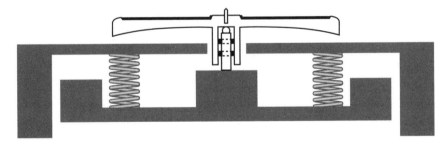

Courtesy Audio Advisor, Inc. and SOTA Industries

Whichever technique is used, the goal of all sprung designs is to isolate the platter and tonearm from external vibration. Any vibration picked up by the supports on which the turntable rests won't be transferred as effectively to the platter and tonearm. The primary sources of structure-borne vibration are passing trucks, footfalls, air conditioners, and motors attached to the building. Structure-borne vibration is much less of a problem in a single-family home with a concrete floor than in an apartment building or frame house with suspended floors.

Fig. 9-3 The sub-chassis can also be mounted in open air, with no base.

Courtesy Basis Audio, Inc.

The suspension on which the sub-chassis is mounted is carefully tuned to a very low frequency. The vertical resonant frequency of the suspension can also be tuned to a slightly different frequency than the horizontal resonant frequency. In addition, the suspension can be immersed in a viscous fluid to damp any remaining vibration. An advantage of viscous damping over mechanical damping such as foam or Sorbothane (a rubberlike material) is that the viscous fluid doesn't compress, retaining its damping properties under all conditions. (The turntable shown in Fig.9-3 uses this technique.)

You can judge a suspension's effectiveness by putting the stylus on a stationary record and tapping on the stand on which the turntable is mounted. The volume should be turned up to what would be a moderate listening level if the record were spinning. You should start by gently tapping the stand, then gradually increasing the force. The less sound you hear from the loudspeakers, the more effective the turntable's suspension. With the best models, you can even hit the stand as hard as you like with a hammer and hear no sound from the loudspeakers; the suspension completely isolates the platter and tonearm from the hammer blow. In less effective designs, a small tap on the stand can be heard through the loudspeakers.

A small minority of turntable designers believe, however, that the springs used in suspended turntables can resonate and actually introduce vibration into the platter and arm. They believe the answer is the *unsprung* turntable, in which the platter and tonearm are mounted directly to the base. If the base is made rigid and non-resonant enough, they argue, the platter and arm won't vibrate—and you don't have to worry about springs resonating (spring vibration can be eliminated with fluid damping). Unsprung turntables sometimes use constrained layer damping in the base to dissipate mechanical energy before it reaches the platter and tonearm. Constrained layer damping, however, is more effective at high frequencies than at low frequencies. A prime example of an unsprung design is the very popular Well-Tempered Turntable.

The Platter and Bearing Assembly

The platter not only provides a support for the record, it also plays two other important roles: as a flywheel, to smooth the rotation; and as a "sink," to draw vibration from the record. Many platters are very heavy (up to 30 pounds), with most of their mass concentrated toward the outside edge to increase their moment of inertia. This high mass also counters bearing friction and stylus drag. Irregular (non-linear) bearing friction can create rapid irregularities in the platter's speed, which frequency-modulates the recovered audio signal. Massive platters greatly reduce the audible effects of bearing friction.

Most platters are made of a single substance such as acrylic, stamped metal (in the cheaper turntables), cast and machined aluminum (in better turntables), or exotic materials such as ceramic compounds. The platter sometimes has a hollowed-out ring around the outer edge that is filled with a heavy material to increase the platter's mass, or is loaded with a damping substance to make the platter more inert and resistant to vibration.

These techniques also attempt to make the platter act as a "sink" for record vibration. When the record is clamped to the platter, any record vibration will be transferred to the platter. The platter's material and geometry is thus an important design consideration: The platter should have no resonant peaks within the audioband. Some platters use constrained layer damping, and combinations of different materials to provide the ideal sink for record vibration.

I recently heard the difference that a layer of damping material applied to a platter can make to sound quality. The Well-Tempered Turntable was recently upgraded to include a platter with a layer of highly effective damping material put into a recess machined into the platter's underside. With the two platters side by side, I auditioned each and heard an enormous improvement. My review of the damped platter in *Stereophile* read, in part: "Seconds into the first record, I was stunned by the difference the Black Damped Platter made. It was like listening to a different turntable! . . . First, there was a huge increase in dynamic contrast. The music seemed to jump out of the loudspeakers with an effortless, unfettered quality . . . Transients seemed to "line up" together instead of being smeared slightly over time." Other characteristics I heard from just adding a layer of damping material to the platter included tighter and better-defined bass, deeper low-frequency extension, a more transparent soundstage, and greater resolution of fine detail.

Because the platter spins on a stationary object (the rest of the turntable), there must be a bearing surface between the two. With one technique, the bearing is mounted at the end of a shaft to which the platter is attached (Fig.9-4). This shaft—often made of stainless steel—extends down a hollow column in the base. The shaft has some form of bearing on the end, either a chrome-hardened steel ball, tungsten-carbide, Zirconium, ceramic, or even a very hard jewel such as sapphire. The bearing often sits in a layer of lubricant.

Fig. 9-4 A platter bearing at the bottom of the shaft

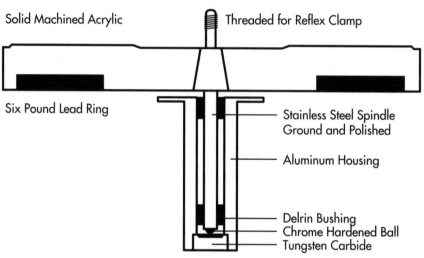

Solid Machined Acrylic   Threaded for Reflex Clamp

Six Pound Lead Ring

Stainless Steel Spindle Ground and Polished

Aluminum Housing

Delrin Bushing
Chrome Hardened Ball
Tungsten Carbide

Courtesy Audio Advisor, Inc. and VPI Industries

A second technique puts the bearing surface on top of a stationary shaft, with the bearing surface between the platter and shaft (Fig.9-5).

Fig. 9-5 A platter bearing at the top of the shaft

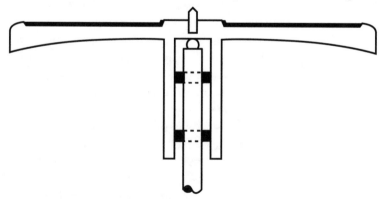

Courtesy Audio Advisor, Inc. and SOTA Industries

Whichever technique is used, the bearing must provide smooth and quiet rotation of the platter. Any noise or vibration created by the bearing will be transmitted directly to the platter. Turntable bearings are machined to very close tolerances, and are often highly polished to achieve a smooth surface.

A bearing that suffers none of the traditional mechanical problems is the *air bearing*. The platter rides on a cushion of air rather than on a mechanical bearing. A pump forces compressed air into a very tiny gap between the platter and an adjacent surface. This air pressure pushes the platter up slightly so that the platter literally floats on air. Air-bearing turntables are, however, very expensive and can be difficult to set up.

Platter Mats, Record Clamps, and Vacuum Hold-Down Systems

Platter mats are designed to minimize record vibration, and then to absorb what vibration remains. Designers of soft mats suggest that an absorbent felt mat works better in drawing vibration away from the record. Designers of hard mats contend that a stiffer mat material better couples the record to the platter. Finally, some turntable manufacturers discourage using any mat at all, believing that their platter design provides the best sink for record vibration.

Record clamps couple the record to the platter so that the record isn't allowed to vibrate freely. The platter acts as a vibration sink, draining vibration from the record. By more intimately coupling the record to the platter, the record clamp improves the sound.

Record clamps come in three varieties. First, the clamp can simply be a heavy weight put over the spindle. The clamp's weight squeezes the record between clamp and platter. Other clamps have a screw mechanism that threads down onto the spindle. The third type is the "reflex" clamp, in which a locking mechanism pushes the clamp down onto the record. Which type works best should be decided by your listening, the turntable manufacturer's recommendations, or your local dealer's suggestion. Note that very heavy clamps can put a strain on some sprung turntables, compressing the springs (or expanding them if the sub-chassis is hung from the plinth). Some form of record clamping is, however, a must for any high-end turntable.

Another technique for coupling the record to the platter is the *vacuum hold-down system*. An external pump creates a vacuum that is transferred by tubes to the platter. The vacuum holds the record tightly to the platter surface so that vibration is drained away from the record. A vacuum hold-down also makes the record more flat, even if it is mildly warped. Vacuum pumps can be noisy, however, and benefit from some form of acoustic isolation from the listening room. Bright Star

Audio makes a small acoustic isolation chamber, called "The Padded Cell" (their motto: "Every audiophile needs a padded cell"), for isolating vacuum hold-down and air-bearing pumps. (A vacuum hold-down system is shown in Fig.9-6.)

Fig. 9-6 A vacuum hold-down system

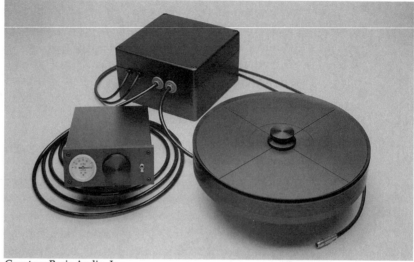

Courtesy Basis Audio, Inc.

The Drive System

A turntable's drive system transfers the motor's rotation to the platter. Virtually all high-end turntables currently made are belt-driven; the platter is spun by a rubber belt or silken thread stretched around the motor pulley and outer rim of the platter (Fig.9-7).

Fig. 9-7 A belt-drive turntable showing the drive motor, belt, and platter.

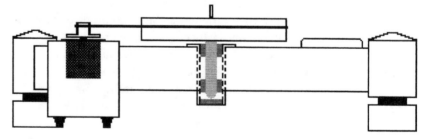

Courtesy VPI Industries

Mass-market mid-fi turntables are usually direct-drive; i.e., the motor is connected directly to the platter. The motor's spindle is often the spindle over which you place the record. Direct drive was sold to the public as superior to belt drive—there are no belts to stretch and wear, and a direct-drive motor can be electronically controlled to maintain precise speed and have low wow and flutter. Indeed, the wow and flutter specifications of a direct-drive turntable are generally better than those of a belt-drive turntable. Direct-drives often have an electronic speed control and sometimes a Phase Locked Loop (PLL) servo mechanism to assure perfect speed stability. In a servo system, the platter's speed is sensed and a signal is fed back to the motor, which responds to keep the platter turning at a precisely constant speed. Direct-drive turntables also have high-torque motors, allowing them to come up to speed instantly.

But, without question, belt-drive turntables sound far better than direct-drive units. Rather than directly couple the motor's vibration to the platter as in direct-drive, the drive belt acts as a buffer to decouple the platter from the motor. Motor noise is isolated from the platter, resulting in quieter operation than is possible from a direct-drive turntable. Belt drive also makes it easier to suspend the platter and drive system on a sub-chassis.

No elaborate speed controls are used on belt-drive turntables; the motor just sits there spinning at a fairly high speed (as fast as 1000rpm). This high-speed rotation is coupled to the large platter with a small pulley, resulting in 33 1/3rpm rotation of the platter. Belt-drive motors are usually *AC-synchronous*, meaning that their rotational speed is determined by the frequency of the AC voltage driving them. But because the AC line is subject to noise and fluctuation, the platter's speed can be very slightly affected by dirty AC power. Although this speed variation is minute, it doesn't take much to destroy the music's pitch definition, timbre, and image stability. Consequently, some manufacturers synthesize their own 50Hz or 60Hz AC sinewave with an outboard drive unit. This device creates a pure, stable sinewave with a precision oscillator, then amplifies it to 120V to drive the turntable's AC synchronous motor. The Linn Lingo power supply for the Linn LP12 turntable is the most notable example of this technique. Some AC-synchronous motors run on voltages lower than 120V.

The drive motor can be a source of turntable vibration. As the motor spins, it produces vibration that can be transferred to the other components in the turntable, producing a low-frequency rumble. Even if you don't hear rumble directly, motor vibration can still degrade the sound. The motor assemblies of some turntables are completely separate from the base and encased in damping material. Other designs mount the motor to the sub-chassis, and isolate its vibration from the other turntable components.

The Tonearm

The tonearm's job is to hold the cartridge over the record and keep the stylus in the groove. We want the tonearm to be an immovable support for the cartridge, yet also be light enough to follow the inward path of the groove, track the up-and-down motions of record warps, and follow any record eccentricity caused by an offset center hole—all without wreaking undue wear on the delicate grooves themselves. As we'll see, this is a challenging job.

Tonearms come in two varieties: *pivoted* and *tangential-tracking*. A pivoted tonearm allows the cartridge end of the arm to traverse the record in an arc while maintaining a fixed pivot point. A tangential tonearm (also called a *linear tracking* tonearm) moves the entire tonearm and bearing in relation to the record.

Let's look at the pivoted tonearm first; its fundamental limitations will explain the reason for the tangential tonearm's existence.

The ideal tonearm would allow the cartridge to maintain the same angular relationship with the record groove as the record-cutting stylus had with that groove. LP cutting lathes are all tangential-tracking—the cutting head moves in a straight line across the lacquer master. But in a pivoted tonearm, the cartridge end swings in an arc over the record, causing the playback stylus to turn slightly in relation to the groove. The stylus/groove relationship is constantly changing with a pivoted tonearm. The result is *tracking error*, defined as a difference in the stylus/groove relationship between the cutting stylus and the playback stylus.

Tracking error is minimized by putting a bend in the tonearm, called the *offset*. Offset can be a sudden angle at the end of the tonearm, or a gradual bend that gives the armtube a "J" or "S" shape. The offset angle in modern tonearms is 25°, which provides the least tracking error. Note that adding an offset to the tonearm doesn't eliminate tracking error. Instead, the offset produces a small tracking error toward the outside of the record, which gradually decreases until the cartridge reaches a midpoint in the record. At this midpoint, the playback stylus and cutting stylus share the same geometric relationship with the groove, and the tracking error is zero. As the arm continues its arc toward the record's center, the tracking error gradually increases again.

The tonearm offset needed to reduce tracking error introduces a problem in pivoted arms called *skating*. Skating is a force that pulls the tonearm toward the record center. The result is a force acting on the stylus that must be compensated for by applying an equal but opposite force on the cartridge. This compensation, called *anti-skating*, counteracts the skating force caused by tonearm offset. Anti-skating allows the stylus to maintain equal contact pressure with both sides of the groove, and prevents the cartridge's cantilever from being displaced from its center position in the cartridge. Anti-skating can be generated by springs, weights with pulleys, or mechanical linkages. (I'll talk about anti-skating adjustment later in this chapter under "LP Playback System Setup.")

On a more technical level, skating is caused solely by the friction between the groove and stylus. Frictional force always acts in the direction of the attempted motion; the frictional force of the record pulling the stylus is in the tangential direction of the record groove. This force vector doesn't pass through the tonearm pivot. As with any vector quantity, this force can be resolved into two component forces at right angles to each other. Because one of the component forces is in-line with the pivot, the second (and much smaller) force is at a right angle to the primary force, causing the arm to skate inward.

As you can see, the problems of pivoted tonearms—tracking error and skating—don't exist with tangential-tracking arms. By moving the entire arm across the record, the stylus/groove relationship is identical to that of the LP cutting lathe at any record radius. And because the arm has no offset, no skating force is generated. Tangential-tracking arms have another advantage: Because they're generally very short, tangential-tracking arms can have lower vertical mass than pivoted arms. Tangential-tracking arms, however, have *higher* horizontal mass. Because they don't pivot, the effective horizontal mass of a tangential arm is the arm's actual mass, which is higher than the effective horizontal mass of a pivoted arm. Tangential arm design is a compromise between too-low vertical mass and too-high horizontal mass.

One the down side, tangential tracking is much more complex, and consequently more expensive to execute well. The entire arm must be moved along a track tangent to the record—a difficult engineering challenge. In mid-fi tangential-tracking turntables, the arm is driven by a servo motor whose motion may not exactly match the record's *pitch* (spacing between record grooves), forcing the stylus first against one side of the groove, then the other. Although the servo system attempts to correct for this error, servo systems by their very nature work only *after* an error has occurred.

The solution in high-end tangential-tracking arms is the *air bearing*, in which the arm rides on a cushion of air surrounding a tube. The only force moving the tonearm is the gentle force of the stylus. Owing to the air bearing, the friction between the arm and the tube on which it is mounted is practically zero. (The turntable in Fig.9-3 is fitted with a tangential-tracking, air-bearing tonearm.)

Tangential-tracking arms are more difficult to correctly set up, require periodic adjustment, and have air pumps that can become audible if not properly isolated from the listening area. Proponents of pivoted tonearms argue that the inherent geometric advantages of tangential arms are far outweighed by concerns over the tangential arm's rigidity and resonance damping. They suggest that the distortion produced by tracking error isn't a significant source of sonic degradation.

Let's take a closer look at the pivoted tonearm, by far the most popular type of arm. Its major components are, from back to front, the counterweight, bearing, armtube, and headshell. (These elements are shown from left to right in the photograph of Fig.9-8.) The *counterweight* counteracts the weight of the arm tube and cartridge; its weight and position determine the downward force of the stylus in the groove. The *bearing* provides a pivot point for the arm, in both the vertical and horizontal planes. The *arm tube* extends the cartridge position away from the pivot point to an optimum position over the record. The *headshell* is attached to the end of the arm tube and provides a platform for mounting the cartridge to the arm tube. The small, flat disc above the bearing in Fig.9-8 sets the anti-skating compensation.

Fig. 9-8 A high-quality pivoted tonearm

Courtesy Linn Products

A tonearm's bearing is an important aspect of its design. The bearing should provide very low friction and not impede the arm's movement. If the bearing is sticky, the stylus will be forced against the groove wall, causing distortion. Loosening the bearings reduces friction, but can cause the bearings to "chatter" as the tonearm is rattled by the motion of the stylus in the groove, or by other sources of tonearm vibration. Remember, any movement of the tonearm in relation to the stylus in the groove is interpreted by the cartridge as a groove modulation, and is converted into an electrical signal that appears at the cartridge output along with the musical signal. Tightening the bearings decreases chatter, but also increases friction. Tonearm designers must balance these trade-offs.

The most common type of tonearm bearing is the *gimbal*, in which a set of rings attached to bearings allows the arm to move in any direction. Gyroscopes are sometimes mounted in gimbal bearings. Another bearing type, called the *unipivot*, has recently come back into favor, partially from its exemplary use in the Graham tonearm. A unipivot bearing is similar to a ball within a cup, allowing motion in any direction. The unipivot is the simplest design, and offers the lowest friction of any bearing (except an air bearing). Gimbal and unipivot bearings are lubricated internally, and some are immersed in a silicon fluid to damp resonances.

An innovative approach to tonearm bearings is the Well-Tempered Tonearm. The tonearm is attached to a vertical post and horizontal paddle suspended in a cup of silicon by monofilament line. In essence, the WTA has no bearing; the arm moves in a fluid with no hard connection between the arm and the rest of the turntable.

A tonearm's arm tube is designed to be rigid, low in mass, resistant to vibration, and have the ability to damp any resonances that do occur. Arm tubes are often made of exotic materials to combine rigidity with low mass (carbon fiber is a popular arm-tube material). Arm tubes can be filled with damping material to kill resonances, and one particular arm (the Graham) is even made of concentric tubes separated by damping material to form a constrained-layer-damping design. The goal is to make the arm inert and less likely to ring and transmit vibration to the cartridge. A well-damped arm tube correlates with an improved retrieval of low-level musical detail.

A tonearm's effective mass (defined earlier in this chapter) is carefully chosen to strike a balance between the ability to hold the cartridge as its stylus is moved from side to side (which requires mass), and the ability to follow record warps (where low mass is desired). When a massive tonearm encounters a record warp, it will increase the downward force of the stylus on the "uphill" side of the warp, then tend to reduce the downward force of the stylus on the "downhill" side. In some cases, the stylus can even fly out of the groove. Although this phenomenon occurs with all tonearms, it is magnified by high effective tonearm mass.

A tonearm's *effective length* is the distance from the pivot point to the stylus tip. Most tonearms measure between 210 and 230 millimeters of effective length. (Note that the effective length is shorter than the actual length due to the tonearm's offset.) The technical definition of *overhang* is the distance the stylus extends past the spindle. In general parlance, "overhang" means where the stylus falls in relation to the pivot point. Overhang can be adjusted by moving the cartridge forward or backward in the headshell. Some tonearms have adjustable-length arm tubes for setting overhang. These alignment procedures are described later in this chapter.

The Phono Cartridge

The phono cartridge has the job of converting the modulations of the record groove into an electrical signal. Because the cartridge changes one form of energy into another (mechanical into electrical), the cartridge is called a *transducer*. There's one other transducer in your system—the loudspeakers at the other end of the playback chain.

A phono cartridge consists of the cartridge body, stylus, cantilever, and generator system. The *body* is the housing that surrounds the cartridge, and comprises the entire surface area. The stylus is a diamond point attached to the cantilever (the tiny shaft that extends from the bottom of the cartridge body). The stylus is moved back and forth and up and down by modulations in the record groove. This modulation is transferred by the cantilever to the *generator system*, the part of the cartridge where motion is converted into an electrical signal.

Moving-Magnet and Moving-Coil Cartridges

Cartridges are classified by their principle of operation: moving-magnet or moving-coil. In a *moving-magnet* cartridge, tiny magnets attached to the cantilever move in relation to stationary coils in the cartridge body. The movement of the magnetic field through the coils induces a voltage (the audio signal) across the coils. (This phenomenon is explained in detail in Appendix B.) Less common variations on the moving-magnet cartridge are the *induced magnet* and *moving-iron* types. (Fig.9-9 shows the essential elements of a moving-magnet cartridge.)

A *moving-coil* cartridge works on exactly the same physical principles, but the magnets are stationary and the coils move. A moving-coil cartridge generally has much less moving mass than a moving-magnet cartridge. Consequently, a moving-coil cartridge can generally track better than a moving-magnet type, and also have better transient response. With less mass to put into motion (and less mass to continue moving after the motivating force has stopped), moving-coil cartridges can better follow transient signals in the record. Because of their construction, moving-coil cartridges generally don't have user-replaceable styli; you must return the cartridge to the manufacturer.

Cartridge output voltage varies greatly between moving-magnet and moving-coil operation. A moving-magnet's output ranges from 2mV (two thousandths of a volt) to about 8mV; a moving-coil cartridge's output is typically between 0.15mV and 2.5mV. Although moving-coil cartridges generally have lower output voltage than moving-magnet types, some so-called "high-output" moving-coils have higher output voltage than some moving-magnet cartridges. A cartridge's output voltage is specified when the stylus is subjected to a recorded lateral groove velocity of 5cm per second RMS at 1kHz.

Fig. 9-9 Moving-magnet cartridge construction

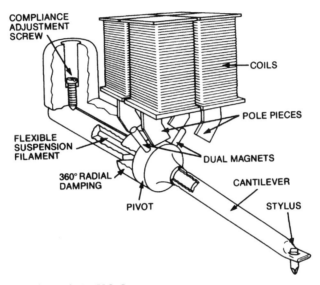

COMPLIANCE ADJUSTMENT SCREW

COILS

POLE PIECES

FLEXIBLE SUSPENSION FILAMENT

DUAL MAGNETS

360° RADIAL DAMPING

CANTILEVER

PIVOT

STYLUS

Courtesy Audio-Technica U.S., Inc.

This wide range of cartridge output voltage requires that the phono preamplifier's gain be matched to the cartridge's output voltage. The lower the cartridge output voltage, the higher the gain needed to bring the phono signal to line level. (A full discussion of matching cartridge output voltage to phono stage gain is included in Chapter 5.)

A moving-coil's output voltage is determined largely by the number of turns of wire on the coil. The greater the number of turns, the higher the output voltage. More turns means less gain is needed in the phono preamp, but most designers use the minimum number of turns possible to keep the moving mass low.

The method of generating the audio signal, whether moving-magnet or moving-coil, affects how sensitive the cartridge is to the effects of preamplifier "loading." The cartridge output "sees" an electrical load of the preamplifier's input impedance and capacitance, and the tonearm cable's capacitance. The load impedance is in parallel with the capacitance.

The frequency response of a moving-magnet cartridge is greatly influenced by the amount of capacitance in the tonearm cable and preamplifier input. A moving-magnet cartridge terminated with the correct impedance (47k ohms), but with too much capacitance, can have frequency-response errors in the upper midrange and treble of 5dB. Most cartridge manufacturers specify the ideal load impedance and capacitance for their cartridges. A typical load for a moving-magnet cartridge is 47k ohms in parallel with 200-400pF (picofarads) of capacitance. Moving-coil cartridges are nearly immune to capacitance loading effects.

Stylus Shapes and Cantilever Materials

Styli (the plural of stylus) come in a variety of shapes, the simplest and least expensive of which is the *conical* or *spherical* tip. The conical stylus is a tiny piece of diamond polished into a cone shape. Because the stylus tip must be smaller than the record groove, the radius of a conical stylus tip is about 15μm, or about 0.0006".

The conical stylus, however, cannot perfectly track the groove's modulations because it is a different shape than the cutting stylus used to make the record. As shown in Fig.9-10, the conical stylus contacts different points on the groove wall compared to the cutting stylus, causing distortion. In a related problem, called *pinch effect*, the stylus is pushed up out of the groove. Although the cutting stylus created a groove of equal width, the conical playback stylus may see a narrower groove because it touches different places on the left and right groove walls in relation to the cutting stylus. Pinch effect most likely to occur where there are large high-frequency groove modulations.

Fig. 9-10
Comparison of conical and elliptical styli in relation to the cutting stylus

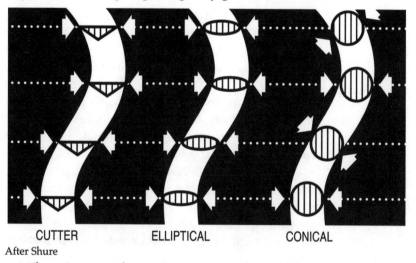

CUTTER   ELLIPTICAL   CONICAL

After Shure

The solution to these two related problems is the elliptical stylus. Instead of using a rounded tip to track the groove modulations, an elliptical stylus has an oval cross section, with two flat faces. Because this shape more closely approximates the shape of the cutting stylus, it results in lower tracking distortion and eliminates the pinch effect. An elliptical stylus can also track high-frequency modulations better, and distributes its force over a wider area to reduce record wear. (Fig.9-10 compares the stylus/groove relationships of cutting, conical, and elliptical styli.)

A third type of stylus takes the elliptical shape one step further by making the tip even narrower. These styli shapes are called *Shibata, line-contact, fine-line, van den Hul,* and *hyperelliptical*. A cartridge with any of these stylus shapes requires more precise alignment and setup than conical or standard elliptical types.

A variation of the elliptical stylus is the *microridge,* which has a tiny groove cut into each edge. As the stylus wears, the microridge stylus maintains the same shape, and thus its relationship to the record groove.

Keeping your stylus clean is of paramount importance: The stylus should be cleaned before every record side. A speck of dust or dirt is like a boulder attached to the stylus, grinding away at the groove walls. An appreciation of the enormous pressure a stylus imposes on the groove further highlights the need for a clean stylus. For example, a tracking force of 1.4 grams applied to a typical stylus contact area (0.2×10^{-6}") results in a pressure of nearly four tons per square inch. This pressure is enough to momentarily melt the outer layer of the groove wall. It's easy to see how stylus motion through the groove is much smoother with a clean stylus, and produces much less record wear. A clean stylus sounds better, too.

A stylus should be cleaned with a back-to-front motion so that the brush follows the record's motion. Some manufacturers recommend that no cleaning fluid be used; other suggest that a fluid is essential to removing accumulated dirt. There is also debate over the best type of brush. Some have short, stiff bristles, while other cleaners resemble nail-polish brushes. Your best bet is to follow the cartridge manufacturer's cleaning instructions. And don't clean the stylus with the tonearm locked in place; you could apply too much force and damage the stylus.

With good maintenance, a stylus should last for about 1000 hours of use. It's a good idea to have the stylus examined microscopically after about 500 hours, then again at 800 hours to check for irregular wear that could damage records.

Because the cantilever transfers stylus motion to the generator, its construction is extremely important. Cantilevers are designed to be very light, rigid, and non-resonant. The lower the cantilever mass, the better the cartridge's trackability, all other factors being equal. To obtain stiffness with low mass, exotic materials are often used in cantilever design, including boron, diamond, beryllium, titanium, ceramic, ruby, and sapphire. Cantilevers are often hollow to reduce their mass, and are sometimes filled with a resonance-damping material.

The cantilever is mounted in a *compliance* inside the cartridge body at the end opposite to that which bears the stylus. The compliance allows the cantilever to move, yet keeps it in position. Because this compliance is stiff when the cartridge is new, it takes many hours of use for the cartridge to break-in and sound its best. It isn't unusual for a cartridge to continue to sound better after 100 hours of use. (Cartridge compliance is described earlier in this chapter under "Technical Aspects of Choosing an LP Front End.")

Some audiophiles remove the cartridge body to run the cartridge "naked." The body can be a source of resonance, and adds a fair amount of effective mass to the tonearm. Removing a cartridge body should be attempted only by those very skilled in working with tiny precision devices, and then only if they are willing to risk destroying their cartridge.

LP Playback System Setup

Correctly playing back a record is a delicate art. It takes patience, skill, a keen ear, a delicate touch, an appreciation for the forces involved—and a high-quality LP front end. Doug Sax, co-founder of Sheffield Lab and the pioneer of the modern direct-to-disc recording, has said, "Probably the easiest thing in the world is to play an LP record incorrectly."

What prompted Doug Sax's observation is the great variability in setup possible with a turntable, tonearm, and cartridge. When you add to the equation how the phono preamp loads the cartridge, the turntable stand, and its placement in the room, you have the potential for not getting all the music out of the record grooves.

But this situation also offers the promise of improving the sound of your LP front end without spending any more money. By just setting up the system correctly, you can realize far better sound from a modest turntable than from a poorly set-up front end costing thousands more. Great musical rewards await those willing to tweak their LP front ends.

The best sources of advice for LP system setup are the manufacturers of the components in the LP playback system, and your dealer. The dealer will have undoubtedly set up many turntable/tonearm/cartridge combinations like yours, and will have the techniques down pat. A good dealer will set up your system when you buy a product from him.

Nonetheless, you should know the procedure for getting the best sound from your LP front end. This will let you converse with the dealer from a position of knowledge, and also allow you to set up your system if you just change cartridges or move your turntable from one location to another.

The first rule of LP system setup is to put the turntable on a good platform. I can't emphasize this enough; a flimsy rack, or one prone to resonating, will seriously degrade the sound of your system. The less good the turntable's suspension, the more important the rack. The very best turntables (those having superlative isolation from structure-borne vibration) are affected very little by the stand. With all but the very best turntables, you won't hear your system at its best without a solid, non-resonant support structure for your turntable. Many stands and racks are made specifically for turntables. Invest in one.

The most massive racks can, however, put too much stress on a suspended wood floor. In addition, footfalls and other vibrations can be transmitted right through the rack and to the turntable if the turntable has inadequate suspension. If you live in a building with a shaky floor, you have several options. The first is to use a turntable shelf that mounts to the wall instead of to the floor. The second option is to locate the rack directly above the point in your room where the floor joists meet the foundation. The third alternative, which can be used in conjunction with the second option, is to support the joists with house jacks. Put a concrete block on the ground below the floor joists, put the house jack between the concrete block and the joist, and raise the jack to meet the joist. Continue raising the jack about half a turn past where contact is made between the jack and the joist. Don't try to move the joist; all you want to do is provide a stable support. Finally, you can further increase the turntable's isolation from vibration by using a commercially available isolation system such as the Marigo Turntable Isolation System. These products decouple the turntable from the stand. Finally, the best solution is to buy a turntable with a superior suspension system.

Once you've got a good rack, where you place it in the room can have a large effect on the sound. Here's why: When the air in a room is excited by sound from the loudspeakers, the pressure isn't evenly distributed throughout the room. Instead, there are pockets of high and low pressure. You can demonstrate this by playing an organ recording and walking around the room; you'll hear the sound get louder and softer. Moreover, the pressure tends to build up along walls and in corners. If the turntable is in an area of high pressure, it will be more prone to resonating from the acoustic energy impinging on it. Conversely, a turntable located in a room "null" won't be as affected by sound from the loudspeakers striking it. Sitting Duck Software's "The Listening Room" program can identify null points for specific loudspeaker placements. If you don't use the software, you can avoid the worst turntable placements with a few simple rules. First, don't put the turntable in a corner where bass tends to build up. Second, keep the turntable away from the wall, if possible. An extra 8" or 12" can make a difference.

With the turntable on your stand, make sure that the turntable is level by using a pair of small round bubble levels and adjusting the turntable's feet. If you have a sprung turntable, make sure the tonearm cable doesn't impede the motion of the sub-chassis.

I'll assume you've followed the manufacturer's directions for installing the tonearm and are ready to mount the cartridge. After you've attached the four tiny tonearm cable clips to the cartridge pins, mount the cartridge to the headshell with minimal torque on the bolts—we'll be adjusting the cartridge position in the headshell later.

Move the counterweight forward or backward until the arm floats, then move it slightly forward to apply some tracking force. Use a *stylus pressure gauge* (also called a *vertical tracking force gauge*) to set the tracking force to the cartridge manufacturer's tracking-force specification. (Some tonearms include built-in calibrated tracking-force gauges.)

The next step roughly sets the *vertical tracking angle* (VTA), also called the stylus *rake angle*. Adjusting the VTA changes the angle at which the stylus enters the groove. Ideally, the VTA of the playback stylus should match the VTA of the cutting stylus. Most cartridges work best when the cartridge body is exactly parallel with the record surface (Fig.9-11a). VTA is adjusted by moving the tonearm rear up or down at the pivot point. Negative VTA is when the cartridge rear is *below* the level of the cartridge front (Fig.9-11b). Positive VTA is when the cartridge rear is *above* the level of the cartridge front (Fig.9-11c). Follow the cartridge manufacturer's suggestions for rough setting of VTA. (We'll fine-tune the VTA later.)

Fig. 9-11 a,b,c
Vertical Tracking
Angle (VTA)
adjustments

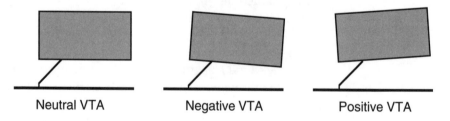

Neutral VTA   Negative VTA   Positive VTA

If the tonearm manufacturer provides a protractor, place it on the spindle and make sure the stylus reaches the indicated point on the protractor. If necessary, move the cartridge body forward or backward in the headshell. This is called the *overhang* adjustment.

The protractor will have an alignment grid on it for setting the correct angle of the cartridge in the headshell relative to the tonearm. Getting this adjustment right minimizes tracking error.

Azimuth describes the cantilever's perpendicular relationship to the record groove. A cantilever with perfectly aligned azimuth will form a right angle with the record (Fig.9-12). Notice that I said the *cantilever's*—not the *cartridge's*—relationship to the groove. Many cantilevers are slightly skewed in their mountings, making it impossible to get perfect azimuth alignment by looking at the cartridge body alone. Instead, you can put the stylus tip on a small mirror and look for a perfectly straight line through the cantilever and its reflection. If there's a bend in the reflection at the mirror, the azimuth is wrong. Some tonearms are designed to allow for ease of azimuth adjustment; those that aren't require you to insert tiny shims between headshell and cartridge. Azimuth alignment is vital to correct left-right channel balance, and consequently to soundstaging and imaging. Azimuth can also be checked with a dual-trace oscilloscope and a test record. With each channel feeding one input of the 'scope, play a test record with a pure tone. Perfect azimuth alignment will produce identical amplitudes from both 'scope channels.

Fig. 9-12
Azimuth is the perpendicular relationship of the cantilever to the record.

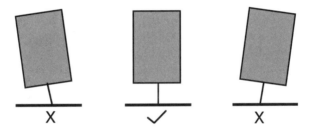

Recheck the cartridge alignment and overhang with the protractor; when these are correct, gently tighten the cartridge mounting bolts. The tightness of the bolts should strike a balance between making the cartridge tight in the headshell and distorting the cartridge body. Don't overtighten them.

Following the tonearm manufacturer's instructions, set the anti-skating force. If you don't have the instructions, and the tonearm doesn't have a calibrated anti-skating scale, you can set the anti-skating with a grooveless record (test pressings always have one grooveless side), or a sheet of Mylar cut into the shape of a record with a spindle hole. Put the stylus about halfway between the spindle and the outer edge, and spin the grooveless record or Mylar sheet. Adjust the anti-skating so that the arm moves very slowly toward the outside of the record. If the anti-skating is set incorrectly, mistracking on loud passages will occur more in one channel than in the other. Too much anti-skating will cause the left channel to distort first; too little will make the right channel distort first.

Another trick for setting the anti-skating force is to sum the left and right channels into mono, and invert the phase of one channel. When playing a record, the anti-skate will be properly set when the least sound is heard from the loudspeakers. Correct anti-skating adjustment will produce equal output from both channels; when one channel is inverted, the greatest cancellation will occur (the least sound heard) when the output levels are most closely matched. To make an inverting cable, buy a "Y" adapter with two female jacks and one male. Cut off one lead and reverse the shield and center conductor to invert the phase. The turntable output drives the two female jacks, and the single output feeds one phono input on the preamplifier. This method works very well, and costs about $3 for the "Y" adapter.

The next step is to fine-tune the VTA by listening. Mark on the tonearm rear the position that produces a parallel line between the cartridge bottom and the record. Raise the tonearm rear a few millimeters, then listen. Lower the tonearm rear a few millimeters below the parallel line and listen again. Find the position that provides the smoothest tonal balance and best imaging. Use several records for setting VTA, not just one or two.

There are many more ways to improve the sound of your LP front end. You can replace the stock tonearm cable with a high-end one; place isolation feet under the turntable; put contact enhancer on the cartridge pins; or put damping material on the tonearm tube, cartridge, finger lift, and counterweights. Damping material should be applied with care; it may upset the careful balance and resonance tuning designed into the turntable and tonearm.

Finally, I highly recommend an excellent booklet on turntable setup: *How to Set Up and Tune Your Turntable and Tonearm*, by George Merrill. The booklet, which includes a protractor, is filled with lots of useful information, and is available for $8.95 from Underground Sound, Memphis, TN 38104, (901) 272-5495.

10 Tuners

Overview

Atuner is a source component that receives radio transmissions from the air and converts them into a line-level audio signal that feeds an input on a preamplifier. The tuner has an antenna input (or inputs) and usually one pair of unbalanced line-level outputs.

Compared with other source components, the tuner plays a different role in a high-end system. On one hand, FM is a lower-quality source than LP and CD, and doesn't let your system live up to its full sonic potential. On the other hand, a tuner is an unending source of free music, and an invaluable way of being exposed to new musical forms and artists you may not have otherwise heard. How important a tuner is in your listening life is greatly influenced by the musical programming of stations in your area, how far away you live from transmitters, the care (or lack of care) taken by the station in achieving good sound, and the quality of your tuner.

The limiting factor in broadcast sound quality is often the radio station, not the FM transmission format or even the tuner. FM broadcasts of live concerts by radio stations that care about sound, and received by a good tuner, can be spectacular. I haven't any firsthand experience, but the live broadcasts by WGBH in Boston of the Boston Symphony Orchestra reportedly sounded superb.

Further, it's possible to set up a closed-circuit FM broadcast in a listening room using the highest-quality source components, then receive that broadcast signal with a tuner under evaluation. The source signal can thus be compared directly with the closed-circuit FM transmission. Listening tests and demonstrations of this technique reveal that FM is capable of extremely high sound quality. (For a full exposition of how tuners are evaluated with closed-circuit FM, see Larry Greenhill's review of the Day-Sequerra FM Reference tuner in the December 1991 issue of *Stereophile*.)

How to Choose a Tuner

Choosing a tuner for your system is a little different from choosing other components. When auditioning other components, we're primarily concerned with their sound quality, not their technical performance. If, for example, a preamplifier under audition sounds good, we don't need to worry much about its technical performance—if it sounds good, it's probably working well.

Tuners, on the other hand, exhibit great variability in their technical performance. We're interested not only in aspects of a tuner's sound—tonal balance, soundstaging, portrayal of timbre, etc.—but also in more basic characteristics such as the ability to pick up weak or distant stations, reject adjacent stations, provide a noise-free audio signal, and stay tuned to a station without drifting. A tuner's performance in these areas can be accurately characterized by measurement; this makes tuner specifications much more meaningful than those of other audio components. There is a direct correlation between a tuner's specifications and its sonic performance. You'll still need to listen to the tuner before you buy, but you can often separate poorer-performing models from better units by looking at the specification sheets. And unlike most audio products, in which the highest-performance units have the fewest features, the best high-end tuners have more features, front-panel controls, and displays than the lower-end products.

How much of your audio budget you should allocate to a tuner varies greatly with the individual. Some listeners just want a tuner for background music and National Public Radio, not for serious music listening. If this describes you, or if you listen to FM only occasionally, you may consider a tuner from a mid-fi company. The performance will be acceptable (if you choose wisely), and you can put more of your budget into components that matter more to you musically and sonically.

Those listeners who want the best possible technical and musical performance from FM will opt for a tuner designed and made by a high-end company. Several companies have dedicated themselves exclusively to the design and manufacture of tuners: their products are often superb, but expensive. Without the economies of scale provided by a factory making an entire line of audio products, the dedicated tuner company must charge more for its products. It can, however, focus its talents and engineering expertise on making the best tuner possible. If you want the highest performance and are willing to pay for it, seek out companies that have established reputations for making superlative tuners.

The price range for a good tuner from a mass-market manufacturer is between $400 and $1000. Some of the higher-end models from mass-market companies offer excellent performance. The price range from $750 to $1200 is very competitive, with many superb units to choose from. The very best tuners cost as much as $5000.

Although we'll discuss tuner specifications in detail later in this chapter, I'll briefly describe here the primary differences between mediocre and excellent tuners.

Good tuners are characterized by their *sensitivity*, or ability to pull in weak stations. The greater a tuner's sensitivity, the better it can pick up weak or distant stations. This aspect of a tuner's performance is more important in suburban or rural areas that are far from radio transmitters.

A tuner characteristic of greater importance to the city dweller is *adjacent-channel selectivity*—the ability to pick up one station without interference from the station next to it on the dial. The *alternate-channel selectivity* specification defines a tuner's ability to reject a strong station two channels away from the desired channel. When stations are packed closely together, as they are in cities, adjacent-channel and alternate-channel selectivity are more important than sensitivity.

Equally important to all listeners is the tuner's signal-to-noise ratio, a measure of the difference in dB between background noise and the maximum signal strength. A tuner with a poor signal-to-noise ratio will overlay the music with an annoying background hiss.

In short, a poor tuner will have trouble receiving weak stations, may lack the ability to select one station when that station is adjacent to another station, have high background noise, and be overloaded by nearby FM transmitters or other radio signal sources (taxi dispatchers, for example).

Tuners can be roughly divided into two categories: analog tuning and digital tuning (the latter is more correctly called *frequency-synthesized* tuning). If the tuner has a dial and pointer moved with a flywheel knob, it uses analog tuning. Frequency-synthesized tuners move in discrete jumps; from say, 88.1MHz to 88.3MHz. A frequency-synthesized tuner will lock on to the station and can't be mistuned (unless the tuner is misaligned). (Note that the presence of a digital station readout doesn't mean that the tuner is synthesized, only that the display is digital.) Synthesized tuners provide features such as *seek*—to move to the next station—and the ability to store many stations in a preset memory, recalled at the touch of a button. Another common feature of synthesized tuners is *scan*, which stops briefly at each station until you find a station you want and tell it to stop. *Memory scan* samples only the stations preset in the tuner's station.

Although it would appear that synthesized tuners have a big advantage over analog tuners, the very best tuners are all analog. Analog tuners have lower noise, and also allow fine-tuning to find the center of a station. Synthesized tuners jump in discrete steps of at least 25kHz, precluding the precise degree of fine-tuning possible with an infinitely variable analog tuner.

Better tuners have a feature called *selectable IF bandwidth* that adjusts the bandwidth in the tuner's intermediate frequency (IF) stage for best sound quality and minimum interference from adjacent stations. When in the "wide" mode, the audio quality improves at the expense of lower selectivity (less adjacent-channel rejection) and lower sensitivity. Specifically, a wide IF bandwidth provides the lowest distortion and the best high-frequency audio response. The high-frequency audio response of some tuners isn't affected by IF bandwidth, but all tuners have better imaging with wider IF bandwidths: phase shift in the IF filter may compromise stereo separation (and add distortion) at high frequencies. Wide bandwidth is used when no strong adjacent stations are present; narrow bandwidth is selected when the dial is crowded near the desired station. The best tuners have three selectable IF bandwidth settings.

Nearly every tuner has a *signal-strength meter* to indicate the strength of the received signal. The meter, usually a row of Light Emitting Diodes (LEDs), is helpful in positioning an antenna for best reception. The most sophisticated tuners have an oscilloscope display that provides a means of perfectly locating the center of a station. This expensive feature is found only on analog tuners.

Another useful tuner feature, used in conjunction with the signal-strength meter, is a *multi-path indicator*. Multi-path occurs when the broadcast signal reaches the tuner's antenna directly, in addition to reflections of that same signal off objects such as buildings. The slight delay between the two signals causes loss of audio-channel separation and increased distortion. In a car stereo, multi-path distortion is sometimes called "picket-fencing": the signal swells and fades as the car travels quickly in and out of multi-path reflections. A tuner's multi-path indicator allows you to rotate your antenna for least multi-path. A signal-strength meter alone doesn't discriminate between a clean signal and a signal with multi-path, making a multi-path indicator a very useful feature.

The high-end tuner shown in Fig.10-1 has a multi-path indicator (the meter on the left side of the front panel). The middle meter shows center tuning (how closely to the station's center frequency the tuner is set). The right-hand meter indicates signal strength.

Fig. 10-1 A high-end analog tuner

Courtesy Magnum Dynalab

Nearly all tuners have a *local/distant* switch. When in the Local position, the tuner simply attenuates the antenna's signal level before it gets to the tuner's input circuit, and prevents the tuner from being overloaded by strong stations.

A tuner's *muting* function mutes the audio output when the signal received by the tuner drops below some defined level. Muting prevents a blast of noise through your system when the tuner is between stations, or on a very weak station. A tuner's muting can be turned off (if the tuner has a muting on/off switch) to receive very weak stations.

The *mono/stereo* button found on most tuners allows you to reduce noise from weak stations by making the signal mono instead of stereo. The complete loss of left/right stereo separation is more than offset by the significant reduction in noise.

Many tuners have a *high-blend* circuit that automatically switches the signal to mono when the signal strength falls below a certain level. The difference between high-blend and the mono/stereo switch just described is that the high-blend circuit puts only the treble into mono, leaving the rest of the spectrum in stereo. This gets rid of most of the noise, but maintains stereo separation through most of the midrange and bass.

Some tuners have a switch marked "MPX" that invokes a 19kHz filter to remove the 19kHz pilot tone from the broadcast signal. This feature is necessary when recording on a cassette deck: the 19kHz pilot tone can interfere with the cassette deck's Dolby noise-reduction tracking. Some cassette decks have a switchable 19kHz filter (also marked "MPX") in case your tuner lacks this feature.

Finally, all good tuners have a 75 ohm coaxial antenna input as well as the more commonly used 300 ohm flat lead input. The coaxial input should be used for best signal transmission between the antenna and tuner.

What to Listen For

If the tuner has high technical performance standards—particularly sensitivity and selectivity—we can then characterize the tuner's musical performance using the listening techniques described in Chapter 3.

In addition to the usual sonic checklist, tuners should be auditioned with an ear to certain qualities unique to tuners. Many tuners overlay the music with a whitish haze that makes listening fatiguing. This sound isn't perceived as noise, but as a fuzz that rides over the music. It sounds as though the channel isn't perfectly tuned, even though it's tuned in as well as the tuner allows.

Better tuners have a more extended and open treble. Lower-quality units tend to sound closed-in, lacking air, and even rolled-off in the treble. This characteristic can obscure low-level detail and make the music bland.

The music's dynamic contrast is also greatly affected by the tuner's audio quality. Some tuners squash dynamics to a point where the sound is lifeless and flat. Others have a much wider variation between loud and soft. Note, however, that most radio stations compress the music's dynamic range before the transmitter to achieve a higher average signal level, making the station seem louder and "stick out" when someone is scanning the dial. The best stations—primarily classical music stations—leave the dynamic range intact. When evaluating a tuner's dynamic range, be sure to use a variety of stations, particularly high-quality classical ones.

A mediocre tuner can compress soundstage depth to the point where the music is a flat, sterile canvas, not a huge, spacious panorama. The music becomes congested, thick, cold, and uninviting. The best tuners can present a deep, spacious soundstage, with real depth and precise imaging.

Many of the negative sonic qualities I've described aren't inherent in the FM format; an excellent radio station broadcasting to a high-end tuner is capable of outstanding musical performance.

When evaluating tuners, keep in mind that a tuner is only as good as the signal supplied to it from the antenna. A high-quality antenna is essential to getting the best technical and musical performance from your tuner. If you're auditioning a tuner at a dealer's showroom or a friend's house, keep in mind that the antenna's quality is a significant variable. Depending on your antenna, you may get better or worse performance than you expect. Further, the very tiny voltages transmitted down the antenna lead, through the connections, and to the tuner input require tight, clean connections. A loose-fitting jack, or some corrosion on the terminals, can greatly degrade a tuner's performance.

Tuner Specifications and Measurements

The earlier part of this chapter described some of a tuner's fundamental specifications and how they relate to choosing a tuner. In this next section, we'll take a closer look at what constitutes good and poor tuner performance.

Sensitivity, or the ability to receive weak or distant stations, is defined technically as the radio frequency (RF) signal strength required to produce an audio signal output with a specified signal-to-noise ratio: the lower the sensitivity specification, the better (less signal required for good reception). Sensitivity is expressed as a voltage across the antenna in microvolts (µV), or as signal power in dBf (decibels referenced to one femtowatt, $10^{-15}W$, or one trillionth of a watt). Two methods of expressing the signal strength across the antenna exist because of the differences between the two antenna impedances (300 ohms and 75 ohms). For example, 30dBf represents 18µV across 300 ohms, but only 9µV across 75 ohms. If you compare dBf specifications, you don't need to worry about this difference. But when looking at microvolts, be certain that the impedance is specified. If one tuner's sensitivity is specified across the 75 ohm input, and the other across a 300 ohm input, simply double the 75 ohm figure and the two specifications will be directly comparable.

Tuner sensitivity is more precisely defined by specifying the voltage across the antenna required to produce an audio signal with a specified signal-to-noise ratio, usually 50dB. This specification is called the 50dB *quieting sensitivity*. A less stringent specification, called *usable sensitivity*, is the voltage required to achieve a 30dB signal-to-noise ratio—which is barely listenable. When comparing tuner specifications, be sure that the manufacturer specifies the 50dB quieting-sensitivity figure.

Sensitivity is different for mono and stereo reception: Mono requires less RF signal strength to achieve a specified quieting sensitivity. In fact, a tuner may require more than double the signal strength to achieve the same quieting sensitivity in stereo than in mono.

The very best tuners have a sensitivity (for 50dB quieting) of 30dBf (stereo) and 10dBf (mono). Usable sensitivity (for 30dB quieting) figures for an excellent tuner are 10dBf (stereo) and 8dBf (mono). Lower-sensitivity tuners may have a 50dB quieting specification of 40dBf (stereo) and 20dBf (mono). The lower the number, the better the tuner.

With alternate-channel selectivity, however, the higher the number, the better. This specification indicates how well the tuner can reject strong stations near the desired station. Technically, alternate selectivity is the ratio (in dB) of the signal strength needed to produce a reference output level on the wanted channel to the signal strength needed to produce an audio output level 30dB below the reference level from a station two channels away. The higher the selectivity, the greater the tuner's ability to reject unwanted adjacent or alternate stations. Selectivity may be the most important tuner specification, particularly in areas with a crowded FM dial.

Selectivity is often specified with both narrow and wide IF bandwidths. The narrower bandwidth improves the selectivity figures, but decreases audio quality. The best tuners have an alternate-channel selectivity of 100dB in narrow mode, and an adjacent-channel selectivity of 40dB (also in narrow mode). In wide mode, a tuner's alternate-channel selectivity may be reduced to 30dB. Lower-quality tuners may have an alternate-channel selectivity specification of 40dB. These tuners generally don't have selectable IF bandwidth.

When a tuner receives two stations at the same frequency, the tuner must suppress the weaker one and capture the stronger one. *Capture ratio* is the difference in dB between the strengths of the two stations needed before the tuner can lock to the stronger station and reject the weaker one. The lower the capture ratio, the better; the stronger station doesn't have to be that much stronger for the tuner to reject the weaker one. Although it is relatively uncommon to receive two stations at the same frequency, a good capture ratio helps in preventing multi-path distortion; the weaker reflected signal is more easily rejected. A capture ratio of 1dB is excellent, 1.5dB is average, and 2dB is poor. This specification, along with adjacent-channel selectivity, is of paramount important to the city dweller who receives strong multi-path reflections from buildings. Capture ratio has a high degree of correlation with sound quality, particularly for those listeners who can't put up a directional antenna to minimize multi-path. Multi-path interference often produces severe amplitude modulation of the FM carrier, an aberration that multiplex stereo decoders are particularly sensitive to.

A tuner's signal-to-noise ratio specifies the level of background noise, usually in both mono and stereo. Signal-to-noise must be specified with a given input signal, usually a very high 65dBf. Some manufacturers specify signal-to-noise ratio at 85dBf, which yields a better number than 65dBf. With a roof antenna located ten miles from a transmitter, many signals may be in the 65dBf range, and the strongest signals may exceed 85dBf. When comparing specifications, be certain that the signal-to-noise ratio is specified with the same signal strength. A good signal-to-noise specification is 90dB (mono) and 80dB (stereo) with a 65dBf signal. The higher the signal-to-noise ratio, the quieter the tuner (all other factors being equal).

Stereo separation is the degree of isolation, measured in dB, between the left and right audio channels. Greater separation correlates with increased spaciousness to the sound. Stereo separation is measured at 1kHz with a 50dB quieting input, and the IF bandwidth adjustment in the wide position (if the tuner has selectable IF bandwidth). A tuner designer can hype a separation specification by tailoring the tuner for wide separation at 1kHz at the expense of the rest of the audio band. It is more difficult to achieve wide separation consistently over the band. This requires excellent phase-linearity in the IF stage, or careful phase-compensation of the feed to the multiplex decoder. The IHF/EIA standards for tuner measurements include separation figures up to a frequency of 6kHz. The separation at 6kHz is a more reliable indicator of a tuner's stereo separation than the 1kHz specification. Unfortunately, not all tuner manufacturers adhere to the IHF/EIA measurement standards. Tuners range from about 40dB of stereo separation, to 70dB in the best models (both are specified at 1kHz).

Digital Audio Broadcasting

The decades-long tradition of broadcasting analog radio signals over the air is about to be overthrown by the distribution of digitally-encoded audio programs. The new technology, known generically as Digital Audio Broadcasting (DAB), delivers digitally-encoded audio via a cable TV-hookup, satellite dish, or over the air along with a conventional AM or FM broadcast.

One such system, Digital Music Express (DMX), is already in operation. The service provides continuous, commercial-free music through an existing cable-TV channel. The user buys the "tuner" (cost: about $200) and pays a monthly fee for the service.

Another proposed method conceals the digitally-encoded audio program beneath existing AM and FM broadcasts. Conventional tuners would receive the signals as they always have, but new digital tuners could decode the so-called "in-band, on-channel" (IBOC) digital signals broadcast at the same frequency as the conventional AM or FM signals.

DAB will provide reasonably high-quality audio without the problems inherent in FM or AM transmission. The sound quality will be less good than that of the compact disc, a result of the low-bit rate coding used in DAB. Low-bit rate coding reduces the number of bits needed to encode an audio signal by ignoring information in the music judged to be inaudible. For example, the Musicam low-bit rate coder proposed for

DAB produces a datastream with a bit rate of 192,000 bits per second, in contrast to the 1,410,000 bits per second needed for CD-quality coding.

Despite the reduction in fidelity introduced by low-bit rate coding, DAB will probably sound better than conventional AM and FM broadcasting. Many of the factors influencing tuner performance described earlier in this chapter will become moot with DAB. It remains to be seen, however, how DAB receivers will respond to weak or interrupted signals, multi-path, and other conventional radio problems.

11   Cables and Interconnects

Overview and Terminology

Loudspeaker cables and line-level interconnects are an important but often overlooked link in the music playback chain. The right choice of loudspeaker cables and interconnects can bring out the best performance from your system. Conversely, poor cables and interconnects—or those not suited to your system—will never let your system achieve its full musical potential. Knowing how to buy cables will provide the best possible performance at the least cost. Moreover, we'll see how the most expensive cables and interconnects aren't always the best.

In this chapter we'll look at all aspects of loudspeaker cables and interconnects. We'll cover balanced and unbalanced lines, bi-wiring, matching cables to your system, and how to get the most cable for your money.

But first, let's start with an overview of cable and interconnect terms.

Cable: Often used to describe any wire in an audio system, "cable" more properly refers to the conductors between a power amplifier and a loudspeaker. Loudspeaker cables carry a high-current signal from the power amplifier to the loudspeaker.

Interconnect: Interconnects are the conductors that connect line-level signals in an audio system. The connection between source components (turntable, CD player, tuner, tape deck) and the preamplifier, and between the preamplifier and power amplifier, are made by interconnects.

Unbalanced Interconnect: An unbalanced interconnect has two conductors and is usually terminated with RCA plugs. Also called a *single-ended* interconnect.

Balanced Interconnect: A balanced interconnect has three conductors instead of two, and is terminated with 3-pin *XLR* connectors. Balanced interconnects are used only between components having balanced inputs and outputs.

Digital Interconnect: A single interconnect that carries a stereo digital audio signal, usually from a CD transport or other digital source to a digital processor.

Bi-wiring: Bi-wiring is a method of connecting a power amplifier to a loudspeaker with two runs of cable instead of one.

RCA Plug and Jack: RCA plugs and jacks are the most common connection termination for unbalanced signals. Virtually all audio equipment has RCA jacks to accept the RCA plugs on unbalanced interconnects. RCA jacks are mounted on the audio component's chassis; RCA plugs are the termination of unbalanced interconnects.

XLR Plug and Jack: XLR plugs are three-pin connectors terminating a balanced interconnect. XLR jacks are chassis-mounted connectors that accept XLR plugs.

Binding Post: Binding posts are terminations on power amplifiers and loudspeakers that provide connection points for loudspeaker cables.

Five-way Binding Post: A type of binding post that can accept bare wire, spade lugs, or banana plugs. Five-way posts are found on most power amplifiers and loudspeakers.

Spade Lug: A flat, pronged termination for loudspeaker cables. Spade lugs fit around power-amplifier and loudspeaker binding posts. The most popular kind of loudspeaker cable termination.

Banana Plug and Jack: Banana plugs are sometimes found on loudspeaker cables in place of spade lugs. Banana plugs will fit into five-way binding posts or banana jacks. Many European products use banana jacks on power amplifiers for loudspeaker connection.

AWG: American Wire Gauge: a measure of conductor thickness, usually in loudspeaker cables. The lower the AWG number, the thicker the wire. Lamp cord has an AWG of 18, or "18 gauge."

Some of these cables, interconnects, and terminations are shown in Fig.11-1.

Fig. 11-1 From left to right: balanced interconnects terminated with XLR connectors, unbalanced interconnects terminated with RCA plugs, a spade lug and a banana plug

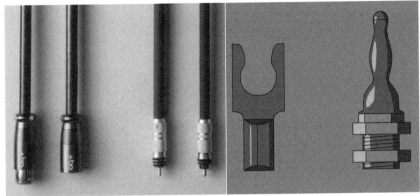

Courtesy AudioQuest

How to Choose Cables and Interconnects

A typical hi-fi system will need one pair of loudspeaker cables (two pairs for bi-wiring), one long pair of interconnects between the preamplifier and power amplifier, and several short interconnect pairs for connections between source components (such as a turntable or CD player) and the preamplifier.

If the power amplifier is located near the loudspeakers, the loudspeaker cables will be short and the interconnects between the preamplifier and power amplifier will be long. Conversely, if the power amplifier is near the source components and preamplifier, the interconnects will be short and the loudspeaker cables long. There is no consensus among the experts about which method is preferable, but I use long interconnects and short loudspeaker cables. Ideally, interconnects *and* loudspeaker cables should be short, but that often isn't practical.

Once you've got a feel for how your system is—or will be—configured, make a list of the interconnects and cables you'll need, and their lengths. Keep all lengths as short as possible, but allow some flexibility for moving loudspeakers, putting your preamp in a different space in the rack, or other possible changes. Although we want to keep the cables and interconnects short for the best sound, there's nothing worse than having interconnects 6″ too short. After you've found the minimum length, add half a meter for flexibility.

Interconnects are often made in standard lengths of 1, 1.5, and 2 meters. These are long enough for source-to-preamplifier connections, but too short for many preamplifier-to-power amplifier runs. These long runs are usually custom-made to a specific length. Similarly, loudspeaker cables are typically supplied in 8′ or 10′ pairs, but custom lengths are readily available. It's best to have the cable manufacturer terminate the cables (put spade lugs or banana plugs on loudspeaker cables, and RCA or XLR plugs on interconnects) rather than trying it yourself.

Concentrate your cable budget on the cables that matter most. The priority should be given to the sources you listen to most. For example, you may not care as much about the sound of your cassette deck or tuner as you do your CD player. Consequently, you should spend more on interconnects between the CD player and preamplifier than between the tape deck and preamp. And because all your sources are connected to the power amplifier through the interconnect between the preamplifier and power amplifier, this link must be given a high priority. But any component—even a cassette deck—will benefit from good interconnects.

Should all your interconnects and loudspeaker cables be made by the same manufacturer? Or is it better to mix and match brands? There are two schools of thought on this issue. The first holds that an entire system with one brand of cable and interconnect is the best route. If one interconnect works well in your system, use it throughout. This argument also suggests that the cable designer made his interconnects and loudspeaker cables to work together to achieve the best possible sound.

The second school of thought suggests that different brands are best. Because each cable or interconnect affects the sound in a certain way, using the same interconnect and cable throughout the system will only reinforce the cable's sonic signature. By using cables and interconnects from different manufacturers, the characteristic sonic signature of a cable won't be superimposed on the music by every interconnect.

This second theory has an analog in the recording world. Engineers will record through one brand of recording console, then mix the record through a different brand of console. They don't want to hear the console's sound in the final product, so they don't subject the signal to the same sonic signature twice.

My experience suggests that the only way to determine the best cable or interconnect for your system is to experiment and listen. In some cases, the best results will be achieved with all the interconnects and cables made by the same manufacturer. In others, a mix of different interconnects will work best. It's impossible to predict which cables will sound best in your system.

Most dealers will let you take home several cables at once to try in your system. Take advantage of these offers. Some mail-order companies will send you many cables to try: you keep the ones you want to buy—if any—and return the others. Compare inexpensive cables with expensive ones—sometimes manufacturers have superb cables that sell for a fraction of the price of their top-of-the-line products.

If you're starting a system from scratch, selecting cables is more difficult than replacing one length in your system. Because different combinations of cables will produce different results, the possibilities are greatly increased. Moreover, you don't have a baseline reference against which to judge how good or bad a cable is. In this situation, the best way of getting the ideal cables for your system is your dealer's advice. Try the cables and interconnects he suggests, along with two other brands or models for comparison.

Ideally, every component in the system—including cables and interconnects—should be absolutely neutral and impose no sonic signature on the music. As this is never the case, we are forced to select cables and interconnects with colorations that counteract the rest of the system's colorations.

For example, if your system is a little on the bright and analytical side, mellow-sounding interconnects and cables can take the edge off the treble and let you enjoy the music more. If the bass is overpowering and fat, lean- and tight-sounding interconnects and cables can firm up and lean out the bass. A system lacking palpability and presence in the midrange can benefit from a forward-sounding cable.

Selecting cables and interconnects for their musical compatibility should be viewed as the final touch to your system. A furniture maker who has been using saws, planers, and rasps will finish his work with steel wool or very fine sandpaper. Treat cables and interconnects the same way—as the last tweak to nudge your system in the right direction, not as a Band Aid for poorly chosen components.

Cables and interconnects won't correct fundamental musical or electrical incompatibilities. For example, if you have a high-output-impedance power amplifier driving current-hungry loudspeakers, the bass will probably be soft and the dynamics constricted. Loudspeaker cables won't fix this problem. You might be able to ameliorate the soft bass with the right cable, but it's far better to fix the problem at the source—a better amplifier/loudspeaker match.

Good cables merely allow the system's components to perform at their highest level; they won't make a poor system or bad component match sound good. Start with a high-quality, well-chosen system and select cables and interconnects that allow that system to achieve its highest musical performance. Remember, a cable or interconnect can't actually effect an absolute improvement in the sound; the good ones merely do less harm.

How Much Should You Spend on Cables and Interconnects?

At the top end of the scale, cable and interconnect pricing bears little relationship to the cost of designing and manufacturing the product. Unlike other audio products, whose retail prices are largely determined by the parts cost (the retail price is typically four to six times the cost of raw parts), cables and interconnects are sometimes priced according to what the market will bear. This trend began when one company set its prices vastly higher than everyone else's—and saw its sales skyrocket as a result. Other manufacturers then raised *their* prices so they wouldn't be perceived as being of lower quality. Although some very expensive cables and interconnects are worth the money, many cables are ridiculously overpriced.

The budget-conscious audiophile can, however, take advantage of this phenomenon. Very often, a cable manufacturer's lower-priced products are very nearly as good as their most expensive models. The company prices their top-line products to foster the impression of being "high-end," yet relies on its lower-priced models for the bulk of its sales. When shopping for loudspeaker cables and interconnects, listen to a manufacturer's lower line in your system—even if you have a large cable budget. You may be pleasantly surprised.

Because every system is different, it's impossible to generalize about what percentage of your overall system investment you should spend on cables and interconnects. Spending 5% of your system's cost on cables and interconnects would be an absolute minimum, with about 15% a maximum figure. If you choose the right cables and interconnects, they can be an excellent value. But poor cables on good components will give you poor sound and thus constitute false economy.

Again, I must stress that high cost doesn't guarantee that the cable is good or that it will work well in your system. Don't automatically assume an expensive cable is better than a low-priced one. Listen to a wide variety of price levels and brands. Your efforts will often be rewarded with exactly the right cable for your system at a reasonable price.

What to Listen For

Cables must be evaluated in the playback system in which they will be used. Not only is the sound of a cable partially system-dependent, but the sonic characteristics of a specific cable will work better musically in some systems than in others. Moreover, personal auditioning is the *only* way to evaluate cables and interconnects. Never be swayed by technical jargon about why one cable is better than another. Much of this is pure marketing hype, with little or no relevance to how the cable will perform musically in your system. Trust your ears.

Fortunately, evaluating cables and interconnects is relatively simple; the levels are automatically matched between cables, and you don't have to be concerned about absolute-polarity reversal. One pitfall, however, is that cables and interconnects need time to break in before they sound their best. Before break-in, a cable often sounds bright, hard, fatiguing, congested, and lacking in soundstage depth. These characteristics often disappear after several hours' use, with days or weeks of use required for full break-in. You can't be sure, however, if the cable is inherently bright- and hard-sounding, or if it just needs breaking-in. Note that break-in wears off over time. Even if a cable has had significant use, it may not sound its best until you've put music through it for a few days.

With those cautions in mind, you're ready to evaluate cables and interconnects. Listen to the first interconnect for 15 minutes to half an hour, then replace it with the next candidate. One way of choosing between them is merely to ask yourself which interconnect allows you to enjoy the music more. You don't need to analyze what you're hearing; just pick the interconnect that makes you feel better.

The other method is to scrutinize what you're hearing from each interconnect and catalog the interconnect's strengths and weaknesses. You'll often hear trade-offs between interconnects: one interconnect may have smoother treble and finer resolution than another, but less soundstage focus and transparency. Another common trade-off is between smoothness and resolution of detail. The smooth cable may lose some musical information, but the high-resolution cable can sound analytical and bright. Again, careful auditioning in your own system is the only way to select the right cables and interconnects. Keep in mind, however, that a better cable can sometimes reveal flaws in the rest of your system.

Cables and interconnects can add some annoying distortions to the music. I've listed the most common sonic problems of cables and interconnects. (A full description of these terms is included in Chapter 3.)

Grainy and hashy treble: Many cables overlay the treble with a coarse texture. The sound is rough rather than smooth and liquid.

Bright and metallic treble: Cymbals sound like bursts of white noise rather than a brass-like shimmer. They also tend to splash across the soundstage rather than sounding like compact images. Sibilants ("s" and "ch" sounds on vocals) are emphasized, making the treble sound spitty. It's a bad sign if you suddenly notice more sibilance. The opposite condition is a dark and closed-in treble. The cable should sound open, airy, and extended in the treble without sounding overly bright, etched, or analytical.

Hard textures and lack of liquidity: Listen for a glassy glare on solo piano in the upper registers. Similarly, massed voices can sound glazed and hard rather than liquid and richly textured.

Listening fatigue: A poor cable will quickly cause listening fatigue. The symptoms of listening fatigue are headache, a feeling of relief when the music is turned down or stopped, the need to do something other than listen to music, and the feeling that your ears are tightening up. This last condition is absolutely the worst thing any audio component can do. Good cables (in a good system) will let you listen at higher levels for longer periods of time. If a cable or interconnect causes listening fatigue, avoid it no matter what its other attributes.

Lack of space and depth: Using a recording with lots of natural depth and ambiance, listen for how the cable affects soundstage depth and the sense of instruments hanging in three-dimensional space. Poor cables can also make the soundstage less transparent.

Low resolution: Some cables and interconnects sound smooth, but they obscure the music's fine detail. Listen for low-level information and an instrument's inner detail. The opposite of smoothness is a cable that's "ruthlessly revealing" of every detail in the music, but in an unnatural way. Musical detail should be audible, but not hyped or exaggerated. The cable or interconnect should strike a balance between resolution of information and a sense of ease and smoothness.

Mushy bass or poor pitch definition: A poor-quality cable or interconnect can make the bass slow, mushy, and lacking in pitch definition. With such a cable, the bottom end is soggy and fat rather than taut and articulate. Low-frequency pitches are obscured, making the bass sound like a roar instead of being composed of individual notes.

Constricted dynamics: Listen for the cable or interconnect's ability to portray the music's dynamic structure, on both small and large scale. For example, a guitar string's transient attack should be quick, with a dynamic edge. On a larger scale, orchestral climaxes should be powerful and have a sense of physical impact (if the rest of your system can portray this aspect of music).

I must reiterate that putting a highly colored cable or interconnect in your system to correct a problem in another component (a dark-sounding cable on a bright loudspeaker) isn't the best solution. Instead, use the money you would have spent on new cables toward better loudspeakers—*then* go cable shopping. Cables and interconnects shouldn't be Band Aids; instead, cables should be the finishing touch to let the rest of your components perform at their highest level.

Binding Posts and Cable Terminations

Binding posts vary hugely in quality, from the tiny spring-loaded, push-in terminal strips on cheap loudspeakers to massive, custom-made, machined brass posts plated with exotic metals. Poor binding posts not only degrade the sound, they also break easily. When shopping for power amplifiers and loudspeakers, take a close look at binding-post quality.

The most popular type is the five-way binding post. It accepts spade lugs, banana plugs, or bare wire. Some five-ways are nickel-plated; higher-quality ones are plated with gold and thus won't tarnish. Five-way binding posts should be tightened with a 1/2" nut driver, not a socket and ratchet or wrench which could easily overtighten the nut. The connection should be tight, but not to the point of stripping the post or causing it to turn in the chassis. When tightening a five-way binding post, watch the inside ring or collar next to the chassis; if it begins to turn, you've overtightened the post and are in danger of damaging the power amplifier or loudspeaker.

Custom posts of heavy-duty machined metal are more robust than five-way posts—they can accept more torque without stripping or coming loose in the chassis. Custom posts are often found on the most expensive equipment. The amplifier rear panel shown in Chapter 6 (Fig.6-6) uses high-quality custom posts.

Some binding posts have such a large center post that spade lugs won't fit around them. These posts have large holes in the center for accepting large bare wires or banana jacks. Although these posts are expensive and appear to be of high quality, they're inconvenient to use. If your equipment has this sort of post, the best solution is to terminate your loudspeaker cables with oversized spade lugs. Most spade lugs have a distance between the prongs of 1/4" to 3/16"; oversized spades have prongs 5/16" apart—enough of a difference to fit the large-holed posts.

If you have a choice of bare wire, banana plug, or spade lug on loudspeaker cable terminations, go with the spade lug. It forms the best contact with a binding post and is the most standard form of connection. Many European products provide only banana jacks, forcing you to use sonically inferior banana-plug terminations.

You should be aware that any termination slightly degrades the sound of your system. Consequently, some audiophiles have gone to the trouble of removing all plugs, jacks, spade lugs, and binding posts from their systems and hard-wiring everything together. This is an extreme measure and makes switching equipment difficult or impossible. Hard-wiring is an option, but not one that should be undertaken without considerable deliberation and technical expertise.

Bi-Wired Loudspeaker Cables

Bi-wiring is running two lengths of cable between the power amplifier and loudspeaker. This technique usually produces much better sound quality than conventional single-wiring. Most high-end loudspeakers have two pairs of binding posts for bi-wiring, with one pair connected to the crossover's tweeter circuit and the other pair connected to the woofer circuit. The jumpers connecting the two pairs of binding posts fitted at the factory must be removed for bi-wiring.

In a bi-wired system, the power amplifier "sees" a higher impedance on the tweeter cable at low frequencies, and a lower impedance at high frequencies. The opposite is true in the woofer half of the bi-wired pair. This causes the signal to be split up, with high frequencies traveling mostly in the pair driving the loudspeaker's tweeter circuit and low frequencies conducted by the pair connected to the loudspeaker's woofer circuit. This frequency splitting reportedly reduces magnetic interaction in the cable, resulting in better sound. The large magnetic fields set up around the conductors by low-frequency energy can't affect the transfer of treble energy. No one knows exactly why bi-wiring works, but on nearly all loudspeakers with bi-wiring provision, it makes a big improvement in the sound. Whatever your cable budget, you should bi-wire if your loudspeaker has bi-wired inputs, even if it means buying two runs of less expensive cables.

You can bi-wire your loudspeakers with two identical single-wire runs, or with a specially prepared bi-wire set. A bi-wire set has one pair (positive and negative) of terminations at the amplifier end of the cable, and two pairs at the loudspeaker end of the cable. This makes it easier to hook up, and probably offers slightly better sound quality.

Loudspeakers can also be connected with a *single bi-wire* set in which a single cable with multiple internal conductors has two pairs of terminations on one end and a single pair of terminations at the other end. Although this approach is much less expensive than two runs of cable, you lose the benefit of magnetically isolating the low- and high-frequency conductors from each other. A bi-wired set and single bi-wire set are shown in Fig.11-2.

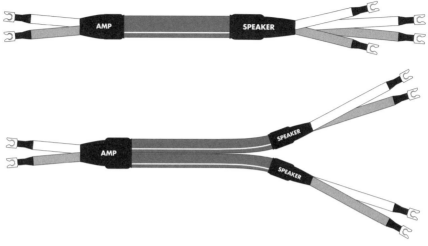

Courtesy AudioQuest

Most bi-wired sets use identical cables for the high- and low-frequency legs. Mixing cables, however, can have several advantages. By using a cable with good bass on the low-frequency pair, and a more expensive but sweeter-sounding cable on the high-frequency pair, you can get better performance for a lower cost. Use a less expensive cable on the bass and put more money into the high-frequency cable. If you've already got two pairs of cable the same length, the higher-quality cable usually sounds better on the high-frequency side of the bi-wired pair. If you use different cables for bi-wiring, they should be made by the same manufacturer and have similar physical construction. If the cables in a bi-wired set have different capacitances or inductances, it changes the loudspeaker's crossover characteristics.

Balanced and Unbalanced Lines

Line-level interconnects come in two varieties: balanced and unbalanced. A balanced interconnect is recognizable by its three-pin XLR connector. An unbalanced interconnect is usually terminated with an RCA plug. Balanced and unbalanced lines are shown in the photograph at the beginning of this chapter.

Why do we use two incompatible systems for connecting equipment? At one time, all consumer audio hardware had unbalanced inputs and outputs, and all professional gear was balanced. In fact, balanced inputs are often called "professional inputs" to differentiate them from "consumer" unbalanced jacks. Balanced connection was considered both unnecessary and too expensive for home playback systems.

The emergence of high-end audio changed that thinking. Instead of using the least expensive connection method, high-end product designers started using higher-quality balanced lines and terminations in consumer gear. The better the equipment, the more likely that it has at least some balanced connections in addition to unbalanced jacks. Moreover, more and more manufacturers are offering balanced connections on their equipment. This is why we have two standards—balanced and unbalanced. The technical and sonic advantages of balanced connection, once the exclusive domain of audio professionals, is becoming increasingly available for home playback systems.

But what exactly is a balanced line, and how is it different from a standard RCA cable and jack?

In an unbalanced line, the audio signal appears across the center pin of the RCA jack and the shield, or ground wire. Some unbalanced interconnects have two signal conductors and a shield, with the shield not used as a signal conductor. If this unbalanced interconnect happens to be close to fluctuating magnetic fields—an AC power cord, for example— the magnetic field will induce a noise signal in the interconnect which is heard as hum and noise reproduced through the playback system's loudspeakers.

In a professional application, this hum, buzz, and noise is unacceptable, leading to the development of an interconnection method that is immune to noise interference: the balanced line. A balanced line has three conductors: two carrying signal, and one ground. The two signals in a balanced line are identical, but 180° out of phase with each other. When the signal in one of the conductors is peak positive, the signal in the other conductor is at peak negative (see Fig.11-3). The third conductor is signal ground. Some balanced interconnects use three conductors plus a shield.

When the two identical but opposite polarity signals carried on the balanced line are input to a *differential amplifier* in the component receiving the signal, noise picked up by the interconnect is rejected. Here's why: a differential amplifier amplifies only the *difference* between the two signals (see Fig.11-4). If noise is introduced into the line, the noise will be common to both conductors and the differential amplifier will reject the noise. This phenomenon of rejecting noise signals common to both conductors in a balanced line is called *common-mode rejection*. Differential inputs are specified according to how well they reject signals common to both conductors, a measurement called *Common-Mode Rejection Ratio*, or *CMRR*. Note that a balanced line won't make a noisy signal clean; it just prevents additional noise from being introduced in the interconnect. If the noise is common to both halves of the balanced line, however, common-mode rejection will eliminate the noise.

Fig. 11-3 Signal voltages applied to an unbalanced and a balanced line

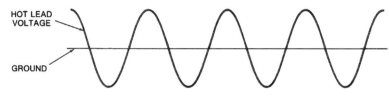

HOT LEAD VOLTAGE

GROUND

(A) Unbalanced line (using two conductors)

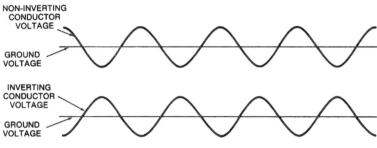

NON-INVERTING CONDUCTOR VOLTAGE

GROUND VOLTAGE

INVERTING CONDUCTOR VOLTAGE

GROUND VOLTAGE

(B) Balanced line (using three conductors)

Fig. 11-4 When the two signals carried by the balanced line are input to a differential amplifier, noise common to both conductors is rejected (bottom).

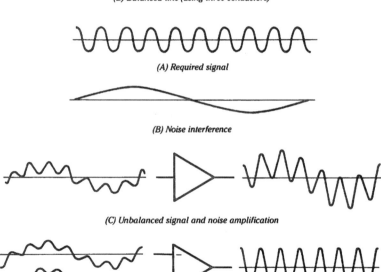

(A) Required signal

(B) Noise interference

(C) Unbalanced signal and noise amplification

(D) Balanced line—signal amplification and noise elimination

Copied with permission from *Audio Technology Fundamentals* by Alan A. Cohen

In professional applications, a transformer sometimes serves the same function as the differential amplifier, passing only the difference between the two signal conductors and rejecting signals common to both conductors. Consumer audio equipment uses differential amplifiers, not transformers, but the concept is identical.

In a balanced line terminated with XLR connectors, pin 1 is always signal ground. There is, however, no convention for which of the two signal conductors carries the non-inverted signal and which carries the inverted signal. The non-inverted conductor is often called the "hot" conductor, with the inverted conductor designated "cold." After decades of no clear standard, the Audio Engineering Society recently adopted the North American tradition of having pin 2 carry the non-inverted ("hot") signal, pin 3 the inverted ("cold") signal.

How the balanced line is wired (pin 2 or pin 3 "hot") can determine if your playback system is inverting or non-inverting of absolute polarity (see the section on absolute polarity in Appendix A). If your system is non-inverting—that is, a positive-going signal on the LP or CD produces a positive-going signal at the loudspeakers—substituting a pin 3 "hot" balanced input power amplifier for a pin 2 "hot" power amplifier will make your system inverting. When switching balanced components— digital processors, preamps, or power amplifiers—you should know if the new component's XLR jacks are wired the same—either pin 2 or pin 3 "hot"—as the existing component. You can also change your system's absolute polarity by rewiring the balanced interconnect to swap the wires going to pins 2 and 3. It's far better, however, to simply reverse absolute polarity by switching red for black and black for red on both your loudspeaker cables if you want to change your system's absolute polarity. The freak interconnect with pins 2 and 3 switched at one end may wind up in another system or application where you don't want the polarity switched.

Quite apart from the advantage of noise cancellation in a balanced line, a balanced connection often sounds better than an unbalanced line. A system connected by balanced interconnects can, however, often sound less good than one connected with unbalanced lines. Say you have a digital processor that takes an unbalanced signal from the digital-to-analog converter chip and converts it to a balanced signal so that the processor manufacturer can tout the product as having "balanced outputs" (see the section on balanced digital processors in Chapter 8). Inside the digital processor, the unbalanced signal is converted to a balanced signal by a *phase splitter*, a circuit that takes a signal of one polarity and turns it into two signals of opposite polarity. Phase splitting subjects the unbalanced signal to an additional active (transistor or op-amp–based) stage and puts more circuitry in the signal path.

The balanced digital processor output is then input to a balanced-input preamplifier. Because all but the very best balanced preamplifiers convert a balanced input signal to an unbalanced signal for the preamplifier's internal gain stages, the preamplifier's input converts this balanced signal to an unbalanced signal—adding yet another active stage to the signal path. After the unbalanced signal is amplified within the pre-amplifier, it is converted back to balanced with another phase splitter.

The preamplifier's balanced output is then sent from the preamplifier output to the power amplifier's balanced input where it's—that's right—converted to unbalanced with yet another active stage. The result of these unbalanced/balanced/unbalanced/balanced/unbalanced conversions is additional electronics in the signal path—just what we don't want. This is why you can't assume that balanced components sound inherently better than unbalanced ones. Magazine reviews of audio components should include musical and technical comparisons of the product's balanced and unbalanced modes.

Some products, however, are truly balanced and don't rely on phase splitters and unbalancing amplifiers. For example, a digital processor may create a balanced signal in the digital domain (at no sonic penalty, and indeed, a sonic gain) and convert that balanced signal to analog with four digital-to-analog converters and analog output stages (left channel + and –, right channel + and –). Similarly, some preamplifiers are truly balanced and have double the circuitry to operate on the non-inverting and inverting signals separately. You can tell a truly balanced preamplifier by the number of elements in the volume control. A preamplifier that operates on an unbalanced signal internally will have two-volume control elements: one for the left channel, one for the right. A fully balanced preamplifier will have four elements: ± left channel and ± right channel. The signal thus stays balanced from before the DACs inside the digital processor all the way to the final stages in the power amplifier.

As in all things audio, the proof is in the listening. When shopping for a component, listen to it in both balanced and unbalanced mode. Let your ears decide if the component works best in your system when connected via the balanced or unbalanced lines.

Digital Interconnects

A digital interconnect carries two channels of digitally encoded audio down a single interconnect, usually between a CD transport and outboard digital processor. A full discussion of digital interconnect methods, cables, and terminations is included in Chapter 8.

Cable and Interconnect Construction

Cables and interconnects are composed of three main elements: the signal conductors, the dielectric, and the terminations. The *conductors* carry the audio signal; the *dielectric* is an insulating material between and around the conductors; and the *terminations* provide connection to audio equipment. These elements are formed into a physical structure called the cable's *geometry*. Each of these elements—particularly geometry—can affect the cable's sonic characteristics.

Conductors

Conductors are usually made of copper or silver wire. In high-end cables, the copper's purity is important. Copper is sometimes specified as containing some percentage of "pure" copper, with the rest impurities. For example, a certain copper may be 99.997% pure, meaning it has three-thousandths of one percent impurities. These impurities are usually iron, sulfur, antimony, aluminum, and arsenic. Higher-purity copper—99.99997% pure—is called "six nines" copper. Many believe that the purer the copper, the better the sound. Some copper is referred to as *OFC*, or *Oxygen-Free Copper*. This is copper from which the oxygen molecules have been removed. It is more proper to call this "oxygen-reduced" copper because it is impossible to remove all the oxygen. In practice, OFC has about 50ppm (parts per million) of oxygen compared to 250ppm of oxygen for normal copper. Reducing the oxygen content retards the formation of copper oxides in the conductor which can interrupt the copper's physical structure and degrade sound quality.

Another term associated with copper is *LC*, or *Linear Crystal*, which describes the copper's structure. Drawn copper has a grain structure that can be thought of as tiny discontinuities in the copper. The signal can be adversely affected by traversing these grains; the grain boundary can act as a tiny circuit, with capacitance, inductance, and a diode effect. Standard copper has about 1500 grains per foot; LC copper has about 70 grains per foot. Fig.11-5 shows the grain structure in copper having 400 grains per foot. Note that the copper isn't isotropic; it looks decidedly different in one direction than the other. All copper made into thin wires exhibits a chevron structure, shown in the photograph of Fig.11-5. This chevron structure may explain why some cables sound different when reversed.

Conductors are made by casting a thick rod, then drawing the copper into a smaller gauge. Another technique—which is rare and expensive—is called "as-cast." This method casts the copper into the final size without the need for drawing.

Fig. 11-5 Copper in cables and interconnects has a grain structure.

Courtesy AudioQuest

The highest-quality technique for drawing copper is called "Ohno Continuous Casting" or *OCC*. OCC copper has one grain in about 700 feet—far less than even LC copper. The audio signal travels through a continuous conductor instead of traversing grain boundaries. Because OCC is a process that can be performed on any purity of copper, not all OCC copper is equal.

The other primary—but less prevalent—conductor material is silver. Silver cables and interconnects are obviously much more expensive to manufacture than copper ones, but silver has some advantages. Although its conductivity is only slightly higher than that of copper, silver oxides are less of a problem for audio signals than are copper oxides. Silver conductors are made using the same drawing techniques used in making copper conductors.

The Dielectric

The dielectric is the material surrounding the conductors, and is what gives cables and interconnects some of their bulk. The dielectric material has a large effect on the cable's sound; comparisons of identical conductors and geometry, but with different dielectric materials, demonstrate the dielectric's importance.

Dielectric materials absorb energy, a phenomenon called *dielectric absorption*. A capacitor works in the same way: a dielectric material between two charged plates stores energy. But in a cable, dielectric absorption can degrade the signal. The energy absorbed by the dielectric is released back into the cable slightly delayed in time—an undesirable condition.

Dielectric materials are chosen to minimize dielectric absorption. Less expensive cables and interconnects use plastic or PVC for the dielectric. Better cables use polyethylene; the best cables are made with polypropylene or even Teflon dielectric. One manufacturer has developed a fibrous material that is mostly air (the best dielectric of all, except for a vacuum) to insulate the conductors within a cable. Other manufacturers inject air in the dielectric to create a foam with high air content. Just as different dielectric materials in capacitors sound different, so too do dielectrics in cables and interconnects.

Terminations

The terminations at the ends of cables and interconnects are part of the transmission path. High-quality terminations are essential to a good-sounding cable. We want a large surface contact between the cable's plug and the component's jack, and high contact pressure between them. RCA plugs will sometimes have a slit in the center pin to improve contact with the jack. This slit is effective only if the slit end of the plug is large enough to be compressed by insertion in the jack. Most high-quality RCA plugs are copper with some brass mixed in to add rigidity. This alloy is plated with nickel, then flashed with gold to prevent oxidation. On some plugs, gold is plated directly to the brass. Other materials for RCA plugs and plating include silver and rhodium.

RCA plugs and loudspeaker cable terminations are soldered or welded to the conductors. Most manufacturers use solder with some silver content. Although solder is poor conductor, the spade lugs are often crimped to the cable first, forming a "cold" weld that forms a gas-tight seal. In the best welding technique, *resistance welding*, a large current is pulsed through the point where the conductor meets the plug. The resistance causes a small spot to heat, melting the two metals. The melted metals merge into an alloy at the contact point, assuring good signal transfer. With both welding and soldering, a *strain relief* inside the plug isolates the electrical contact from physical stress.

Geometry

How all of these elements are arranged constitutes the cable's geometry. Some designers maintain that geometry is the most important factor in cable design—even more important than the conductor material and type.

An example of how a cable's physical structure can affect its performance: simply twisting a pair of conductors around each other instead of running them side by side. Twisting the conductors greatly reduces capacitance and inductance in the cable. Think of the physical structure of two conductors running in parallel, and compare that to the schematic symbol for a capacitor, which is two parallel lines.

This is the grossest example; there are many fine points to cable design. I'll describe some of them here, with the understanding that I'm presenting certain opinions on cable construction, not endorsing a particular method.

Most designers agree that *skin effect*, and interaction between strands, are the greatest sources of sonic degradation in cables. In a cable with high skin effect, more high-frequency signal flows along the conductor's surface, less through the conductor's center. This occurs in both solid-core and stranded conductors (Fig.11-6). Skin effect changes the cable's characteristics at different depths, causing different frequency ranges of the audio signal to be affected by the cable differently. The musical consequences of skin effect include loss of detail, reduced top-octave air, and truncated soundstage depth.

Fig. 11-6 Skin effect causes more of the audio signal to travel on the outside of the conductor.

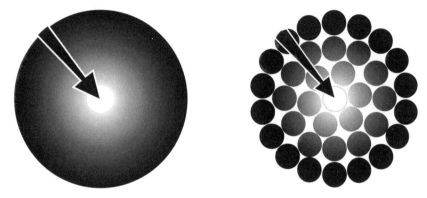

Courtesy AudioQuest

A technique for battling skin effect is *litz* construction, which simply means that each strand in a bundle is coated with an insulating material to prevent it from electrically contacting the strands around it. Each small strand within a litz arrangement will have virtually identical electrical properties. Litz strands push skin-effect problems out of the audible range. Because litz strands are so small, many of them bundled together in a random arrangement are required to achieve a sufficient gauge to keep the resistance low.

A problem with stranded cable (if it isn't of litz construction) is a tendency for the signal to jump from strand to strand if the cable is twisted. One strand may be at the outside at a point in the cable, then be on the inside farther down the cable. Because of skin effect, the signal tends to stay toward the outside of the conductor, causing it to traverse strands. Each strand interface acts like a small circuit, with capacitance and a diode effect, much like the grain structure within copper.

Individual strands within a conductor bundle can also interact magnetically. Whenever current flows down a conductor, a magnetic field is set up around that conductor. If the current is an alternating-current audio signal, the magnetic field will fluctuate identically. This alternating magnetic field can induce a signal in adjacent conductors (see Appendix B), and thus degrade the sound. Some cable geometries reduce magnetic interaction between strands by arranging them around a center dielectric, which keeps them farther apart.

These are just a few of the techniques used by cable designers to make better-sounding cables.

Cable and Interconnect Specifications

There's a lot of hype and just plain misinformation about cables and interconnects. Manufacturers sometimes feel the need to invent technical reasons for why their cables sound better than the competition's. In reality, cable design is largely a black art, with good designs emerging from trial and error (and careful listening). Although certain conductors, dielectrics, and geometries have specific sonic signatures, successful cable designs just can't be described in technical terms. This is why cables should never be chosen on the basis of technical descriptions and specifications.

Nonetheless, some cable and interconnect specifications should be considered in some circumstances. The three relevant specifications are *resistance, inductance,* and *capacitance.* (These terms are explained in detail in Appendix B.)

A cable or interconnect's resistance, more properly called *DC series resistance,* is a measure of how much it opposes the flow of current through it. The unit of resistance is the *Ohm.* The lower the number of ohms, the lower the cable or interconnect's resistance to current flow. In practice, cable resistance is measured in tenths of ohms. Resistance isn't usually a factor in interconnect performance (except in some of the new non-metallic types), but can affect some loudspeaker cables—particularly thin ones—because of their higher current-carrying requirements.

The sounds of interconnects and loudspeaker cables can be affected by inductance. It is generally thought that the lower the inductance the better, particularly in loudspeaker cables. Some power amplifiers, however, need to see some inductance to keep them stable; many have an output inductor connected to the loudspeaker binding post (inside the chassis). When considering how much inductance the power amplifier sees, you must add the cable inductance to the loudspeaker's inductance.

Capacitance is an important characteristic of interconnects, particularly when long runs are used, or if the source component has a high output impedance. Interconnect capacitance is specified in picofarads (pF) per foot. What's important isn't the interconnect's intrinsic capacitance, but the total capacitance attached to the source component. For example, 5' of 500pF per foot interconnect has the same capacitance as 50' of 50pF per foot interconnect. High interconnect capacitance can cause treble rolloff and restricted dynamics. (A full technical discussion of interconnect capacitance is included in Appendix B.)

Cables in the Power Amplifier/Loudspeaker Interface

The interface between a power amplifier and a loudspeaker through a cable is a critical point in a playback system. Unlike interconnects, which carry low-level signals, loudspeaker cables carry much higher voltages and currents. Loudspeaker cables thus react more with the components they are connected to.

Damping factor is an amplifier's ability to control the woofer's motion after the drive signal has ceased. For example, if you drive a loudspeaker with a bass-drum whack, the woofer's inertia and resonance in the enclosure will cause it to continue moving after the signal has died away. This is a form of distortion that alters the music signal's dynamic envelope. Fortunately, the power amplifier can control the motion; the degree of this control, or damping factor, is expressed as a simple number.

Damping factor is related to the amplifier's output impedance. The lower the output impedance, the higher the damping factor. When you connect a power amplifier and loudspeaker with cable, the cable's resistance decreases the amplifier's effective damping factor. For example, an amplifier's damping factor of 100 may be reduced to 40 by 20' of moderately resistive loudspeaker cable. The result is reduced tightness and control in the bass. Loudspeaker cables should therefore have low resistance and be as short as possible.

Getting the Best Sound from Cables and Interconnects

Here are several tricks to help you keep interconnects and cables from degrading your system's sound:

1) Because all wire degrades the signal passing through it, the less wire you have in your system, the better. Keep interconnects and loudspeaker cables short.

2) Keep left and right loudspeaker cables, and left and right interconnects, the same length.

3) If you have excess cable or interconnect, don't wind it into a neat loop behind the loudspeaker or equipment rack. This will make the cable more inductive and change its characteristics. Instead, drape the cable so it crosses other loops at right angles.

4) Periodically disconnect all interconnects and loudspeaker cables for cleaning. Oxide builds up on jacks and plugs, interfering with the electrical transfer. Use a contact cleaner (available at most high-end stores). It works. In fact, switching interconnects sometimes cleans the jacks, making the system sound better even though the interconnect may not be intrinsically better.

5) When connecting and disconnecting RCA plugs, always grip the plug, never the cable. Remember to push the tab when disconnecting XLR plugs.

6) Ensure tight connection of all RCA plugs, and particularly spade lugs on power amplifiers and loudspeakers. Get lots of contact surface area between the spade lug and post, then tighten down the binding posts.

7) Route interconnects and cables away from AC power lines. If AC lines must meet interconnects or cables, cross them at 90° angles. Never allow AC lines and interconnects or loudspeaker cables to run in parallel next to each other.

8) Keep digital interconnects well away from analog interconnects. The high-frequency noise radiated by the digital interconnect can pollute the analog lines.

9) Avoid putting sharp bends in cables and interconnects.

12 High-end Audio Accessories

The vast array and wide availability of audio accessories bears witness to audiophiles' need to "tweak" their systems to squeeze out that last little bit of musical performance. Accessories can not only make your system sound better, they're fun to try. It's quite rewarding to discover some simple trick or product that elevates your system's sound at little cost. This chapter surveys available accessories, describes what they do, and explains how they work.

How to Choose Accessories

Some of the accessories described in this chapter can make your system sound better than you thought it could—and at a modest cost. Conversely, other accessories can not only fail to improve the sound, but can actually degrade your system's musical performance. To make matters even more complicated, many accessories are completely worthless and are nothing more than "snake oil" sold by less-than-honest promoters. Finally, the effectiveness of an accessory can vary from system to system.

Fortunately, there's a simple and effective way of deciding which accessories are worth the money and which aren't: *listen to the accessory in your system before you buy*. Most dealers will let you either borrow the accessory overnight, or return it for a refund if you don't hear an improvement. If you hear an improvement that seems commensurate with the product's asking price, buy it. If you don't, return the product. It's that simple. And if the accessory is inexpensive but not returnable, you can try it at minimal cost. Some CD treatments cost only a few dollars; if they don't work, it hasn't cost you much.

But by all means try some of the devices described in this chapter. They can often make the difference between merely good and superlative sonic performance.

Stands and Racks

The most important accessory for any audio system is the equipment rack. A good rack presents your components in an attractive way, makes your system functional and easy to use, and, most important, helps achieve the best sound possible from your system. If your system includes a turntable, a high-quality rack is absolutely essential to realizing the LP front end's musical potential.

Apart from providing a convenient housing for your equipment, the rack's main job is isolating the equipment from vibration. There is no question that vibrations degrade the sonic performances of preamplifiers, digital processors, CD transports, and particularly turntables. This vibration is generated by transformers in power supplies, motors in turntables and CD transports, and from acoustic energy impinging on the electronics.

Vibration affects electronic products through a phenomenon called *microphony*. A microphonic component emits a small electrical signal when vibrated; in other words, it acts as a microphone, converting mechanical energy into electrical energy. This electrical energy pollutes the audio signal, resulting in degraded musical performance.

Tubed products are particularly susceptible to vibration. In fact, you can shout into a tubed preamplifier and hear your voice come out of the loudspeakers. The preamplifier converts the acoustic energy of your voice into an electrical signal. When the tubed component is vibrated by the sound from the loudspeakers, noise is added to the music.

The sound qualities of digital products are also degraded by vibration, but through a different mechanism. The crystal oscillators in many transports and digital processors change their frequencies slightly when vibrated. Although this frequency shift is slight, even small timing variations can wreak havoc with digital audio systems. Some manufacturers of digital products go to extreme lengths to ensure accurate and stable crystal frequencies, and build some form of vibration isolation around the oscillators.

The LP playback system is the most sensitive to vibration; the vibrational energy is transmitted to the tonearm and cartridge, adding sonic garbage to the tiny signal recovered from the record groove. This vibration comes from the turntable motor, from resonances in the tonearm, and from acoustic energy impinging on the turntable, arm, and cartridge. Clearly, isolating your system from vibration is essential to realizing the best musical performance.

A good equipment rack fights vibration with rigidity, mass, and careful design. The massive, inert structure of a high-quality rack is much less likely to vibrate when in the presence of sound pressure generated by the loudspeakers. Moreover, the equipment rack can absorb, or damp, the vibration created by power transformers and motors. Many equipment racks have built-in vibration-damping mechanisms in their shelves.

When choosing an equipment rack, look for a thick steel frame (14-gauge steel is excellent), welded construction, the ability to be filled with sand, vibration-damping shelves (Medium Density Fiberboard, or MDF, for example), bracing posts around the shelves, and floor spikes. Spikes between the rack and a floor act as a mechanical diode, draining vibrational energy from the rack and providing the best coupling between the rack and floor. For a spiked rack to be effective, the floor must be sturdy and flat so that the rack doesn't rock. The heights of most spikes are adjustable; you can level the rack and get good contact between the floor and all four (or three) spikes. Rack spikes are usually much heavier duty, with more rounded points than loudspeaker spikes. Note, however, that both types of spike will damage wood floors.

Not all good racks will have each of these features, but most will have at least some of them. The ability to fill the rack's posts with sand or lead shot is especially important. Sand is an excellent vibration-absorbing material, and it adds mass to the rack. It's also cheap.

The preceding discussion of high-mass racks, floor spikes, and intimate coupling between components, the rack, and the floor is only one school of thought. The second theory holds that audio components should be *decoupled* from the support surfaces and the floor with lightweight racks and compliant feet. Vibration in the rack and components is thus damped rather than transmitted to the floor. Generally, mass coupling works better for heavy components, and decoupling for lightweight components. The best way to determine which method is best for your system is to try both before you buy, or ask your dealer's advice.

Before installing a heavy rack—particularly one to be filled with sand—make sure the floor structure can support the weight. Suspended wood floors may need additional bracing. Bracing also makes the floor more solid and less prone to vibrating. A concrete slab is the ideal foundation for an equipment rack; you don't have to worry about the weight, and it provides a solid surface for the rack. You should also set up the rack exactly where you want it before filling it with sand.

These features—sand-filled, spikes, vibration-absorbing shelves, thick steel construction, and bracing—are found together in the most elaborate and expensive racks. Many racks without all of these features still provide good performance. Avoid racks with large unsupported shelves, flimsy construction, low mass, and poor vibrational damping. And don't even consider the generic "stereo stands" sold in furniture and department stores. Get a rack specially designed for high-performance audio systems. A rack offering the ultimate in vibration isolation and damping is shown in Fig.12-1. The elaborate rack shown in the photograph is fitted with optional vibration-absorbing blocks that fit below and on top of components, forming a massive structure for maximum vibration isolation.

Fig. 12-1 A braced and damped equipment rack

Courtesy Bright Star Audio

Consider a good equipment rack an essential part of your hi-fi system; it will help your system achieve its full musical potential.

Vibration-Control and -Isolation Accessories: Spikes, Feet, and Cones

Vibration-isolation accessories have the same goals as the specialized audio equipment rack: reduced vibration in the audio component. Isolation devices can be used on their own or in conjunction with an equipment rack.

The field of vibration-control accessories for audio systems was established with a product called Tiptoes, shown in Fig.12-2. Invented by Steve McCormack of The Mod Squad (and now McCormack), Tiptoes are machined aluminum cones with sharp points. When used point-side down to support pieces of audio equipment, they act as mechanical diodes to remove mechanical energy from the audio component. When first introduced, Tiptoes were greeted with scorn—until their effects were heard. Today, Tiptoes and similar products are universally recognized as making an important contribution to high-quality music reproduction.

Fig. 12-2
Tiptoes—the original vibration treatment device

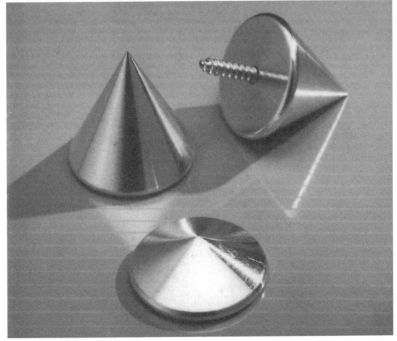

Courtesy McCormack

A different approach to vibration control is supporting the component with compliant feet, or mounting the component on a compliant platform. These devices are made of a rubber-like material (usually Sorbothane) chosen for its excellent damping characteristics. Compliant feet isolate the audio product from external vibration by absorbing the energy before it can get into the product. These devices are also excellent for stacking one component atop another. The feet provide airspace for ventilation, and reduce potential magnetic interaction between components.

The most effective place for Tiptoes or other vibration-control devices is underneath tubed power amplifiers, particularly if the amplifiers are placed near loudspeakers. The acoustic energy from the loudspeakers impinges on the tubes, which convert that energy into an electrical signal that degrades sound quality. These devices also provide a small airspace between the floor and amplifier, increasing ventilation around the amplifier.

One designer of extremely high-quality turntables—who is also a physicist and mechanical engineer—considers vibration control so important that he has had a local tombstone maker cut huge slabs of granite on which to support his equipment.

You probably won't go to that extreme, but you should certainly try some of the available vibration-control devices.

AC Power Conditioners

An AC power conditioner plugs into the wall outlet and provides multiple AC outlets for plugging in your audio equipment. Before we talk about what a power conditioner does, let's look at the AC power line and its relationship to an audio system.

The AC power from the wall outlet is a 60Hz, 120VRMS sinewave that powers the audio system (see Appendix B for more detail on the power line). All your components are connected via the power line. In fact, your audio components are connected to every other electrical device in your house, and to every home and factory also using the power grid.

Power equipment on the AC line generates noise that travels back onto the line where it enters your audio components. The FCC regulates the amount of noise that can be put back onto the power line by appliances and industrial products. This noise is called *electromagnetic interference*, or *EMI*. Light dimmers, refrigerators, and other household appliances put high-frequency junk on the AC line. Vacuum cleaners and electrical power tools are a major source of power-line noise because the fibers in the motors' brushes are continually making and breaking contact. The line is also polluted by AM radio stations; the power lines act as antennae, superimposing the AM signal over the 60Hz line.

Another source of EMI is your audio system. CD players, digital processors, CD transports, and any component using a microprocessor (some preamps, for example) put noise on the power line through their line cords. This noise then gets into preamps and source components to degrade their musical performance. In addition to putting noise on the AC line, audio components with digital circuits pollute other components by radiating *radio frequency* noise, or *RF*, through the air. Digital circuits work with clock pulses and electronic switches that operate in the AM radio frequency range; their operation radiates this RF noise, which is picked up by other components.

In addition to introducing noise on the AC line through the power cord and radiating it into the air, components also transmit noise to other components through the AC ground line. The AC ground connects all the chassis of an audio system together. If you've got a noisy ground on one component, you've got a noisy ground on all your components. Some of this noise gets on the ground by leakage through electrolytic capacitors in power supplies.

All of these problems can be controlled with a well-designed AC power-line conditioner. First, nearly all conditioners filter the incoming AC line to remove the high-frequency garbage generated by factories, neighbors, and your own appliances. The filters allow the 60Hz AC to pass, but remove noise from the line. Second, some filters isolate the components from each other with small isolation transformers on some of the conditioner's AC outlets. These transformers break the physical connection between components, preventing noise from traveling from one component to another. The isolated outputs are often marked "digital" for plugging in digital components, preventing a digital processor from polluting the AC supplying the preamplifier, for example. Third, a good line conditioner will reduce the amount of noise coupled to signal ground. Finally, AC line conditioners can protect components from voltage spikes, lightning strikes, and surges in the power-supply voltage. Not all conditioners perform every function listed here; conditioners vary in their design principles, with some addressing one problem but not another.

Cleaning up the power line for source components and preamplifiers is a different job from conditioning AC power for power amplifiers. Power amplifiers have very different AC requirements and thus must be treated differently. The description earlier of what a good line conditioner should do applies to source components and preamplifiers that draw very little current. Power amplifiers, however, draw enormous amounts of current from the wall. When the power amplifier delivers a significant amount of current to the loudspeaker—a bass-drum whack, for example—the amplifier's power-supply reservoir capacitors are drained to supply the current. The amplifier then draws a huge amount of instantaneous current from the wall outlet to replenish its filter capacitors. The amount of current pulled from the wall can be so great that the AC waveform distorts under the amplifier's current draw; the waveform's tops and bottoms clip under the load. Any isolation transformer or conditioning device in the AC path could limit the amplifier's ability to draw current, and thus degrade the amplifier's performance. The power amplifier needs to be supplied by a low-impedance, high-current source. Power-line filters that remove high-frequency noise can benefit a power amplifier, but transformers in series with the AC supply should be avoided.

Some audiophiles have separate, dedicated AC lines for their power amplifiers. This reduces the chance of distortion of the AC line caused by power-amplifier current draw from affecting the preamplifier and source components. Dedicated lines are often wired with "hospital grade" AC outlets. These are orange in color, and are of higher quality and are more mechanically secure than standard household outlets. Running dedicated lines to your listening room can have a dramatic sonic effect.

Because the AC line voltage varies according to the time of day and the load on the line, one may expect a line conditioner to regulate the voltage and provide a constant 120VAC to your system. Regulation, however, doesn't improve the sound of an audio system, and can actually degrade it if the input voltage moves around the threshold at which a separate transformer tap kicks in. Moreover, most high-end audio equipment is designed to work within the tolerances of the AC line supplied by the electric company. This is why power conditioners for computers—which often incorporate line regulation—shouldn't be used for audio systems.

When choosing a line conditioner, make sure its power capability exceeds the power consumption of the components you'll be plugging into it. Also look for the UL (Underwriters Laboratories) or CSA (Canadian Standards Association) seal of approval, indicating that the power conditioner meets certain safety requirements. Choose a conditioner with a sufficient number of outlets for your present and anticipated needs. As with all accessories, try the power conditioner in your system before you buy. Expect to pay a minimum of $250 for a conditioner with just a few outlets, to several thousand dollars for a state-of-the-art system. Many excellent conditioners cost less than $500. (Fig.12-3 shows an effective yet moderately priced line of power conditioners.)

A new type of power-line conditioning device has recently been introduced, designed to be used in conjunction with a standard conditioner. Instead of plugging your equipment into this new device, the device merely plugs into the wall near your hi-fi system. These products act as noise filters in parallel with the AC line powering your system. In theory, any junk on the line is shunted by the filter.

Fig. 12-3 A range of AC power-line conditioners

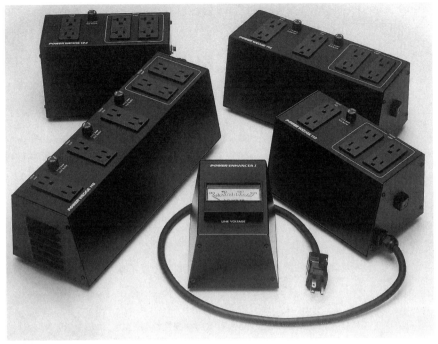

Courtesy Audio Power Industries

A power-line conditioner can't make poor audio components sound good; instead, it merely provides the optimum AC environment for those components so that they may realize their full potentials. The sonic benefits of a good line conditioner include a "blacker" background, with less low-level grunge and noise. The music seems to emerge from a perfectly quiet and black space, rather than a grayish background. The treble often becomes sweeter, less grainy, and more extended. Soundstaging often improves, with greater transparency, tighter image focus, and a newfound soundstage depth. Midrange textures become more liquid, and the presentation has an ease and musicality not heard without the conditioner.

If you haven't tried a power-line conditioner, you may not have heard your system at its best.

AC Power Cords

At first glance, it may seem that several short pieces of wire carrying AC to the components in your audio system—the AC power cords—couldn't affect the sound of the system. But specialty audio power cords have become very popular recently as more and more listeners discover their benefits.

The AC cord is an integral part of the AC delivery system. The noise problems described earlier can be reduced with careful AC cord design. Magnetic interaction and coupling between the conductors is reduced with dedicated audio power cords, resulting in better transfer of AC to the components. This magnetic interaction, addressed in interconnects and loudspeaker cables, affects AC transmission to a greater degree because of the high current flow in an AC cord.

Specialty AC cords also have superior construction, sometimes with Teflon dielectric, silver-plated wire, and high-quality plugs. Some also have an RF (radio frequency) noise suppressor built into the cord. Good AC cords cost between $100 and $200. Again, try them in your system before buying.

CD Treatments

A wide variety of devices are available that claim to improve CD sound quality. These run the gamut from rubber rings that fit around the CD to oils applied to the CD surface. Some CD treatments make a worthwhile improvement to the sound; other are of dubious value.

The main category of CD tweaks is the damping device. This can take the form of a rubber ring stretched around the CD's edge, a flat adhesive ring stuck to the outer perimeter of the CD, or a mat that covers the entire label side of the CD. The theory is, the less disc vibration, the better the sound. One idea holds that a more stable CD results in less servo activity on the part of the transport's electromechanical systems for maintaining focus, tracking, and rotational speed—which means less current demand on the power supply.

Be careful about applying rings that cannot be removed. If they degrade the sound—as some may—you're stuck. In addition, some transports simply won't play discs that are a different size or shape. If you want to experiment with CD rings, use the removable kind. Rings generally cost between $1 and $3 each. Try a few: if they don't make an audible improvement, you're only out a few dollars.

CD mats can improve sound quality, but also stress the CD player's or transport's motor system; the rotational motor was designed to spin the mass of a CD, not a CD and a heavy mat. Adding weight can degrade the transport's or CD player's servo performance and put undue stress on the motor.

The second main category of CD treatments are those intended to improve the CD system's optical performance. These include liquids applied to the CD surface, and colored paint around the disc edge. How these potions work is a mystery, but some of them do improve the sound. Again, you must be careful about what you apply to a CD surface: some chemicals can attack the CD's polycarbonate substrate and ruin the disc. Further, wiping the liquid off the disc can create scratches which may cause mistracking on playback.

Another optical tweak for CD players and transports is the Spatial Filter designed by ASM Labs. This is a tiny doughnut-shaped device that fits over a CD player's lens, making the aperture smaller. Measurements made by the Spatial Filter's designers show less jitter in the recovered datastream with the Filter. Although the Spatial Filter improves sound quality, it can degrade a CD player's ability to track poorly manufactured CDs. Further, attempting to remove the Filter can destroy a player's lens assembly. Note that some CD transports and players have the Spatial Filter installed as standard.

Finally, CD lens cleaners are available to remove dust and dirt from a player's lens. They are the size of a CD, with tiny brushes that wipe the lens as the disc spins. Lens cleaners cost about $20.

LP Accessories

Record-Cleaning Machines

As vinyl records become more scarce, preserving the sound on your LPs becomes even more important. The best way to keep your LPs sounding good and lasting longer is to clean them with a record-cleaning machine. Unlike a brush that removes only some of the dirt, or redistributes it to other parts of the record, a record-cleaning machine uses a motor-driven vacuum to extract dirt and grime from the record grooves. Although some record brushes can help remove dirt, none are nearly as effective as a cleaning machine.

A record cleaned with a vacuum cleaner will have far fewer ticks and pops, and also have a cleaner, more open midrange. By removing the junk in the grooves, the cartridge can extract more musical information from the record. A clean record will also last much longer than a dirty one; the stylus won't constantly be grinding dirt into the groove walls.

Record-cleaning machines vary in price according to their level of automation. Some machines, like the Record Doctor II by Nitty Gritty, require you to apply the cleaning fluid to the record surface, turn the record over (so the fluid side faces the vacuum slot), and spin the record yourself. Semi-automatic machines spin the record with a motor, but still require manual application of the cleaning fluid and turning over the record. Fully automatic machines apply the fluid, spin the record, and even clean both sides of the record at the same time.

Expect to pay about $200 for a bare-bones cleaner, and up to $900 for a state-of-the-art automatic system.

Stylus Cleaners

Cleaning your stylus before every record is essential not only to good sound, but to preserving record life. A dirty stylus will grind junk into the groove walls where it cannot be removed, even by a record-cleaning machine. Stylus cleaners resemble nail polish, with a brush in a bottle of cleaning fluid. The Discwasher brush, by contrast, has short, stiff bristles on which a fluid is applied. Whichever brush you use, the stylus should be cleaned with a gentle stroke from the back of the cartridge to the front. A stylus cleaning kit sells for about $15.

Other LP accessories—stylus pressure gauges, damping devices, record clamps, and alignment protractors—are covered in Chapter 9.

Other Accessories

Cable Enhancers

A cable enhancer is a device that reportedly breaks-in line-level interconnects and loudspeaker cables faster and more completely than running music through the cables. Both ends of the interconnect or cable are connected to the enhancer, which puts out a high-level signal to produce current flow through the cable. Cable enhancers cost about $200. Many dealers, however, will break in your new cables on an enhancer at no charge.

Cartridge Demagnetizers

Cartridge demagnetizers are often referred to generically as "Fluxbusters" after the Sumiko Fluxbuster, the first commercially available demagnetizer. Demagnetizers are about the size of a cassette box and cost less than $100. They generally have two RCA jacks which you connect to your turntable's RCA outputs with a pair of interconnects. When the demagnetizer's power switch is engaged, the demagnetizer puts out a high-frequency signal that slowly diminishes in intensity, removing unwanted residual magnetism in the phono cartridge.

Moving-coil phono cartridges need demagnetizing because the core around which the coils are wound gradually becomes magnetized by the powerful permanent magnets surrounding the coils. Air-cored moving-coil cartridges are not susceptible to accumulated residual magnetism and don't need demagnetizing.

Moving-magnet cartridges build up magnetism on the pole pieces, degrading sonic performance. Note that you must remove the stylus from a moving-magnet cartridge before demagnetizing. Otherwise, the demagnetizer will demagnetize the magnets, reducing the cartridge's output level. If you accidentally demagnetize the magnets, replace the stylus: the stylus assembly contains new magnets.

Cartridges should be demagnetized after each 50 hours of playing time. Note that demagnetizers designed to bulk erase tapes or degauss televisions should not be used to demagnetize cartridges.

RF Filters

An RF filter is a device that fits around cables and AC cords and prevents high-frequency noise from passing. The filter is in essence a "choke" that turns the cable or power cord into a low-pass filter. RF filters can be put around interconnects at the preamp side to prevent RF from getting into the preamp, on interconnects at the power amplifier, or on AC cords. They cost about $25 per pair, are easy to install and remove, and can be an inexpensive improvement to your system. Radio Shack sells a snap-together ferrite core that will fit around cables for $5.50 (part number 273-105).

Contact Cleaners

Contact cleaners remove the residue and oxidation that builds up on RCA plugs and jacks, interconnect terminations, and loudspeaker and power-amplifier terminals. The fluid comes in a small bottle and is usually supplied with pipe cleaners for applying the liquid. Some cleaners come in spray form, but the contacts should still be rubbed to remove oxidation.

A thorough cleaning of all electrical contacts in a system can improve sound quality. Once every two months is a good interval. Make sure, however, that the contact cleaner doesn't leave a residue that could attract dust and end up degrading the connection. Expect to pay about $15 for a bottle of cleaner, which should provide about ten to twenty complete system cleanings.

A related product is the contact enhancer, a fluid applied to electrical contacts in your system. Contact enhancers promote better conductivity between a plug and jack, improving the sound. Contact enhancers work especially well on phono cartridge pins.

Tube Dampers

Tube dampers are devices that fit over vacuum tubes to make them less microphonic. The damper is made from a rubber-like material—often Sorbothane—that damps the tube's vibration and improves sound quality. Some dampers are also claimed to extend tube life by acting as heat sinks, radiating heat away from the tube. Tube dampers cost between $4 and $25 each.

AC Polarity Testers and AC "Cheater" Plugs

The AC plug's orientation in the wall socket can affect a component's sound quality. Most audio components have three-pronged plugs, with the rounded lower pin connected to the component's chassis. This ground lead ultimately ends up at a copper rod buried in the ground outside the electrical service panel. If for some reason the AC voltage touches a component's chassis, the chassis will short that voltage to ground, blowing the breaker fuse and protecting anyone who may touch the chassis. The two other conductors are connected to the component's power transformer, which tends to leak some current to ground. The amount of current leaked depends on the orientation of the AC plug. One direction may produce a lower chassis voltage than the other. The system will sound best with the plug oriented in the direction producing the lower chassis voltage.

Determining which way the AC plug should go can be determined with an AC polarity tester. Just put the polarity tester near the chassis of the component and read the tester's meter. Reverse the AC plug and see if the voltage is lower. Repeat this process on each component until the entire system has been connected for best AC polarity. You can do the same thing with a voltmeter, but the polarity meter avoids direct contact with the AC line. A polarity meter costs less than $30.

Reversing a three-pronged AC plug can be accomplished by adding a "cheater" plug (available at any hardware store) that allows the plug to be inserted upside down. The cheater plug's ground wire (which replaces the rounded pin) must be connected to the screw holding the AC wall cover in place to maintain the safety aspect of a grounded plug and receptacle. If the ground wire isn't attached, the cheater plug "lifts" the ground connection. When this happens, the component is grounded only through the interconnects connecting the ungrounded component to another component that is grounded at the wall. For example, the ground can be lifted on a preamplifier provided the power amplifier is grounded to the wall and the two are connected by interconnects. Ground lifting is sometimes required to eliminate hum and noise in the system created by *ground loops*. A ground loop occurs when there are two paths to ground of unequal resistance. A slight voltage difference is thus created that causes a small current to flow in the ground conductors, producing a hum. By lifting the ground at one component, the ground loop is broken and the hum is removed.

Note that the safety feature of a grounded system is defeated if one component is plugged into a cheater plug and not connected to a grounded component through the interconnects. Further, lifting the ground on all the components is extremely dangerous; if for some reason a high voltage appears on the chassis, you'll have no way of knowing it and could receive a lethal shock. But if the component is properly grounded, the chassis will cause a breaker fuse in your AC wall panel to blow, preventing electric shock.

Ground Isolators

A ground isolator may be needed when a cable TV connection is made to a component audio system, or in a system that includes a tuner for cable-delivered digital radio. The cable TV ground is likely to be different from your audio system's ground, producing hum and buzz when the signal from the digital radio tuner is connected to your preamp. A ground isolator (like Mondial's MAGIC) keeps the two grounds separate.

Vibration Absorbers for Loudspeakers

Several products are said to reduce a loudspeaker's cabinet vibrations and thus improve sound quality. One device that I've found particularly effective is a cloth bag of small but very heavy damping beads— the finished product looks like a bean bag. When put on top of the loudspeaker, the bags absorb vibration, and are especially effective on small, lightweight, stand-mounted loudspeakers. The weight also helps couple the loudspeaker to the stand, and the stand to the floor.

Other vibration devices address the problem with small discs that reportedly absorb vibration through some internal mechanism, or are made of solid wood. The discs are placed on components, loudspeakers, listening-room walls, or equipment racks. These products tend to be quite expensive, however, and reports of their effectiveness are mixed.

Voodoo Accessories and the Lunatic Fringe

Just as there are those who abandon reason in any pursuit, high-end audio has its share of nonsensical, even bizarre accessories. Most of these products are completely worthless.

Examples include an alligator clip attached to the loudspeaker cable that prevents the loudspeaker's "gravitational influence" from affecting the audio signal. Another claims to "energize" the electrons in an audio system with a combination of lithium salts and cobra venom.

We must be careful, however, in branding certain products as fraudulent. Many accessory products whose value is now without question—AC power conditioners and Tiptoes, for examples—were once dismissed as worthless by those who never listened to their effects. In the early days of CD, it was assumed that all CD transports and digital interconnects sounded the same because they all produced the same stream of binary ones and zeros. It was only after much critical listening and closer scientific scrutiny that other mechanisms for creating differences in the sounds of transports and digital interconnects (primarily timing variations called "jitter") were discovered. It is undisputed today that transport and digital-interconnect jitter affects sound quality. We must listen and trust our ears, and not rely solely on pure theories, no matter how elegant or well-argued.

The bottom line with any accessory, as with any audio component, should sound familiar by now: listen before you buy. If the device makes an audible improvement, buy it—regardless of whether or not there's a scientific explanation.

13 Audio for Home Theater

Introduction

Home theater is the combination of high-quality audio *and* video reproduction in the home. The term applies equally to a decent sound system attached to a television, or to a video projection system and elaborate sound system in a dedicated room.

Home theater poses a dilemma for the audiophile and music lover. Integrating a television or video projector into your hi-fi will likely degrade the system's musical performance. Putting an acoustically reflective television or rear-projection system between or even behind your loudspeakers can destroy their imaging and soundstage depth. Conversely, audio systems designed for video soundtrack playback won't have optimum musical performance—they are designed for qualities important to video (dialog intelligibility, for example) rather than recreating musical nuances. Neither of these alternatives is acceptable to the serious music lover. In fact, these alternatives are anathema to the high-end audio ethos of achieving the highest-quality musical playback without compromise.

Fortunately, there are two solutions. The first is to use a front-projection television in which the video image is projected onto a flat screen between the loudspeakers. If a front-projection display is beyond your budget—they're expensive—there's an even better way of having high-quality music reproduction *and* good audio for video: separate systems for music reproduction and home theater. One room contains the high-end music system while another room has a much lower-quality, but still decent, home theater system. Neither system is compromised by the other, and the two distinctly different activities—music listening and film watching—are kept separate. This isn't a practical solution for those with limited space, but for many music lovers solves the dilemma of how to enjoy high-quality presentations of both music and film. Having two separate systems sounds a lot more feasible when you consider that a very satisfying home theater audio system can be had for less than $2000.

In the previous chapters I've emphasized the value of investing a substantial amount of money in a hi-fi system. The return on investment in musical satisfaction, day after day and year after year, justifies spending as much on a hi-fi system as on a decent car. When it comes to audio for home theater, however, I advise against spending a lot of money. Instead, a moderately priced mass-market system should work just fine for most listeners/viewers.

Admittedly, this view reflects my own values and prejudices: I find listening to music more enjoyable, rewarding, and fulfilling than watching films. Moreover, audio reproduction for music needs to be at a much higher level of quality than audio for film. The visual element of home theater shifts the emphasis away from auditory perception. Small improvements in the sound quality of a hi-fi system can have large musical significance; improvements on a similar scale in a home theater system probably wouldn't be noticed. This is why I recommend putting the vast majority of your total budget into a music system, and only a small amount into audio for home theater. Of course, if money is no object, you can have a superlative music system *and* a first-rate home theater.

This chapter is a guide to understanding and assembling an audio system for a home theater. The principles outlined apply equally to someone spending $800 as to someone investing many thousands of dollars.

Dolby Surround and Dolby Pro Logic

The heart of any home theater audio system is a Dolby Surround decoder. Dolby Surround is a means of re-creating the multi-channel cinema sound experience in the home. "Dolby Surround" encompasses Dolby Surround decoding as well as the very similar but more sophisticated Dolby Pro Logic decoding. Because Pro Logic is rapidly superseding standard Dolby Surround, the following discussion is based on Pro Logic. A comparison of the two processes is included later in this chapter.

The Dolby Surround process is a *matrix* system that combines four audio channels into two channels for storage on video tape or laserdisc (or for television broadcast), then separates those two channels into four channels during playback in the home. A Dolby Pro Logic decoder takes a Dolby-encoded two-channel audio program (from a video tape or laserdisc) and converts it into four separate audio channels for reproduction from five loudspeakers (plus an optional subwoofer). (Fig.13-1 shows how Dolby encoding makes possible multi-channel playback in the home.)

Fig. 13-1 Dolby Surround matrixes four audio channels into two channels for storage or transmission; Dolby decoding recovers the four audio channels for home playback.

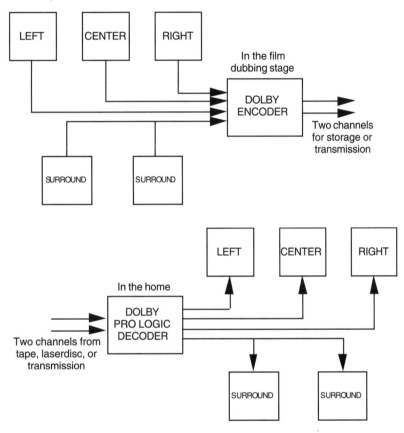

The four audio channels and five loudspeakers in a Dolby Pro Logic system are left, center, and right across the front of the viewing area, and two "surround" loudspeakers beside or behind the listener/viewer. The two monaural surround loudspeakers are fed from the same audio channel; thus, the five loudspeakers from four audio channels. On the other hand, a Dolby Surround decoder produces three channels—left, right, and surround—for reproduction from four loudspeakers (Dolby Surround lacks the center channel).

Fig.13-2 shows a typical arrangement of the five loudspeakers in a home theater system. The left and right channels reproduce the main stereo information in the film soundtrack—mostly music and effects. The center channel reproduces sounds that seem to originate on the screen, usually dialog and effects. The center-channel loudspeaker also ensures a stable central image, even for listeners not sitting in the "sweet spot" between the left and right loudspeakers. The two surround loudspeakers provide a sense of depth and envelopment in the sound.

Fig. 13-2 A home theater audio system consists of three loudspeakers across the front and two side or rear loud-speakers.

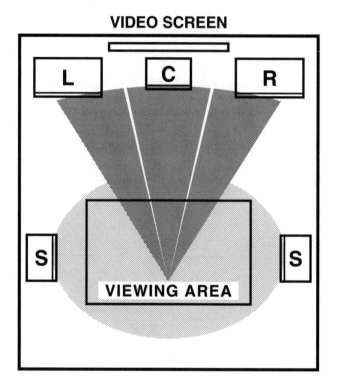

Courtesy Dolby Laboratories

Dolby Pro Logic also creates a mono sum of the left- and right-channel information below 100Hz for driving a subwoofer. Dolby Pro Logic is sometimes referred to as a "5.1"-channel system, with the ".1" channel being the bandwidth-limited subwoofer channel.

Pro Logic decoders can be stand-alone units, or incorporated into home-theater preamplifiers, or integrated into multi-channel receivers. Note that Dolby Laboratories doesn't manufacture the decoders; instead, it licenses the decoding technology to many manufacturers. This is why you'll see Dolby Surround and Pro Logic decoders included in products from different manufacturers. Dolby Surround processors are marked with the logo in Fig.13-3a, and Dolby Pro Logic decoders carry the logo shown in Fig.13-3b.

Dolby-encoded stereo programs contain the center and surround channels necessary for multi-channel playback. In fact, virtually all video tapes and laserdiscs produced in the past ten years are Dolby

Surround–encoded. Even some television broadcasts are now encoded with Dolby Surround. All Dolby Surround–encoded software (video tapes and laserdiscs) bears the Dolby Surround logo.

Fig. 13-3 a and b
Dolby Surround
(top) and Dolby
Pro Logic
(bottom) logos

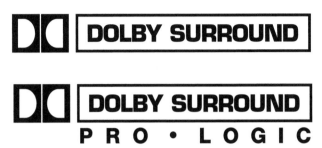

Courtesy Dolby Laboratories

Surround Channel Processing

All Dolby Surround decoders (Surround and Pro Logic) incorporate a short time delay in the surround channel. This delay is either fixed at 20ms (milliseconds) or is adjustable, usually between 15ms and 30ms to accommodate a wider range of room sizes. The delay improves front-to-rear channel separation by a psychoacoustic phenomenon called the *Haas Effect*. Here's how the Haas Effect works: When exposed to two identical sounds slightly delayed in time, the ear tends to localize the sound source in the direction of the sound that arrives first, and ignore the sound that arrives second. Delaying the signal to the rear surround channels psychoacoustically reduces the crosstalk (unwanted front-channel information) appearing in the surround channels.

Reducing leakage of front-channel information into the rear surround channels is of utmost importance for film soundtracks; sounds accompanying a visual image in front of us—particularly dialog—are extremely distracting if we hear them originating from behind us.

The optimum surround-channel delay time is determined by the relationship of the listener's distances from the front and surround loudspeakers. The time-of-arrival difference between the front and surround loudspeakers should be great enough so that the Haas Effect works, but no so long that the surround signal is heard as an echo or discrete sound. The chart in Fig.13-4 shows how to calculate the best delay time for several loudspeaker-to-listener distances.

The surround-channel signals are bandwidth-limited to 7kHz in the treble, and often to 100Hz in the bass. In other words, no treble above 7kHz, or bass below 100Hz, is sent to the surround loudspeakers. Bandwidth-limiting the surround channel has several advantages. First, keeping the upper treble out of the surround loudspeakers improves the front-to-surround separation. The Dolby decoding system can introduce high-frequency errors that cause front-channel information to appear in the surround channels. This is not good—watching actions or conversations on the screen in front of you, and hearing the accompanying sounds coming from *behind* you, is distracting to say the least. By rolling off the surround-channel treble, these errors are made less audible. The overall spectral balance of the system is relatively unaffected.

Fig. 13-4 The optimum surround delay times for different listening and loudspeaker positions

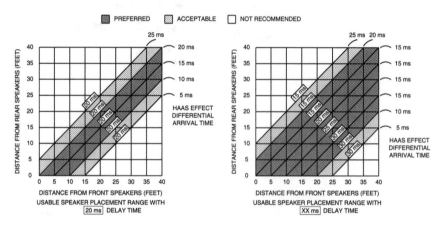

Courtesy Dolby Laboratories

In addition, rolling-off the treble to the surround loudspeakers reduces the ear's ability to pinpoint sounds coming from the surround loudspeakers. The goal of surround loudspeakers is envelopment in a soundfield; if we can identify a specific location as the source of surround information, the feeling of envelopment is reduced. By keeping treble out of the surround channels, the sense of diffusion and "atmosphere" is enhanced, and with it, our immersion in the film.

Rolling-off bass below 100Hz in the surround channels reduces the demands on the surround power amplifiers and loudspeakers. Because the front channels and subwoofer reproduce the soundtrack's low-frequency content, bass from the surround channels is unnecessary. However, full-range surround loudspeakers, or a subwoofer connected to the surround channel, provides smoother bass reproduction than is possible with a single front-channel subwoofer because of the reduction in standing waves and lessened excitation of room modes.

Note that this bandwidth-limiting of the surround channels is employed when the film is mixed in the dubbing stage. You hear the same mix and spectral balance at home as did the director, sound mixer, and sound designer in the dubbing stage.

Finally, Dolby Surround and Pro Logic use a modified version of Dolby B noise reduction on the surround channels. Dolby B is the noise-reduction system most often used in cassette decks. Processing the surround channels with Dolby B noise reduction improves the signal-to-noise ratio of the surround channels and further reduces high-frequency crosstalk from the front channels to the surround channels. This technique is especially good at preventing dialog sibilants ("s" and "ch" sounds) from appearing in the surround channels. Dolby B encoding of the surround channels is performed on all Dolby Surround–encoded software, whether or not B-type noise reduction is applied to VHS audio channels.

Other Aspects of Dolby Surround

The Dolby Surround license specifies that products using Surround decoding incorporate certain features that allow the user to optimize the system. All Dolby Surround and Pro Logic decoders, as well as receivers and preamplifiers with Surround or Pro Logic decoding, must have a master volume control that adjusts all channels simultaneously. They must also include separate volume controls for individual channels. An input balance control is also required to optimize decoding accuracy. If you see the Surround or Pro Logic logos on a product incorporating a Dolby decoder, you can be assured that the product meet Dolby's specifications.

Products with Pro Logic must incorporate a noise source that is routed to the left, center, right, and surround loudspeakers in sequence to allow quick level-matching between channels. (There is usually a button on the remote control that starts the test sequence.) The noise is heard in each channel for a few seconds so that the relative levels between channels can be adjusted.

Pro Logic products may also have an automatic input-balance control. This feature eliminates the need to set the left/right input balance for best decoding accuracy. If the left/right balance input to the Dolby decoder is skewed, decoding errors can result which increase crosstalk between channels. Products with automatic input-balance control ensure correct decoding, whatever the left/right balance fed to the decoder.

A Pro Logic decoder may have other features, such as *Dolby 3 Stereo*. This mode is optimized for playback without surround loudspeakers, while maintaining left, center, and right channels.

The control marked *Center Mode*, or *Phantom Center*, is used when no center-channel loudspeaker is available. It splits the center-channel signal and sends it equally to the left and right channels. This creates a "phantom" center speaker, or speaker image, from which the dialog will seem to emanate. Analogous to punching the mono button on a stereo system, this channel-summing applies *only* to the center-channel signal;

the rest of the soundtrack continues to be reproduced in stereo from the left and right loudspeakers.

Finally, some decoders allow the user to switch between a full-bandwidth center channel and one that is rolled off below 100Hz. The normal mode for Dolby Surround is with bass below 100Hz removed from the center channel. The so-called "wide" mode (for wide bandwidth, not wide soundstage) restores the full bandwidth to the center channel.

How Dolby Pro Logic Differs from Dolby Surround

At the time of this writing, Dolby Surround decoding is being rapidly replaced by the superior Dolby Pro Logic system. The widespread availability of Pro Logic decoding chips has made Pro Logic the system most often included in stand-alone decoders, home-theater preamplifiers, and receivers.

Dolby Surround is a passive decoding system that produces left, right, and surround channels from an encoded two-channel source. A center-channel loudspeaker can be used with Dolby Surround, but the signal fed it is merely a mix of the left- and right-channel signals. This reduces the "hole-in-the-middle" effect, but narrows the soundstage width.

Dolby Pro Logic is a much more sophisticated system. It uses an active, variable matrix that greatly improves the separation between channels. The Pro Logic decoder senses the dominant signal at any given time and redistributes the non-dominant signals. Pro Logic also has a discrete center-channel output, separate from the left and right channels. Of course, Pro Logic incorporates the surround-channel processing (delay, bandwidth limiting, and noise reduction) described earlier. Pro Logic provides better separation, greater localization of on-screen sounds, and allows a wider listening/viewing area. (A block-diagram comparison of Dolby Surround and Dolby Pro Logic is shown in Fig.13–5.)

Note that the term "Dolby Surround" includes both Dolby Surround and Dolby Pro Logic decoding. Pro Logic is merely a higher-quality implementation of the Dolby Surround format, providing better performance and the additional center-channel signal. Dolby-encoded software works on both Dolby Surround and Dolby Pro Logic decoders.

Fig. 13-5 A comparison of Dolby Surround and Dolby Pro Logic decoders

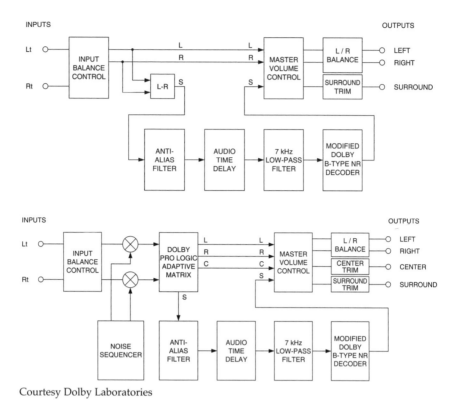

Courtesy Dolby Laboratories

Dolby Surround Decoders and Power Amplifiers for Home Theater

Dolby Surround and Pro Logic decoders are available as stand-alone units, in audio/video preamplifiers, or incorporated into an audio/video receiver which may also contain five power-amplifier channels. Stand-alone decoders typically have a two-channel input (fed from the audio channels of your VCR or laserdisc player) and six line-level outputs. The six line-level outputs (left, center, right, two monaural surrounds, and subwoofer) drive six power amplifiers. A preamplifier with built-in Dolby Pro Logic decoding has multiple stereo inputs (fed by different source components) and six line-level outputs that drive power amplifiers.

Some home-theater products offer a Pro Logic decoder and a three-channel amplifier in one chassis. The idea is to use your existing stereo amplifier and loudspeakers for the left and right channels, and the decoder/amplifier for the center and surround channels. This is the least expensive way of adding home theater to your audio system. Because nearly any amplifier is good enough to reproduce the surround channel, look for a three-channel amplifier with a center channel amplifier of equal power to your main stereo amplifier.

A full audio-for-home-theater system requires a minimum of five amplifiers (six, if a subwoofer is used). These amplifiers can be all in one home-theater receiver, or five separate monoblocks, or a five-channel home-theater amplifier, or two stereo amplifiers with an additional mono amplifier for the center channel. If separate amplifiers are used, the Dolby Surround decoder will probably be a stand-alone unit, or be incorporated into a preamplifier. If the Surround decoder is built into a receiver, the receiver's rear panel will have six pairs of loudspeaker terminations to directly connect the left, center, right, and surround loudspeakers, plus an optional subwoofer.

The amount of amplifier power required varies among the five channels. The surround channels, for example, are band-limited (100Hz-7kHz) and receive a much lower signal level than the main left and right speakers. Consequently, the surround amplifier can be of much lower power than the left-, right-, and center-channel amplifiers. The center channel is also band-limited (a 100Hz high-pass rolloff), but carries a much larger portion of the signal than the surrounds. Specifically, the center channel reproduces dialog and on-screen sound effects. The center-channel amplifier must therefore have more power output than the surround amplifiers, and should be equal in power to the left and right amplifier channels. A typical power distribution may be 100W each to the left and right loudspeakers, 80W to the center channel, and 40W each to the surround channels. Many five-channel amplifiers have the same power output for the center channel as for the left and right channels—a decided advantage, considering how much of the total acoustic energy is produced by the center channel.

The overall amount of power required in a home theater depends on many factors that are discussed in detail in Chapter 6 ("Power Amplifiers"). Remember that the variables involved music playback—loudspeaker sensitivity, room size, playback volume requirements—are identical for home theater and music reproduction.

Loudspeakers for Home Theater

The technical and aesthetic requirements of soundtrack playback make music loudspeakers less than ideal for home theater. Conversely, most loudspeakers designed for soundtrack reproduction don't perform well on music. The video loudspeakers' dispersion and response have been optimized for factors such as dialog intelligibility and a boom in the bass, not conveying musical detail. This is why it's best to have separate music and home theater systems rather than a compromise setup that reproduces music and video programs equally poorly. A few loudspeaker systems do provide excellent performance with both music and video, but these are rare.

When choosing home-theater loudspeakers, you generally have the choice of using large, full-range left and right loudspeakers, or smaller left and right loudspeakers with an additional subwoofer. The subwoofer approach is the better way to go: you have greater placement freedom with the smaller loudspeakers, and the bass performance of a subwoofer is often better. Moreover, a subwoofer allows the main loudspeakers to be rolled off in the bass; relieved of their bass-handling chores, they can concentrate on what they do best: increasing midrange clarity and power handling. Active subwoofers also have the advantage of adding additional amplifier power, which increases the system's dynamic range.

The three front loudspeakers—left, center, right—should all be the same model, made by the same manufacturer. Many loudspeaker companies offer matched sets of three loudspeakers just for this purpose. The center-channel loudspeaker is usually short and wide, designed to be laid horizontally atop a television monitor or rear-projection system. It is also magnetically *shielded* so that the magnetic fields created by the loudspeaker's drive units don't interfere with the television picture. Using three identical (or nearly identical) loudspeakers ensures that there will be no change in tonal balance as a sound moves from one side of the picture, across the center, and to the other side. For example, if a character talking off-screen moves to the center, the timbre of the voice should remain constant. If the center loudspeaker isn't matched to the left and right loudspeakers, a sound's timbre will be dependent on where it is placed in the soundstage—and change as it moves.

The center-channel loudspeaker's quality will largely determine the clarity and intelligibility of dialog—an essential element of the film soundtrack. The center loudspeaker should be flat through the midband, extend in frequency response to 100Hz, and have high power-handling capability. A bright or ragged treble will make dialog unpleasant and distracting. The wide dynamic range of film sound effects puts additional stress on the center loudspeaker. Because many home-theater amplifiers provide less output power for the center than for the left and right channels, look for a center loudspeaker with slightly greater sensitivity than the left and right loudspeakers. This will let you get plenty of acoustic output from the center channel from even underpowered center-channel amplifiers.

Although some televisions have a "Center Channel In" jack that drives the television's internal loudspeakers, it should be avoided in favor of a single dedicated center-channel loudspeaker.

The surround loudspeakers can be of lesser quality than the left, center, and right loudspeakers. Not only do they cover a narrower frequency range (100Hz-7kHz), they are also played very quietly in relation to the other loudspeakers. They should, however, have a smooth midband and no serious peaks or dips in the frequency response.

Most surround loudspeakers are small to make placement easier. They can be mounted on wall brackets, flush with the wall, or on stands. The last method is preferred, with the loudspeakers to the sides of the listeners. In some wall-mounted surrounds the midrange and tweeter are positioned at angles to create a more diffuse soundfield.

Surround loudspeakers are sometimes bi-polar in their radiating patterns. A bi-polar loudspeaker emits energy equally from the front and back. Bi-polars are preferred for surrounds because they produce a greater sense of envelopment and make it more difficult to tell where the sound is coming from.

Perhaps the greatest challenge in surround loudspeakers is running cables to them. Surrounds are often at the opposite end of the room from the power amplifier driving them, which makes hookup difficult. Some surround loudspeakers are wireless, but using these requires buying an entire system from one manufacturer.

A complete home-theater loudspeaker system is shown in Fig.13-6. The center loudspeaker uses the same drivers as the left and right loudspeakers, and in a very similar cabinet. The slim design makes the left and right loudspeakers less obtrusive, while allowing the center loudspeaker to fit easily atop a TV monitor. The subwoofer is powered by an external amplifier (included in the system). The surround loudspeakers are bi-polar.

When choosing loudspeakers for home theater, listen to video soundtracks that have music, effects, and dialog. The dialog should be clear and easy to understand. Listen at fairly high levels, and don't be distracted by the visual image accompanying the sound—some of your auditioning should be with the video monitor turned off.

Subwoofers

Home-theater subwoofers add greatly to the sonic impact of film soundtracks, increasing the power of sound effects and giving more body to the musical score. Every good home theater should have a subwoofer.

The easiest way to incorporate a subwoofer into your home theater is to use a *powered* subwoofer (also called an *active* subwoofer). A powered subwoofer has a built-in amplifier and accepts a line-level input, usually the "Subwoofer Out" jack of a Pro Logic decoder or receiver. This line-level subwoofer output has already been low-pass–filtered (cutting frequencies above 100Hz), so you don't need an external crossover. The amplifiers of some powered subwoofers are built right into the subwoofer enclosure; others use a separate box for the power amplifier. (An example of a separately powered subwoofer is shown in Fig.13–6 following.)

Fig. 13-6 A home theater loudspeaker system including a powered subwoofer

Courtesy NHT

A passive subwoofer requires a separate power amplifier to drive it. If you're using a Dolby Pro Logic decoder with a Subwoofer Out jack, you don't need an external crossover; the Subwoofer Out signal has already been low-pass–filtered.

Setting Up a Home Theater Audio System

Just as loudspeaker placement is crucial to realizing the highest performance from a music system, locating your home-theater loudspeakers is essential to getting the best sound. If you haven't already read the section on loudspeaker placement in Chapter 4, I suggest you do so before setting up a home theater system—many of the principles are identical.

First, the left and right front loudspeakers should be even with each other, and slightly in front of, the television monitor. When the center loudspeaker is placed on the monitor, it will be the same distance from the listener as are the left and right loudspeakers. This placement also puts the monitor behind the left and right loudspeakers, where it is less likely to degrade imaging. The center loudspeaker's front baffle should be flush with the monitor screen to avoid acoustic reflections from the monitor top that could reduce clarity.

The left and right loudspeakers can be placed farther apart than with a music playback system because the center loudspeaker will fill in the middle to create a continuous soundstage. Left and right loudspeakers spaced far enough apart can create a very wide soundstage, but be careful not to create an unrealistically wide image.

The surround loudspeakers should be behind or to the sides of the listening/viewing position. Position the surrounds so that they don't sound like discrete sound sources, but instead create a diffuse sound field around the listening position. Positioning the surrounds above ear level can help to ensure this.

Where you put a subwoofer can have a great influence on how much bass you hear from it. A room corner will reinforce bass and make the subwoofer seem more powerful, but may cause boominess. This boominess, however, is much less objectionable on film soundtracks than on music. Experiment with subwoofer placement to get the best integration between the subwoofer and the three front loudspeakers.

Once the loudspeakers are correctly placed, set the delay time (if it's adjustable). Use the chart shown in Fig.13-4 to find the optimum delay time for your particular loudspeakers and listening position. If you sit far from the three front loudspeakers and close to the surrounds, increase the delay time.

The next step is balancing the channels. A Dolby Surround system will have three channels (left, right, and surround), a Dolby Pro Logic system four (left, right, center, and surround). The "Test" button on a Dolby Pro Logic decoder sends a few seconds of a noise signal through each loudspeaker in turn. (Because the surround channels are monaural, they are fed the noise signal simultaneously.) The remote control allows you to adjust the center and surround levels to match the main left and right channels. The left-right balance control usually remains in its center position.

After the four channels seem to have equal loudness, play part of a film soundtrack and adjust the subwoofer level to match the rest of the system. The subwoofer's output should add power and depth to effects and music, yet not constantly intrude on the soundtrack. Avoid the (almost irresistible) temptation to set the subwoofer level too high.

If your Dolby decoder doesn't have automatic input-balance adjustment, you'll need to set it by ear. With a Dolby Surround decoder, play a section of dialog from the film soundtrack and adjust the input level control so that the dialog output from the surround loudspeakers is minimal. If you're using a Dolby Pro Logic decoder, play a section of dialog with the center channel turned off. Adjust the input balance control for minimum dialog from the left and right loudspeakers.

Once these rough calibrations are made, don't be afraid to adjust them so that the soundtrack sounds better. Very often when using the calibration method, the center channel will be too weak and the surrounds too loud. It's difficult to have too much center channel—that's where so much of the audio information comes from. On the other hand, it's very easy to set the surround channels too high and hear them as discrete sources. If you hear sound directly from the surround loudspeakers, they're too loud.

Source Components and Software

All home-theater audio systems have a source component at the front end of the playback chain. This is usually a stereo VCR (with Hi-Fi tracks) or laserdisc player. (Note that monaural VCRs cannot carry Dolby-encoded soundtracks.)

All laserdiscs carry a stereo pair of analog audio tracks. These tracks typically have a bandwidth of 15kHz and a signal-to-noise ratio of about 55dB. Virtually all recently manufactured laserdiscs also include a stereo pair of digital audio channels. The digital tracks, identical in format and sound quality to a CD's, provide 20kHz bandwidth and a 98dB signal-to-noise ratio.

These digital tracks can be converted to analog by the laserdisc player's onboard D/A converter, or with a separate digital processor. The integral D/A converters found in most laserdisc players, chosen for low cost and simple circuitry rather than sound quality, are mediocre at best. These converters can be replaced with the higher-quality converters available in outboard digital processors. This is realized by connecting the laserdisc player's digital output jack to the digital input on the outboard processor. Most laserdisc players have only TosLink optical output, requiring a processor with TosLink input. Because TosLink is significantly inferior to the other digital interface types (see Chapter 8), the sound quality from an outboard converter may not be much better than the laserdisc player's integral converters.

A solution to the problem is an outboard device connected between the laserdisc player and the digital processor. This will accept TosLink input, and outputs the signal on a coaxial RCA jack. These devices also re-clock the digital signal, reducing jitter in the datastream and improving the sonic performance of the laserdisc player/outboard processor combination. These devices are available for as little as $200, and can greatly improve your home theater's sound quality.

The THX Standard

THX is the name given by LucasArts Entertainment to a quality standard for film sound playback, either in a movie theater (THX) or the home (Home THX). It isn't a product, system, or components, but a set of technical criteria for the reproduction of film soundtracks.

A THX system can theoretically allow a listener/viewer to re-create, as closely as possible, the sound heard in the studio when the film was mixed. A manufacturer can design such a system by adhering to the THX standards established by LucasArts for playback components (amplifiers and loudspeakers, for example), system setup, playback level, and the acoustic environment in which the soundtrack will be played. The idea is to have the same loudness, same loudspeaker directivity, same spectral balance, same amplifier power, etc. as in the film studio. If the movie theater or home theater meets these standards, the listener has a better chance of hearing exactly what the director intended. Without such technical standards, the listener could hear a very different tonal balance, a different mix of dialog, music, and effects, and not hear the directional cues that were created on the soundtrack. Movie theaters displaying the THX logo must conform to THX standards to advertise themselves as THX theaters.

Although THX started as a certification program for movie theaters, the concept has been extended to home theater. Manufacturers of home-theater products can send samples to LucasArts for testing and possible certification. Home theater components bearing the THX logo have been tested to meet THX specifications and are certified for use in a home THX system. These specifications include amplifier power, loudspeaker directivity, subwoofer crossover frequency and slope, and myriad other factors. THX-certified processors also decorrelate the signals feeding the surround speakers.

Decorrelation simply means making the two signals driving the surrounds slightly different, either by directing some frequency components to one loudspeaker more than the other, or by changing the phase relationship between the two signals. These techniques diffuse the soundfield so that the surround loudspeakers cannot be located by ear. THX processors also re-equalize the signal by applying a slight treble cut to remove the excess brightness engineered into most film soundtracks to compensate for sound losses unavoidable in large theaters. The surround channel is also re-equalized by rolling off the treble to compensate for the human ear's directivity, and also to match the timbre of the surrounds to that of the front channels. (This is called "timbre equalization.")

Dolby Surround and Pro Logic are integral parts of THX. A THX-certified home theater system uses the multi-channel output from a Dolby Pro Logic decoder as the signal source. Dolby and THX are not competing systems; instead, Dolby Surround decoding is the first step in a THX-certified system.

Finally, the THX designation has been expanded to apply to laserdiscs and tapes containing high-quality audio signals.

The Home Theater of the Future: Dolby Stereo Digital

Dolby Laboratories plans to replace the matrixed Dolby Surround and Pro Logic systems with an entirely discrete digital system called Dolby Stereo Digital (DSD). The new format puts six discrete digitally encoded audio channels (five full-bandwidth, one bandwidth-limited low-frequency) into a digital datastream that can be broadcast (when HDTV, or High-Definition Television, becomes a reality) or stored on a laserdisc.

Because DSD provides a separate audio channel for each of the five loudspeakers in a home theater, the old problems of Dolby Surround are eliminated. With DSD, each channel can be full-bandwidth, the surrounds can be driven by different signals, and there is no chance of sounds in one channel leaking into other channels. Moreover, the digital nature of DSD makes the system more robust than analog carriers.

DSD is now in use at selected movie theaters around the world. Dolby sees this as the first step toward making DSD the worldwide standard in film-sound reproduction in both the movie theater and the home.

DSD is made possible by a digital encoding technique called *perceptual coding*. Perceptual coders decide which parts of the audio signal are audible and which are not, and encode only the audible portions. New, more efficient coding schemes are also used in perceptual coders. The result is a vastly lower number of bits required to code an audio signal, allowing six discrete audio channels to occupy a space normally used by just two channels of linearly coded digital audio. For example, a standard digital audio signal like that found on CDs (and stereo laserdiscs) consumes about 700,000 bits per second per channel. DSD encodes 5.1 channels with a data rate of 320,000 bits per second. Although this corresponds to an average data rate per channel of 64,000 bits per second, those bits are allocated to the channels with dominant energy (left, right, and center). In addition, the joint coding technique (allocating the available "bit pool" to whatever channel needs the bits) results in an effective bit rate of 128,000 bits per second for the dominant channels at any moment. The drawback of perceptual coding is somewhat reduced fidelity to the original signal.

Pioneer Corporation is working closely with Dolby Laboratories to create a laserdisc format containing DSD sound and conventional digital audio on the same disc. The name *Laser Digital* will identify discs carrying both DSD and two-channel Dolby encoded digital audio. When films made with DSD for theatrical release are transferred to video for home viewing, the DSD coding will be included in the transfer. Films made with competing in-theater digital audio soundtrack formats (DTS and SDDS) will be transferred to DSD coding for home video. The first DSD-based decoders and Laser Digital laserdiscs should be for sale by 1995.

DSD has officially been selected as the audio standard for HDTV, with the first broadcast of HDTV and DSD scheduled for the 1996 Olympics. DSD may be available in homes sooner than 1996: 5.1-channel DSD film soundtracks may be distributed via new cable-TV decoders, and through cable-delivered digital radio services such as Digital Music Express and Digital Cable Radio. DSD will also be provided to subscribers of the RCA/Hughes DirecTV DBS service.

Dolby sees their discrete six-channel–encoded format as a replacement for conventional stereo for music reproduction. In this scenario, a CD-like disc would contain six channels rather than two, and all playback systems would need DSD decoders. To audiophiles, however, two good channels are far better than six channels that have been compromised by perceptual coding. Without strong support from Sony or Philips, these new discs may not become commercial realities.

Appendix A: Sound and Hearing

Introduction: What is Sound?

Sound is a series of physical disturbances in a medium such as air. When an object vibrates, it sends out a series of waves that propagate through the air. These waves are composed of fluctuations in air pressure above and below the normal atmospheric pressure of 14.7 pounds per square inch. When a loudspeaker cone moves forward, for example, it compresses the air in front of it, creating an area in which the air molecules are denser than normal atmospheric pressure. This portion of the sound wave is called a *compression*.

When the loudspeaker cone moves backward, it creates an area in front of it in which the air molecules are less dense than atmospheric pressure. This portion of the sound wave is called a *rarefaction*. Sound is made up of a series of alternating compressions and rarefactions moving through the air.

Sound waves are transmitted through the air by passing on the moving molecules' momentum to adjacent molecules. The original compressed molecules return to their original positions because of the elastic properties of air. The air molecules don't move very far; instead, their "bumping into each other" is what transmits sound energy.

When these compressions and rarefactions strike our eardrums, we perceive the phenomenon as sound. The greater the change in air pressure above and below normal atmospheric pressure, the greater the *amplitude* of the sound.

Because most objects vibrate with a periodic back-and-forth motion, or oscillation, most sound waves (and nearly all musical sounds) have a periodic repetition. The sound wave is a replica of the object's motion. Consequently, sound waves have a regular, periodic pattern of compressions and rarefactions.

This periodic pattern is illustrated in Fig.A-1. The loudspeaker at one end of the tube of air is driven by a periodic signal, such as that made by the cyclic back-and-forth motion of a tuning fork. Fig.A-1 (b) shows the movement of the loudspeaker diaphragm as a function of time. When the cone moves forward, a compression is created; when it moves backward, a rarefaction is formed. This pattern moves down the tube at 1130 feet per second, the speed of sound. The resulting pattern of pressure change, shown in A-1(c), is called a *sinewave*, the most basic periodic repetition. Fig.A-1 (c) shows the instantaneous pressure distribution over the tube's length. Fig.A-1 (d) represents the change in atmospheric pressure as a function of time at some point along the tube.

Fig. A-1 The relationship between a loudspeaker moving back and forth, pressure distribution in a tube, wavelength, and period

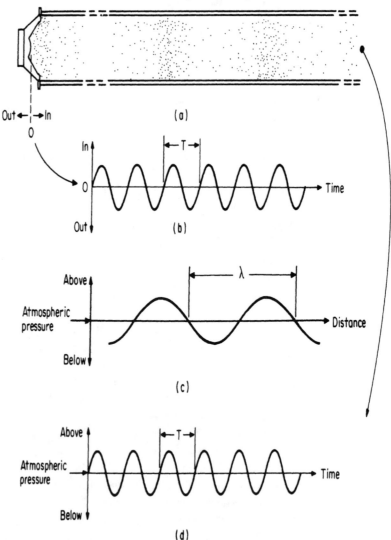

Courtesy *Audio Engineering Handbook*, K. Benson, McGraw-Hill, Inc., 1988

Another way of relating periodic motion to a sinewave is to imagine a tuning fork with a pen attached to it, with the pen touching a moving strip of paper. As the paper moves under the pen, the tuning fork's oscillations trace a sinewave on the paper.

Period and Frequency

The time it takes to complete one cycle of a sinewave (indicated by the "T" in A-1(b)) is called its *period*. The *frequency* of a sinewave is the number of periods per second. A sound's frequency largely determines the sound's *pitch*, our subjective impression of frequency.

The unit for expressing frequency is the *Hertz*, abbreviated *Hz*. This unit of measurement is named after Heinrich Hertz, the German physicist who established that light and heat are electromagnetic radiations. The use of the unit Hz is relatively recent; the older unit of frequency was the more descriptive *cycles per second*, or *cps*.

Frequency is the reciprocal of time, expressed in the equation $F = 1/T$, where F is the frequency in Hz and T is the wave's period in seconds. For example, a sinewave with a period of 0.01 seconds (one one-hundredth of a second) has a frequency of 100 cycles per second, or 100 Hertz (100Hz). Because each period occupies one one-hundredth of a second, there are one hundred periods in a second, or 100Hz.

A sinewave with a period of 0.001 seconds (one one-thousandth of a second, or one millisecond) has a frequency of 1000Hz. The shorter the period, the higher the frequency.

Wavelength

If a wave's period is the *time* it takes to complete one cycle, a wave's *wavelength* is the *distance* between successive cycles. Wavelength, represented by the Greek letter lambda (λ), is shown in Fig.A-1 (c).

A sound's wavelength in air is directly related to frequency: the shorter the wavelength, the higher the frequency. To calculate wavelength, we simply divide the wave's frequency into the speed of sound in air. The formula is $\lambda = V/F$, where λ is the wavelength in feet, V is the speed of sound in feet per second, and F is the frequency in Hz. A sinewave with a frequency of 100Hz has a wavelength of 11.3' (1130 divided by 100). At a very high audio frequency of 10,000Hz (10kHz), the wavelength is about an inch.

Notice that a sound's wavelength is dependent on the speed of sound in the medium. For most applications, the speed of sound in air (1130 feet per second) is all we're concerned about. Because sound travels about five times faster in water than in air, the wavelengths are five times longer.

Phase

The term *phase* describes the fraction of a period that has elapsed in a sinewave. Phase is expressed in degrees, with one complete cycle of a sinewave represented by 360° (see Fig.A-2). Although phase can be measured from any arbitrary point along the sinewave, 0° is usually where the wave begins its positive-going zero crossing.

Fig. A-2 The phase of a wave is its time relationship to a reference point.

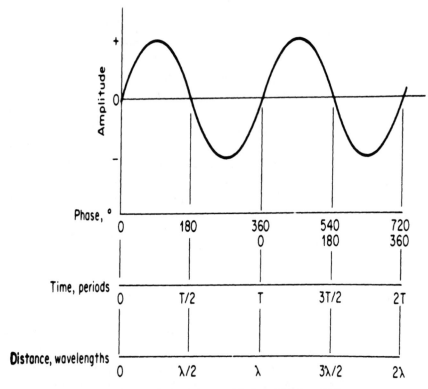

Courtesy *Audio Engineering Handbook*, K. Benson, McGraw-Hill, Inc., 1988

The term *phase shift* describes a time displacement of the sinewave relative to a fixed point. For example, if the sinewave in Fig.A-2 were delayed by half its period, we would say it experienced a 180° phase shift (because one cycle is 360°, half a period is 180°).

Phase can also describe the time relationship between two or more sinewaves. If one wave is delayed by half a period in relation to a second wave, we say the second wave lags the first wave by 180°. If one wave is delayed by one whole period (360°) in relation to another wave, it as though the phase shift never occurred—the wave is returned to its original phase relationship with the first wave. This is analogous to a clock's second hand returning to the same location every minute.

Phase shift has important consequences when waves are combined. If two waves of equal frequency and the same phase are superimposed, their combination will create a wave of greater amplitude. Specifically, two waves of equal amplitude, equal frequency, and the same phase will yield an increase of 6 decibels (dB) when combined. (Decibels are explained later in this appendix.) These waves are said to *reinforce* each other. If, however, one of these waves is phase-shifted by 180°, the two waves will *cancel* each other and produce no signal. When one wave is at peak positive, the wave shifted by 180° is at peak negative, producing the cancellation.

This is exactly what happens in a hi-fi system if *one* loudspeaker is connected with the loudspeaker cables reversed (the red amplifier terminal is connected to the loudspeaker's black terminal, and the black amplifier terminal is connected to the loudspeaker's red terminal). Reversing the leads to one loudspeaker "flips" that signal over, making positive into negative and negative into positive. This is similar to a phase shift of 180°. Now, when one woofer cone pushes forward to create a compression, the second loudspeaker's woofer pulls back to make a rarefaction. When the compressions and rarefactions are combined, they cancel; the compression from one loudspeaker "fills in" the rarefaction from the second loudspeaker, and less sound is heard. Because the two waves don't perfectly coincide, they don't completely cancel, but they do greatly reduce the acoustic output in the bass. If these two signals were combined electrically, however, complete cancellation would occur. Note that if you reverse the red and black leads on *both* loudspeakers, there is no phase shift between the left and right signals, and thus no cancellation occurs.

Absolute Polarity

Some audio products (primarily preamplifiers and digital processors) have switches marked "polarity," "phase," or "180°." These invert the polarities of *both* audio channels. The switch "flips" the signals over, making positive into negative and negative into positive. The switch inverts the stereo signal's *absolute polarity*.

Absolute polarity shouldn't be confused with *phase* reversal *between* channels (described earlier). In that case, there was a 180° phase shift in one channel with respect to the other—with severe audible consequences.

Absolute polarity, however, describes a polarity reversal of *both* channels. If musical waveforms were completely symmetrical—that is, identical in the positive- and negative-going halves—absolute polarity would make no difference. You could flip the signal upside-down and never be able to detect the difference, either by listening or by measuring.

But most musical signals aren't symmetrical, and are degraded if reproduced with inverted absolute polarity. When a recording is played back with correct absolute polarity, a compression from the musical instrument or voice at the original acoustic event causes a compression from the loudspeaker; a rarefaction from the instrument causes a rarefaction from the loudspeaker. Conversely, playing a recording with inverted polarity results in a compression from the instrument or voice to be reproduced as a rarefaction from the loudspeaker.

It may seem obvious and intuitive that all recordings and playback systems should maintain correct absolute polarity, but that isn't the case. An audio signal undergoes many reversals of absolute polarity during the recording and reproduction chain—reversals that no one keeps track of. Some recordings have correct absolute polarity and others don't—it's about a 50-50 chance that it's right. Similarly, some playback systems invert absolute polarity and others don't. The only thing that matters is that the sum total of all the polarity reversals results in correct polarity at the loudspeaker output. If a recording with inverted absolute polarity is played on a system that inverts absolute polarity, the result is correct polarity at the loudspeaker end of the playback chain.

The only way to ensure correct absolute polarity for each recording is by throwing the polarity switch and listening for which position sounds better. You can mark your records and CDs as to their polarity, and put the polarity switch in the appropriate position for each recording without listening every time. Reversing the red and black leads on the cables going to *both* loudspeaker will also invert absolute polarity.

Note that it doesn't do any good to have a non-inverting playback system: roughly half your records and CDs will be reproduced with incorrect polarity whether your system is inverting or not. Moreover, many recordings have no single correct polarity; the disc contains a mix of inverted and non-inverted tracks. Finally, music recorded with multitrack techniques often contain a mix of inverted and non-inverted signals in the same piece of music, making moot the entire issue of absolute polarity.

Some listeners report radical degradation of the sound when absolute polarity is reversed; others never notice the difference. The audibility of absolute polarity is highly variable, depending on the listener's polarity sensitivity, the instruments on the recording (some instruments produce a less symmetrical wave shape than others), whether or not the recording has a mix of inverted and non-inverted signals (from different microphones), and the phase coherence of the loudspeakers. Loudspeakers with poor time-domain performance can obscure the difference between correct and incorrect polarity.

There's an entire book devoted to absolute polarity. *The Wood Effect*, by R.C. Johnsen, is available from The Modern Audio Association, 23 Stillings Street, Boston, MA 02210.

Complex Waves

Real sounds and musical signals are made up not of sinewaves, but of *complex waves*. Complex waves are many sinewaves of different frequencies superimposed on one another. A vibrating object will produce a *fundamental* frequency (its lowest frequency) overlaid with *overtones* or *harmonics* which are mathematically related to the fundamental frequency. For example, a guitar string vibrating at 440Hz (middle A) will also vibrate at multiples of 440Hz. The second harmonic has a frequency of 880Hz, the third harmonic is at 1320Hz, the fourth at 1760Hz, and so forth.

It is the presence of these harmonics that give an instrument its *timbre* or tonal color. If a piano and a violin both play middle A, both instruments produce the same fundamental frequency of 440Hz. They sound very different because they have different *harmonic structures*: the violin produces stronger harmonics that extend higher in frequency than the piano's.

Harmonics can be *even-order* or *odd-order*. Even-order harmonics are the second, fourth, sixth, eighth, and so on. Odd-order harmonics are the third, fifth, seventh, ninth, etc.

The phase relationships of these harmonics and the fundamental have a great influence on the resulting complex wave. The top of Fig.A-3 is a complex wave composed of a fundamental, a third harmonic, and a fifth harmonic, all shown below the fundamental. Just by changing the phase relationship between the fundamental and its harmonics, we get a very different-looking complex wave (top of Fig.A-4). In this case, the fundamental was shifted by 90° (one quarter of a period) in relation to the third and fifth harmonics.

A squarewave is a sinewave with the addition of the entire series of odd-order harmonics. The shape of the complex wave in Fig.A-3 looks somewhat like a squarewave, even though only the third and fifth harmonics are present.

Fig. A-3 A complex wave is composed of multiple sinewaves.

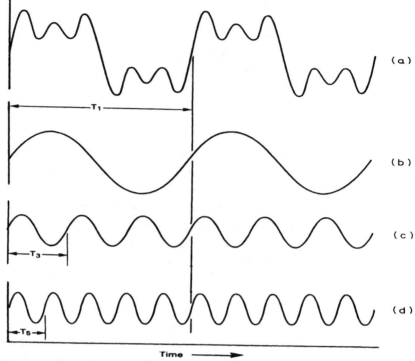

Courtesy *Audio Engineering Handbook*, K. Benson, McGraw-Hill, Inc., 1988

Fig. A-4 Changing the phase relationship between the constituent sinewaves greatly changes the complex wave's shape.

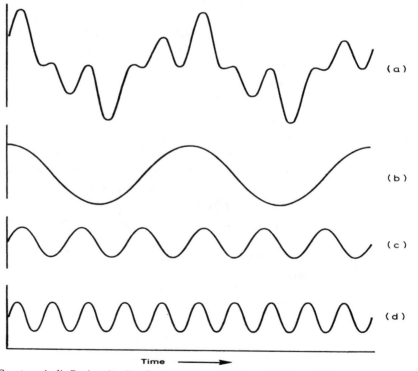

Courtesy *Audio Engineering Handbook*, K. Benson, McGraw-Hill, Inc., 1988

Comb Filtering

A waveform can also be altered if it is combined with a slightly delayed version of itself. This situation occurs when a loudspeaker is placed near a sidewall of a listening room: the listener receives the direct sound from the loudspeaker, and a reflection from the sidewall. The additional distance the reflected sound travels causes the delay. When these two sounds combine and interact, they reinforce at some frequencies and cancel at others. This phenomenon, called *comb filtering*, is a sequence of peaks and notches—hence its similarity to a comb—in the frequency response caused by constructive and destructive interference between the direct and reflected sounds. Chapter 4 includes a detailed description of comb filtering's effects on reproduced sound.

Absorption, Reflection, and Diffusion

When sound strikes a surface, it is absorbed, reflected, or diffused by that surface—or some combination of all three. A soft surface such as carpet or drapes absorbs energy because sound can enter its porous surface to be dissipated by being reflected off the material's fibers. In this mechanism, sound energy is converted into a minute amount of heat within the absorbing material.

Reflective surfaces are hard and thus don't allow sound to penetrate the surface; nearly all the energy is reflected back toward the source. Sound is reflected at the same angle at which it struck; i.e., "the angle of incidence equals the angle of reflection." Light and other electromagnetic waves behave similarly.

Diffusion is a scattering of sound. A diffuser converts a sound traveling in one direction into many lower-amplitude sounds moving in many directions. An irregularly shaped surface tends to diffuse sound, provided that the irregular structures are similar in size to the wavelength of sound striking them. A convex surface acts as a diffuser, but a concave surface does the opposite, concentrating sound into a point.

Diffraction

Diffraction is the bending of sound waves around an object and the re-radiation of energy through an opening. Diffraction makes it possible to hear sounds around corners and behind walls, or through a small opening in an obstruction.

The way sound behaves when it encounters an obstruction, or an opening in an obstruction, changes according to the obstruction's or opening's size in relation to the sound's wavelength. For example, low frequencies encountering an obstruction such as a large wall will bend around that wall, while high frequencies will not. If the obstruction is small compared to the impinging wavelength, it is almost as though the obstruction isn't there; sound just bends around it. The same-sized obstruction would, however, be a barrier to high frequencies.

Diffraction is easily demonstrated by standing behind your loud-speakers; you'll hear bass but no treble. This is because low frequencies can diffract around the loudspeaker cabinet, but mid and high frequencies cannot. The loudspeaker cabinet is small compared to the bass wavelengths, but large in relation to midrange and treble wavelengths.

This phenomenon is shown in Fig.A-5. The following quote is the caption accompanying Fig.A-5, reprinted from the McGraw-Hill *Audio Engineering Handbook* by K. Benson, with permission:

Fig. A-5 How sound behaves when it encounters an obstacle or opening depends on the obstacle's or opening's size in relation to the wavelength of sound.

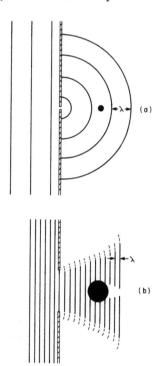

Courtesy *Audio Engineering Handbook*, K. Benson, McGraw-Hill, Inc., 1988

"Stylized illustration of the diffraction of sound waves passing through openings and around obstacles. The sound waves are depicted by their wavefronts. The distance between successive wavefronts is the wavelength λ. The sound waves approaching the barriers are shown as plane waves, as is approximately the case when the source of sound is far away. (a) The wavelength is large compared with the size of the opening and the obstacle. The sound radiates from the small opening as a spherical wave, dispersing equally in all directions and displaying no shadowing behind the small obstacle. (b) The wavelength is small compared with the size of the opening and the obstacle. The plane wave continues through the opening with only slight spreading, and there is a substantial shadow zone behind the obstacle. Although it is not shown, some of the sound would also be reflected back toward the source."

Diffraction can cause problems in loudspeaker performance: When sound from the drivers reach the cabinet edge, the energy is re-radiated, as shown in Fig.A-6. This makes it appear acoustically as though the sound is coming from more than one source (the driver and the cabinet edges). Because this energy re-radiated from the cabinet edges is delayed in relation to the driver's output (it travels slightly farther), the two signals combine to produce peaks and dips in the loudspeaker's frequency response due to constructive and destructive interference (similar to the comb-filtering effects described earlier). Diffraction can be reduced in loudspeakers by rounded baffles, recessed driver mounting bolts, low-profile grille frames, and absorbent material around the drivers.

Fig. A-6
Diffraction causes
re-radiation of the
sound from cabi-
net edges.

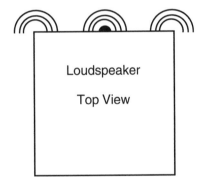

The Decibel (dB)

An understanding of the decibel is essential to understanding many aspects of sound and audio. Decibel notation is a convenient way of expressing very large numbers, and also corresponds closely with our perception of sound. A figure in decibels can describe the magnitude of voltages, electrical powers, acoustic powers, and sound pressure levels.

The decibel doesn't express an absolute value, but a *ratio* between *two* values. When we say that one CD player has 2.5dB higher output voltage than another, we are expressing the *difference* in output voltages *between* the players. In the case of our CD players, the decibel notation expresses the *ratio* of their respective output voltages. Any time a decibel notation is used, it must be accompanied by a reference level—either to another level, as with the two CD players, or against a standard reference.

This is where the dB notation's suffix comes into play. The letters after the number of dB (80dB SPL, or –20dBFS, for examples) denote the reference level to which the expressed value is referenced. If we say a certain *sound pressure level* (SPL) is 80dB SPL, "SPL" tells us that the sound pressure is referenced to 0dB SPL, the threshold of hearing. By saying "80dB SPL," we mean that the sound is 80dB greater in magnitude than the threshold of hearing. Note that 0dB SPL isn't absolute silence, but the softest sound an average person can hear in a very quiet environment.

The decibel scale is logarithmic, meaning that as the number of dB increases arithmetically, the value that number expresses increases exponentially. For example, each doubling of sound pressure level represents an increase of 6dB, as shown in Table 1.

Sound or electrical power ratio	Decibels	Sound pressure, voltage, or current ratio	Decibels
1	0	1	0
2	3.0	2	6.0
3	4.8	3	9.5
4	6.0	4	12.0
5	7.0	5	14.0
6	7.8	6	15.6
7	8.5	7	16.9
8	9.0	8	18.1
9	9.5	9	19.1
10	10.0	10	20.0
100	20.0	100	40.0
1,000	30.0	1,000	60.0
10,000	40.0	10,000	80.0
100,000	50.0	100,000	100.0
1,000,000	60.0	1,000,000	120.0

Let's say you were in a very quiet room and measured the sound of fly buzzing at 40dB SPL. We can see in Table 1 that 40dB represents a pressure ratio of 100; the sound of the buzzing fly produces a pressure 100 times greater than a sound at 0dB SPL, the threshold of hearing. The threshold of hearing, represented by the reference level of 0dB SPL, has been established as a pressure of 0.0002 dynes per square centimeter (dynes/cm^2). A dyne is a unit of force. The letters "SPL" after the decibel notation tell us that 0.0002 dynes/cm^2 is the reference level. Knowing this, we can calculate that the sound a buzzing fly produces is a pressure

100 times that of the pressure at 0dB SPL, or 0.02 dynes/cm^2 (100 × 0.0002).

Two flies would produce a sound pressure level of 46dB—double the pressure, and an increase of 6dB over the 40dB one fly produces. Because 40dB represents a pressure of 0.02 dynes/cm^2, 46dB represents a pressure of 0.04 dynes/cm^2. (For the purposes of this illustration, we'll assume the flies produce the same sound pressure, and that their sounds are perfectly in-phase with each other. In reality, the phase relationship between the two sounds will be random, producing a sound *power* increase of 3dB.)

Now consider another example: Let's say that a jet taking off produces an SPL of 120dB. Looking at Table 1, we see that 120dB represents a ratio of 1,000,000—in other words, the jet creates a pressure on our eardrums a million times greater than the pressure at the threshold of hearing. Multiplying 1,000,000 by the reference pressure (0.0002 dynes/cm^2), we know that the jet creates a pressure of 200 dynes/cm^2 (0.0002 × 1,000,000).

If we add a second jet taking off, we know that the number of dB SPL will increase from 120dB to 126dB, and also that the pressure will double from 200 dynes/cm^2 to 400 dynes/cm^2. (Again, we'll assume for illustrative purposes that the jets produce equal loudness and are in-phase.)

Obviously, the sound of the second jet taking off is much greater than that of the second fly. But both increased the sound pressure level by the same *ratio*: 6dB. The same 6dB increase represented an increase of only 0.02 dynes/cm^2 in the case of the buzzing fly, but a whopping 200 dynes/cm^2 with the jet.

This logarithmic nature of the decibel makes handing very large numbers easier. These very large numbers are needed to express the vast range of sound pressure levels we can accommodate, from the threshold of hearing to the threshold of pain. The threshold of pain, 140dB SPL, is a pressure on your eardrum of 2000 dynes/cm^2, or ten million times the pressure at the threshold of hearing. Rather than saying that the threshold of pain is 10,000,000 times louder than the threshold of hearing, it's easier to represent this value as 140dB.

Moreover, this exponential increase parallels our subjective impression of loudness. If we asked a person listening to music at 60dB SPL to turn up the volume until it was "twice as loud," the person would increase the volume by about ten dB. If the person were listening at 100dB SPL and was asked to turn up the volume until it was twice as loud, he would also increase the volume by 10dB. As we can extrapolate from the fly and jet examples, the increase in pressure from 60dB to 70dB is far less than the pressure increase from 100dB to 110dB. Both increases, however, produce similar subjective increases in loudness.

This phenomenon is analogous to the way we perceive pitch: We hear each doubling of frequency as an octave, yet each ascending octave spans a frequency difference twice that of the next lower octave. The octave span between 20Hz and 40Hz is perceived as the same musical interval as the octave between 10kHz and 20kHz, although the latter is a much larger change in frequency.

We can calculate the number of dB between two values with the following formula: $NdB = 20 \log P1/Pr$ where NdB = the number of dB, $P1$ is the measured pressure, and Pr is the reference pressure. Expressing this formula verbally, we say, "The number of dB equals twenty times the logarithm of the ratio between the two pressures (or voltages, or currents)." This formula works for voltage, electrical current, or sound pressure level. Just as a doubling in SPL is represented by an increase of 6dB, a doubling of voltage is represented by an increase of 6dB.

Using this formula, we can calculate the difference in dB between two CD players having different output voltages. We'll say CD player A puts out 3.6V when playing a full-scale, 1kHz test tone, and CD player B puts out 2.8V with the same test signal. How much difference in dB is there between the two players?

We first find the ratio between the two voltages by dividing 3.6 by 2.8. The ratio is 1.2857. By pressing the "log" key on a calculator with 1.2857 in the display, we get the logarithm of the ratio (0.0109). Then we multiply the result by 20, giving us the answer in dB. CD player A's output voltage is 2.18dB higher than that of CD player B.

Calculating power ratios is slightly different. With acoustic or electrical power, an increase of 3dB represents a doubling of power. This is given by the following formula: $NdB = 10 \log P1/Pr$ where $P1$ is the measured power and Pr is the reference power. If we want to find the difference in power output in dB between two amplifiers, we multiply the logarithm of the ratio of the two values by 10, not by 20 as in voltage, current, and sound pressure.

Let's say one power amplifier has a maximum output power of 138W, and another has a maximum output power of 276W. What is the decibel difference between them? First find the ratio between the two powers by dividing 276 by 138. The answer is 2. Find the logarithm of 2 (0.301) and multiply by 10. The answer is that the second amplifier has 3dB more output power than the first amplifier. Note that a doubling of power yields an increase of 3dB.

Frequency, Loudness, and Equal Loudness Contours

So far, we've looked at only the purely physical properties of sound and how it behaves. But sound is meaningless without its perception. *Psychoacoustics* is the study of the interaction between the physical properties of sound and our perceptions of those physical properties.

Humans can perceive a frequency range of sound from about 16Hz to 18kHz. The commonly cited range of 20Hz-20kHz is less accurate but easier to remember and express. In reality, most people can hear tones below 20Hz, but few can hear above 18kHz. Teenagers and young to middle-aged women can hear above 18kHz, but that sensitivity decreases with age. It has been proved that women have a greater ability to hear high frequencies than men, and that they retain this ability longer.

This frequency range is wider than it first appears; the frequency span is huge when considering the wavelength of sound. A 16Hz tone has a wavelength of more than 70'; an 18kHz tone has a wavelength of about 3/4".

One of our most fundamental auditory perceptions is *loudness*, the term that describes the magnitude of an auditory event. Loudness is a *perception* that is influenced by factors other than the physical amplitude of sound. In fact, we perceive loudness very differently depending on the sound's frequency. This was first established by two researchers, Fletcher and Munson, who produced a set of curves called the *equal-loudness contours*, also known as *Fletcher-Munson curves*.

The equal-loudness contours (Fig.A-7) show how much difference in sound pressure level is required to make all frequencies have the same perceived loudness as the 1kHz reference tone. The numbers running down the middle above each curve are *phons*, a measure of loudness. At the reference frequency of 1kHz, phons are equal to dB.

Fig. A-7 The perception of loudness is affected by a sound's frequency and volume.

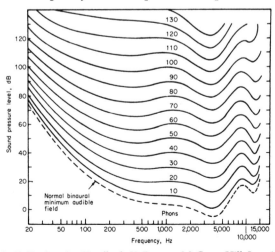

Courtesy *Audio Engineering Handbook*, K. Benson, McGraw-Hill, Inc., 1988

For example, at a very quiet level of 30 phons (30dB SPL at 1kHz), a bass tone of 50Hz would have to be reproduced at 60dB SPL to be perceived as having the same loudness as the 30dB SPL 1kHz tone. In other words, our ears are less sensitive at the bass and treble frequency extremes than in the midrange.

This large disparity in sensitivity with frequency is more acute at low sound pressure levels, shown by the steep slope of the curves at the graph bottom, and by the gradual flattening of the curves toward the graph top. As the SPL increases, our ears become nearly equally sensitive at all frequencies. At 110 phons (110dB at 1kHz), a 50Hz tone would need to be reproduced at 120dB to be perceived as being of equal loudness to the 1kHz tone—quite a difference from the 30 phon example.

Everyone has heard this effect; when you turn up the volume on your hi-fi, you hear more bass and treble. The bass seems to extend lower in frequency, and there's more of it. Conversely, if you turn down the volume to where it's barely audible, you hear only midrange sounds. The "Loudness" button on mid-fi receivers boosts the bass and treble to compensate for the ears' reduced sensitivity to bass and treble at low volume.

Weighting Filters

SPL measurements, and measurements of noise in audio equipment, often invoke a *weighting filter* to remove some bass and treble from the reading. Weighting filters attempt to simulate our reduced sensitivity to bass and treble and produce a measurement that more accurately reflects the perceived sound or noise level. Fig.A-8 shows the three weighting curves used in SPL and noise measurements.

Fig. A-8
Weighting curves applied to SPL or noise measurements approximate the ear's varying sensitivity with frequency.

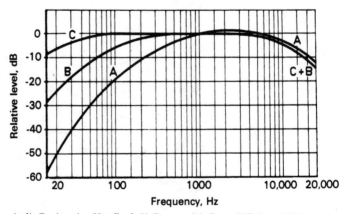

Courtesy *Audio Engineering Handbook*, K. Benson, McGraw-Hill, Inc., 1988

A signal-to-noise specification for a preamplifier, for example, may read "85dB, ~`A' weighted." This means the noise was filtered with the curve with the characteristics of curve "A" in Fig.A-8 *before* the preamplifier's noise level was measured. Consequently, applying the weighting curve makes the signal-to-noise ratio appear higher. Similarly, a weighting curve applied to an SPL measurement makes the measured SPL seem lower than the physical magnitude of the sound.

The Dynamic Nature of Music

So far we've only talked about sound in the context of steady, continuous tones. But music is dynamic, constantly changing in level, and is composed of impulsive sounds as well as steady ones. A basic understanding of this dynamic quality is important to learning about music reproduction.

We can divide a dynamic sound into three components: *attack, internal dynamics*, and *decay* (see Fig.A-9). These three aspects of a sound are called the sound's *envelope*. Attack is the way in which a sound begins. The attack can be sudden (a snare drum, for example) or gradual (the build-up of an organ note in a large room). Decay is the way a sound ends. Internal dynamics are the main portion of the sound between the attack and decay. The envelopes shown in Fig.A-9 could be for a snare drum (left figure) or an organ (right). The snare drum has a very sudden attack; it takes very little time for the sound to reach its highest volume. It also has a very short duration and a rapid decay. By contrast, the organ has a very slow attack, taking a longer time to reach its full amplitude. The internal dynamics are very long, and define the note's sound. Similarly, the decay is slow and gradual.

Fig. A-9 Musical sounds are composed of an attack, internal dynamics, and decay.

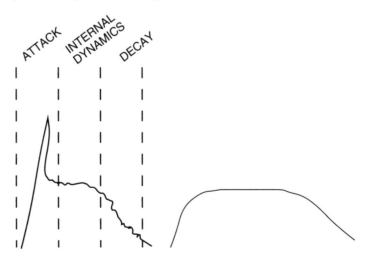

A sound characterized by sudden attack and rapid decay is a *transient* signal. *Transient response* refers to an audio component's or system's ability to reproduce the steep attack of transient signals. This type of signal has a high *peak-to-average ratio*, meaning that the peaks are much higher in level than the average level. Conversely, the organ has no peaks, so it has a very low peak-to-average ratio. A sound's peak-to-average ratio greatly influences the perceived volume; the ear tends to integrate the sound so that peaks add very little to the overall perceived volume.

Another way of expressing the dynamics of a musical signal is the term *dynamic range*—the difference between the loudest and softest sounds. Technically, a piece of audio equipment's dynamic range is the difference in dB between the device's noise floor and its maximum undistorted signal level. Subjectively, dynamic range is the contrast between a piece of music's quietest and loudest passages.

Localization

Localization is our ability to identify the spatial position of a sound. This ability to localize sounds derives in part from the fact that we have two ears, and that sounds arriving at each ear differ slightly from one another. The brain uses these differences (and other cues) to construct a three-dimensional representation of where a sound source is located.

The most basic mechanism for localizing a sound source is attenuation of high frequencies by the head. Low frequencies can diffract around the head more easily than high frequencies, causing one ear to receive a signal with a gradual attenuation of the midrange and treble. The brain interprets this high-frequency rolloff at one ear as a cue that the sound originates closer to the other ear.

At low frequencies (below about 700Hz), there is virtually no amplitude difference between the left and right ears for a sound emanating from one side. The sound diffracts around the head and the treble-rolloff localization cue doesn't exist. At these low frequencies, a second mechanism takes over in which the phase difference between the left and right ears is analyzed. Because low frequencies have long wavelengths compared to the size of the head, one ear receives a slightly different phase of the sound wave. This information is another cue as to the location of a sound source.

The head, upper body, and outer ear (called the *pinna*) also modify the acoustic signals before they reach the ear. The pinna's unusual shape reflects sounds from its structures into the ear. These reflections combine with sounds directly striking the eardrum, causing comb-filter effects.

The brain processes the resultant cancellations and reinforcements to determine a sound source's direction.

The Listening Environment Diagnostic Recording (LEDR) on the first Chesky Test CD (Chesky JD37) is a synthetic percussion instrument that appears in one loudspeaker, then slowly moves across to the other loudspeaker. Another LEDR test moves the image from the loudspeaker up to a plane above the loudspeaker. The third LEDR test moves the image in an arc from one loudspeaker to the other. These special signals, used to evaluate a listening room, were created by simulating the frequency and amplitude cues imposed by the pinna. By creating notches in the signal's spectrum at precisely calculated frequencies, the signal simulates the effect of a sound source's movement.

You can conduct a simple experiment that demonstrates the pinna's effect on localization. Close your eyes and have a friend jingle keys about four feet away from you, either at head level, waist level, or knee level. Point to where the sound is coming from. Now repeat the experiment with your hands folding your outer ears forward. This eliminates the pinna cues that aid in localization, making it much more difficult to tell where the sound of the keys is originating.

Other Psychoacoustic Phenomena

An interesting phenomenon occurs when we hear a direct sound and a delayed version of that sound (as we would hear an echo). If the echo occurs within about 30ms (milliseconds) of the first sound, the echo isn't perceived as a discrete sound, but instead slightly modifies the sound's timbre. This first 30ms is called the *fusion zone*, and the phenomenon is called the *Haas Effect*.

Similarly, when exposed to a direct and a delayed sound that originate from different directions, we hear the sound as coming from the direction of the first sound. The ear ignores the second sound.

Masking is a psychoacoustic phenomenon that renders one sound inaudible when accompanied by a louder sound. Our inability to hear a conversation in the presence of loud amplified music is an example of masking; the music masks the conversation. Similarly, we hear tape hiss or record-surface noise only during quiet passages, not during most of the music. Masking is particularly effective when the masking sound has a similar frequency to the masked component. This kind of masking is called *simultaneous masking*.

Masking also occurs when two sounds are close together in time, an effect called *temporal masking*. The ear/brain tends to hear only the louder of the two sounds—oddly, within a limited time window, it doesn't matter if the louder sound occurred earlier or later than the softer sound. Although it seems logically impossible that a later sound could mask an earlier sound, this occurs because it takes time for the auditory system to process the signal and send it to the brain. When confronted by a louder sound slightly later in time, the louder sound takes precedence.

A Final Note

This appendix is meant only as a cursory survey of the basics of sound and hearing for the interested audiophile; the subject can be studied in great depth. For those interested in learning more about sound and hearing, I recommend the superb introduction to the subject by Dr. Floyd Toole in *Audio Engineering Handbook*, published by McGraw-Hill, ISBN 0-07-004777-4. Further references are included in Dr. Toole's chapters.

Appendix B: Audio and Electronics Basics

A knowledge of electronics and audio technology isn't necessary to choosing and enjoying a high-end music system. You can just select a system, set it up, and not worry about what's going on inside those mysterious black boxes.

Some audiophiles, however, want at least a basic understanding of how audio products work. They have an inherent fascination with audio equipment and want to broaden their knowledge of high-end audio to include a basic conception of electronics and audio circuits. This Appendix is by no means a comprehensive treatment of the subject—that could fill many books. Instead, it provides an overview of audio technology for the interested audiophile.

Moreover, it bridges the gap between the technical descriptions of products published in some high-end audio magazines and the reader who feels intimidated by all the technical jargon. So next time you read that a particular power amplifier has a transformer with dual secondary windings, three full-wave bridge rectifiers, a discrete, direct-coupled JFET class-A input and driver stage, with a push-pull output stage that switches to Class B operation at 20W RMS, you'll know what it means.

But before we get to that, let's take a look at the basic vocabulary of electronics and audio technology.

Voltage, Current, Resistance, and Power

The most basic elements of electronics are voltage, current, and resistance. Let's look first at voltage.

A *voltage* exists between two points when one point has an excess of electrons in relation to the other point. A battery is a good example: the negative terminal has an excess of electrons in relation to the positive terminal. When this happens, we say the battery is *charged*.

Voltage is also called *potential difference*, because it has the *potential* to do work and because voltage is always the *difference* in the electrical charges between two points. This is why we say a voltage exists *across* two points, such as a pair of loudspeaker terminals (when driven by an amplifier), or the positive and negative terminals of a battery. One point is more negative (an excess of electrons) than the other point. The *volt* is the unit of measurement that expresses just how great the difference in electrons between two points is. Another way of thinking of voltage is as electrical pressure, like the pressure in a water faucet.

When an electrical *conductor* such as a wire connects two points that have a voltage across them, *current* flows. Current is the electron charge moving through the conductor. The electrons travel through the conductor from the negative charge to the positive charge. If we put a wire across a battery's terminals, current will flow until both terminals have the same number of electrons; the potential difference no longer exists and the battery is discharged, or "dead." Current from a battery is called *direct current*, or *DC*, because the voltage pushing the electrons produces a steady, non-fluctuating electron flow.

If voltage is analogous to water pressure in a faucet, current flow is analogous to water moving through a hose (the conductor). Just as water in the hose is pushed by the pressure of the water behind it, current flows through a conductor pushed by voltage. Current is measured in *amperes*, or *amps* for short.

Resistance is opposition to current flow. If our hose had a kink in it, the flow of water would be reduced. Similarly, an electrical resistance opposes current flow, reducing the number of electrons flowing through the conductor. The higher the resistance, the less the current flow in the conductor (given the same voltage). The unit of electrical resistance is the *ohm*.

Ohm's Law

With that introduction, let's look at a simple circuit involving voltage, current, and resistance. Fig.B-1 is schematic diagram of a battery connected to a resistor by a conductor. The dashed arrow shows the direction of current flow *through* the resistor, and the two solid arrows point to the voltage *across* the resistor. The voltage source supplies electrons which flow through the conductor and resistor, returning to the positive battery terminal. The current flow will be maintained as long as the voltage exists across the battery.

The amount of current flow is determined by two things: the resistor's resistance value and the battery's voltage. More resistance will decrease current flow. Conversely, a higher voltage will increase current flow. This relationship is expressed by *Ohm's Law*, which states that one volt of charge across one ohm of resistance will push one ampere of current. Mathematically, Ohm's Law is $E = I \times R$. E is *electromotive force* (another term for voltage), I is current (for "intensity" of electron flow), and R is resistance. If we know any two values, we can calculate the third using Ohm's Law. For example, if we know the voltage and current and want to find the resistance, the formula is $R = E/I$. If we want to find the current from the voltage and resistance, we use $I = E/R$.

Fig. B-1 A simple series circuit. Electrons from the negative battery terminal flow through the resistor to the positive battery terminal.

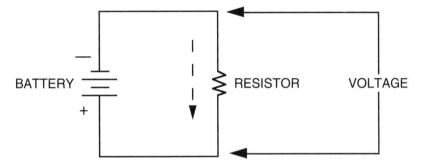

Let's put some units on our schematic diagram (Fig.B-2). We'll say the voltage is 10V and the resistance is 100 ohms. How much current flows through the resistor? Using $I = E/R$, we divide 10 by 100, getting 0.1 ampere, also expressed as 100 milliamps (100mA). If the resistance is doubled, the current is halved. Similarly, doubling the voltage doubles the current flow. This relationship between voltage, current, and resistance is perfectly linear.

Fig. B-2 With an applied voltage of 10V and a resistance of 100 ohms, the current flow through the resistor is 0.1 ampere (100mA).

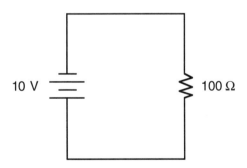

There's another factor here that particularly concerns us in audio—*power*. Power is an expression of the amount of work done by the voltage and current, measured in watts. Power is the product of voltage and current, expressed by Ohm's Law as $P = I \times E$ (power equals the current times the voltage). Power is dissipated as heat in the resistor. A resistor is also called the *load*. Going back to our schematic of Fig.B-2, we can calculate the power dissipated by the resistor. We know that the voltage across the resistor is 10V, and the current through the resistor is 0.1A. Multiplying the voltage by the current tells us that the power dissipated by the resistor is 1 watt (10 x 0.1). Again, the relationship between power, voltage, current, and resistance is linear.

A power amplifier's output power is a product of its output voltage and current. It describes how much *voltage* the amplifier can develop *across* the load (the loudspeaker input), and how much *current* it can drive *through* the load. Current flows through voice coils in the loudspeaker's drive units make the cones move back and forth, producing sound.

A perfect amplifier would double its power as the load resistance is halved: it would maintain its voltage and double its current. We know from Ohm's Law that if the voltage is kept the same and the current is doubled, the power will double. Most amplifiers, however, can't maintain the same voltage across a low-impedance load as it can across a higher impedance, thus reducing the power available to drive the loudspeaker. Amplifiers can also run out of current, again limiting the power delivered to the load.

Series and Parallel Circuits

So far we've discussed a type of circuit called a *series* circuit. In a series circuit, there is only one path through which current can flow. A *parallel* circuit provides multiple paths for current flow. If we add another resistor to our series circuit, we've turned it into a parallel circuit (Fig.B-3). Some of the current flows through the first resistor, some through the second resistor.

Fig. B-3 A parallel circuit provides more than one path for current.

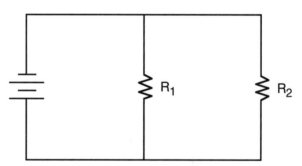

Let's look at series and parallel circuits from the standpoint of a power amplifier driving loudspeakers. An amplifier driving a single loudspeaker is shown in Fig.B-4. The amplifier and loudspeaker form a series circuit; there is only one path for current. If we want to add another loudspeaker to this amplifier channel, we can do it two ways. The first is to put the second loudspeaker in series with the first one (Fig.B-5). The same current flows through both loudspeakers. In a series circuit, the individual resistances are added to find the total resistance. If each loudspeaker presents a resistance of 8 ohms, the total load the amplifier must drive is 16 ohms.

Fig. B-4 An amplifier driving a loudspeaker is a series circuit.

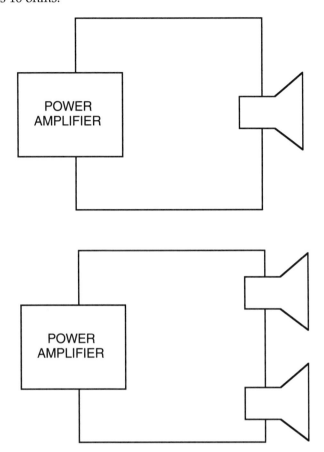

Fig. B-5 Two loudspeakers in series

Another way to connect the second loudspeaker is to wire it in parallel with the first one (Fig.B-6). We've now provided more than one path for current; some current flows through loudspeaker 1, some through loudspeaker 2. Unlike a series circuit, in which the resistances are added to find the total resistance, adding a parallel resistance *lowers* the total resistance (R_T). In the case of our two 8-ohm loudspeakers in parallel, the total resistance the amplifier must drive is 4 ohms. When two equal resistances are in parallel, the total resistance is half that of one resistance. The total resistance (R_T) in a parallel circuit can also be found with the formula $1/R_T = 1/R_1 + 1/R_2 + 1/R_3$, etc.

Parallel circuits differ from series circuits in that the voltage across each branch of a parallel circuit is the same as the applied voltage. If we put ten resistors of different resistance values in parallel and apply a source voltage of 20V, that 20V will appear across all ten resistors. However, the current flow will be different through each resistor. It's the current that changes in parallel circuits, not the voltage.

Conversely, in a series circuit, the current remains the same while the voltage across each resistor is different. As current flows through each resistor in series, some of the applied voltage is dropped across each resistor. The amount of that voltage drop is determined by the resistor's resistance value. The sum of the voltage drops across each resistor equals the applied voltage.

Fig. B-6 Two loudspeakers in parallel

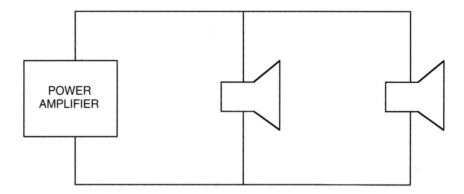

Let's work through examples of series and parallel circuits using Ohm's Law. We'll build two circuits with identical components, one of them a series circuit and the other a parallel circuit. Fig.B-7 is a series circuit with three resistors. To find out how much current flows through this circuit, and how much voltage exists across each resistor, we first find the circuit's total resistance. In a series circuit, the total resistance is the sum of the individual resistances. By adding R_1, R_2, and R_3, we know that R_T = 60 ohms. Because we know the applied voltage (12V), we use Ohm's Law to find the current, specifically $I = E/R$ (current equals voltage divided by the resistance). By dividing the applied voltage by the total resistance, we know that the current flowing through this circuit is 0.2 amperes, or 200mA (200 milliamps). And because current flow is the same in all parts of a series circuit, 200mA flows through all three resistors.

Fig. B-7 Current flow is the same in all parts of a series circuit.

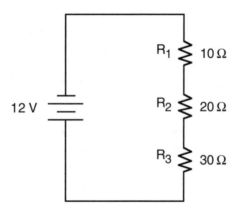

As just mentioned, current flow through the resistors produces a voltage drop across each resistor. To find the individual voltage drops, we turn again to Ohm's Law. Using the formula $E = I \times R$ (voltage equals current multiplied by the resistance), we can calculate the voltage drops. We know that R_1 is 10 ohms, and that the current flowing through it is 0.2A. The voltage drop across R_1 is therefore 2V. Similarly, the voltage drop across R_2 is the current multiplied by the resistance (0.2 x 20), or 4V. Repeating the process for R_3 tells us that 6V is dropped across the third resistor. This illustrates that current flow is the same in all parts of a series circuit, but that the voltage across each resistor changes. Also, the sum of the voltage drops equals the applied voltage.

Fig.B-8 shows the same applied voltage and resistors of the same value, but connected in parallel. In this case, the voltage across the three resistors remains the same, but the current flow through each is different. Using the formula $1/R_T = 1/R_1 + 1/R_2 + 1/R_3$, we see that this circuit's total resistance is 5.45 ohms. The current flow through R_1 will be 12V/10 ohms, or 1.2A. The current through R_2 is 12V/20 ohms, or 0.6A. The current through R_3 is 12V/30 ohms, or 0.4A.

Fig. B-8 In a parallel circuit, the voltage across each resistor is the same, but the current through each resistor changes.

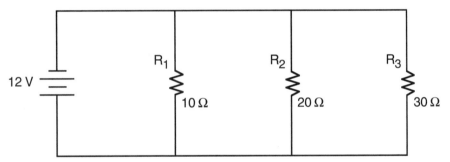

Note that, at each resistor in the parallel circuit, the voltage stayed the same while the amount of current flow was different—the opposite of the series circuit.

Alternating Current (AC)

So far we've only talked about circuits using direct current (DC). Another type of current, called *alternating current*, or *AC*, is the basis for all audio circuits. An audio signal is an example of an AC voltage. An AC voltage reverses polarity, producing current that reverses direction. The principles of DC circuits and Ohm's Law described earlier still apply, but AC circuits use additional elements we'll discuss later.

Let's use the AC power line from a wall outlet as an example of AC voltage and current. The 120 volts from the wall socket appear across the socket's two vertical slots. The voltage's polarity (which slot is positive, which negative) reverses itself at the rate of 60 times per second, or 60 Hertz (*Hz*). If we looked at this 120V, 60Hz voltage we'd see the waveform in Fig.B-9.

Fig. B-9 The 120V 60Hz AC from a wall socket is a sinewave.

Starting at the left side of Fig.B-9, the voltage increases until it reaches its positive peak, then decreases to the zero crossing line (no voltage). The voltage then increases again, but in the opposite polarity. After reaching its negative peak, it decreases again. This represents one complete cycle of a *sinewave*, sixty of which occur every second. The reversing-polarity voltage causes current to reverse direction in whatever conductor is attached to it—usually an AC power cord and power transformer.

An audio signal is also an AC signal, but unlike our simple 60Hz sinewave, an audio signal is a *complex* AC voltage because it's composed of many frequencies. The AC audio signal is an electrical analog of the sound-pressure wave that created the original audio event. Just as a sound wave is composed of compressions and rarefactions, the audio signal is composed of positive and negative polarity phases.

AC voltage can be expressed in two ways: peak-to-peak (p-p) and root mean square (RMS). In a p-p expression, the voltage between the waveform peaks is measured. The more commonly used RMS value specifies the voltage at roughly 70% of the peak voltage. RMS better describes the "effective" voltage, or the ability of the voltage to do work. The 120V AC power line has a peak value of 170V, but an RMS value of 120V. Whenever you see an audio signal expressed as a voltage—a preamplifier output level, for example—it is virtually always an RMS value.

Manufacturers of power amplifiers sometimes exploit this difference between peak and RMS to overstate a product's power output. An amplifier can deliver more power on peaks than continuously. Chapter 6 ("Power Amplifiers") has a more complete discussion of power-amplifier output ratings.

Electromagnetic Induction, Inductance, and Capacitance

We've learned how voltage is equivalent to electrical pressure, current is the flow of electrons "pushed" by the voltage, and resistance is the opposition to current flow. Now let's look at three more electrical properties very important in audio: electromagnetic induction, inductance, and capacitance.

Electromagnetic induction is the relationship between moving electrons and magnetism; moving electrons produce a magnetic field, and a moving magnetic field causes electrons to flow through a conductor. Many audio devices, from phono cartridges to loudspeakers, rely on electromagnetic induction to work.

Let's first look at how a moving magnetic field causes electrons to flow. If you have a conductor, a magnetic field, and relative motion between them, a current (electron flow) will be *induced* in the conductor. For example, if we move a magnet upward through a coil of wire (the conductor), a voltage will be induced across that wire. A pointer on a voltmeter across that coil will swing in one direction when the magnet is moved. When the magnet stops moving, the pointer will return to its original position—no more voltage is being induced across the coil. Now, if we move the magnet in the opposite direction, a voltage will also be induced, but of opposite polarity to that of the voltage induced by moving the magnet up. The voltmeter pointer will now swing to the opposite side of the meter while the magnet is moving. When the magnet stops moving, the pointer will return to its center zero position.

This is exactly how a phono cartridge works. In a moving-coil cartridge, the coils (left and right audio channels) are attached to the cantilever; the cantilever is moved back and forth by the stylus as the stylus follows the modulations in the record groove. The coils sit in a fixed magnetic field. As the coil moves back and forth, a voltage is induced across the coil—the audio signal. The coil cuts through *magnetic lines of flux* surrounding the magnets, inducing a voltage across the coil. The faster the coil cuts these magnetic lines of flux, the higher the induced voltage. The more turns on the coil, the more lines of flux are cut, and the higher the induced voltage. High-output moving-coil cartridges have more turns on their windings than low-output moving-coils. A moving-magnet cartridge works on exactly the same principle, but with the roles reversed: the magnets move and the coils are fixed.

There's another interesting phenomenon of electromagnetic induction: electrons flowing through a conductor create a magnetic field around that conductor. A conductor connected across a battery's terminals will be surrounded by a magnetic field. If we make current flow in the opposite direction by reversing the battery terminals, the north-south magnetic field will also reverse polarity. The magnetic field's density can be increased by coiling the wire to concentrate the magnetic lines of flux, creating a device called an *inductor*, which creates a property called *inductance*. Inductance is measured in henrys (the unit of inductance) and is represented by the letter L. (The schematic symbol for an inductor is shown in Fig.B-10).

Fig. B-10 The schematic symbol for an inductor.

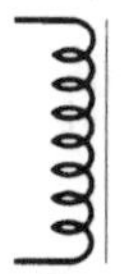

A loudspeaker works on this principle. When current flows through a loudspeaker's voice coil, a magnetic field is set up around that coil. This magnetic field reacts with the fixed magnetic field generated by the magnets surrounding the voice coil. One polarity of the signal-generated magnetic field makes the loudspeaker cone more forward; the opposite polarity makes it move backward. By applying an AC audio signal to the loudspeaker, AC current flow through the voice coil causes a reversing magnetic field to be set up around the voice coil, making the voice coil move back and forth, and with it, the loudspeaker's cone.

Let's look more closely at what happens when alternating current flows through a coil of wire (an inductor). The AC current flow creates a magnetic field around the coil that expands, collapses, expands in the opposite polarity, and collapses again. The constantly changing magnetic field follows the AC sinewave voltage applied across the coil.

We've just satisfied the requirements for electromagnetic induction: a conductor, a magnetic field, and relative motion between them. The relative motion results from the expanding and contracting magnetic field. This fluctuating magnetic field causes magnetic lines of flux to move through the coil, inducing a voltage across that coil.

This induced voltage opposes the applied voltage, reducing current flow. The higher the alternating current frequency, the greater the induced voltage and the greater the opposition to the applied voltage. At DC, there is no expanding and collapsing magnetic field, and thus no induced voltage and no opposition to current flow—the inductor looks electrically just like a simple piece of wire. At a very low frequency, say 5Hz, the magnetic field expands and collapses very slowly, inducing only a very low voltage across the coil to oppose the drive signal. Conversely, at very high frequencies, the rapidly expanding and collapsing magnetic field induces a much higher voltage across the coil to oppose the drive signal.

This opposition to AC current flow in a coil is called *inductive reactance*. The term *reactance* describes how the coil *reacts* to the applied voltage: the higher the frequency of the applied voltage, the greater the opposition to current flow (the higher the reactance). An inductor can be thought of as a frequency-dependent resistor. The higher the frequency, the more it resists current flow.

Inductive reactance is represented by the term X_L. Inductive reactance is proportional to frequency, expressed in the formula $X_L = 2\pi fL$, where f is frequency in Hertz and L is inductance in henrys. For example, a 2-millihenry (2mH) inductor has an inductive reactance of 125.7 ohms at 10kHz. At 20kHz, the inductor's reactance is 251.3 ohms. The higher the frequency, the greater the reactance to the applied voltage.

A power transformer dramatically illustrates how inductive reactance reduces AC current flow. A power transformer is two coils of wire placed next to each other, with one coil connected to a 120V AC power line. The DC resistance of that coil is probably about an ohm. If we put 120V DC across one ohm of resistance, Ohm's Law tells us that a huge amount of current will flow (120A), which would instantly burn up the transformer. But because that applied voltage is AC, the coil's inductive reactance opposes current flow and prevents the transformer coil from burning. At the 60Hz AC line frequency, the transformer looks like an impedance higher than one ohm.

Another reactive element is called *capacitance*, represented by the letter C and shown schematically in Fig.B-11. Just as inductance produces a reactance to an AC signal, capacitance also reacts to AC. While an inductor becomes more reactive at *high* frequencies, the capacitor becomes more reactive at *low* frequencies. The capacitor acts as a resistor that increases its resistance as frequency decreases, exactly the opposite of an inductor. A few paragraphs ago we saw that inductive reactance could be calculated with the formula $X_L = 2\pi fL$. To calculate capacitive reactance (X_C), we use the formula $X_C = 1/2\pi fC$. Note that capacitive reactance is a reciprocal function; as frequency increases, capacitive reactance decreases. The unit of capacitance is the *farad*.

Fig. B-11 The schematic symbol for a capacitor

Filters

We can exploit inductive and capacitive reactance to perform specialized functions in audio circuits. In a two-way loudspeaker, for example, we want only low frequencies to reach the woofer and only high frequencies to reach the tweeter. Consequently, we may design a circuit that looks something like Fig.B-12.

Fig. B-12
Inductors and capacitors filter the audio signal, as in this loud-speaker crossover.

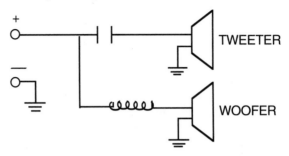

At low frequencies, the capacitor's high reactance opposes current flow. As the frequency increases, the reactance decreases and the capacitor begins to let current flow to the tweeter. At the highest frequencies, the capacitor virtually disappears electrically, allowing maximum current flow. The tweeter is thus protected from low frequencies while high frequencies are allowed to pass. Conversely, the inductor in series with the woofer has a very high reactance at high frequencies, and virtually no reactance at low frequencies.

The capacitor forms a *high-pass filter* and the inductor is a *low-pass filter*. We've just created a simple loudspeaker crossover (practical loudspeaker crossovers are more complex).

A single capacitor or inductor is called a *first-order filter*, producing a *rolloff* of 6dB per octave. Because inductive reactance doubles as the frequency is doubled, the passed voltage is halved when the signal frequency is increased by one octave. Similarly, capacitive reactance is doubled as the frequency is halved by one octave. Because a halving of voltage represents a decrease of 6dB, first-order filters have a rolloff of 6dB per octave. Another term for rolloff is *slope*. First-order filters are also called *single-pole* filters.

Steeper rolloffs can be realized with more inductors and capacitors. *Second-order filters* have a rolloff of 12dB per octave, *third-order filters* roll off at 18dB/octave, and *fourth-order filters* exhibit a 24dB/octave rolloff. Virtually all loudspeaker crossovers have slopes between first-order and fourth-order. These rolloffs are shown in Fig.7-18 on page 200 in the chapter on loudspeakers.

In another combination of a capacitor and an inductor, a *bandpass* filter is created. The bandpass filter will roll off frequencies on either side of the *passband*. A three-way loudspeaker crossover will have a high-pass filter on the tweeter, a low-pass filter on the woofer, and a bandpass filter on the midrange driver.

A filter's *cutoff frequency* is the frequency at which the amplitude is reduced by 3dB. Similarly, the *bandwidth* of an audio device or filter is the frequency span between the –3dB points. All the filters described here are called *passive filters* because they aren't built around an amplifier. Filters that use amplifying devices are called *active filters*.

Capacitors are also used to block direct current, yet pass alternating current. As we'll see later in this chapter, many audio circuits mix DC with the AC audio signal. Putting a capacitor in series with the signal blocks the unwanted DC component and allows the desired AC audio signal to pass. The capacitor looks like an infinitely high resistance at DC, but a low-value resistor to AC signals.

Capacitors can also store a voltage. In fact, the definition of capacitance is the ability to store a charge. If we put a battery across a capacitor, electrons flow from the battery's negative terminal to the capacitor's plate. The voltage source redistributes electrons from one plate of the capacitor to the other. The applied voltage stays across the capacitor even after the battery is removed.

This stored charge can be lethal. A power amplifier with large power-supply capacitors can kill you even if the amplifier hasn't been plugged in for years. Even small capacitors can give you a shock. The storage ability of capacitors can be demonstrated by turning off your power amplifier while it is reproducing music. It takes several seconds for the music to fade after the amplifier's power source has been removed. The amplifier is running off the charge stored in its capacitors.

Impedance

Impedance is the opposition to current flow in an AC circuit, specified in ohms and represented by the symbol Z. Impedance is to an AC signal what resistance is to DC. If we're dealing with DC, opposition to current flow is resistance. If the voltage is AC, opposition to current flow is impedance. Because loudspeakers are driven by AC signals, they have an impedance, not a resistance.

Impedance differs from resistance in that impedance implies that the load is not a simple resistance, but a combination of resistance, inductive reactance, and capacitive reactance.

An audio playback chain is a series of impedances. Every component with an input presents an impedance to the signal driving it. The impedance a component presents to the drive signal is called its *input impedance* (also called *load impedance*). A digital processor's analog output drives the preamplifier's input impedance, the preamplifier drives the power amplifier's input impedance, and the power amplifier drives the loudspeaker's impedance. Impedance can be thought of as the load through which the component must force current.

Components in an audio chain also have an *output impedance, or source impedance*. If you think of a component—a CD player, for example—as an audio signal generator, its output impedance is like a resistance in series with that signal generator. There isn't actually a resistor in series with the output, but the resistor exists conceptually.

Generally, audio products have output impedances of between a few tens of ohms and a few hundred ohms. Input impedances, however, are very high, usually between 10,000 ohms (10k ohms) and 1,000,000 ohms (one Megohm, or one million ohms). The product with a 1M ohm impedance will draw less current through it than one with a 10k ohms input impedance. The higher the input impedance, the easier it is for the source component to drive; the input impedance is less of a load on the source component.

Let's combine our knowledge of Ohm's Law, capacitance, and impedance to examine the interaction between a preamplifier and a power amplifier through a long run of interconnect. Fig.B-13 shows this circuit pictorially and schematically. Because all cables and interconnects have some inherent capacitance, we can represent the interconnect capacitance by the symbol for a capacitor between the signal conductor and ground. The preamp's output impedance is represented by the resistor in series with the signal generator. The power amplifier's input impedance is represented by the resistor inside the power amplifier outline.

Fig. B-13 A pre-amplifier to power amplifier connection shown pictorially and schematically. The interconnect's capacitance is shown as the capacitor in parallel with the power amplifier's input.

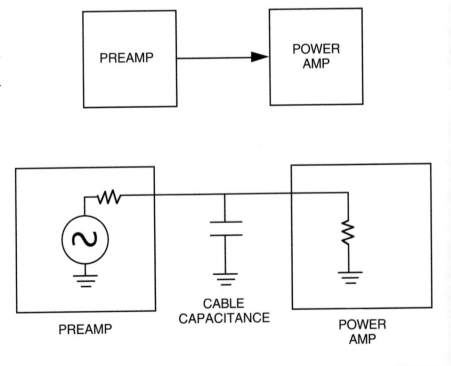

Let's say that the preamp has a very low output impedance, the power amplifier has a high input impedance, and the cable capacitance is low. All these are ideal conditions. The power amplifier's high input impedance means very little current will flow, causing very little voltage drop across the preamplifier's output impedance. Because the cable's capacitance is low, its reactance will remain high up to a very high frequency. Everything works just fine.

But if the preamplifier has a high output impedance and the cable is excessively capacitive, we run into problems. At low frequencies, the cable capacitance has no effect: its capacitive reactance is extremely high. In fact, it's almost as if the capacitor weren't there. But as frequency rises and the capacitive reactance drops, the capacitor looks like a resistor connected to ground. The higher the frequency, the lower the value of the "resistor" connected between the signal and ground. Consequently, as the signal frequency increases, more and more of the drive signal is dropped across the source impedance and less and less across the load (the power amplifier's input). We've just created a low-pass filter. The result is high-frequency rolloff across the power amplifier's input terminals. The capacitor provides high frequencies with an easier path to ground than does the amplifier's input circuit.

Moreover, the greater current flow caused by the power amplifier's low input impedance and the cable capacitance causes the preamplifier's output stage to work harder, perhaps even becoming *current-limited*. This condition occurs when the source can no longer supply the current through the load, resulting in a clipped waveform.

The result of an impedance mismatch and high interconnect capacitance between a preamplifier and power amplifier is a rolled-off treble, lack of air and extension, mushy bass, and loss of dynamics.

We can calculate the –3dB rolloff point for our low-pass filter using the formula $F = 1/2\pi RC$. F is the –3dB point, R is the power amplifier's input impedance in parallel with the source impedance, and C is the interconnect capacitance in farads. Interconnect capacitance is measured in picofarads (10^{-12} farads) per foot, with less than 100pF per foot considered low capacitance.

This example illustrates what can happen with an impedance mismatch between components, particularly if the cable is capacitive. Source components should have an output impedance of less than a few hundred ohms, preferably a few tens of ohms. Input impedances should be at least 47k ohms (a standard value).

Loudspeaker Phase Angle

Another application of our knowledge of impedance, capacitance, and inductance is understanding the concept of *phase angle* in a loudspeaker's impedance. Phase angle describes how reactive a load is compared to the load's resistance.

A loudspeaker impedance measurement includes the impedance magnitude plotted in ohms, but also a separate plot of how reactive the loudspeaker is to the drive signal as a function of frequency. This reactance is caused by the inductors and capacitors in the loudspeaker's crossover. Fig.B-14 is a loudspeaker's impedance magnitude and phase-angle plot. If we performed this measurement on a resistor (which exhibits no inductive or capacitive reactance), we would see straight lines on the impedance-magnitude and phase-angle traces (the latter is dotted). A pure resistor has no phase angle. But because the loudspeaker is reactive, its phase angle and impedance change with frequency.

Fig. B-14 A loudspeaker's impedance magnitude and phase angle

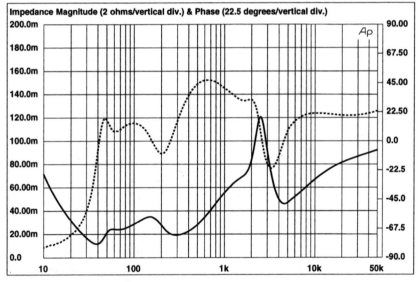

Courtesy *Stereophile*

Phase angle is introduced because capacitive reactance causes voltage to lag slightly behind the current flow in time. In an inductor, the opposite occurs: current lags voltage. Capacitive reactance creates a phase angle of −90°, while inductive reactance creates a phase angle of +90°. When capacitive and inductive reactance are combined, the phase angle may be anywhere between ±90°. When the dotted line on a phase angle plot is above the 0° center line, the loudspeaker is primarily inductive. When the dotted line dips below the 0° center line, the loudspeaker is primarily capacitive. The less severe the phase-angle swings (deviations from a flat line), the less reactive the loudspeaker and the easier it is for the amplifier to drive. A phase-angle trace that stays near the 0°

center line makes the loudspeaker look more like a simple resistor to the power amplifier.

Capacitor Types

Capacitors are critical elements in audio circuit design and manufacture. They are used everywhere in audio products, and can significantly influence the product's sound. Capacitors vary greatly in their physical and electrical properties; some are better than others for use in audio circuits. There are also huge price differences between good and poor capacitors.

Capacitors are formed of two plates separated by an insulator called the *dielectric*. The dielectric can be air, Mylar, ceramic, paper, polystyrene, polypropylene, foil, Teflon, tantalum, or other materials. Capacitors are referred to by their dielectric material: we may say a particular preamplifier uses Teflon capacitors throughout. The best audio capacitors are Teflon, polystyrene, and polypropylene.

One type of capacitor found in power supplies is the *electrolytic* capacitor. These are usually large metal cans that have very high capacitance values. Electrolytics work well in power supplies, but are poor choices for capacitors in the signal path. One manufacturer even gets rid of all electrolytics from the power supply, using much more expensive polypropylene caps instead.

Anatomy of an Audio Product

With this basic knowledge of electronics, let's see how these principles are applied in audio products.

The Power Supply

Every audio component that plugs into a wall outlet contains a power supply. The power supply converts 120V, 60Hz AC power from the wall outlet into the lower DC voltages needed by audio circuits. This is a critical job in high-end audio: the power supply has a large influence on the product's sound quality. Often, the power supply accounts for much of a component's size, weight, and cost. The general thinking in high-end product design is to have extremely simple audio circuits and extremely elaborate power supplies. We want a pure and simple path for the audio signal to follow, and a very clean and stable DC supply.

The first component in the power supply is the *power transformer*. This device *steps down* the 120V AC powerline to a lower AC voltage, perhaps ±30V (we'll see how it does this in a minute). The transformer's schematic symbol is an accurate representation of its construction: it consists of two coils of wire placed next to each other (Fig.B-15).

Fig. B-15 The schematic symbol for a transformer represents its physical structure.

A little earlier we learned that whenever current flows through a conductor, a magnetic field is set up around that conductor. We also learned that whenever we have a conductor, a magnetic field, and relative motion between the two, a voltage is induced. Both principles are in operation in a transformer. When the 60Hz AC flows through the transformer's first coil, called the *primary winding*, an expanding and collapsing magnetic field is set up around this coil. This expanding and collapsing field created around the primary winding induces a voltage across the second coil, called the *secondary winding*. The 60Hz AC signal thus appears across the secondary winding, even though there is no physical connection between this winding and the AC wall outlet.

The voltage induced across the secondary is determined by the *turns ratio* between the primary and secondary. By changing the turns ratio, any value of output voltage can be obtained. Some transformers have multiple secondary windings to supply different circuits. The transformer thus converts 120V, 60Hz AC to a lower 60Hz AC voltage or voltages. The transformer also *isolates* the component from the power line.

Transformers are rated by power capacity, called a *VA* rating (Volt/Amperes). A transformer rated at 1kVA (1000VA), for example, can deliver 100V at 10A (assuming a 1:1 turns ratio). Transformers in low-signal components (preamps, CD players) are typically rated at a few tens of VA, while the largest power amplifier transformers may reach a whopping 5kVA. Such a transformer may weigh more than 100 pounds.

Many audio products use *toroidal* transformers instead of the more conventional *laminated* type. Toroidal transformers are round, and concentrate their magnetic field in a tighter configuration. Toroidals are more expensive than laminated types, but are more efficient and radiate less noise into the surrounding circuitry. Just as the magnetic field surrounding the primary winding induces a voltage across the secondary winding, audio circuitry near the transformer can pick up 60Hz *hum*. Toroidal transformers reduce this risk.

The stepped-down voltage from the transformer's secondary winding is still AC, but we need DC to supply the audio circuits. The next element in the power supply is the *rectifier*, a device that turns AC into DC. Rectifiers are made from diodes, the most basic *semiconductor* element. A diode allows current to flow in one direction but not the other. Fig.B-16 shows the effect of putting a single diode on a transformer's output. The diode allows one polarity to pass, but blocks the 60Hz sinewave's other half (which half it passes—positive or negative—is determined by the diode's direction). In effect, the diode removes one polarity of the signal. Because the resultant voltage never changes polarity, it is technically direct current. This method, called *half-wave rectification*, isn't very efficient. But by putting four diodes together, we can make a *full-wave bridge rectifier* (Fig.B-17). In effect, the other sinewave polarity is "flipped over." The full-wave rectifier produces smoother DC and delivers more power to the supply.

Fig. B-16 A half-wave rectifier passes only one phase of the AC powerline.

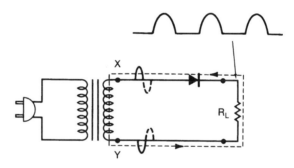

(A) Transformer feeding a half-wave rectifier

Fig. B-17 A full-wave rectifier "flips" over one polarity of the AC powerline.

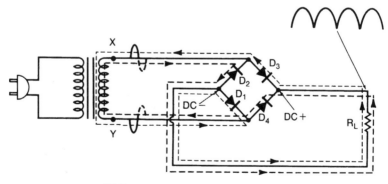

(C) Transformer feeding a bridge rectifier

Copied with permission from *Audio Technology Fundamentals,*, by Alan A. Cohen

The rectifier output is DC (it never changes polarity), but still has AC *ripple* riding on it. Ripple consists of vestiges of the AC signal superimposed on the DC; the DC shifts up and down at 120Hz. Note that a full-wave rectifier produces ripple at 120Hz, not 60Hz, because the negative phase of the sinewave is "flipped" over (shown earlier in Fig.B-17). Ripple is reduced by adding *filter capacitors*, whose storage function smoothes the AC ripple riding on the DC voltage. In fact, filter capacitors are also called *smoothing* capacitors.

The filtered output is now DC with much less ripple, but it still isn't ready to supply our audio circuits. Any changes in the input line voltage will affect the DC voltages supplying the audio circuits—an unacceptable condition. The job of making this DC more stable and at the correct voltage falls on the *voltage regulator*. A voltage regulator maintains a constant output voltage regardless of changes to its input voltage. The voltage regulator's input is DC that may have some ripple and be subject to fluctuation and drift; the regulator's output is a pure, stable, and unwavering DC source. Voltage regulators are fed a voltage slightly higher than the desired output voltage; they can thus maintain a stable output voltage even if the input voltage changes slightly. A typical 12V regulator (the output voltage) may have an input voltage of 15V. This 12V is now good enough to become the power-supply *rail* for the audio circuits. Voltage regulators usually have heat sinks attached to them; the difference between input and output voltage is dissipated as heat.

All these elements—power transformer, rectifier, filter capacitors, and a voltage regulator—are shown schematically in Fig.B-18, and pictorially in Fig.B-19. These drawings are simplified for clarity; a schematic of an actual power supply used in a preamplifier is shown in Fig.5-8 on page 126.

Fig. B-18 A simple power-supply schematic

Fig. B-19 The power supply shown pictorially

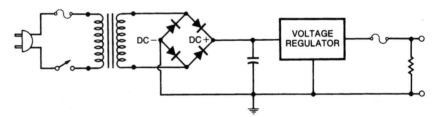

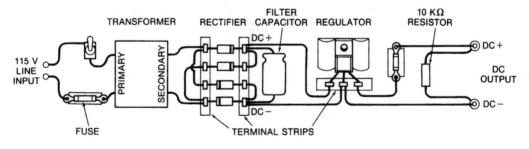

Copied with permission from *Audio Technology Fundamentals* by Alan A. Cohen

The power supply will often produce several DC voltages of different polarities (positive and negative) to supply different parts of the circuit. At the very minimum, a digital processor will need +5V to the digital circuits and ±12V to the analog stage. Most processor have at least four *regulation stages*, with some having up to 15 separately regulated supply voltages. Multiple regulation stages help *isolate* circuits from each other. Different audio circuits can interact with each other through a common regulation stage, degrading performance. For example, if a CD player's tracking servo power supply also fed the analog output stage, the supply voltage would *droop* when the tracking servo demanded current, affecting the analog circuit's performance. Designers agree: the more regulation stages, the better.

Most regulators are integrated circuits (see Fig.B-19). Conversely, some regulation stages are called *discrete* because they use separate transistors, resistors, and capacitors to form the regulator. Discrete regulation is much more expensive to implement, but is generally considered to produce better-sounding products than those using IC regulation. Some very elaborate products use *cascaded* regulation, in which the output of one regulator supplies the input to the second regulator. This ensures a purer, more stable DC supply. The ultimate power supply uses many cascaded discrete regulation stages.

The regulated DC voltages are often *bypassed* with very-low–value (0.01µF) high-quality capacitors. The capacitor is placed physically next to the supplied circuit, and electrically between the power-supply rail and ground. The capacitor provides a path to ground for noise or power-supply–rail disturbances.

Other techniques that contribute to good power-supply performance are high values of filter capacitance, with some of the capacitors located next to the audio circuits they supply. A large transformer is also a plus, even though the VA rating may already exceed the circuits' current requirements. Most designers agree that the bigger the transformer, the better. Separate transformers are also an advantage, further isolating individual circuit elements from each other.

Power supplies are a critical element in the music reproduction chain. Although mediocre supplies will still make the product work, the very finest components are distinguished by elaborate and expensive power supplies. Much of what you pay for in high-quality audio products is in the power supply.

Now let's look at some circuits that the power supply feeds.

Amplifier Circuits

Amplifier circuits are the basic building blocks of preamps, power amps, phono stages, and CD players. If you understand a simple, one-transistor amplifier, you'll have a good grasp of how all amplifiers work.

A transistor is a solid-state semiconductor that has three elements: the *base, emitter,* and *collector.* It can be thought of as a sandwich of these three layers, shown schematically in Fig.B-20a and b. The transistor converts a small signal at the base to a large signal at the collector. If you think of a hose with water flowing through it, the water source is the emitter, and the base is a kink in the hose that opens and closes to allow more or less water to flow.

Fig. B-20 a and b
A transistor's
schematic symbol
(NPN and PNP
types)

(A) NPN transistor   *(B) PNP transistor*

Copied with permission from *Audio Technology Fundamentals* by Alan A. Cohen

Let's see how this works by looking at the single-stage transistor amplifier shown in Fig.B-21. The DC power supply is connected to the collector at the top of the figure. The emitter is at ground potential, meaning it is negative with respect to the collector. Because a voltage exists between the emitter and collector, current wants to flow up through the transistor. The base can prevent or permit current flow, depending on the base voltage. The base is like a control valve that can turn current flow on and off. When the transistor is *turned on* by a tiny base current, a large current flows from the emitter, through the base, and into the collector. When the transistor is *turned off* by a lower base current, no current flows from the emitter to the collector.

Fig. B-21 A simple
one-transistor
amplifier

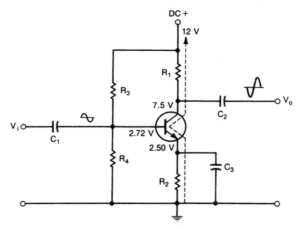

Copied with permission from *Audio Technology Fundamentals* by Alan A. Cohen

If we put an audio signal on the base, current flow from the emitter to the collector will be controlled by that audio signal. When the audio signal is of higher amplitude, the transistor will be more turned on, allowing more current to flow from the emitter to the collector. A low-amplitude audio signal will allow less current to flow through the transistor. A tiny base current thus controls a large current through the emitter and collector. This is how a transistor amplifies an audio signal.

The amount of amplification provided by a transistor is called *gain*, expressed either as the ratio between the input and output voltages, or in decibels (dB). A gain of 10 means that the output signal has ten times the voltage of the input signal; a 1kHz sinewave with an amplitude of 10mV applied to the base will produce a 1kHz sinewave at the collector with an amplitude of 100mV.

In practice, the transistor is partially turned on all the time. A small base current, called the *bias current*, is always present. Bias is essential to making the transistor work. Bias makes the transistor conduct *quiescent current* through the emitter and collector. Quiescent current is the current that flows through the transistor's collector when no input signal is applied to the base. The amount of bias current is carefully selected so that the transistor operates in its linear operating region (Fig.B-22). Bias allows the transistor to amplify both positive and negative phases of the audio signal; because the supply voltage is positive and the emitter is connected to ground, the transistor can never produce a negative voltage at the collector. By making the transistor conduct all the time with bias, the zero crossing point is some voltage between ground and the supply voltage (determined by the values of the emitter and collector resistors). When the input signal swings negative, the output voltage is simply "less positive" than this zero crossing voltage.

Fig. B-22 Bias makes the transistor operate in its linear region.

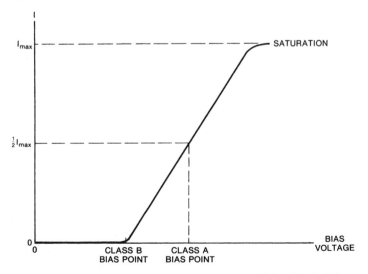

Copied with permission from *Audio Technology Fundamentals* by Alan A. Cohen

As explained in the section on series circuits, two resistances in series will produce a voltage drop across the resistors. This is what happens in a transistor circuit: current flow through the collector and emitter resistors form a *voltage divider*, producing a DC voltage at the collector. When we apply an AC audio signal on top of the bias current, the transistor becomes more and less turned on, amplifying the base current. The signal at the collector is thus a DC voltage with the audio signal riding on it. The final output is an amplified replica of the signal input to the base. In the configuration shown here, called a *common-emitter* amplifier, the output signal is 180° out of phase with the input signal.

Note that the large signal at the output is simply the DC power supply converted to an AC audio signal by the transistor. This is an important point for audio products: the power supply is effectively in the audio signal path. It's easy to conceptualize the power-supply rails as a static DC supply outside the audio signal path. But because the audio signal appears at the collector, and the power supply is also connected to the collector, anything that happens to the power supply—noise, high output impedance, fluctuations—also happens to the audio signal. This is why high-end amplifiers have such elaborate power supplies.

In Fig.B-21, R_1 is the load resistor, R_2 is the emitter resistor that stabilizes the transistor's operation, R_3 and R_4 create a voltage divider that applies the correct bias to the base, and C_3 is a bypass capacitor. C_1 and C_2 are *coupling capacitors*, which block DC from getting into the transistor (C_1) and the next amplification stage (C_2). Because capacitors in the signal path are generally not a good thing, some designers prefer to remove them. An amplifier circuit without coupling capacitors is called *direct-coupled*. If no coupling capacitors are used, DC can be prevented from reaching the amplifier's output with an active device called a *DC servo*.

A technique for decreasing distortion in amplifiers is called *negative feedback*, or just *feedback*. A portion of the amplifier's output signal is returned to the input, reducing distortion. When the feedback *loop* is around a single or several gain stages, the feedback is called *local*. When the feedback is taken from the amplifier's final output and returned to the input stage, the feedback is called *global*. Excessive feedback produces lower distortion figures, but often makes the amplifier sound worse. High-end amplifier designers try to use as little feedback as possible.

Going back to Fig.B-21, we can see that the transistor amplifies the entire audio signal; consequently, it's always turned on—i.e., always conducting current. Because the transistor is always turned on, this amplifier operates in *class-A* mode. Class-A simply means that the transistor amplifies the entire audio signal and is always turned on.

Although it may seem intuitive that transistors would work this way, virtually all power-amplifier output stages use a more efficient technique called *class-A/B*. Class-A/B operation produces less heat and is more efficient than class-A, making class-A/B stages more economical in circuits that must handle lots of current.

In Class A/B, transistors are arranged in *complementary pairs*. One half of the complementary pair is an *NPN* transistor, the other half is a *PNP* transistor. The NPN/PNP designation refers to the transistor's internal structure, which determines the voltage polarities needed to operate the transistor. In a complementary pair, an NPN transistor is connected to a PNP transistor (Fig.B-23). The "top" transistor will handle the positive half of the audio signal, and the bottom transistor will amplify the negative portion of the signal. When the top transistor is conducting, the bottom transistor is turned off, and vice versa. This technique keeps the transistors turned off half the time, producing less heat and reducing stress on the transistors.

Fig. B-23 A complementary output pair of transistors driven by a class-A driver stage

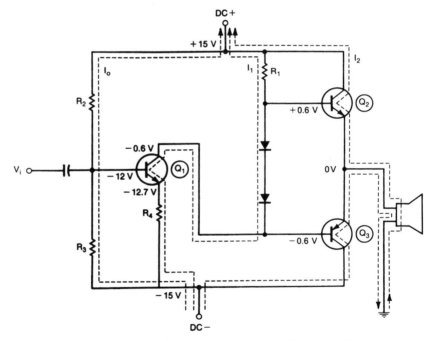

Copied with permission from *Audio Technology Fundamentals* by Alan A. Cohen

The signal driving the complementary pair has been processed by a *phase splitter* before the transistor bases. A phase splitter splits the audio signal into positive and negative phases; the positive phase drives the NPN transistor of the complementary pair, and the negative phase drives the PNP half of the pair.

A Class A/B amplifier is also called a "push-pull" output stage because one transistor "pulls" current while the other transistor "pushes." Current flow is indicated by the directions of the arrows in Fig.B-23.

A true push-pull amplifier actually operates in pure class-B, but virtually all power amplifiers operate in class-A up to a few watts, then switch to class-B operation, hence the "class-A/B" designation. At low signal levels, both halves of the complementary pair always conduct, meaning that the output stage is operating in class-A. The power output level at which the amplifier switches into class-B is determined by the bias current applied to the output transistor bases. More bias current turns the transistors on harder, allowing them to handle both phases of the audio signal up to a higher power output. There's a limit to how much power the amplifier will deliver in class-A; the designer just can't keep increasing the bias current. Maximum class-A power output is determined by how much current the transistors can handle, how well heat is removed from the transistors, and how much current the power supply can deliver. Pure class-A amplifiers are huge, very heavy (massive power transformers), generate lots of heat, and are very expensive in terms of "dollars per watt."

Class-A operation produces less distortion than class- A/B, and generally sounds better. A kind of distortion in class-B amplifiers called *crossover distortion* can produce a waveform discontinuity at the zero crossing point where one transistor turns off and the other turns on. The two halves of the complementary pair aren't biased identically, producing crossover distortion. This condition can't occur in class-A amplifiers. Class-A output stages have other another big advantage: the transistors are always at the same temperature regardless of the signal they are amplifying, making the output stage more stable and linear.

(Chapter 6 contains a discussion of amplifier output stages and their musical qualities.)

The NPN and PNP transistors described previously are called *bipolar* devices because current can flow in two directions through the transistor. Another type of transistor, called the *Junction Field Effect Transistor* (JFET), is often used in small-signal applications. The JFET is called a *unipolar* device because current can flow in only one direction. A JFET, shown schematically in Fig.B-24, has a *gate*, a *source*, and a *drain*, which correspond to the base, emitter, and collector in our NPN and PNP transistors. JFETs are often used in amplifier input stages for their high input impedance and low noise. JFETs are generally quieter than bipolar transistors, which makes them ideal for circuits that need lots of gain. They are also turned on (biased) by voltage rather than by current, as are bipolar transistors. JFETs are found only in small-signal circuits. In addition, JFETs are also used as electronic switches.

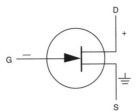

Fig. B-24 A JFET's gate, source, and drain correspond to the bi-polar transistor's base, emitter, and collector.

Another type of field-effect transistor is called the MOSFET (MOS stands for Metal Oxide Semiconductor). MOSFETs are sometimes used in power-amplifier output stages.

Amplifier Distortion

All the amplifier circuits we've talked about produce distortion—their output signals aren't exact replicas of their input signals. Instead, the signals are changed in certain ways. In *harmonic distortion*, harmonics of the input signal appear in the output. For example, if a 100Hz sinewave is input to the amplifier, the output will be a 100Hz sinewave, but with the harmonics of 100Hz (the second harmonic at 200Hz, third harmonic at 300Hz, fourth at 400Hz, etc.) added to the signal.

Harmonic distortion is expressed as a percentage of the output signal. The term *Total Harmonic Distortion*, or *THD*, is an expression of the percentage of all the harmonic components combined. For example, if the amplifier puts out 10V and the harmonic distortion products are 10mV, the amplifier has 0.1% THD. Although THD is a common amplifier specification, a more instructive analysis of harmonic distortion involves examining *which* harmonics are produced by the amplifier. Second- and third-harmonic distortion components aren't nearly as objectionable as upper-order harmonic distortion components such as the fifth, seventh, and ninth. In fact, 10% second-harmonic distortion is less musically objectionable than 0.5% seventh-harmonic. We can quickly see that a single THD figure tells us very little about the audibility of an amplifier's distortion. All amplifiers produce different harmonic distortion spectra—one possible reason why they sound different.

Another distortion in amplifiers is called *intermodulation distortion*, or *IMD*. When a signal of two frequencies is input to an amplifier, the amplifier will output the two frequencies, plus the *sum* and *difference* of those frequencies. For example, if we drive an amplifier with a mix of 100Hz and 10kHz, the amplifier's output will be 100Hz and 10kHz, *plus* 9.9kHz (the *difference* between 100Hz and 10kHz) and 10.1kHz (the *sum* of 100Hz and 10kHz). In fact, intermodulation distortion produces a infinite number of intermodulation products. Like harmonic distortion, intermodulation distortion is expressed as a percentage of the output signal.

Amplifiers can also distort the audio waveform's transient character, a distortion called *slew-rate limiting*. If the steepness of the input signal's attack is faster than the amplifier's ability to respond, slew-rate limiting will occur. An amplifier's slew rate, measured in volts per microsecond (V/μs), describes how much voltage the amplifier can swing in a specified time period (1μs). If the amplifier can swing 20V/μs and the input signal has transient signals that swing faster than 20V/μs, the amplifier will distort the music's dynamic structure. Slew rate is often referred to as an amplifier's "speed."

Vacuum Tube Amplifiers

Vacuum tube amplifiers are very similar in operation to transistor amplifiers, but are generally much simpler. The three elements in a tube are the *control grid*, *cathode*, and *plate*, shown schematically in Fig.B-25. These correspond to the base, emitter, and collector of the bipolar transistor. The cathode emits electrons, the plate collects them, and the control grid controls how many electrons flow through the tube from cathode to plate. This most basic form of tube is called a *triode*.

Fig. B-25 The three elements of a vacuum tube are the grid, cathode, and plate.

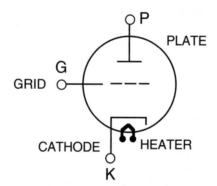

One more element is needed to make the tube work: the *filament*, or *heater*. The heater is the part of the tube that glows, heating the cathode to a high temperature. When the cathode is heated, electrons are given off, a phenomenon called *thermionic emission*. These electrons "boiling" on the cathode surface want to flow through the vacuum to the positively charged plate, but the grid is in the way. The voltage applied to the grid determines how many electrons jump from the cathode to the plate. The grid is a mesh of wire that produces an electric field that controls the flow of electrons, yet doesn't impede them on their way to the plate. By applying an audio signal to the grid, we can control a large current flow though the tube.

In addition to amplifying audio signals, triodes are also used as *output buffer* amplifiers in a configuration called a *cathode follower*. The cathode follower has a voltage gain of less than one (meaning it provides no amplification), but has other attributes, such as a high input impedance and low output impedance. In tubed digital processors and preamplifiers, cathode followers are often the last stage before the output jacks.

Another tube type, called a *pentode*, is often used in amplifier output stages. A pentode is essentially a triode with two additional elements, called the *screen grid* and the *suppressor grid*. Both of these elements are between the control grid and plate. When connected to a voltage, the two additional grids affect the electric field within the tube, and provide much higher voltage gain than is possible with a triode. While triode voltage gain may be between 10 and 50, pentodes can provide voltage gains of up to 500. Most low-level tubed circuits—such as preamplifier input, gain, and output stages, and power-amplifier input and driver stages—use triodes for their better sound. Pentode stages are usually reserved for tubed output stages where high amplification is needed. Some tubed power amplifiers use triode output stages, but their power output is relatively low. However, they sound extremely good.

Tubed amplifiers usually have much higher power-supply voltages than do transistor amplifiers. Where the collector supply voltage in a transistor amplifier may be 15-100V, tube plate voltages can run as high as 800V. The plate voltage is often called the "B+" supply. Further, tubed amplifiers need a high current supply—usually 6V or 12V—for the tubes' heaters.

(See Chapter 6 for more discussion of tubed power amplifiers.)

Operational Amplifiers

An *operational amplifier*, or *op-amp*, is an integrated circuit capable of amplifying audio signals. The op-amp replaces many transistors, capacitors, and resistors with a tiny plastic or metal package. Very few external components are needed to build an audio circuit based on op-amps—just supply them with a DC power supply, a *feedback resistor*, and an input signal, and they work. A typical op-amp circuit for audio signal amplification is shown in Fig.B-26.

In theory, an op-amp is ideal for audio circuits: it has a very high input impedance, very low output impedance, and can provide high gain over a wide bandwidth. They are much easier and cheaper to implement than *discrete* circuits made of transistors, capacitors, and resistors. Unfortunately, most of them don't sound as good as discrete circuits. The very best audio components use discrete circuitry, while budget and moderately priced products usually use op-amps. Some products employing op-amps have sounded superb, however.

Fig. B-26 A simple op-amp circuit

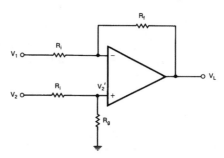

Copied with permission from *Audio Technology Fundamentals* by Alan A. Cohen

An op-amp has two inputs, one output, and pins for the DC power supply. The op-amp is typically supplied with ±12V DC from the power supply. It has two input terminals, marked + and –, called the *non-inverting input* and the *inverting input*, respectively. A signal input to the non-inverting input will produce an output signal of the same polarity as the input signal. Conversely, an input signal at the inverting input will produce an output signal of opposite polarity to the input signal. Op-amps can thus function as inverting or non-inverting amplifiers. The value of the feedback resistor determines the op-amp's gain.

Op-amps can be used as voltage amplifiers, active filters, or output buffer amplifiers (they also have thousands of uses not applicable to audio circuits).

The op-amp's two inputs make it ideal for circuits that need a *differential input*. A differential signal, also called a *balanced* signal, is composed of two signals of opposite polarity. These two signals are 180° out of phase with each other; when one is at peak positive, the other is at peak negative. (Balanced signals are explained in detail in Chapter 11.) When fed signals at both inputs, the op-amp will amplify and pass only the *difference* between those two signals. The two out-of-phase signals will be amplified and combined into one signal at the op-amp's output, but any noise, distortion, or spurious junk common to both polarities will be not be amplified by the op-amp. The phenomenon by which a differential amplifier rejects signals common to both channels is called *common-mode rejection*; the op-amp's ability to reject signals common to both channels is called its *common-mode rejection ratio*, or *CMRR*.

The op-amp driven with a differential signal naturally converts a balanced signal to an unbalanced signal. Many audio components with balanced inputs have a differential amplifier at the input, which converts the balanced signal to a single-ended (unbalanced) signal that the component then amplifies.

Digital Electronics

Digital electronics are becoming increasingly important in audio recording and reproduction. Not only CD players and digital processors use digital electronics: more and more control and switching functions in preamps and power amps are being handled by digital circuits.

Simply, digital circuits operate in one of two states: on or off. The "On" state is represented by a voltage (such as +5V), and "Off" is represented by no voltage (also called *ground*). The terms *high* and *low*, or *one* and *zero*, also describe the two conditions in digital circuits. Unlike an analog signal that has a continuously varying amplitude, digital signals are a train of high and low pulses. Digital circuits are also called *binary* circuits to describe the two-state nature of a digital signal.

In digital signals, information is represented as a series of high and low states. Each state carries one piece of information, or *bit*. (Appendix C explains how binary coding can represent numbers, which in turn can represent an audio signal. Binary coding can store virtually any sort of information; this book's text and graphics were stored as binary code.)

The building blocks of digital electronics are called *logic gates*. A logic gate has more than one input, but only one output. Logic gates are made with tiny transistors that are either fully turned on or fully turned off. Simple logic gates can make basic decisions. For example, an *OR gate* will produce a high output if either input #1 *or* input #2 is high. A two-input *AND gate* will produce a high output if input #1 *and* input #2 are high. Digital electronics use many other types of logic gates.

Logic gates can be arrayed to perform nearly any mathematical task. In practice, many hundreds of thousands of gates comprise digital circuits. These gates are combined into *integrated circuits*, or ICs. Several hundred thousand gates can be put on a single IC.

In the next appendix, we'll see how an audio signal can be stored in digital form.

Appendix C: Digital Audio Basics

Introduction

Throughout the history of recorded sound, the goal has been to capture an acoustic event by storing a mechanical or magnetic representation of the original acoustic waveform. The modulations in an LP groove, for example, are an analog of the acoustic wave that was originally heard as music. The more alike the groove modulations and the acoustic waveform, the higher the fidelity. Tiny changes in the shape of that squiggly line—inevitably introduced in record cutting, pressing, and playback—produced an almost infinite variability in sound quality.

The advent of digital audio has fundamentally changed the way audio is encoded, stored, and played back. Rather than attempting to preserve the acoustic waveform directly, digital audio converts that waveform into a numerical representation. The numbers representing the waveform are stored and later converted back into an analog signal. Because those discrete numbers can be stored and recovered more precisely than the infinitely variable analog signal, digital audio has the potential to exceed the musical performance of analog media.

I say "potential" because, in many respects, digital audio has yet to sound better than the best analog formats. Virtually anyone who's listened to a live microphone feed, then the same signal played back both from analog tape and after encoding into digital form, will attest that the analog tape produces a truer representation of the music. Similarly, a comparison of a properly played LP and the CD of the same music reveals musical virtues in the analog representation not heard from the digital medium.

This isn't to say that analog is without flaw; rather, it suggests that the distortions generated by digital audio are less sonically benign than those from analog media.

Fortunately, this state of affairs is only temporary; digital audio is still in its infancy and will undoubtedly improve. We are only now beginning to discover that building digital audio products is a vastly more exacting process than theory suggests. Although some audiophiles shun digital, it's shortsighted to summarily reject all digital audio based on the crude sound provided by the technologies of digital's first decade. The future promises much more than that.

With that background, let's take a look at how music can be converted into numbers and back into music again.

Binary Number System

All digital audio systems—and digital electronics in general—use the *binary* number system. "Binary" means "two," reflecting the two possible values in the binary, or base 2, number system: 0 and 1. A binary number of these two values strung together can represent any quantity we want, as can the ten values of the decimal system we're so familiar with.

When we count in decimal and reach the highest digit (nine), the ones place is reset to zero and the sum is carried to the next column, producing the number 10. This number is a code that represents a 1 in the tens column and a 0 in the 1s column—one ten, no ones. The position of a digit indicates the weight given that digit.

Just as there is no single digit greater than nine in decimal notation, there is no single digit greater than 1 in binary notation. Consequently, when we count in binary, we reset and carry with every count. For example, the number 01 in binary represents the decimal number 1. If we add the binary numbers 01 and 01, we reset the ones column and carry to the next column, producing the binary number 10. This represents a 1 in the twos column and a 0 in the 1s column, or the number 2 (expressed in decimal). Binary addition works like this:

01	10	11
+01	+01	+01
10	11	100

Just as the position of a digit within a decimal number changes its value by a factor of ten (ones, tens, hundreds, thousands, etc.), the position of a binary digit changes its value by a factor of 2. For example, the binary number 0101 indicates a 1 in the 1s column, a 0 in the 2s column, a 1 in the 4s column, and a 0 in the 8s column. The binary number 0101 thus represents the decimal quantity 5. (Fig.C-1 shows binary and decimal equivalences.)

	Binary	Decimal
Fig. C-1 Binary and decimal equivalences	**Binary**	**Decimal**
	0000	0
	0001	1
	0010	2
	0011	3
	0100	4
	0101	5
	0110	6
	0111	7
	1000	8
	1001	9
	1010	10
	1011	11
	1100	12
	1101	13
	1110	14
	1111	15

Any decimal number can be represented by binary notation, provided the binary number is long enough. The highest number that can be represented in binary notation is 2^x, where x is the number of places. For example, a binary number with four places can represent any decimal number between 0 and 15 (2^4). The number 15 in binary is 1111: a one in the 8s column, a one in the 4s column, a one in the 2s column, and a one in the 1s column.

Each of these positions in a binary number is called a *bit*, short for *binary digit*. The greater the number of bits, the higher the number we can represent. The bit in the position of highest value in a binary number (usually at the far left) has the greatest effect on the number's value and is called the *Most Significant Bit*, or *MSB*. The bit in the position of lowest value in the binary number (usually the far right column) is called the *Least Significant Bit*, or *LSB*.

Binary notation makes computers and electronic circuits simpler and more practical. The electronic circuit or device need operate in only two states: one or zero, on or off, yes or no. If a voltage is present, we call that binary 1; if no voltage is present, that represents binary 0. These conditions relate to a transistor being fully biased on (binary 1) or fully biased off (binary 0). Similarly, a north-south polarization of a magnetic medium could represent binary 1, and a south-north polarization might indicate binary 0.

In digital audio, the analog signal is represented by a stream of these binary numbers. In the next sections, we'll see exactly how music can be represented by binary numbers.

Sampling and Quantization

Sampling and quantization are the cornerstones of digital audio. The two distinct but interrelated processes form the basis for all digital audio systems. To see how sampling and quantization can preserve an analog audio signal as a series of numbers, let's first look at an audio signal's characteristics.

An analog audio signal is a voltage that varies over time. The faster the variation over time, the higher the audio signal's frequency. The greater the amplitude swings, the louder the signal. The audio signal thus has two properties—time and amplitude—that must be encoded to correctly preserve that signal.

An LP record is a good example of how time and amplitude information are preserved. The side-to-side modulations in the record groove encode the amplitude information; the greater the modulation, the higher the signal amplitude. The time information is encoded by the LP's rotation, which must be the same on playback as when the disc was recorded. If we change the speed of the LP, we change the time relationship and thus the audio signal's frequency.

Digital audio must also preserve the time and amplitude information of an audio signal. But instead of encoding and storing those characteristics continuously as in an LP groove, digital audio preserves time and amplitude in discrete units.

A digital audio system encodes the signal's time information by *sampling* the audio signal at discrete time intervals. The amplitude information is encoded by generating a number at each sample point that represents the analog waveform's amplitude at sample time—a process called *quantization*. Time sampling and amplitude quantization are the foundations of digital audio: sampling preserves the time information, quantization preserves the amplitude information.

Sampling and quantization produce a series of binary numbers—called *words*—that represent the analog waveform. When those binary words are converted back into voltages with the same timing reference as when they were first sampled, the analog audio waveform is roughly reconstructed. The original waveform is recovered by smoothing the staircase with a low-pass filter. Sampling and quantization thus convert a continuous analog function (the continuously varying voltage of the analog waveform) into a series of discrete binary numbers. Fig.C-2 shows how a continuous analog waveform is converted into binary numbers, then back into a continuous analog waveform.

Fig. C-2 Graphical representation of the signal flow in a complete PCM digitization system

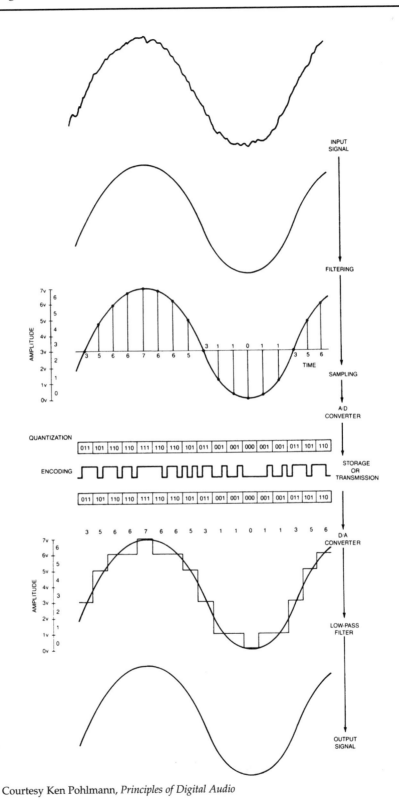

Courtesy Ken Pohlmann, *Principles of Digital Audio*

Sampling Rate, Nyquist Theorem, and Aliasing

The speed at which the samples are taken is called the *sampling rate,* or *sampling frequency.* The sampling rate determines the highest audio frequency that can be correctly encoded. Specifically, the sampling rate must be at least twice as high as the highest audio signal to be preserved. The compact disc format, for example, samples the analog signal at 44,100 times per second (44.1kHz), which provides an audio bandwidth of about 20kHz.

This fundamental relationship between sampling frequency and audio bandwidth was stated in the now-famous Nyquist Theorem. In 1928, telegraph engineer Harry Nyquist postulated that in any sampled system, the sampling rate must be at least twice as high as the highest frequency we want to encode.

If we violate the Nyquist theorem and sample a signal with a frequency higher than half the sampling rate, a form of distortion called *aliasing* occurs. Aliasing creates new frequencies in the sampled signal that weren't present in the original signal. Specifically, if we sample a 33kHz sinewave with a 48kHz sampling frequency, a new signal at 15kHz (48kHz minus 33kHz) is created. Once aliasing occurs, there is no way to remove the spurious alias components from the signal. The term *alias* comes from the fact that the incorrectly sampled signal assumes a completely new identity as a lower-frequency signal. Aliasing is sometimes called "foldback" because the incorrectly sampled high-frequency signal folds back into the audioband.

The only way to prevent aliasing is to never let the sampler see a signal higher in frequency than half the sampling rate. This is accomplished with an *input low-pass filter* that removes all energy above half the sampling frequency. This input filter, called an *anti-aliasing filter,* is an essential part of all digital audio systems. It allows audioband frequencies to pass, but rapidly attenuates the signal just below half the sampling rate. These filters have been a significant source of sonic degradation in digital audio, particularly in early CD releases, when the filters were more crude.

Armed with this knowledge that the input signal is band-limited, we can address the common question of newcomers to digital audio: What happens to the information *between* the samples? If there are squiggles in the waveform between samples, won't that information be lost by the sampling process?

The answer is that there is *no* information between samples. If the input signal is properly band-limited, those squiggles will be removed by the anti-aliasing filter. And if the appropriate sampling rate is chosen for the filter's cutoff frequency, the sampler will perfectly encode any waveform input to it. In Fig.C-2 shown earlier, the input filter removed all energy above 20kHz (squiggles in the uppermost sinewave) before the signal was sampled.

Let's take the case of a 40kHz sampling frequency and a 20kHz sinewave. Even though the sampler sees only two samples per waveform, that's enough information to perfectly encode that 20kHz sinewave. Fig.C-3 shows the original 20kHz waveform (top) and the resultant waveform after sampling (the squarewave). We know from Appendix A that a squarewave is a sinewave combined with all its odd-order harmonics; these harmonics are represented as the four high-frequency waveforms below the 20kHz square wave. When these harmonics are removed by an output low-pass filter, we're left with a 20kHz sinewave—the same signal we started with.

Fig. C-3 A 20kHz sinewave sampled at 40kHz produces a square wave. Low pass filtering removes the harmonics above 20kHz, recovering the 20kHz sinewave.

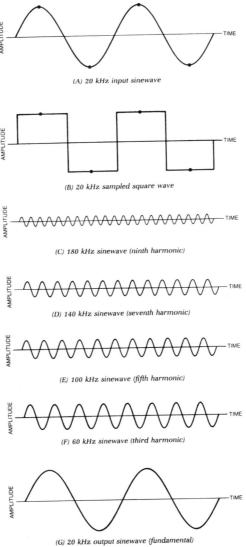

(A) 20 kHz input sinewave

(B) 20 kHz sampled square wave

(C) 180 kHz sinewave (ninth harmonic)

(D) 140 kHz sinewave (seventh harmonic)

(E) 100 kHz sinewave (fifth harmonic)

(F) 60 kHz sinewave (third harmonic)

(G) 20 kHz output sinewave (fundamental)

Courtesy Ken Pohlmann, *Principles of Digital Audio*

We can see from this worst-case example that sampling is a perfectly lossless process: the reconstructed waveform is theoretically identical to the input waveform. This is true provided that the input signal is properly band-limited and an appropriate sampling rate for the filter's characteristics is chosen. Digital audio has its problems (which I'm about to discuss), but sampling theory isn't one of them.

One mechanism, however, by which today's digital audio degrades musical quality is too low a sampling frequency. Although our upper limit of hearing is 20kHz (if you're over 30, 16kHz is a more accurate figure), research has shown that increasing the bandwidth from 20kHz to 40kHz improves musical reproduction. Although we can't hear 40kHz sinewaves, removing energy above 20kHz from the signal reduces the music's sense of openness, transient attack, and natural quality.

Quantization

We've seen how sampling preserves the time information in an audio signal; now let's look at how quantization encodes the amplitude information.

Quantization generates a binary number that represents the analog waveform's amplitude at sample time. The binary number is a digital representation of the audio signal's analog voltage when the sample is taken.

The number of bits available to encode the audio waveform's amplitude is called the *quantization word length*. Just as the sampling rate determines the digital audio system's bandwidth, the quantization word length determines the digital audio system's dynamic range, resolution, and distortion level. Most digital audio systems today use a minimum of 16-bit words, with state-of-the-art systems using 20-bit words. The longer the word length, the greater the fidelity to the original signal.

Quantization word length defines the number of steps available to encode the audio signal. Specifically, the number of steps is 2^x, where x is the number of bits in the word. For example, 16-bit quantization provides 2^{16} steps (65,536) to quantize the analog signal amplitude. An 18-bit system quadruples this figure to 262,144, and a 20-bit quantization word length provides 1,048,576 quantization steps. The longer the word length, the wider the dynamic range, the lower the distortion and noise, and the higher the resolution.

Unlike sampling, which is a lossless process, quantization produces errors in the encoded signal. Converting an infinitely variable analog function into a discrete number is inherently an approximation. This error occurs because the amplitude represented by a given quantization word is virtually never the signal's exact analog voltage. The difference between the analog signal's actual amplitude and the amplitude represented by the quantization word is called *quantization error*.

Fig.C-4 shows how quantization error occurs. The analog amplitude values don't exactly coincide with the values represented by the quantization words. For example, the first sample (the vertical dotted line to the far left) falls between the quantization levels 100111 and 101000. There is no value "100111.25," so the quantizer simply rounds off to the nearest discrete quantization value (100111), even though that number isn't quite correct. The difference between the voltage represented by 100111 (1.3V) and the audio signal's actual voltage (1.325V) represents quantization error. When the audio signal is reconstructed, the slightly wrong binary number 100111 will generate a slightly wrong analog amplitude. The result is a distortion of the original waveform.

Fig. C-4
Quantization error is limited to one-half LSB.

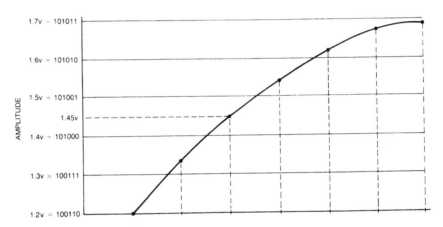

Courtesy Ken Pohlmann, *Principles of Digital Audio*

The worst case is when the analog amplitude falls exactly between two quantization levels as occurs at the second sample in Fig.C-4; the difference between the analog amplitude and the quantization word representing that amplitude is the greatest.

Quantization error can be expressed as a percentage of the least significant bit (LSB). At the first sample, the quantization error was one-quarter of an LSB. At the second sample, the error was one-half of an LSB. Note that quantization error can never exceed half the amplitude value of an LSB. Consequently, the smaller the quantization step size, the less the quantization error. Adding one bit to the quantization word length doubles the number of quantization steps and halves the quantization error. Because such a halving represents a difference of 6dB, the signal-to-noise ratio of a digital system improves by 6dB for each additional bit in the quantization word. A digital system with 18-bit quantization will have 12dB less quantization noise than a system with 16-bit quantization.

We can also approximate the signal-to-noise ratio of a digital system by multiplying the number of bits in the quantization word by 6. Sixteen-bit quantization provides a theoretical dynamic range of about 96dB. A 20-bit digital audio system has a dynamic range of about 120dB, or 24dB higher than a 16-bit system.

Quantization error is audible as a rough, granular sound on low-level signals, particularly reverberation decay. Instead of hearing the sound decay into silence, the reverberation decay grows in coarseness and grain as the signal decays. This is because the quantization error becomes a greater percentage of the signal as the signal's amplitude decreases.

This increase in distortion as the signal level drops is unique to digital audio; all analog recording formats exhibit higher distortion at *high* signal levels. This situation presents unusual challenges: an increase in distortion as signal level decreases makes that distortion much more audible. Increasing the word length to 20 from 16 bits significantly reduces this problem.

Note that signal-to-noise ratio and distortion figures specified for a digital audio system are with a full-scale signal. Most of the time, a music signal is well below full-scale and therefore closer to the noise floor. The distortion isn't a function of how many bits the system has available, but the number of bits used by the signal at any given moment. This is why distortion and noise are inversely proportional to signal amplitude, and why digital audio has problems with low-level signals.

These factors make setting recording levels in a digital system an art completely different from setting analog recording levels. Ideally, the highest peak over the entire audio program should just reach full-scale digital (using all the bits). If the recording level is set so that the highest peak reaches –6dB, this is equivalent to throwing away one bit of the quantization word, with the attendant 6dB reduction in signal-to-noise ratio. And if the analog signal amplitude is higher than the voltage represented by the highest number, the quantizer simply runs out of bits and repeats the highest number, making the waveform peaks flat. This highly distorted waveform produces an unacceptable "crunching" sound on peaks. If you have a DCC or DAT machine, you can look at the recording levels on compact discs by taking the digital output from a CD transport and plugging it into the digital recorder. The recorder's meters will show the exact levels recorded on the CD. If the highest peaks never reach full-scale, some resolution has been needlessly lost.

Note that an audio program with a very wide dynamic range will be closer to the quantization noise floor more of the time than a signal with limited dynamic range. The peaks on the wide dynamic range signal will be set just below full-scale, and the much lower level signal will consequently be encoded with fewer bits. This is a strong incentive for recording or mastering engineers to compress the music's dynamic range.

Digital signal levels are referenced to a full-scale signal, which occurs when all the bits are used and no higher signal can be coded. This reference level is called 0dBFS, with FS standing for "full-scale." We may refer to a signal as –20dBFS, meaning it is 20dB below full scale.

Dither

The most extreme case of quantization error occurs when the signal amplitude is less than one LSB (Fig.C-5). This low-level signal isn't encoded at all by the quantizer: the quantizer outputs the same code at each sample point and the information is completely lost (C and D). If the signal does traverse quantization steps, the encoded signal is a squarewave, which represents a significant distortion of the original signal. This suggests that any information lower in amplitude than the LSB will be lost.

Fig. C-5
Quantization error is large relative to a signal traversing only a few quantization steps.

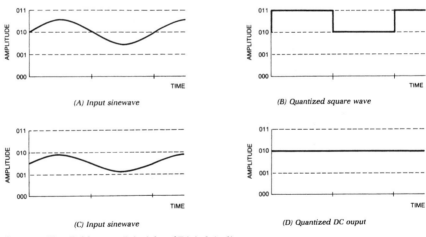

(A) Input sinewave

(B) Quantized square wave

(C) Input sinewave

(D) Quantized DC ouput

Courtesy Ken Pohlmann, *Principles of Digital Audio*

Fortunately, this limit can be overcome by adding a small amount of noise, called *dither*, to the audio signal. Dither allows a quantizer to resolve signals below the LSB, and greatly improves the sound of digital audio.

Fig.C-6 is identical to Fig.C-5 shown earlier, but this time we've added a small amount of white noise to the audio signal. This noise causes the audio signal to traverse quantization levels, allowing the signal to be encoded. The original sinewave is better preserved in the pulse width modulation signal of Fig.C-6.

Fig. C-6 Dither can alleviate the effects of quantization error.

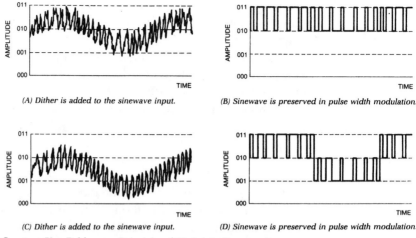

(A) Dither is added to the sinewave input.

(B) Sinewave is preserved in pulse width modulation.

(C) Dither is added to the sinewave input.

(D) Sinewave is preserved in pulse width modulation.

Courtesy Ken Pohlmann, *Principles of Digital Audio*

Dither reduces quantization artifacts, allows the system to resolve information lower in amplitude than one-half the least significant bit, and makes a digital audio system sound more like analog. Among other benefits, dither improves low-level resolution and smoothes reverberation decay. Without dither, reverberation decay gets granular in texture, then seems to drop off into a black hole. It's ironic that a small amount of analog white noise can greatly improve the performance of digital audio. Still, despite the great advantages of dither, we do end up paying a small penalty in decreased signal-to-noise ratio.

Digital Audio Storage

Once the audio signal is in the digital domain, we must store it on some medium. Common storage formats include the compact disc, magnetic tape, magneto-optical discs, and computer hard disks.

One may intuitively conceptualize a digital audio recording system as storing the binary information representing the audio signal directly on the medium. For example, a reflective spot on a CD could represent binary one, a non-reflective spot binary zero. In practice, however, digital audio is always encoded with a modulation scheme. Further, a significant amount of additional information is added to the raw audio data.

Every encoding scheme increases the storage capacity of the medium and facilitates data recovery. The Eight-to-Fourteen Modulation (EFM) encoding scheme used in the CD is a good example of encoding. The disc surface is a spiral track of small indentations called *pits* and flat areas called *land*. A transition from pit-to-land or land-to-pit represents binary one; all other surfaces (pit bottom or land) represent binary zero. The pattern of pit and land is created by the EFM encoding: 8 audio bits are converted into 14 bits for storage on the CD. These 14-bit words are linked by 3 "merging" bits to produce 17 bits for 8 audio bits. The result is a specific pattern of ones and zeros that follow certain rules. For example, each binary one is separate from other binary ones by a minimum of two zeros and a maximum of ten zeros. Although EFM encoding more than doubles the number of bits to be recorded, it actually increases the storage capacity of the CD compared to unmodulated coding. Note that both left and right audio channels as well as this additional information are encoded into a single serial datastream.

The compact disc is also a good example of how audio data are mixed with non-audio data and stored on the medium. The CD datastream is formatted into structures called *frames*. A CD frame (Fig.C-7) contains a synchronization pattern to identify the beginning of a block, bits that contain information about the signal (pre-emphasis, elapsed time, data format, etc.), and error-correction information. Between EFM coding, error correction, subcode, and synchronization, only about a third of the data stored on a CD are actual audio data. All digital audio-storage formats add non-audio data and structure the data into clearly defined blocks.

Fig. C-7 The CD frame format prior to EFM modulation

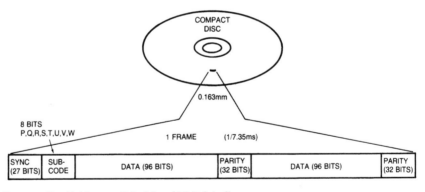

Courtesy Ken Pohlmann, *Principles of Digital Audio*

For a full discussion of how audio data are stored and recovered from the compact disc, see the section in Chapter 8 on how CD transports work.

Error Correction

No storage or transmission medium is perfect. LPs have ticks and pops, and analog magnetic tape has imperfections in the magnetic coating that causes a momentary loss of high frequencies. In analog recording, nothing can be done about these errors; we must live with their sonic imperfections.

Digital audio, however, provides an opportunity to make the audio signal virtually impervious to media imperfections. Lost or damaged data can be reconstructed with error-correction techniques. Error correction doesn't merely approximate the missing data; in most cases it can precisely restore the lost information bit for bit. For example, the compact disc's error-correction system can completely correct for up to nearly 4000 consecutive missing bits. These errors could result from poor-quality disc manufacturing, or scratches on the disc from mishandling. Without error correction, the CD simply wouldn't function. The official CD specification—called the "Red Book"—allows a Block Error Rate (BLER) of 220 errors per second.

The two principles on which error correction is based are *redundancy* and *interleaving*. Redundant data is information added to the signal that isn't necessary to decode the signal—unless that signal is corrupted. The crudest form of redundancy is simply to store the data twice. Data corrupted in one spot is unlikely to be corrupted at the second storage location. A more efficient technique transmits a *checksum* with the data that indicates if the data has been reliably retrieved. In practice, error-correction schemes are enormously complex.

Digital audio media are subject to two kinds of errors: *bit errors* and *burst errors*. Bit errors are short in duration and easy to correct. Burst errors, however, affect long, consecutive streams of data. Not only is a large chunk of data missing, but the redundant information accompanying that data is also lost and the chance of correction is reduced.

A technique called *interleaving* increases the possibility that a burst error can be corrected. Interleaving scatters data to different areas of the media. After deinterleaving, a long burst error is broken up into many shorter errors which are more easily corrected.

If the error is so large that it cannot be completely corrected, the error is *concealed* by approximating the missing data. Some concealed errors may be audible as a click or pop sound. This is a rare occurrence; the CD's error-correction system is so good that very few discs—even those abused and scratched—have uncorrectable errors.

Digital-to-Analog Conversion

The digital-to-analog conversion process requires recovering the digital audio data from the medium and converting it to analog form.

The recovered datastream must first be demodulated. In the CD format, this involves converting the 14-bit EFM-coded words back into their original 8-bit form. The data are deinterleaved and error correction performed. Synchronization information—essential to data recovery—is no longer needed and is discarded. The subcode information is stripped out of the data stream and handled separately from the audio data. All of these functions are performed by the CD transport, which outputs a formatted datastream to the digital processor which actually converts the signal to analog. (A full description of how a digital processor converts digital data to an analog signal is included in Chapter 8.)

Jitter Explained

In analog recording, speed variations in the recording media cause audible distortion. The classic case is a tape machine's "wow and flutter", speed fluctuations that cause the music's pitch to shift up and down slowly ("wow") or quickly ("flutter"). Digital audio doesn't suffer from wow and flutter; digital audio data can be read from the medium at a varying rate, yet be clocked out at a constant speed. But digital audio suffers from a distortion-producing mechanism conceptually similar to wow and flutter called *clock jitter*.

Jitter—timing variations in the clocks that serve as the time base reference in digital audio systems—is a serious and underestimated source of sonic degradation in digital audio. Only recently has jitter begun to get the attention it deserves, both by high-end designers and audio academics. One reason jitter has been overlooked is the exceedingly difficult task of measuring such tiny time variations—on the order of tens of trillionths of a second. Another reason jitter has been ignored is the mistaken belief by some that if the ones and zeros that represent the music are correct, then digital audio must work perfectly. Unfortunately, getting the ones and zeros correct is only part of the equation. Those ones and zeros must be converted back to analog with extraordinarily precise timing to avoid degrading the signal.

As described in Chapter 8, the series of discrete audio samples are converted back into a continuously varying signal with a digital-to-analog converter (DAC) chip. A DAC takes a quantization word and converts it to a voltage—exactly opposite the function of the A/D converter. All that is required for perfect conversion (in the time domain) is that the samples be input to the DAC in the same order they were taken *and with the same timing reference* as when the samples were created. In theory, this sounds easy—just provide a stable clock to the A/D converter and a stable clock of the same frequency to the D/A converter.

It isn't that easy in practice. If the samples aren't converted back to an analog waveform with the identical timing with which they were taken, distortion of the analog waveform will result. These timing errors between samples are caused by variations in the clock signal that controls *when* the DAC converts the digital words to an analog voltage.

Let's take a little closer look at how the DAC decides *when* to convert the digital samples to analog. In Fig.C-8, the binary number at the left is the quantization word that represents the analog waveform's amplitude when it was first sampled. The bigger the number, the higher the amplitude (this is only conceptually true—in practice, the data are in 2's complement form, a code this is easier to handle by circuits). The squarewave at the top is the "word clock," the timing signal that tells the DAC *when* to convert the quantization word to an analog voltage. Assuming the original sampling frequency was 44.1kHz, the word clock's frequency will also be 44.1kHz (or, if the processor uses an oversampling digital filter, some multiple of 44.1kHz). On the word clock's *leading* edge, the next sample (quantization word) is loaded into the DAC. On the word clock's *falling* edge, the DAC converts that quantization word to an analog voltage. This process happens 44,100 times per second (without oversampling). If the digital processor has an 8x-oversampling digital filter, the word-clock frequency will be eight times 44,100, or 352.8kHz.

Fig. C-8 The word clock tells the DAC when to convert the quantization words to an analog voltage.

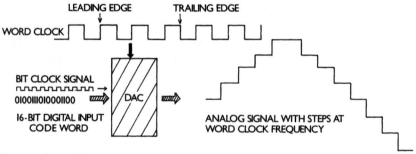

Courtesy *Stereophile*

It is here at the word clock that timing variations affect the analog output signal. Specifically, clock jitter is any time variation between the clock's trailing edges. Fig.C-9 shows perfect and jittered clocks (exaggerated for clarity).

Fig. C-9 Word-clock jitter consists of either a random variation or a variation which has a periodic component.

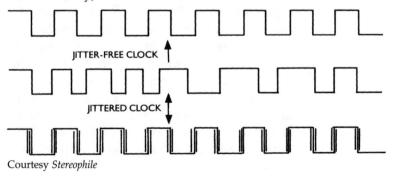

Courtesy *Stereophile*

Now, look what happens if the samples are reconstructed by a DAC whose word clock is jittered (Fig.C-10). The sample amplitudes—the ones and zeros—are correct, *but they're in the wrong places*. The right amplitude at the wrong time is the wrong amplitude. A *time* variation in the word clock produces an *amplitude* variation in the output, causing the waveform to change shape. A change in a waveform's shape is the very definition of distortion. Remember, the word clock tells the DAC *when* to convert the audio sample to an analog voltage; any variations in its accuracy will produce an analog-like variability in the final output signal—the music.

Fig. C-10 An analog waveform is reconstructed correctly with a jitter-free word clock (top); word-clock jitter results in a distortion of the analog wave-form's shape.

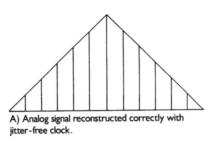

A) Analog signal reconstructed correctly with jitter-free clock.

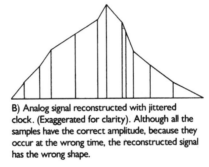

B) Analog signal reconstructed with jittered clock. (Exaggerated for clarity). Although all the samples have the correct amplitude, because they occur at the wrong time, the reconstructed signal has the wrong shape.

Courtesy *Stereophile*

Clock jitter can also raise the noise floor of a digital converter and introduce spurious artifacts. If the jitter has a random distribution (called "white jitter" because of its similarity to white noise), the noise floor will rise. If, however, the word clock is jittered at a specific frequency, artifacts will appear in the analog output as sidebands on either side of the audio signal frequency being converted to analog. It is these specific-frequency artifacts that are the most sonically detrimental; they bear no harmonic relationship to the music, and may be responsible for the hardness and glare often heard from digital audio.

Fig.C-11a is a spectral analysis of a computer-simulated digital processor's output when reproducing a full-scale, 10kHz sinewave with a jitter-free clock. Fig.C-11b is the same measurement, but with 2 nanoseconds (two billionths of a second) of jitter with a frequency of 1kHz on the clock. The plot in Fig.C-11b reveals the presence of discrete-frequency sidebands on either side of the test signal caused by jitter of a specific frequency. The amplitude of these artifacts is a function of the input signal level and frequency; the higher the signal level and frequency, the higher the sideband amplitude in the analog output signal.

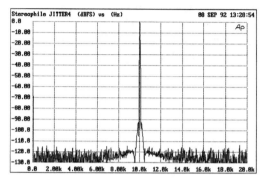 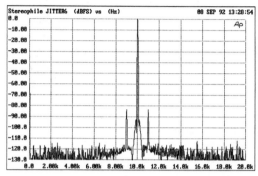

Fig. C-11a and b Computer-simulated spectral analysis of a digital processor's output with a jitter-free clock (left), and with 2ns of jitter (right) (Courtesy *Stereophile*)

How much jitter is audible? In theory, a 16-bit converter must have less than 100 picoseconds of clock jitter if the signal-to-noise ratio isn't to be compromised (there are 1000 picoseconds in a nanosecond). Twenty-bit conversion requires much greater accuracy, on the order of 8ps. One hundred picoseconds is one-tenth of a billionth of a second (10^{-10})—about the same amount of time it takes light to travel *an inch*. Moreover, this maximum allowable figure of 100ps assumes that the jitter is random (white), and not having a specific frequency which would be less sonically benign. Clearly, extraordinary precision is required for accurate conversion.

Where does clock jitter originate? The primary source is the interface between a CD transport and a digital processor. The master clock signal is embedded in the S/PDIF (Sony/Philips Digital Interface Format) signal that connects the two devices (though it's more accurate to say that the audio data are embedded in the clock). The digital processor recovers this clock signal at the input receiver chip (usually the Yamaha YM3623B, Philips SAA7274, or the Crystal CS8412 chip). The typical method of separating the clock from the data and creating a new clock with a *Phase Locked Loop* (PLL) produces *lots* of jitter. In a standard implementation, the Yamaha chip produces a clock with 3-5ns of jitter, about 30 to 50 times the 100ps requirement for accurate 16-bit conversion (the Crystal CS8412 input receiver reportedly has 150ps of clock jitter, and the UltraAnalog AES 20 low-jitter receiver has 40ps). Even if the clock is recovered with low jitter, just about everything inside a digital processor introduces clock jitter: noise from digital circuitry, processing by integrated circuits—even a pcb trace.

It's important to note that the only point where jitter matters is at the DAC's word-clock input. A clock that's recovered perfectly but is degraded just before it gets to the DAC is no better than a high-jitter recovery circuit that's protected from additional jitter on its way to the DAC. Conversely, a highly jittered clock can be cleaned up just before the DAC with no penalty.

Digital Signal Processing (DSP)

DSP is the manipulation of an audio signal in the digital domain. DSP opens vast and exciting new possibilities for improving the quality of reproduced sound—possibilities unimaginable with analog techniques.

DSP is nothing more than the mathematical processing of the digital data representing an audio signal. This processing can take many forms, allowing DSP chips to be configured in a wide range of applications. For example, DSP chips can be programmed to be a high-pass and a low-pass filter, thus replacing the capacitors, resistors, and inductors in a loudspeaker crossover. Some loudspeakers accept a digital input, implement the crossovers with DSP, then convert the signal to analog inside the loudspeaker. The advantages of DSP crossovers are vast: the designer can make the crossover frequency and slope exactly as he or she wants it without regard for the limitations of analog crossover components—capacitors, resistors, and inductors. Moreover, the phase response can be precisely controlled, as can the time offset between drivers. In addition to this added control, DSP crossovers get analog components out of the signal path for better sound. The Meridian D6000 loudspeaker is an example of a product using DSP-based crossovers.

Distortions in conventional loudspeakers can be corrected by DSP. If we know that a particular loudspeaker has amplitude errors and departures from linear phase response, those errors can be corrected in the digital domain by DSP.

The first commercial consumer product of this genre was the Celestion DLP-600. The DLP-600 is a digital input/output device connected between a CD transport and digital processor that corrects for time and amplitude anomalies in the Celestion SL-600si loudspeaker. The DLP-600 even corrects for reflections from driver mounting bolts and cabinet diffraction by introducing "anti-impulses" that cancel the acoustic reflections.

DSP-based Room Correction

A new and promising field in audio, called *room correction*, is also made possible by DSP. As we saw in Chapter 4, the listening room exerts a significant influence on the reproduced sound. Room resonance modes and standing waves can cause 15dB peaks and dips in the bass. In essence, the room acts as an equalizer between the loudspeakers and your ears. These peaks and dips are time-dependent and cannot be removed with analog equalization (which introduces a whole host of other problems anyway).

DSP-based room-correction systems seek to remove the listening room's peaks and dips. They do this with a series of adaptable digital filters that create an "inverse room" in the digital domain that counteracts the listening room's characteristics. For example, if the room has a peak at 100Hz, the filters are configured to create a notch at 100Hz. The signal fed to the loudspeakers is preconditioned to correct for the room's peak at 100Hz.

Fig.C-12a shows a particular loudspeaker's measured in-room response. The huge peak at 100Hz and dip at 50Hz are caused by interaction between the loudspeaker's direct sound and reflections from the room's walls. Fig.C-12b is the correction filter's response that will precondition the signal to counteract the room's effect.

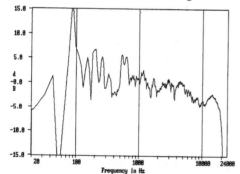
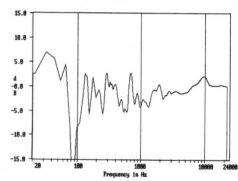

Fig. C-12a and b Measured in-room response at the listening position (left), and response of DSP correction filter (right). (Courtesy Snell Acoustics, Inc.)

That isn't the end of the story. If we look at the loudspeaker's in-room response over a longer time window to see the effects of room resonance modes and standing waves, we can see that the excess energy at 100Hz and lack of energy at 50Hz is more pronounced during the 50ms period after the direct signal from the loudspeaker has stopped. The 100Hz energy "hangs" in the room for a longer period, and energy centered at 50Hz is truncated prematurely in relation to the rest of the spectrum. The result will be thick midbass and an absence of low bass.

This is shown in the waterfall plot of Fig.C-13a. A waterfall plot, more correctly called a "cumulative spectral-decay" graph, shows the loudspeaker/room's frequency response at discrete slices of time after the stimulus has been removed. We can see that the lower curves (later in time) have much more excess 100Hz energy, caused by a room resonance mode at that frequency.

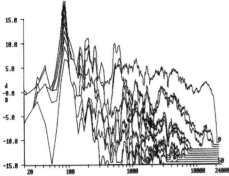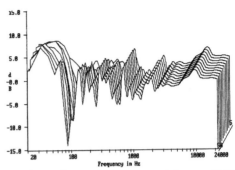

Fig. C-13a and b Uncorrected cumulative spectral-decay (left), and cumulative spectral decay of DSP correction filter (right) (Courtesy Snell Acoustics, Inc.)

DSP-based room-correction systems must therefore act in a time-dependent way to correct these delayed resonances. The music signal driving the loudspeakers is preconditioned to contain signals that have the same time delay as the wall reflections (at the listening position), but of opposite polarity. The wall reflections are thus canceled by a series of delayed waves from the loudspeaker that have a polarity opposite to that of the wall reflections.

A cumulative spectral-decay plot of the DSP filter's response is shown in Fig.C-13b. When applied to the uncorrected cumulative spectral-decay plot (Fig.C-13a), the result is a much flatter in-room response (Fig.C-14a). Not only was the loudspeaker's amplitude response corrected for that room, but the delayed resonances caused by standing waves were removed (Fig.C-14b). In essence, the DSP room-correction system removed the listening room's detrimental effect on the reproduced sound.

In practice, room-correction systems will work like this: Your dealer visits your listening room with a computer and measurement microphone. After you've got your loudspeakers correctly positioned and you know where you will sit, the microphone is put at the listening position and the loudspeaker/room is excited by an impulse. The measured impulse response contains all the information about the system frequency response, and about how that response changes over time. The computer then generates the filter coefficients that will correct for that particular loudspeaker at that particular listening position in that particular room. The filter coefficients are stored in an Erasable Programmable

Read-Only Memory (EPROM) chip that is then installed in your room-correction box. Every time you turn on the room-correction box, the filter coefficients are loaded into the DSP memory. The computer and measurement microphone are no longer needed. If you change loudspeakers, loudspeaker position, listening position, or move to a different house, the process must be repeated.

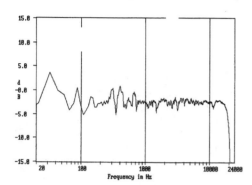 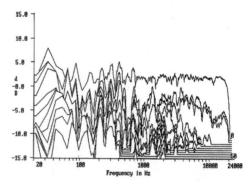

Fig. C-14a and b Corrected in-room response (left) and corrected cumulative spectral decay (right) (Courtesy Snell Acoustics, Inc.)

The first commercially available DSP-based room-correction systems cost about $10,000, but prices are dropping rapidly. Before buying a room-correction system, be aware that this field is in its very early stages and subject to rapid development. Fortunately, most improvements will be in software, which is more easily updated than hardware improvements.

It is important to stress that DSP room correction won't make a poor loudspeaker or room sound great. You must start with excellent loudspeakers, a decent room, and correct loudspeaker placement. DSP should be used to correct small problems rather than tackle massive response anomalies.

DSP in Professional Audio

DSP technology is rapidly being applied to all kinds of audio technology. For example, DSP can replace the racks of equipment used for sound reinforcement at amplified concerts. Currently, the equipment in those racks must be patched together with cables to configure the system. If the engineer needs an equalizer, for example, it must be physically patched into the system.

In a DSP-based system, however, there are no racks of specific equipment, only DSP chips that can be configured to perform any task required. The engineer assembles the sound-reinforcement system by dragging icons of particular devices with a mouse across a computer monitor. If he needs an equalizer, he just drags the equalizer icon into the signal path. This action reconfigures the DSP chips to perform equalization. The system's complexity is limited by the number of DSP chips. This concept is a revolution in how audio signals are handled and processed. The first of these DSP-based sound reinforcement systems was shown at the October, 1993 Audio Engineering Society Convention.

New Directions in Digital Audio

Although the digital audio techniques and systems discussed in this appendix appear extremely advanced and sophisticated, digital audio is actually in its infancy. In the past few years, new and highly imaginative techniques have been developed to improve the technical and musical performance of digital audio. These techniques seek to maximize the quality available from existing formats rather than overthrow the current standards in favor of higher sampling rates and longer word lengths. In other words, designers are trying to make the best of what we have. The constraints of 16-bit, 44.1kHz digital audio has forced designers to innovate in their attempts to squeeze the highest performance from the limitations of the CD standard.

One technique, called *in-band noise shaping*, takes a 20-bit digital input and outputs a 16-bit word length for storage on CD. The technique shifts quantization noise away from the midrange (where such noise is most audible) to the treble (where it's less audible). Through the critical midrange, the noise floor is nearly at the 20-bit level, and the subjective dynamic range approaches 20-bit performance. Noise shaping doesn't reduce the noise level; it merely redistributes it to a portion of the audio band where it is less audible. In-band noise shaping is known by various trade names. Sony Corporation's Super Bit Mapping is an example of in-band noise shaping. Meridian Audio's 618 Digital Mastering Processor is an extremely sophisticated noise shaping device that greatly improves the sound of 16-bit compact discs.

Another—and much more elaborate—technique for improving digital audio is called High Definition Compatible Digital, or HDCD. The process was developed by Pacific Microsonics of Berkeley, California, and is the brainchild of Keith O. Johnson and Michael Pflaumer. HDCD is a sophisticated analog-to-digital converter and proprietary encoding process that produces a digital signal compatible with all existing digital formats and hardware—including the compact disc. The second part of HDCD is an optional decoder to be included in some CD players and digital processors. Discs encoded with HDCD will still play back on standard hardware without the decoder and sound better than conventional CDs, but the process's full potential is realized only by playing HDCD-encoded discs through a CD player or digital processor equipped with an HDCD decoder. Note that the decoder is not a requirement, but an enhancement.

At the time of this writing (Spring 1994), HDCD is yet to become a commercial reality. I have, however, heard the process, and believe it is a revolutionary leap forward in digital audio sound quality.

A Final Note

Those readers interested in learning more about digital audio are directed to the excellent *Principles of Digital Audio* by Ken Pohlmann.

Bibliography

Avalon Acoustics Inc., Ascent Owner's Manual.

Ballou, G. (Editor) *Handbook for Sound Engineers: The New Audio Cyclopedia*. Sams, 1987.

Benson, K. (Editor) *Audio Engineering Handbook*. McGraw-Hill, 1988.

Berger, I. and Fantel, H. *The New Sound of Stereo*. Plume, 1986.

Cohen, A. *Audio Technology Fundamentals*. Sams, 1989.

Colloms, M. *High Performance Loudspeakers, Fourth Edition*. Halstead Press, 1991.

Dearborn, L. *Good Sound*. Quill, 1987.

Encyclopædia Britannica. 1989.

Everest, F.A. *Acoustic Techniques for Home and Studio, Second Edition*. Tab, 1984.

Graf, R. *Modern Dictionary of Electronics, Sixth Edition*. Sams, 1984.

Grob, B. *Basic Electronics, Fourth Edition*. McGraw-Hill, 1977.

Johnsen, R. *The Wood Effect: Unaccounted Contributor to Error and Confusion in Acoustics and Audio*. The Modern Audio Association, 1988.

Lee, N. "Life is Tough for an Audio Signal: A Primer on the Audibility of Cables and Monster Cable Technologies." Monster Cable Products, Inc. (white paper, 1992).

Low, B. "Cable Design: Theory vs. Empirical Reality." AudioQuest (white paper, 1993).

Malvino, A. *Digital Computer Electronics, Second Edition*. McGraw-Hill, 1983.

Malvino, A. *Resistive and Reactive Circuits*. McGraw-Hill, 1974.

Manley, D. *The Vacuum Tube Logic Book*. Blue Book Enterprises, 1986.

Merrill, G. "How to Set-up and Tune Your Turntable and Tonearm." Underground Sound, 1988.

Metzler, R. *Audio Measurement Handbook*. Audio Precision, 1993.

Pohlmann, K.C. *Principles of Digital Audio, Second Edition*. Sams, 1989.

Pohlmann, K.C. *The Compact Disc: A Handbook of Theory and Use*. AR Editions, 1989.

Polanyi, M. *Personal Knowledge*. Harper Torchbooks, 1957.

Rosenberg, H. *Understanding Tube Electronics: A Study in Natural Harmonics Audio*. New York Audio Laboratories, 1984.

Stereophile, Vol.7 No.7 to Vol.17 No.1.

Woram, J. *The Recording Studio Handbook*. Sagamore, 1977.

Index

A

A/A paradox, 64

Absolute polarity, 65, 167, 234, 367-369

Accessories, 32, 329-344
    choosing, 329-330
    "voodoo" accessories, 344

AC ground isolators, 343

Acoustic
    absorption, 82-86, 371
    absorption coefficients, 101-103
    diffraction, 196-198, 371-373, 380
    diffusion, 82, 371
    dimensional ratios, 89, 95-98
    feedback, 276
    isolation, 104-105
    optimum dimensional ratios table, 98
    reflection, 82, 371
    resonance, 93-95
    treatments, 30, 69, 79, 82-88, 90, 92, 102-104, 106-108

Acoustic Sciences Corporation, 75

Acoustic Techniques for Home and Studio, 108

AC polarity testers, 242

AC power conditioners, 17-18, 31, 334-337

AC power cords, 337-338

AC power line, 334-337, 389-390

AC-synchronous motors, 283

AES/EBU digital interface, 218, 243-244, 246

Aliasing, 420

"Allison Effect", 82

Allison, Roy, 82

Alternating current (AC), 389-390

Amplifier circuits, 404-409
    distortion in, 409-410

Anti-aliasing filters, 420-422

Apogee Acoustics, 2, 182, 184

ASC Tower Traps, 84, 86-87, 90, 92, 106, 107

ASC Tube Traps, 107

ASM Labs Spatial Filter, 339

Atkinson, John, 207

ATRAC perceptual coding, 253

Audio Advisor, 106, 277, 280

Audio Engineering Handbook, 81, 364, 366, 370, 372, 377-378

Audiophile values, 34-37

Audiophilia nervosa, 38

An Invitation to Join the High-end Audio Community

Become a Member of the Academy for the Advancement of High-end Audio

The Academy for the Advancement of High-end Audio is an international organization formed to represent and further the interests of music lovers everywhere. The Academy has established itself as the voice of the high-end audio community, with members in 23 countries around the world.

One of the Academy's main goals is providing consumer education about high-end audio equipment. The organization also recognizes outstanding achievement in high-end audio, and sets standards for the audio industry. By educating consumers to the joy of high-quality music reproduction in the home, the Academy brings benefits to everyone in our special community of music lovers—-manufacturers, distributors, retailers, the high-end audio press, and, most importantly, consumers.

Although the Academy's voting membership consists of manufacturers and distributors, we also provide programs for high-end audio retailers and opportunities for consumers to meet the manufacturers and designers of high-end audio equipment. As an Academy member, you will receive our quarterly newsletter that keeps you up-to-date on activities within the high-end audio community, and receive invitations to special events that give you an opportunity to meet other Academy members and equipment designers. With the Academy Golden Note Awards and the High-end Hall of Fame, outstanding achievements of our industry are being recognized and preserved for our High-end Audio Archives.

Through much hard work by the Academy member companies, high-end audio has grown into a serious, half-billion dollar business worldwide. As implied by the word "Advancement" in our name, our mission is to identify opportunities offering the greatest potential to expand awareness of the high-end audio industry.

Consumer memberships are $25 per year. This gets you the newsletter and invitations to all our functions throughout the year. Send your check to AAHEA, P.O. Box 373, Dana Point, CA 92629. For more information, call (714) 443-9395, or fax us at (714) 443-9396.

A

ORDER FORM

Acapella Publishing
P. O. Box 80805
Albuquerque, NM 87198-0805

Name and address: **Ship to:**

_____   _____

_____   _____

_____   _____

_____   _____

Contact: _____

Telephone Orders: Call Toll Free 1 (800) 848-5099. Have your VISA or
MasterCard ready.

Quantity		Unit Cost	Total Amount
	The Complete Guide to High-end Audio-Soft Cover	$29.95	
	The Complete Guide to High-end Audio-Signed Hard Cover	$39.95	
	Subtotal		
	Shipping and Handling ($4.95 total)		
	Total (enclosed)		

Payment:

☐   **Check or Money Order, sorry no COD**

☐   **VISA**

☐   **MasterCard**

_____   _____

Card Number   **Expiration Date**

_____   _____

Signature   **Name on Card**